COMICS and the U.S. South

COMICS and the U.S. South

Edited by Brannon Costello and Qiana J. Whitted

University Press of Mississippi / Jackson

www.upress.state.ms.us

The University Press of Mississippi is a member of
the Association of American University Presses.

Copyright © 2012 by University Press of Mississippi
All rights reserved
Manufactured in the United States of America

First printing 2012
∞
Library of Congress Cataloging-in-Publication Data

Comics and the U.S. South / edited by Brannon Costello and
Qiana J. Whitted.
   p. cm.
   Includes bibliographical references and index.
   ISBN 978-1-61703-018-5 (cloth : alk. paper) — ISBN 978-1-
61703-019-2 (ebook) 1. Comic books, strips, etc.—History and
criticism. 2. Southern States—In literature. 3. Race in literature. I. Costello, Brannon, 1975– II. Whitted, Qiana J., 1974–
   PN6725.C647 2012
   741.5'973—dc22   2011017734

British Library Cataloging-in-Publication Data available

Contents

Introduction

—Brannon Costello and Qiana J. Whitted

In an early installment of Alan Moore, Stephen Bissette, and John Totleben's ambitious run on the DC Comics horror title *Saga of the Swamp Thing*, a mad villain with the power to control plants—Jason Woodrue, the Floronic Man—decides to cleanse the earth once and for all of the humans whose careless attitude toward the ecosystem has imperiled the planet's safety. His master plan unfolds quickly, largely because the staging ground for his assault on humanity—Lacroix, Louisiana—is completely off the radar of DC's high-profile defenders such as Superman, Batman, and Wonder Woman. As the Justice League, floating high in their satellite headquarters, ponders the severity of the threat posed by Woodrue, the team's gadfly, Green Arrow, rails, "Man, I don't believe this! We were watching out for New York, for Metropolis, for Atlantis . . . but who was watching out for Lacroix, Louisiana?" (figure 1.1; *Saga of the Swamp Thing* 24:3).

Green Arrow's complaint speaks to a larger issue both within the superhero comics genre and in comics studies generally. Superman's "never-ending battle for Truth, Justice, and the American Way" is most likely to take place in a major northern city, a fantasy landscape, or the far reaches of the galaxy, with Mississippi, Tennessee, and Louisiana usually all but invisible until a lesson on the need for tolerance is in the offing. Of course, the existence of *Swamp Thing* is evidence that exceptions to this rule exist, but they are typically treated *as* exceptions, as deviations from an unarticulated norm. This norm draws substantially from the medium's own origins amid the urban skyscrapers of the Northeast United States and among the pulp genres of the western frontier and suburban Midwest. Southern locales, generally reserved for folktales and local color peculiarities, are often subject to limiting assumptions about the region's aesthetic complexity, storytelling potential, and modern relevance, making the South a provincial enclave on the comics landscape.

Beyond mainstream adventure comics, the United States South has perhaps been more frequently represented on the pages of alternative and

1.1. From *Saga of the Swamp Thing* #24 (May 1984). Written by Alan Moore with art by Stephen Bissette and John Totleben. Copyright © 1984 DC Comics. All Rights Reserved.

underground comics and in daily comic strips. Indeed, the South looms large in such seminal newspaper strips as *Li'l Abner*, *Pogo*, and *Kudzu*. However, scholars working in the burgeoning field of comics studies have in general not closely attended to the historical, literary, and ideological contexts that inform that regional setting. *Comics and the U.S. South* seeks to fill this silence, bringing together a variety of essays on comics in a range of genres and styles to demonstrate how comics studies can participate in, and even suggest new avenues for, the ongoing transformation of southern studies, as well as to demonstrate how engaging key questions in southern studies can contribute to comics studies, opening up alternate ways of reading new and familiar texts. Our understanding of comics in this regard will include serial comic books, graphic novels, comic strips, editorial comics, webcomics, and other forms of visual narrative.

The past decade has seen a radical and energizing transformation of the study of the literature and culture of the United States South. Works such as Michael Kreyling's *Inventing Southern Literature* (1998), Houston Baker's *Turning South Again* (2001), and Scott Romine's *The Real South: Southern Narrative in the Age of Cultural Reproduction* (2008) urge critics to question the ideological implications of the conventional southern literary canon and to seek new approaches in attempting to understanding the South and its literature, while works such as Leigh Anne Duck's *The Nation's Region* (2006), Suzanne Jones and Sharon Monteith's *South to a New Place* (2002), and Jon Smith and Deborah Cohn's *Look Away: The U.S. South in New World Studies* (2004) have sought to revise deeply entrenched understandings of the South's relationship to the rest of the nation and to other parts of the world. The result has been a dramatic widening of the field of inquiry about southern literature, and about the South generally, that emphasizes the complex, multiple nature of southern culture(s). Indeed, the very notion of what constitutes "southern" writing has been radically altered. Once southern studies was guided by a usually unarticulated exceptionalism—the notion that the South was a region possessed of certain distinct and essential qualities and that its only true literature was that which explored (and maybe even celebrated) these values. But in addition to revising critical consensus about the works of William Faulkner, Eudora Welty, and others, in recent years critics have turned greater attention to texts that are *about* the South rather than focusing exclusively on texts written by authors who can provide their southern *bona fides*. In *The Scary Mason-Dixon Line* (2009), Trudier Harris refers to the act of confronting the United States South through narrative as a "rite of passage" for African American writers, no matter their place of birth (2). Surely we could extend this sentiment to any American artist who sees within the South's history and evolution a ritual proving ground for the nation's fundamental ideals and aspirations. In these cases, the question becomes about the uses to which representations of the South are put—in narratives of United States nationalism, in models of race, class, and gender, in political rhetoric, or even in constructions of individual selfhood.

Clearly, then, southern studies is in the midst of an intensely exciting period of reexamining its most fundamental assumptions and, in doing so, placing itself at the center of the most important movements in contemporary literary and cultural studies. As Jon Smith argues, "United States southern studies, far from gazing into the navel of memory, is pushing the boundaries of American and inter-American studies, postcolonial theory, queer studies, cultural studies, and media, visual culture, and globalization studies" (550). Although each of the individual essays in the collection engages with the representation of the South in comics in its own way, the collection, taken as a whole, makes an important contribution to one of the most significant revisions of southern studies: redefining the South as a visual, rather than primarily an oral, culture. The notion of the South as a uniquely and dominantly oral culture is widespread. But in *Ordering the Facade: Photography and Contemporary Southern Women's Writing* (2007), Katherine Henninger argues that, while the importance of the oral tradition in the South is not to be dismissed, placing too much emphasis on the oral dimensions of southern culture blinds us to the ways in which the South is an intensely *visual* culture. Writes Henninger, "In a culture where visual signs—the shape of a lip, a skin's shade, external sex characteristics, the carriage of one's body, the condition of one's clothing—determine 'place' (and may literally mean the difference between life and death), surely the visual may be said to reign supreme" (16). Henninger goes on to note that while her focus is on photography, other visual texts such as film, television, paintings, and newspapers play a key role in the South's visual culture (28). Mass culture produced both within and outside of the South would seem to be a natural focus for exploring this visual culture. Yet while there is considerable work on, for example, the South in film, there has been virtually no sustained treatment of the varied and complex representations of the South in comic books, comic strips, and graphic novels. We would be remiss if we did not note the major exception to this trend: the work of M. Thomas Inge, a contributor to this volume, whose writing on subjects from Al Capp's *Li'l Abner* to comics adaptations of the work of Edgar Allan Poe to the role of comics and cartooning in the work of William Faulkner pioneered the exploration of this critical territory. Despite Inge's important work and his active participation in both southern studies and comics studies, few critics have to this point joined the exploration. As the essays included here reveal, however, the territory is rich with potential.

Indeed, the comics form itself offers enormous potential for revising conventional understandings of the South. In *Reconstructing Dixie: Race, Gender, and Nostalgia in the Imagined South* (2003), Tara McPherson coins the phrase "lenticular logic" to describe an important tendency in representations of the South in mass culture and even in academic discussions of the South. Her metaphor is that of the lenticular card familiar from Cracker Jack boxes and coin-operated toy dispensers: two pictures printed together so that, by turning the card, the viewer can see one picture at a time (25–26). Ruminating on the implications of a particularly striking lenticular post-card that alternates an image of a southern belle before a columned mansion with the "stereotypical image of the grinning, portly mammy," McPherson writes, "a lenticular logic is capable of representing both black and white; but one approaches the limits of this logic when one attempts to understand how the images are joined or related" (26). McPherson argues that many representations of the South fall victim to this lenticular logic, with the effect that "the lenticular restricts our descriptions of the places we inhabit and of the people we meet," and the resulting impoverished vocabulary lim-its our ability to understand the complex and multiple nature of southern culture: We see parts, but the whole eludes us (27). In her wide-ranging sur-vey of representations of the South in mass culture, McPherson does touch on comics, offering a brief and insightful analysis of the 1980s independent series *Captain Confederacy*. Yet of all the media she surveys, comics have the greatest inherent potential to refute this lenticular logic. The comics page, after all, is frequently a collection of images that are at once separate and interdependent—the quality that Thierry Groensteen terms "iconic solidar-ity" (18)—and can thus represent an infinitely wide range of places and times both serially and simultaneously and can suggest an enormously complex tangle of connections and relationships. The very act of reading a comics page requires the very sort of interpretive work on the part of the reader—"closure," in Scott McCloud's terminology—for which McPherson calls (63). As Charles Hatfield puts it, "The fractured surface of the comics page, with its patchwork of different images, shapes, and symbols, presents the reader with a surfeit of interpretive options, creating an experience that is always decentered, unstable, and unfixable. . . . The very discontinuity of the page urges readers to do the work of inference, to negotiate over and over the passage from submissive reading to active interpreting" (*Alternative Com-ics* xiii–xiv). The essays in this collection combine formal and ideological concerns to model a method of reading that works against the limitations of lenticular logic to engage with the South in all its complexity.

While comics studies has much to offer southern studies, the reverse is true as well. The recent boom in academic comics scholarship comes as no surprise to scholars and critics working in the field who have long champi-oned the unique power of the comics medium to bring together form and theme in surprising and powerful ways. As is to be expected in a relatively new field, the majority of books on comics have been fruitfully engaged in the ongoing process of definition. Indeed, as Hatfield puts it, a "rage for definition has fairly swept the field" ("Defining Comics" 19). Charting the medium's histories, demonstrating its richness and complexity, and considering the achievement of its most accomplished artists has been the dominant task to this point. The work of defining the field is not over and must continue—after all, in any field, canons are perpetually in revision (and the value of canons perpetually in question), and new understandings of history or new theoretical tools lead critics to redraw boundaries. Yet at this moment, there is also a sense that the invigorating discussions about comics studies are happening primarily *within* comics studies. That is, it has not always been clear how productively comics scholarship can speak to (and with) other academic fields. Through close engagement with the major issues in southern studies, these essays offer fresh perspective on some of the key questions that shape our understanding of graphic narrative. While this collection is wide-ranging—considering such disparate topics as the role of the "redemptive South" in the national imagination in Walt Kelly's *Pogo*, the formally innovative exploration of the America's racial history in Kyle Baker's *Nat Turner*, and the multimedia, hyper-linked attempt to understand Hurricane Katrina and its aftermath in Josh Neufeld's webcomic *A.D.: New Orleans After the Deluge*—it is by no means exhaustive. We hope that it will be the beginning, not the end, of a long and fruitful conversation about the relationship between comics and the South, and between comics studies and southern studies.

Although these essays speak to one another in varied and complex ways, we have grouped essays most intimately in conversation with each other into four sections: "The South in the National Imagination," "Emancipation and Civil Rights Resistance," "The Horrors of the South," and "Revisualizing Stories, Rereading Images." The first section, "The South in the National Imagination," takes part in one of the most crucial developments in the field of southern studies in recent years: the corrective move away from traditional narratives of the U.S. South's exceptionality—its supposed fundamental and essential difference from other regions—and toward investigations of the role such narratives play in constructions of United States national identity. Various constructions of "the South" have enabled what Barbara Ladd terms a "willed amnesia" about U.S. history: In order to maintain a coherent national narrative that the U.S. is the land of life, liberty, and the pursuit of happiness, the myriad and threatening exceptions to that narrative—illiteracy, poverty, and violence against African Americans and women—are imagined to be contained within the regional Other of the South

(1637). And yet, at the same time the South has stood for an array of positive attributes that the nation is purported to be losing as it grows ever more modern—tradition, folkways, communal values. The essays in this section examine this double vision and the uses to which ideas of the South are put in understanding the ways in which "southern" images and artifacts signify in national discourses about politics, race, gender, and identity. M. Thomas Inge examines the ways in which the once enormously popular comic strips *Li'l Abner* and *Snuffy Smith* blended research, conjecture, and stereotype in their representations of Appalachian culture, representations which were crucial in shaping their national audience's imagination of the South; Brian Cremins offers a new way of thinking about race and region in Walt Kelly's *Pogo* by reading the strip's Okefenokee Swamp setting as an idiosyncratic entry in the discourse of the "redemptive South" prevalent in various forms throughout the mid-twentieth century—a discourse that held out the hope that the South would become a national model of racial healing; Brannon Costello examines how a storyline in which the original Captain America is replaced by a reactionary and violent southerner exposes and interrogates 1980s anxieties about the growing centrality of the South in the nation's political and cultural life; and Christopher Whitby considers how the ambivalence evident toward the evolving South in Doug Marlette's long-running newspaper strip *Kudzu* offers a useful way of thinking about the circulation of the concept of southern authenticity within the region and in U.S. culture generally.

Explorations of African American life in graphic narratives have undergone a fascinating resurgence in the last two decades, with the prevailing trend emphasizing the historical antagonisms of the United States South as a brutal social, cultural, and spiritual landscape. The comics discussed in the second section on "Emancipation and Civil Rights Resistance" seek to upset traditional configurations of heroism through carefully crafted counter-narratives that reframe black enslavement, segregation, and Civil Rights resistance through the voices of insurrectionists, activists, and bystanders. In her reading of *Nat Turner*, Conseula Francis makes a strong case for Kyle Baker's visual rendering of the fugitive slave narrative form through a strategically violent aesthetic that takes issue with Thomas Gray's 1831 account. Tim Caron's analysis of narratives of passing and lynching in Mat Johnson and Warren Pleece's *Incognegro: A Graphic Mystery* reveals how the comic critiques socially constructed ideas of race during Jim Crow. Finally, Gary Richards problematizes the manner in which race and sexual identity intersect in Howard Cruse's *Stuck Rubber Baby* by framing the graphic novel through the conventions of the "coming-out novel" and the "white southern racial conversion narrative." These essays not only continue the previous section's critical conversation about the influence of the southern past, but they also confront the comic book industry's history with stereotypical depictions of the Other during a time in which, as Will Eisner has stated, "humor consisted in our society of bad English and physical difference in identity" (Arnold). Perhaps, then, we might argue that the modern comics under investigation in this section, with their diverse representations of race, sexuality, and resistance, signify a different kind of "Golden Age." These comics explore the complexities of identity in the South in ways never seen before.

Each of the essays in the third section on "The Horrors of the South" scrutinize comics within horror and fantasy genres that deploy elements of supernatural terror in their exploration of the region's mythos. At issue for these investigations are the unresolved spiritual fears, psychological consequences, and monstrous manifestations of the historical contradictions often central to southern identity. While strong preternatural characters like Swamp Thing, Bayou, Hellboy, and *Preacher*'s Jesse Custer constitute the moral centers of their series, each also wrestles his (or its) own demon in an evolving personal struggle. What is particularly valuable about this section's essays are the critical and theoretical approaches that illuminate subtextual meanings in a way that places horror comics in conversation with southern studies: Qiana Whitted's analysis demonstrates how EC Comics-style zombie horror informs postmodern neo-slave narrative conventions in the work of Alan Moore and Jeremy Love; Joseph Michael Sommers examines how Mike Mignola demystifies Appalachian witchcraft lore in *Hellboy* through the subversions of Bakhtinian laughter; and Nicolas Labarre's argument about the South as a "way of seeing the world" in Garth Ennis and Steve Dillon's *Preacher* draws support from the meta-fictional comic's obsession with popular culture.

The contributors to our final section, "Revisualizing Stories, Rereading Images," answer Katherine Henninger's call for understandings of the South that do not uncritically reiterate the claim that the region is primarily and definitively an oral culture. As Henninger argues, "dominant narratives of southernness, black and white, privilege oral over visual expression, word over picture" (21–22). These essays examine texts that explore the intersections of oral, visual, and textual cultures, using innovative formal strategies to blur the boundaries between such categories in order to offer a richer and more complex understanding of their interdependence as well as of particular southern experiences. Alison Mandaville's consideration of Randall Kenan's postmodern prose novel *A Visitation of Spirits* reveals how that novel's adaptation of comics elements represents the attempts of the protagonist—a gay African American teenager in a conservative religious community—to imagine an alternative way of being in the world and also suggests the dense imbrication of visual and oral southern cultures. Anthony Dyer Hoefer's analysis of Josh Neufeld's *A.D.: After the Deluge*, a "multimedia, multimodal graphic oral history" of Hurricane Katrina and its aftermath in New Orleans, examines how Neufeld revises "official" images of that event by viewing them through the perspective of individuals and by reaching outward to encompass sound and video recordings and online discussion threads. Hoefer demonstrates how Neufeld's webcomic-turned-graphic-novel challenges the received narratives of that event and suggests the limits of official discourse to represent trauma on such a vast scale.

We would like to thank all our colleagues who helped us to realize this project—and who also helped make the process such a pleasure. First, our thanks to the contributors for their willingness to share their insightful essays and for their diligence throughout the editorial process. Many of our friends and colleagues offered sage advice, patient ears, and encouragement from the very beginning, including Charles Hatfield, Bob Brinkmeyer, Robert Hamm, and Sue Weinstein. We also appreciate the opportunity to discuss portions of the project at the Society for the Study of Southern Literature Conference and the International Comic Arts Forum, and we gratefully acknowledge the support of a grant from the Institute of African American Research at the University of South Carolina. Thanks as well to Johnny Lowe, our well-informed and sharp-eyed copy editor, and to Bob Ellis, our expert indexer. We are grateful to Walter Biggins at the University Press of Mississippi for his invaluable guidance at every stage, and to Anne Stascavage and Shane Gong for their work on the latter stages of production. Finally, our appreciation to Jeremy Love for use of the image from *Bayou* that adorns the cover, and to the press's design team, including John Langston, for integrating it into such a handsome volume.

Works Cited

Arnold, Andrew D. "Never Too Late: An Interview with Will Eisner." *Time Magazine.* 19 September 2003. http://www.time.com/time/columnist/arnold/article/0,9565,488263,00 .html

Groensteen, Thierry. *The System of Comics*. Trans. Bart Beaty and Nick Nguyen. Jackson:
UP of Mississippi, 2007.

Harris, Trudier. *The Scary Mason-Dixon Line: African American Writers and the South*. Baton
Rouge: Louisiana State UP, 2009.

Hatfield, Charles. *Alternative Comics: An Emerging Literature*. Jackson: UP of Mississippi,
2005.

———. "Defining Comics." *Teaching the Graphic Novel*. New York: Modern Language
Association of America, 2009. 19–27.

Henninger, Katherine. *Ordering the Facade: Photography and Contemporary Southern
Women's Writing*. Chapel Hill: U of North Carolina P, 2007.

Ladd, Barbara. "Literary Studies: the Southern United States, 2005." *PMLA* 120.4 (2005):
1628–39.

McCloud, Scott. *Understanding Comics*. New York: Harper, 1994.

McPherson, Tara *Reconstructing Dixie. Race, Gender and Nostalgia in the Imagined South*.
Durham: Duke UP, 2003.

Moore, Alan (w), Stephen Bissette (p) and John Totleben (i). *Saga of the Swamp Thing #24*
(May 1984). New York: DC Comics.

Smith, Jon. "The State of United States Southern Literary Studies." *PMLA* 121 (2006): 549–50.

I.

The South in the National Imagination

Li'l Abner, Snuffy, and Friends

The Appalachian South in the American Comic Strip

—M. Thomas Inge

The comic strip in the United States has largely been an urban-oriented newspaper feature in terms of setting and character, beginning with the Yellow Kid and his urchin friends in *Hogan's Alley* in 1894. During the first few decades of development, only occasionally would the rural South enter the comics as coincidental or background material, as in Clare Victor Dwiggins's *Tom Sawyer and Huck Finn* in 1918 (which paid little allegiance to Mark Twain's novels), or as an exotic identification for a character, like Captain Easy, who hailed from Savannah, Georgia, in Roy Crane's rollicking adventure epic *Wash Tubbs*, beginning in 1924. By the early 1930s, however, United States popular culture was filled with references to the South, such as the widely distributed records of the band from North Carolina and Virginia who called themselves "The Hill-Billies," or Paul Webb's panel cartoons about lazy mountain folk in *Esquire* magazine.

The honor of creating the first successful comic strip specifically set in the South fell not to a cartoonist from below the Mason-Dixon Line but to a young artist from New Haven, Connecticut, named Alfred Gerald Caplin, later abbreviated to Al Capp, who went to work for Ham Fisher in 1933 to help draw the popular strip about a prizefighter named *Joe Palooka*. While Fisher was on vacation, Capp introduced to the cast a hillbilly boxer from Kentucky named Big Leviticus and his country kin in November 1933.

The characters captured the public's fancy, so when Capp left Fisher he carried with him the basic idea for his own strip that began as *Li'l Abner* on August 13, 1934. Fisher tried to lay claim to the characters and initiated one of the most acrimonious feuds in comic strip history which, like the Hatfields and McCoys, took no prisoners. Nevertheless, Capp went on to enormous fame and fortune with his 43-year saga of the denizens of Dogpatch, which eventually reached 60 million readers in over 900 U.S. newspapers

"About the time my first crop of whiskers began to come up, I took a walking trip through the Kentucky mountains. Take it from me, it was thumb experience!"

"I sketched the hillbilly people there, the prototypes of Li'l Abner and the folks of his world. My skill amazed them—till they saw the drawings."

2.1. From a United Features Syndicate promotional book by Al Capp, 1937. Reprinted in *Li'l Abner Dailies* vol. 1. Northampton, MA: Kitchen Sink Press, 1988.

and 100 foreign papers in 28 countries. Capp arguably had a profound influence on the way the world viewed the United States South.

What would a young man from Connecticut, schooled mainly in the ways of city life, know about southern character and culture? Several sources of information have been suggested. Capp himself reported:

> About the time my first crop of whiskers began to come up, I took a walking trip through the Kentucky mountains. . . . I sketched the hillbilly people there, the prototypes of Li'l Abner and the folks of his world. In Greenwich Village later, between wondering where the next meal was coming from, I tore my hair searching for a comic strip idea. I remembered my hillbilly. And I knew nobody had ever built a comic strip around one. So I did. (figure 2.1; Capp 1:6)

Al Capp's brother, Elliott Caplin, tells a slightly different version in his memoir, *Al Capp Remembered*. According to Elliott, when Capp was sixteen, he and a friend hitched a ride to a grocery store for cigarettes in Bridgeport. When it turned out the driver was headed for Baltimore, with a little over ten dollars in their pockets, the two boys decided to join him and ten days later ended up in Memphis, Tennessee, at the home of Al's Uncle George, an orthodox rabbi. "When 'Li'l Abner' became a success," added Elliott, "Alfred would resolutely maintain that the trip to Memphis was but a preliminary tour of the hillbilly country so that the future cartoonist could research the characters who wound up populating his wildly successful comic strip." Elliott also tactfully labeled the entire story a typical piece of Capp "mythology" (61–63).

How the two hitchhikers completed a journey of over 1,100 miles, crossing several states in ten days, and yet found time to absorb local color in the Appalachian mountains remains a question, especially when we must make allowance for the fact that Capp had to walk on a wooden leg as a result of an accident at age nine. Clearly it was no "walking trip through the Kentucky mountains," as Capp described it, but few doubt that he actually made the trip to Memphis. It is his own embellishments that are questionable, since he was known for his skills in the art of exaggeration.

His wife, Catherine, identified a more specific cultural source for his idea:

One night while Al was working for Fisher, we went to a vaudeville theatre in Columbus Circle. One of the performances was a hillbilly act. A group of four or five singers/musicians/comedians were playing fiddles and Jews harps and doing a little soft shoe up on stage. They stood in a very wooden way with expressionless deadpan faces, and talked in monotones, with Southern accents. We thought they were just hilarious. We walked back to the apartment that evening, becoming more and more excited with the idea of a hillbilly comic strip. Something like it must have always been in the back of Al's mind, ever since he thumbed his way through the Southern hills as a teenager, but that vaudeville act seemed to crystallize it to him. (qtd. in Capp 1:4)

This seems to be the most likely story of how it all started, because in fact he didn't have to look very far into the culture around him, on the vaudeville stage or elsewhere, to have a hillbilly experience.

It is no exaggeration to say that culture in the United States, high and low, had been obsessed with things southern and Appalachian since the turn of the century. Even before then, in the late nineteenth century, periodicals in the U.S. had proven an insatiable market for southern local color fiction by such writers as George Washington Cable, Kate Chopin, Alice Dunbar-Nelson, and Grace King from Louisiana; Mary Noailles Murfree from Tennessee; Charles Chesnutt from North Carolina; James Lane Allen from

Kentucky; and Joel Chandler Harris and Richard Malcolm Johnson from Georgia. Readers were fascinated by the exotic locales, peculiar characters, and distinct language used in these chronicles of rural and mountain life in remote communities. As the century turned, novelists like Thomas Nelson Page, Mary Johnston, and Ellen Glasgow from Virginia, and John Fox, Jr. from Kentucky, among many others, mined the same material for best-selling historical romances. In fact, the last of these was of special importance to Capp.

Young Alfred enjoyed visiting his grandparents, according to his brother, because of their extensive library. Elliott reports that "On the scrupulously dusted bookshelves, Alfred found the complete works of John Fox, Jr., who wrote such temporary classics as *The Kentuckians, The Little Shepherd of Kingdom Come, The Trail of the Lonesome Pine*, and many others that Alfred adored—until the age of 13" (Caplin 30). Fox focused on the pre- and post-Civil War lives of both the Kentucky mountaineer and the bluegrass country people and largely defined for general readers the mountaineer stereotype: proud, hospitable, and good-natured but also sometimes lazy, vengeful, and murderous when insulted. Largely Scotch-Irish in origin, they practiced a sturdy individualism, but because of their intentional isolation, they were ill educated, unsophisticated, and suspicious of new ways. Feuding, making moonshine liquor, and pursing romance seemed to be their major occupations.

According to one Fox critic, "the usual pattern in this fiction is to have an educated, gentlemanly outsider—most often a geologist, engineer, or teacher—come into the mountain community and there meet an unlettered, unmannered, and naturally well-endowed young mountain girl; to have them fall in love with each other; and to record the problems that such a love poses because of their contrasting backgrounds" (Titus 29). Except for the fact that the Yokums would venture out into the larger world as often as entertain visiting outlanders, this defines a very common pattern in *Li'l Abner*. There are numerous episodes in which a young man—a painter, a doctor, or a wealthy playboy—ventures into Dogpatch to fruitlessly fall in love with Daisy Mae. Capp's special and unusual twist on this mountain romance is to have Daisy Mae already hopelessly in love with Abner and Abner always resisting and denying his love for her. Thus the desired outcome is held in a state of unresolved suspense and keeps the reader coming back day after day.

Fox also dwelt upon the feud as a central element in Appalachian social culture and once described it as reflective of "ignorance, shiftlessness, incredible lawlessness, a frightful estimate of the value of human life," which encouraged, Fox said, "the horrible custom of the ambush, a class of cowardly assassins who can be hired to do murder for a gun, a mule, or a gallon of moonshine" (qtd. in Titus 60). With the third episode in *Li'l Abner*, beginning December 13, 1934, Capp introduced a feud that would extend throughout the history of the strip between the Scragg and the Yokum families, resisted by the latter but relentlessly pursued by the former, and complicated by the fact that Daisy Mae is a Scragg herself (Capp 1:65). Of course, the romantic tragedies about star-crossed lovers from opposing families run throughout the literature of Appalachia directly from Shakespeare's *Romeo and Juliet*. In any case, Fox's characterization of those who enact feuds clearly applies to the cold-blooded, cruel, and murderous patriarch Romeo Scragg and his sons Lem and Luke, who maim and kill for the pure pleasure of it.

It is interesting to note that because the mountaineers cut themselves off from the rest of the world about the time of the American Revolution, Fox believed that they remained devoted to those principles. Thus, "when the Civil War came, these people knew allegiance only to the Stars and Stripes; their loyalties were still to the nation forged by Revolution" (Titus 59). When Capp shows the Yokums as highly patriotic and Li'l Abner as fiercely devoted to the representatives and institutions of the United States government then, he is reflecting what was true of the southern Appalachian life. In one strip published during the Cold War on July 4, 1949, Mammy Yokum gives an "o-ray-shun" on the importance of safeguarding the freedoms won in 1776 at a time when "th' enemies o' freedom is harder t' reckanize now, becuz they pretends t'be th' friends o' freedom" (Capp 15:93).

While Capp seems to have borrowed little from Fox in terms of specific plots or characters, he obviously absorbed the ethos and social codes of Fox's fictional world, as well as his stereotypical portrayals of mountain men and women. But there is an even earlier literary tradition to which Capp owes allegiance, although his acquaintance with it may have been primarily through Mark Twain, who himself learned how to write humor under its influence.[1] This was the frontier humor of the Old South produced by a group of professional men primarily for their amusement and published first in the sporting papers of the mid-nineteenth century: Augustus Baldwin Longstreet's *Georgia Scenes* (1835), Johnson Jones Hooper's *Some Adventures of Captain Simon Suggs* (1845), and George Washington Harris's *Sut Lovingood Yarns* (1867) are among those collected in book form. They wrote bawdy, vulgar, and often brutal tales but realistic and written in a language and style close to the backwoods idiom and point of view of everyday people. The literary elite found their work repulsive.

   Like these frontier humorists, Capp relied on comic dialect, exaggeration of the tall-tale variety, grotesque examples of human nature, and lively narrative action for his humor. Many a con-man of the Simon Suggs type shows up in Dogpatch to outwit Abner, and when Available Jones, the odd-job tycoon of Dogpatch, posts on his wall a sign saying, "I can be had—for a price" (Capp 8:28), this is a distant echo of Simon Suggs favorite maxim, "It's good to be shifty in a new country." Honest John, who runs the Dogpatch general store, is like many a tight-fisted and untrustworthy shop keeper in frontier humor, and when he engages with Pappy Yokum in a horse swap on his first appearance in February 1, 1938, he reenacts one of the most common comic situations in southern folklore and fiction (Capp 4:31).

Perhaps the liveliest and most riotous of the characters to emerge from frontier humor was Sut Lovingood, a hell-raising hillbilly from the Knoxville mountains of Tennessee. A drawing of Sut by Justin H. Howard for the collected *Sut Lovingood Yarns* in 1867 (see figure 2.2) may have been one of the earliest visual images to establish the hillbilly stereotype in appearance: slouch hat, loose-fitting shirt, denim overalls, and bare feet (Inge, "Sut and His Illustrators" 26–35; Williamson, *HillbillyLand* 33–34). There are more than passing similarities between a riot instigated by Sut Lovingood, which brings destruction and physical harm if not death in its wake, usually at a public gathering, a dance, a wedding, or an evangelical meeting, and Marryin' Sam's eight-dollar wedding ceremony:

   Eight dollahs! This entitles yo' t' a puffawmence fum which ah may nevah recover!! Fust—ah strips t' th' waist, an' rassles th' four biggest guests!! Ah follows thet by playin' th' "Mad Scene" fum "Lucia" on mah moosical comb—wifout removin' mah uppers!! But Thass only th' beginn'!! A eight-dollah weddin' entitles yo' t' plenty more!! Next a fast demon-stray-shun o' how t' cheat yore friends at cards!! Follyed by four snappy jokes, guaranteed t' embarrass man or beast, an' then comes th' real action!! Ah climbs a tree, pours gasoline on mah head, sets mah-self afire, an' jumps, whistlin' "Th' Burnin' o' Rome"!! An', while ah is in mid-air, Weakeyes Yokum shoots a apple off mah haid!! . . . After ah dances thet jig wif th' pig, ah yanks out two o' mah teeth, an' presents 'em t' th' bride an' groom, as mementos o' th' occasion!! Then ah really gits goin'!! Ah offers t' remove any weddin' guest's appendix, wif mah bare hands—free!! Yo' spread-eagles me, fastens mah arms an' laigs t' four

2.2. Justin Howard's drawing of Sut Lovingood
from the collected *Sut Lovingood's Yarns*, 1867.

wild jackasses, an' Bam!! Yo' fires a gun!! While they tears me t' pieces, ah puffawms th' weddin' ceremony!!²

When Marryin' Sam asks Mammy Yokum "How's thet?", she responds with her typical brand of deadpan one-upmanship, "It's all right—but, it seems t' me, thet fo' eight dollahs, we oughta git somethin' onusual!!" (Capp 15:74).

Marryin' Sam himself bears resemblance to a frequent target of satire in frontier humor—the circuit rider. These early representatives of Christian evangelism were often opportunists and confidence men out to fleece believers in the name of the Lord by collecting money for missionary efforts among the pirates, seeking free chicken dinners, or seducing the family daughters, when not stirring entire congregations at camp meetings into sensual frenzies. The stories of Sut Lovingood and Simon Suggs contain such hypocritical preachers and scoundrels, with Mark Twain making his own contribution to the tradition in the Duke and Dauphin, who complicate the escape of Huckleberry Finn and Jim through their several con games.

While Capp dresses Marryin' Sam in the traditional clerical garb of the hill preacher and gives him certain pastoral characteristics, he takes pains to identify him as a justice of the peace and never identifies the large book he carries as a Bible. That he is a confidence man, however, is made clear just five weeks after his first appearance in *Li'l Abner* when on March 2, 1935, he reappears disguised as a medicine show Indian selling a bottled remedy for any illness. Pappy Yokum and Abner reveal him by his bulbous red nose and his pious tendency to say "Bless me!", and they rescue him from an angry mob, while he publicly confesses, half naked, "Alas! What a spot my sins have brought me to!" (Capp 1:99–101). That he is a fraud enables Capp to rescue Abner from the first of many seeming marriages to Daisy Mae on February 14, 1935, when it turns out that his marrying license has expired (Capp 1:92–94).

Religion in general is an important element of southern culture Capp chose to ignore entirely, and for good reason. Any satire of religious institutions, southern or otherwise, would generate controversy and alienate newspaper editors. Instead, Capp invests Dogpatch with a rich and imaginative set of folk superstitions, such as Mammy's visions that require the blood of an innocent lamb (either Abner or Pappy are sacrificed) so she can conjure up what is happening elsewhere or commune with a spirit; the Yokum death warning which means a family member will die within 24 hours (lightning has to strike the left-handed branch of a crab-apple tree, which falls on the head of a skunk, which slowly walks away in a daze while whistling "Swing Low, Sweet Chariot," and exactly in that order); or such compelling characters as Joe Btfsplk who brings misfortune with his presence, Evil-Eye Fleegle and his disastrous double whammy, and Nightmare Alice with her effective practice of voodoo.[3]

A world of spirits and powerful supernatural forces clearly inform the beliefs of the people of Dogpatch and are not out of accord with traditional southern folk belief; most local color fiction had its soothsayers, healers, and granny conjurers often central to the plot. Capp wrote two somber sequences early on which easily might have been written by a Mary Noailles Murfree or a John Fox, Jr. One is the story of the howling hound of October 27 to November 4, 1937. Trapped in an isolated cabin with strange twin brothers and a dog that howls only when someone in the cabin will die, Abner waits out the night to see if the prediction will come true. It does, and the conclusion is an O. Henry-style surprise ending (Capp 3:148–51). The other is the story of the old grandfather clock that bears Young Yancey's curse, a sequence that ran from July 20 to August 15, 1942. When Yancy's bride stood him up, he cursed the clock to play the funeral march, and any beautiful girl who happened to be near the clock when it strikes twelve is found murdered. But the clock is transported to the city of Mammy Yokum's society matron sister, and the resolution is handled in a slapstick rather than suspenseful manner (Capp 8:112–24).

Another popular theme in the frontier humor of the antebellum South is the conflict that occurs when a country bumpkin comes to the big city for the first time. In typical versions of the story, the unsophisticated mountaineer or farm boy stays in a bordello thinking it a boarding house where young ladies are welcome (a situation used by William Faulkner in *Sanctuary* to great comic effect), or he attends an opera or a play and stands up in the middle of the performance to berate or shoot the villain who is mistreating the heroine. In one story as narrated by a nineteenth-century actor, during a performance of *Othello*, a canal boatman attending a play for the first time stood up and shouted at Iago, "You damned-lying scoundrel. I would like to get a hold of you after the show and wring your infernal neck" (qtd. in Levine 30).

Capp must have been familiar with this comic construct since he began the strip in 1934, after a preliminary week of introducing the characters, by sending Abner to New York to stay with his wealthy Aunt Bessie who undertakes to educate and civilize him. Much of the humor in the sequence arises from the interaction between Abner and Bessie's sophisticated friends. On November 7, 1934, however, she offers to take Abner to the opera, but when he learns there are no acrobats in it, he declines to attend, puzzled why anyone would want to see a stage show without acrobats (Capp 1:16–65).

For the first few years of the strip, Capp would repeat this situation, such that a good deal more occurs outside rather than inside Dogpatch. Perhaps Capp was working with a more familiar environment until he could develop more fully the less familiar and more exotic world of rural Dogpatch. He would occasionally change the conventions too by having Abner outwit the city sophisticate, as for example in a series of bets over the years, beginning on August 19–21, 1937, with "Bet-a-Million" Bashby, the millionare who never bets on anything but a sure thing (Capp 3:105–6). While successful in every other bet in his career, Bashby loses to Abner no matter how unlikely or impossible the odds.

In addition to John Fox, Jr., and frontier humor most likely by way of Mark Twain, another best-selling author of the regional romantic school Capp must have read as a child, perhaps in his grandparents' library, was

Harold Bell Wright, a native New Yorker and clergyman whose visits to the Ozark Mountains of Arkansas and Missouri provided him with material for a series of melodramatic and religious, but extremely popular novels, especially *The Shepherd of the Hills* in 1907. The plot concerns an older, well-educated man who enters a mountain community anonymously to make up for a series of injustices perpetrated by his son some fifteen years earlier, especially his seduction and abandonment of a young mountain girl who bore him a child. The son was a painter, Howard Howitt, and he carried away with him a portrait of the girl, which brought him instant recognition: "The people stood before it in crowds when it was exhibited in the art gallery; the papers were extravagant in their praise; the artist became famous; and wealthy patrons came to his studio for their portraits. The picture was of a beautiful girl, standing by a spring, holding out a dripping cup of water" (Wright 327).

Capp appears to have borrowed this premise in the second year of *Li'l Abner*. In a sequence beginning on February 11, 1936 (through April 4), artist Eric Travers wanders into Dogpatch in search of the perfect American beauty and finds Daisy Mae, of course. He paints her portrait and falls deeply in love with her, but finally leaves unable to defy the force of the love between Daisy and Abner (Capp 2:30–52). Four months later, beginning December 11, 1936, the story continues when we find Eric Travers in New York having achieved fame through his painting of Daisy, now called "Mountain Girl" and hanging in an art gallery, as depicted in figure 2.3 (Capp 3:11). The picture would reappear in the comic strip from time to time in later years, passing through the hands of other owners, and usually the cause of a new plot development. Eric Travers too would reappear, including a touching sequence March 5 to April 14, 1941, in which he is stunned by a blow to the head from one of the Scraggs and begins to lose his vision. He travels to Dogpatch so that his last sight will be Daisy Mae, and playing upon her sympathy for a blind man, he seduces her into agreeing to care for and marry him. The sudden return of his sight at the last minute precludes the marriage (Capp 7:48–65). This was one of Capp's few descents into sentimental melodrama before irony gained the upper hand.

Capp need not have read *The Shepherd of the Hills* to have encountered the premise. The novel was filmed twice as a silent film in 1920 and 1928 (Williamson, *Southern Mountaineers* 261–62, 290). A sound Technicolor version in 1941 starred John Wayne but omitted the part about the painter and famous portrait. Several of John Fox, Jr.'s novels were also filmed. *The Little Shepherd of Kingdom Come* became a silent film in 1920 and 1928, while *The*

2.3. *Li'l Abner*, December 11, 1936, by Al Capp. © Capp Enterprises, Inc.

Trail of the Lonesome Pine was adapted four times in 1914, 1916, 1923, and 1936 (the last in sound and Technicolor with Henry Fonda), and a stage version ran successfully on Broadway four times between 1912 and 1922 (Williamson, *Southern Mountaineers* 8, 160–61, 218–19, 259–60, 276, 290). *The Heart of the Hills* was filmed in 1914 and 1919, and *The Kentuckians* in 1921 (Williamson, *Southern Mountaineers* 132–33, 249–50, 267). These were part of a larger trend—for more than twenty years, between 1908 and 1928, Hollywood found a steady market for movies about hillbillies, moonshine, and mountain romance.

Before 1908, producers experimented with just a few films about illegal stills, mountain love triangles, and feuding, but beginning in 1908, they developed into a crescendo such that by 1928, at least 475 known features had been released—an average of more than 22 films a year, nearly two a month. During the peak years of 1910 to 1918, 350 of the total were produced, and in the major year of 1914, 70 appeared, or more than one new film a week. That year *The Trail of the Lonesome Pine* combined most of the plot elements in these hillbilly films in general: "moonshining, treachery for the sake of coal profits, jealousy, attempted kidnapping, battles, woundings, false arrests, dynamiting, and multiple murders" (Williamson, *Southern Mountaineers* 2, 8). How many such films Capp might have seen as a child, we do not know, but his brother has testified that "the one joy we all shared with equal gusto was the weekly trip to the movies," and that Alfred dearly loved every minute he spent in the movie palaces, which thoroughly stirred his imagination: "They were the interplanetary vehicles that transported Alfred and the rest of us to the wonderful places we couldn't begin to imagine without the images on the screen proving that, yes, there was an existence beyond the ones we led" (Caplin 7–9).

Later, while Capp was creating and developing *Li'l Abner*, contemporary sound films continued to reflect a nationwide interest in all aspects of not only mountaineer but southern life and culture in general. In 1932, *Cabin in the Cotton* and *I Am a Fugitive From a Chain Gang* brought controversial attention to southern mistreatment of sharecroppers and criminals, and in 1934, both *Carolina* and *Judge Priest* provided romanticized versions of a depleted South possessed by memories of the Civil War. The last was a comedy with Will Rogers, who would also appear a year later with humorist Irvin S. Cobb in a Mark Twain-inspired film, *Steamboat 'Round the Bend*.

In fact, 1935 proved to be a bumper year for popular films about the South, such as *So Red the Rose*, based on the novel by Mississippian Stark Young, which created great sympathy for the Confederacy and its sacrifices during the Civil War; *Harmony Lane*, a biography of Stephen Foster, composer of such songs as "Oh, Susanna" and "My Old Kentucky Home"; *Mississippi*, a musical comedy in which Yankee Bing Crosby pursued belle Joan Bennett amidst antebellum plantation splendor and which encouraged theatres, as a promotional ploy, to hire a black man to play banjo tunes while sitting on a cotton bale in the lobby; and *The Little Colonel* and *The Littlest Rebel* in which Shirley Temple and her faithful black butler Bill "Bojangles" Robinson tap danced their way through war and peace in Dixie. Within the next few years such blockbuster films as *Show Boat* (1936) with Paul Robeson, *Jezebel* (1938) with Bette Davis (attempting to prove she should have won the part of Scarlett O'Hara), and *Gone With the Wind* (1939) all defined for the popular imagination a South that never existed but which would influence all portrayals to come (Campbell).

An interesting sub-genre of films set in the South were the "hillbilly" musicals, such as *Mountain Music* (1937) and *The Arkansas Traveler* (1938) with vaudevillian Bob Burns, *Grand Ole Opry* (1940) with a comedy group called the Weaver Brothers and Elviry, or a long-running series featuring comedienne Judy Canova from *Sis Hopkins* (1941) to *Lay That Rifle Down* (1955). These were a direct result of another popular phenomenon, a new presence on the music scene that what would come to be known as country music.

String bands, banjo players, fiddlers, and gospel singers had always been a part of southern folklife, but with the establishment of southern radio stations after 1920, their songs of rural life were heard by the nation through such performers as Vernon Dalhart, Uncle Dave Macon, the Skillet Lickers, and the Fruit Jar Drinkers. The National Barn Dance from Chicago and the Grand Ole Opry from Nashville reached ever-growing audiences after 1925, and commercialization brought the Carter Family from Virginia and Jimmie Rodgers, "The Singing Brakeman," from Mississippi, into recording studios in 1927 (Malone 1002–3).

The first group of performers to reach New York in 1923 called themselves "The Hill Billies," a name that from then on was applied to that entire music genre for years. Other bands and comedy teams would follow to the New York vaudeville houses, one of which Alfred and Catherine Caplin visited one evening in 1933. Could that group have been the Weaver Brothers and Elviry, who performed in a "drawling, deadpan comedy style"? Elviry was called by a critic for the New York *American* newspaper "the best straight-faced comedienne in captivity" (Williamson, *Hillbillyland* 47–49). Their style suited Catherine's description, but it could have been any one of dozens of such groups.

Capp did undertake in one instance a direct satire of country music and its penchant for sad lyrics about death and disaster. In a 1940 sequence, two Chicago con men overhear Daisy Mae as she baby-sits and sings a typical song about the execution of a prisoner whose pardon came too late. They find it so affecting that they hire her every evening for ten cents from 7:15 to 7:30 to sing while baby-sitting one of the con men, a midget disguised as an infant. With a hidden microphone they parlay this into a $5,000-a-week contract with a major Chicago radio station, and soon the entire nation is weeping nightly to the sad lyrics of "Sorrowful Sue." A "Sunshine Sue" Workman was beginning her broadcast career at about that time in Chicago and elsewhere and would eventually become the star of the Old Dominion Barn Dance in Richmond, Virginia, after 1946 and be crowned "Queen of the Hillbillies" in 1949 by the state governor (Ward 290).

By the end of the six-week sequence, Daisy Mae had parodied all the major types of country tunes, including "The Prisoner's Song," "Little Rosewood Casket," and "The Letter Edged in Black," and even a swing tune of the period that went "Oh, Johnny, Oh, Johnny, How you do love," and which came out as "Oh, Li'l Abner, Oh, Li'l Abner, How yo' don't love." A good example of these lachrymose lyrics is Daisy Mae's rendition of "The Letter Edged in Black":

"Ah was seated by th' window yester mawnin',
Wifout a tho't o' worry or o' care,
When ah spied the postman comin' up th' pathway,
Wif *sech* a jolly smile an' happy air!!

He whistled gaily as he rang th' doorbell,
An' then he said 'Good mawnin' t' yo' Jack!'
He did-unt know th' sorrow thet he brought me-e,
When he handed me thet let-ter edged in *black*!

Wif tremblin' hands ah took th' letter fum him,
Ah opened it, an' this is whut I read,
'Come home, come home, mah boy, yo' are fo'given,
Come home, come home, *yo' pore ole mother's daid*!'"

Everyone falls in love with the plaintive voice of "Sorrowful Sue," including the murderous Black Rufe, who loses the will to kill when she sings, and Li'l Abner, whose love disappears, of course, when he finds out that she is really Daisy Mae. She becomes so overjoyed with the mere fact that Abner had loved her voice, she begins singing happy songs and promptly loses her audience, sponsors, and broadcaster (Capp 6:75–94). The entire episode was a keen piece of satire directed at the fickle taste of Americans in popular music and the extreme sentimentality of early country song lyrics.

Another powerful source of southern rural stereotypes of which Capp was undoubtedly aware during the early years of *Li'l Abner* were the novels of Erskine Caldwell. Both *Tobacco Road* (1932) and *God's Little Acre* (1933) sold in the millions in paperback and brought him national notoriety. His steamy treatment of poor whites and their irresistible sexual urges spoke to the worst suspicions of readers about life in isolated southern communities at the same time that they offered erotic delight. One novel reached millions more through the 1933 play version of *Tobacco Road*, which became by 1939 the longest running play in Broadway history, with 3,180 performances. A movie adaptation followed in 1941, and *God's Little Acre* was filmed in 1958 (Miller).

There appears to be a slight satiric glance at Ty Ty Walden of *God's Little Acre* in the February 6, 1941 strip when Abner digs into the ground, his own God's little acre, and unlike Ty Ty, actually finds $42 buried there. When Moonshine McSwine learns this, he rushes to persuade his daughter to seduce and marry Abner for his fortune. This is the introduction of Moonbeam McSwine, the dirtiest, laziest, but most sexually appealing woman ever

2.4. *Li'l Abner*, October 4, 1942, by Al Capp. © Capp Enterprises, Inc.

to appear in the comic strip. She would have been perfectly at home in a Caldwell novel, as would her daddy willing to use his daughter's sex appeal and body to make his own life more comfortable (Capp 7:36).

Like the rest of the nation, by 1939 Capp had apparently read Margaret Mitchell's *Gone With the Wind* (1936) and could not resist satirizing the obsession over who would play Scarlett O'Hara in the film version. Thus in a *Li'l Abner* sequence in April of 1939, Capp has a fictional actress named Marge Mars, who has won the role, decide to back out of the commitment because she has a chance to marry a European prince who has appeared incognito in Dogpatch. Capp portrays the scene on the film set of "Pfft With the Breeze" as the actors incredulously discuss Mars's willingness to give up the role of "Heartless O'Tara," which would make her "Hollywood's number one star."

Apparently Mitchell didn't notice this or decided to let it pass, but this would not be the case three years later when Capp decided to lampoon the novel itself with what he thought was affectionate parody. It began in a series of Sunday pages on October 4, 1942 (figure 2.4) under the title "Gone Wif' th' Wind" with Abner playing "Wreck Butler," Daisy Mae "Scallop O'Hara," and Hannibal Hoops "Ashcan Wilkes." When Mitchell saw it, she was horrified. What happened next was fully recounted by Capp himself over ten years later on a forum at a meeting of the National Cartoonists Society:

I think the most luxurious trouble a strip ever got into was some years ago when I read a book which along with all America I was enchanted with—*Gone With the Wind* by Margaret Mitchell. I think it was the most suspenseful thing ever written in our time. At every chapter end, you wondered would she be raped, or what's worse, wouldn't she be. It was a thriller—a sort of *Dick Tracy* without pictures. I loved *Gone With the Wind* and decided to send it flowers in my own way which was to disembowel it in a series of four Sunday pages.

Like all of you, I work five or six weeks ahead. The morning after the first of these burlesques appeared, my phone in Boston rang . . . and the operator told me I was being called from Atlanta, Georgia, by a John Marsh. Does anybody here know that name? I didn't. I didn't know that Mr. John Marsh was Miss Mitchell's husband and a libel lawyer without much to do at the time. He asked me, "Are you Al Capp, suh?" in a Southern drawl, and I told him yes that was my privilege. He said, "Suh"—I must tell you that he called me "Suh" throughout the conversation and at first I thought it a term of Southern respect. Later, I found out that it was an abbreviation for what he deeply felt about me—he said, "Suh, my wife read your Sunday page, and suh, she didn't like it, suh."

Well, I was touched. To think that people in far Atlanta were so concerned about my career that they went to the expense of calling me when they felt I wasn't doing so well, and I said, "Gee, I'm sorry. Maybe she'll like it better next Sunday." (Then I really murder it!) He said, "No suh." I advised that she read *Rex Morgan, M.D.* until the whole thing blew over. As a matter of fact, *Rex Morgan* was having a most hilarious sequence then about leprosy; it didn't tell how to cure it but how to enjoy it.

But he kept nagging me and said that the only way I could please his wife was to cancel the entire series. I patiently tried to explain the facts of syndicate life; that they were irrevocably in the papers and no power on earth . . . could possibly stop the pages. But he kept nagging, and as I had to go back to work, I ended the conversation with a short Anglo-Saxon phrase of two words. It's very useful for getting rid of pests—and for beginning lawsuits.

About an hour later, United Features called me from New York to reveal for the first time that the gentleman to whom I had just spoken was Miss Mitchell's husband and that my closing remark had somehow irritated him and that he intended to sue United Features and me jointly for one dollar for every newspaper in which this burlesque had appeared. We had actually infringed on their copyright. I had used an arrangement of English words—Gone With the Wind—which then belonged to the Mitchells, as I've since always thought of them.

He was going to sue for one buck for every newspaper in which this infringement had appeared. Seventy-six million dollars! And in the opinion of the United Features lawyers, he had a damn good chance of collecting it. That didn't scare me although it is true that my half would have amounted to somewhat more than a year's pay. But I tell you this in confidence—United Features is very cheap about sums like $36,000,000. ("The Comic Page" 16-17)

Two corrections are in order: John Marsh was actually Director of Advertising for the Georgia Power Co., not a libel lawyer. Also, the title of a work or novel cannot be copyrighted, so the actual grounds for the threatened lawsuit are not clear. Perhaps Mitchell simply wanted to coerce Capp from parodying or ridiculing her characters.

They eventually settled out of court, although because of advanced distribution two more weeks in the series appeared before it was stopped in mid-sequence. According to Finis Farr in *Margaret Mitchell of Atlanta* (1965), a legal stipulation required that the copyright in the series be transferred to Mitchell. Farr cites no source for this information. This seems unlikely, however, since United Features Syndicate could not give up any part of a property copyrighted and trademarked since 1934. Capp was required to apologize for his indiscretion, but in his usual whimsical manner, he decided to do it on his own terms.

On December 27, 1942, in what would become a continuing practice in the years to follow, Capp drew himself into a Sunday page of *Li'l Abner* at the drawing board. Abner says, "Befo' goin' on wif *this* story, Mistah Capp—rec'lect thet story yo' did a *while back*, good-naychurdly kiddin' a sartin book?" Mammy Yokum continues, "Wal—sartin parties objected—sartin parties got thar feelin's hurt! Yo gotta make it *right*, Mistah Capp!! *It's the Code of the Hills*!!" A handwritten apology appears in the final panel. Most authors would have been happy over the free publicity generated by the most widely read comic strip in the nation, but not Mitchell. Capp would steer clear of living southern authoresses after this.

If the producers of popular U.S. fiction, film, and music were absorbed with southern culture in the 1930s and 1940s, so too were those writers of a belletristic or serious turn of mind. Beginning with the work of the Fugitive poets in Nashville in 1922, the fiction of William Faulkner with *Soldiers' Pay* in 1926, and the early drama of Tennessee Williams in 1940, soon mainstream U.S. literature was largely dominated by major writers using their southern experience as material for creative expression in what has come to be called the Southern Literary Renaissance. Writers such as Thomas Wolfe, Robert Penn Warren, Richard Wright, Flannery O'Connor, Eudora Welty, John Crowe Ransom, and hundreds of others explored the South from every conceivable angle, while at Vanderbilt University a select group of writers and intellectuals organized a symposium published as *I'll Take My Stand* in 1930 to articulate a philosophy of economic Agrarianism for the South that pitted it politically against the Industrial North and the New South.

While Capp reflects little of this cultural discourse, he does display an awareness of the issues. Dogpatch is a distinctly agrarian or agricultural community whose sole means of support is the annual crop of turnips, which means that like so much of the South during the 1930s, failure to practice crop rotation has left the soil depleted. But the biggest threat is the annual invasion of turnip termites that will wipe everything out unless the farmers are able to buy exterminator poison from Honest John, who uses the situation mercilessly to his advantage. The termites are not unlike the boll weevils that infected cotton in the South and were celebrated in folk song and story.

The inhabitants of Dogpatch also express many of the sentiments of the Agrarians in their devotion to home and family and love of the soil. On May 27, 1937, Mammy Yokum provides another of her occasional orations that embodies the Agrarian attitude (figure 2.5). Abner comments on how quickly Dogpatch has been restored after a destructive flood. "Thet, son," replies Mammy, "is becuz ev'ry man, woman, an' chile h'yar has been sweatin' thar hearts out buildin' it up! Floods might wash our homes away, but nuthin' kin ever wash us Dogpatchers off th' earth o' Dogpatch itself. It's whar we was all born 'n' raised, it's the place we loves better'n any place on earth—it's *home!*" (Capp 3:82). The Agrarian mistrust of technology is also evident in Dogpatch. Every time an automobile, a telephone, or a mechanical improvement of any kind enters the community, it is usually soon dispatched because of the trouble it brings.

Like William Faulkner, who created in his fiction an extended self-contained community known as Yoknapatawpha County, so too has Capp created a similar fictional community in Dogpatch, in which a complex set of family connections and recurring characters provide a historical structure. So well defined was Faulkner's sense of his imaginary world that he could

2.5. *Li'l Abner*, May 27, 1937, by Al Capp. © Capp Enterprises, Inc.

draw a map of it with statistics attached: "Area, 2400 square miles. Population: Whites, 6298; Negroes, 9313" (Brooks 500). Capp provides only brief glimpses of the terrain and physical layout of Dogpatch, but on September 14, 1942, a character outlines the area as "Th' free an' independent commoonity o' Dogpatch, garden spot o' th' mountains—no taxes, no roads, no water power, no modern sanitation—in fact, no nuthin'—also, hay grain, an' feed, cheap at Softhearted John's—popoolayshun two hunderd," but minus one since Abner is about to be hanged for a murder he did not commit (Capp 8:136).

There is one obvious and important southern presence missing in Li'l Abner's world, and that is the African American. When blacks appear at all, they are merely background characters, like the porters who appear at the train station when Abner arrives in New York for the first time in the tenth and eleventh daily strips published in August 1934 (Capp 1:17–18). There is no black culture in the strip, although Daisy Mae does reiterate in 1940 a popular phrase from one of the great blues songs of the period when Abner is about to marry another woman at sunset: "How ah hates t' see thet evenin' sun g-go down!!" (Capp 6:109). Capp largely avoided humor based on immigrant or ethnic stereotypes, unlike much of American graphic comedy.

Southern politics were avoided too, except in general ways, as in the introduction of Senator Jack S. Phogbound, an unscrupulous politician who blackmails his fellow Washington senators to appropriate two million dollars to establish Phogbound University in Dogpatch, to be known fondly as "P. U." Most of the money goes to build a brass statue of the Senator, but as Mammy Yokum says, "Bet Harvard hain't got as fine a statchoo o' Phogbound as *thet*!!" (Capp 13:138–40). There are echoes here of the career of

Louisiana demagogue Huey P. Long, who entered the U.S. Senate in 1932, was gunned down by an assassin in 1935, but left behind as one of his legacies the development of Louisiana State University into a major national educational institution. A statue of Long stands before his grave in Baton Rouge at the state capitol building, not far from the university.

Also missing are references to the Civil War, an all-consuming preoccupation and topic of conversation in the South, except for the statue dedicated to General Jubilation T. Cornpone, who won undying fame in a vague series of military defeats and routs generally known as "Cornpone's Hoomiliation" (Capp 13:145). The whole business of erecting statues to leaders of the lost cause has been a common southern practice—witness Monument Avenue in Richmond, Virginia, where Robert E. Lee, Jefferson Davis, J. E. B. Stuart, and Stonewall Jackson stand today. We already know, of course, that the Yokums are fierce patriots of the United States, so any lack of lament over the Confederacy is not surprising. Capp was smart enough to realize, too, that like religion, race, politics, and the Civil War were dangerous subjects for satire and more likely to irritate than amuse certain readers.

Some critics and commentators on southern culture are not happy with the way cartoonists have portrayed mountain people and Appalachian life, especially Capp as the most widely read in his day. In a 1971 attack on television for its portrayals of hillbillies, James Branscome called it "the most intensive effort ever exerted by a nation to belittle, demean, and otherwise destroy a minority people within its boundaries" (overlooking obviously the treatment of blacks in America, as well as the Holocaust). Branscome went on to include in his indictment the work of "that hillbilly-maligning patriot, Al Capp" (Branscome 25–32). David Whisnant called Dogpatch part of "a broader pattern of cultural imperialism" in America in 1973, and John Egerton and Frye Gaillard found *Li'l Abner* alarming and full of "dim-witted yokels and pig-sty-wallowing ignoramuses" in 1974 (Whisnant 124–38; Egerton 8–13). A 1984 documentary produced by Herb E. Smith for Appalshop Films called *Strangers & Kin: A History of the Hillbilly* criticized Capp's stereotypes, even as the producers utilized drawings from *Li'l Abner* to make their promotional flyer attractive (according to a note, with Elliott Caplin's permission).

But few readers saw things this way. *Li'l Abner* was as popular in the South as he was elsewhere, and southern newspaper readers never for a moment believed that Dogpatch was anything but a fictional community. Capp's world was not meant to be a faithful representation of a real, historical South, though it did draw upon many of the qualities his readers would have associated with the region: an emphasis on the family and blood kin as a source of loyalty; a reliance on violence when social order is threatened; an acceptance of individuality in personal behavior which sometimes borders on eccentricity and the grotesque; and a faith in the land and home as a source of morality and self-sufficiency. It was also perfectly evident the comic strip had a clear sense of morality that always saw justice done and goodness, no matter how naïve, rewarded. This is what Frank Stack, former underground cartoonist and art professor at the University of Missouri, seems to be saying in his comment on Capp:

> Li'l Abner was the authentic public persona of Al Capp. For me, and for millions of others, reading Li'l Abner was an exciting, exuberant, positive experience. As an artist, creating a world ruled by poetic justice in which foolishness is exposed, evil is punished, and innocence is rewarded, Capp was a good friend and mentor: loyal, warm, witty and wise.
> . . . Southerners are notoriously touchy, and conjure insults to their honor in every Southern reference originating north of the Mason-Dixon Line. One would expect the south in general to take umbrage at the satire it suffered from Li'l Abner and [Walt Kelly's] Pogo. But it seems to me that Southerners, in particular, took both of those innocent heroes to heart. (qtd. in Capp 16:6)

Capp's South was no different from the one already extant in the larger popular culture from which it derived, and his intent was neither to exploit Appalachian people nor address the genuine economic and social problems from which they have suffered under industrial exploitation. Dogpatch had less in common with reality than Lubberland and its worthless inhabitants as described by William Byrd II in his eighteenth-century comic history of establishing the dividing line between Virginia and North Carolina. Humor about the South reaches far back into our culture. The name Dogpatch has entered our vocabulary as any community, North or South, that is hopelessly backward in its economy and attitudes. Capp's satire was directed at the national scene rather than the South and at man's inhumanity to man rather than regional characteristics. That is why John Steinbeck thought Capp deserved the Nobel Prize. As has been true with all great satirists, from Jonathan Swift and Voltaire to Mark Twin and James Thurber, it is our failure to live up to our ideals and principles that brings upon us their sublime ridicule, and Capp, who knew how to puncture our pretensions in grand style with mere pen and India ink, belongs among them.

The same year that Capp began *Li'l Abner*, another important southern comic strip character appeared in an already successful feature about the sporting life, *Barney Google*, celebrated in Billy Rose's song, "Barney Google with his goo goo googly eyes." Billy DeBeck of Chicago premiered the strip on June 17, 1919, and soon the bulb-nosed, pop-eyed, dumpy little bummer and his unlikely race horse Spark Plug took the nation by storm and generated millions of dollars worth of merchandise and three stage musicals. In 1934 the plot line led into the Kentucky hills, and on November 17, an equally dumpy and scruffy bootlegger named Snuffy Smith and his wife Loweezy appeared. Snuffy, his mountain friends, and their often grotesque adventures soon stole the spotlight away from Barney, who became only an occasional visitor. After DeBeck's death in 1942, his assistant, Fred Lasswell, shifted the strip entirely into the fictional Appalachian community and would maintain it for another fifty years as one of the most popular strips in comics history.

DeBeck's creation of Snuffy was no incidental excursion into a currently popular topic, nor was it an imitation of *Li'l Abner*. Indeed, he was deeply fascinated with the life and culture of the southern mountaineer. DeBeck, as an examination of his personal library (on deposit at Virginia Commonwealth University in Richmond) demonstrates, read deeply into the literature and fiction of Appalachia, especially the works of Tennessee writers George Washington Harris and Mary Noailles Murfree, and the Ozark folklore collections of Vance Randolph, among dozens of others. The cartoonist traveled into the mountains of Kentucky and Virginia, talked with the local people, and made numerous sketches of faces, scenes, and places.

The single book that inspired DeBeck the most was an 1867 edition of George Washington Harris's *Sut Lovingood Yarns*, which he purchased and inscribed in 1935. Every page of the volume is annotated, and many contain sketches illustrating passages in the stories. The book was ranked number one in his library and was so marked on the spine. Inside the back cover, DeBeck drew a deftly detailed miniature portrait of Snuffy, his contribution to the tradition of Simon Suggs and Sut Lovingood.

Folklorist Vance Randolph took note of the fact that DeBeck was borrowing his material and sent him a letter dated January 25, 1939, which noted:

Dear Mr. Debeck:
    A Texan named Wood writes me that you read some of his Ozark rhymes, and sent him a signed cartoon.
    Well by God you can send me a signed cartoon—a good big one! You certainly have used a lot of my Ozark stuff in "Barney Google."

A subsequent letter, tucked inside a copy of Randolph's *From an Ozark Holler* along with the above one, indicates that DeBeck complied. Randolph also offered to share with him even better material "than the items you so flatteringly crib out of my books."

Like Li'l Abner, Snuffy Smith has also been charged with contributing to the stereotyping of southern mountaineers as backwards, dumb, lazy, and unable to cope with the modern world. Neither Capp nor DeBeck made any claim to realism or accuracy, and as noted above, their humor remains no less flattering than the numerous films, fiction, and cartoons of the times. In the case of DeBeck, however, under his hand the adventures of Snuffy reflected a brilliant use of Appalachian language, folklore, customs, themes, and stories inspired by experiences and reading in southern culture.[4]

While DeBeck showed no influence of *Li'l Abner*, Capp's success did inspire at least two similar features—*Ozark Ike* and *Long Sam*. Ray Gotto of Tennessee began *Ozark Ike* as a baseball sports strip in 1945. While the naïve and shy Ike bore some resemblance to Abner, his blond girlfriend Dinah had a body like that of Daisy Mae, a hairstyling drawn from movie star Veronica Lake, and a name based on Gotto's Nashville high school classmate Dinah Shore.

Ozark Ike remained less a hillbilly strip as the narrative moved out of the hills and onto the bush league playing fields. Trained as a sports cartoonist, Gotto had a bold and distinctive style that made his strip popular for almost ten years in both newspapers and comic book reprints. When he lost the rights to *Ozark Ike* over a contract dispute, Gotto created a second and very similar version called *Cotton Woods* that ran from 1955 to 1958, after which he turned once again to sports cartoons.

Long Sam was actually created by Al Capp as a female variation of *Li'l Abner* in 1954. Written by his brother Elliott Caplin and drawn by Bob Lubbers, whose style was in the Capp tradition, *Long Sam* was about a beautiful mountain girl of that name whose Mammy spent her time guaranteeing that her daughter never laid eyes on a man. This plot device proved rather limiting, but because of the attractive pen work of Lubbers, the strip lasted for nine years.

An interesting feature of the most popular renditions of the South in American culture in the twentieth century, the comics included, was the fact that most of them were conceived and created by non-southerners. In film, for example, David O. Selznick, who produced the film version of *Gone with the Wind* (1939), was the son of first-generation Jewish immigrants and grew up in Pittsburgh, Pennsylvania. Others were also midwesterners, like Daryl F. Zanuck, producer of *The Littlest Rebel* (1935), a native of Nebraska, and Hal B. Wallis, producer of *Jezebel* (1938), raised in Chicago. These were among the many films of the 1930s that established the mythic pattern for popular views of the South, with their wholesale creation of a cinematic version of the moonlight and magnolias school of fiction. As outsiders who knew only what they had read, seen, or heard in popular fiction, hillbilly movies, and country music on the radio, they understandably objectified the South into a land of high romance, proud defiance, and undeserved defeat and humiliation. Stereotypes were the coin of the realm.

It was not until the 1960s that native southerners became more deeply involved in filmmaking and produced more objective and realistic versions of the region, as in Horton Foote's faithful screenplays for such works as Harper Lee's *To Kill a Mockingbird* (1962) or William Faulkner's *Tomorrow* (1972). The involvement of a southern cartoonist in a comic strip about the South would take longer. The first comic strip entirely southern in creation, content, and orientation would be *Kudzu*, beginning in 1981, by Doug Marlette of North Carolina. The strip ended in 2007 with the untimely death of its creator, and there have been no other such features in the light of its example.

The major features—*Li'l Abner* and *Snuffy Smith*—were created by non-southerners who used the region at first mainly for local color and, except for Billy DeBeck who did his homework, and Capp when he paid attention to his sources, achieved little semblance of southern culture in their renditions. In his thorough and comprehensive study of the "Hillbilly" as an American icon, Anthony Harkins has noted, "From a cynical perspective these comics . . . offered the pleasure of laughing at the misfortunes of others, and even confirmation of the belief that the poor deserved their poverty because of innate laziness and ignorance." He also makes a case, however, for the positive values of reading these strips:

But they could also at times reflect a more sanguine vision of the durability of the American people and the American spirit in the face of adversity. To some readers, they could even be seen as populist celebrations of the hill folk, descendants of white Anglo-Saxon pioneers who preserved colonial life skills and values. From this perspective, hillbilly characters, who rejected a lifestyle driven by the pursuit of monetary gain and who cherished family, kin, and personal independence, might be seen as models of the traditional American values needed to save the nation from the twin threats of unfettered industrial urbanism and unregulated capitalism. (104)

Given Abner Yokum and Snuffy Smith's continued popularity in the United States throughout the struggle for integration and civil rights, probably few readers assumed they were typical southerners. In fact, they may have served to provide some badly needed amusement for the nation throughout a tumultuous century that saw several wars and unending political turmoil, and for that—readers of all regions were grateful.[5]

Notes

1. Caplin 31 documents that Capp probably first read Mark Twain in old bound volumes of *Harper's Weekly* purchased for a quarter each at a used bookstore.

2. This version appears in the sequence for May 19–20, 1949. From its first appearance on September 3, 1937, Marryin' Sam's wedding special increases in complexity and price over the years from $3.00 to $4.00 (June 1940), down to $2.00 (November 15, 1943, and July 6, 1944), then back up to $5.00 (November 22, 1944), and finally $8.00 as above in 1949. Whether these adjustments had anything to do with changes in the cost of living in Dogpatch or with the stock market remains a question.

3. The Yokum death warning first appears on September 13, 1949; Joe Bfstplk on June 11, 1942; Evil-Eye Fleegle October 10, 1947; and Nightmare Alice on July 18, 1951. Nightmare Alice, it should be noted, is white and not African American.

4. These matters are discussed more fully in my essay "Sut Lovingood and Snuffy Smith," also published in *Comics as Culture*.

5. An earlier version of this paper was presented at the 21st Natchez Literary and Cinema Celebration held February 25–28, 2010, in Natchez, Mississippi, on the topic "Humor in the Deep South." Thanks to Director Carolyn Vance Smith for the kind invitation to participate. This revised version incorporates information originally published in "The South in the Comic Strips," *Studies in Popular Culture* 19 (October 1996): 153–66; the introduction to volume 26 of the *Li'l Abner Dailies* reprint project by Kitchen Sink Press (1998); and "Li'l Abner, Snuffy, Pogo, and Friends," *The Southern Quarterly*, 48.2 (Winter 2010/11).

Works Cited

Branscome, David. "Annihilating the Hillbilly: The Appalachians' Struggle with America's Institutions." *Katallagete* 3 (Winter 1971): 25–32.

Brooks, Cleanth. *William Faulkner: The Yoknapatawpha Country*. New Haven: Yale U P, 1963.

Campbell, Edward D. C. *The Celluloid South: Hollywood and Southern Myth*. Knoxville: U of Tennessee P, 1981.

Caplin, Elliot. *Al Capp Remembered*. Bowling Green, OH: BGSU Popular Press, 1994.

Capp, Al. *Li'l Abner Dailies*. Vols. 1–27: 1934–1961. Northampton, MA: Kitchen Sink Press, 1988–1998.

Capp, Al. "The Comic Page is the Last Refuge of Classic Art." *Nemo: The Classic Comics Library*, No. 18 (April 1986): 16–17.

Egerton, John, and Frye Gaillard. "The Mountaineer Minority." *Race Relations Reporter* (March 1974): 8–13.

Farr, Finis. *Margaret Mitchell of Atlanta*. New York: William Morrow, 1965.

Gotto, Ray. *Cotton Woods*. Princeton, WI: Kitchen Sink Press, 1991.

Harkins, Anthony. *Hillbilly: A Cultural History of an American Icon*. New York: Oxford, 2003.

Inge, M. Thomas. *Comics as Culture*. Jackson: UP of Mississippi, 1990.

Inge, M. Thomas. "Sut and His Illustrators." *Sut Lovingood's Nat'ral Born Yarnspinner: Essays on George Washington Harris*. Ed. James E. Caron and M. Thomas Inge. Tuscaloosa: U of Alabama P, 1996. 126–38.

———. "Sut Lovingood and Snuffy Smith." *Barney Google and Snuffy Smith*. Ed. Brian Walker. Wilton, CT: Comicana Books, 1994. 100–105.

Kelly, Walt. *Ten Ever-Lovin' Blue-Eyed Years with Pogo*. New York: Simon and Schuster, 1959.

Levine, Lawrence W. *Highbrow/Lowbrow: The Emergence of Cultural Hierarchy in America*. Cambridge: Harvard UP, 1988.

Malone, Bill C. "Country Music." *Encyclopedia of Southern Culture*. Ed. Charles Reagan Wilson and William Ferris. Chapel Hill: U of North Carolina P, 1989. 1002–3.

Marlette, Doug. *Kudzu*. New York: Ballantine Books, 1982.

Miller, Dan B. *Erskine Caldwell: The Journey From Tobacco Road*. New York: Knopf, 1995.

Time. "Apology for Margaret." *Time* 41 (January 11, 1943): 70–71.

Titus, Warren I. *John Fox, Jr*. New York: Twayne, 1971.

Ward, Harry M. *Richmond: An Illustrated History*. Richmond, VA: Windsor, 1985.

Whisnant, David E. "Ethnicity and the Recovery of Regional Identity in Appalachia." *Soundings* 56 (Spring 1973): 124–38.

Williamson, J. W. *Hillbillyland: What the Movies Did to the Mountains and What the Mountains Did to the Movies*. Chapel Hill: U of North Carolina P, 1995.

———. *Southern Mountaineers in Silent Films*. Jefferson, NC: McFarland, 1994.

Wright, Harold Bell. *The Shepherd of the Hills*. New York: A. L. Burt, 1907.

Bumbazine, Blackness, and the Myth of the Redemptive South in Walt Kelly's *Pogo*

—Brian Cremins

The artist is no freer than the society in which he lives, and in the United States writers who stereotype or ignore the Negro and other minorities in the final analysis stereotype and distort their own humanity. Mark Twain knew that in *his* America humanity masked its face with blackness.
—Ralph Ellison, 1953

There is no need to sally forth, for it remains true that those things which make us human are, curiously enough, always close at hand. Resolve, then, that on this very ground, with small flags waving and tinny blasts on tiny trumpets, we shall meet the enemy, and not only may he be ours, he may be us.
—Walt Kelly, 1953

Nobody loves me—I is hounded all the time—but I'd rather be in the swamp than in the city!
—Kelly's Albert the Alligator, *Animal Comics #5,* 1943

The swamp holds a significant place in the history of American comic strips and comic books ranging from the funny animals of *Pogo* to the grotesque creatures of *Swamp Thing*. Always a territory for alternate realities, magic, and carnivalesque social satire, the swamp's significance in the history of comic art may have its roots in the other-dimensional beasts of H. P. Lovecraft's "The Call of Cthulhu" or in the 3-D camp of *Creature from the Black Lagoon*. As a location always in the process of change or becoming, the swamp appeals to writers and artists looking to explore grand themes ranging from ecological ruin to the final struggle between good and evil. Walt Kelly's vision of the swamp was perhaps less cosmic but no less ambitious. His potent combination of funny animals and editorial-page social satire place the strip within what Leigh Anne Duck describes as "the trope of the backward South" in which "the region was said to maintain social values that modernization was purportedly eroding in the broader nation" (6). While, as Duck argues, the concept of the South as a "region [which] provided a venue through which national audiences could imagine restrictive but stable and sustaining bonds" shifted during the Great Depression (6–7), Walt Kelly's *Pogo* persisted in its depiction of the swamp and, more specifically, the South as territories filled with images of innocence, escape, and magic.

Duck discusses the emphasis some scholars of southern literature have placed on the "analysis of 'imagined geography,' as influentially exemplified in Edward Said's *Orientalism*, [which] holds that fantasies of 'other' spaces depend largely on 'projection,'" a projection that reflects "the psychological needs and material desires of contemplative agents" (Duck 2, Said 55).[1] While Lovecraft and later comic book writers including Steve Gerber and Alan Moore depicted the swamp as a trapdoor to other dimensions and unspeakable evil, Kelly invented an "imagined geography" in which complex social problems including racism, segregation, war, political strife, and environmental blight could be contained and resolved with humor, compassion, and often surreal wordplay (Ong 99, 101). However, a closer analysis of Kelly's work raises significant questions concerning what "psychological needs and material desires" were being satisfied by Pogo and his friends. Kelly, as we shall see, was a northerner, yet he employs a conceptual framework derived—perhaps unconsciously—from discourses on race and geography familiar to scholars of African American and southern literature.

In Kelly's imagined geography, as Norman Hale has argued, Pogo's most human, most endearing, and most transformative qualities were not his own; they were inherited from Bumbazine, the black boy who is the central character of Kelly's earliest Pogo and Albert stories, published in *Animal Comics* in the early 1940s (see Moore 27 and Hale 7–9). Hale's argument is worth closer examination, as it draws readers into the depth and complexity of Kelly's achievement, a comic strip that continues to open lines of inquiry relevant to scholars of African American literature, southern studies, and sequential art. This essay will examine Kelly's appropriation of discourses including blackness as a sign of essential humanity and the South as a region of redemptive power, concepts that gained popularity in American literature and popular culture of the first half of the twentieth century.

Kelly's deployment of these tropes cannot be separated, however, from his work as a cartoonist. His use of imagery derived from the minstrel tradition of the nineteenth century and his depictions, for example, of the horror and violence of the Ku Klux Klan raise significant questions about the limits of representation. At what point does the cartoonist shift from caricature to stereotype? What tools are at the cartoonist's disposal to switch from one to the other? To answer these questions it is necessary to examine how Kelly's work was received over the lifetime of the strip. Any history of *Pogo* is also a history of Kelly's readers, who have analyzed, understood, and enjoyed the strip as everything from children's fable and political satire to pastoral reflection and modernist experiment.

It is perhaps best to start with a discussion of Kelly the cartoonist before embarking upon discussions of Kelly as political satirist or cultural commentator. Even in his art, however, imagined geography plays a significant role that calls to mind Scott McCloud's discussion of the way in which some cartoonists, ranging from Carl Barks to Jaime Hernandez to Dave Sim, blend richly detailed, realistic backgrounds with iconic, almost abstract (or, to use McCloud's less formal phrase, "cartoony") figures (McCloud 43, 56). Kelly was a master of this technique, as he blended comical, simple, child-like figures with lush illustrations of massive live oak trees, cross-hatched vines and tendrils, decaying plantation homes, and dilapidated shotgun shacks. This mixture of the realistic and the iconic, McCloud argues, is most common in American animation, notably in the work of Kelly's one-time employer, the Walt Disney Company. He argues, "This combination allows readers to *mask* themselves in a character and safely enter a sensually stimulating world" (43). The "combination," McCloud suggests, provides readers with "[o]ne set of lines to *see*. Another set of lines to *be*" (43). However, if, as in the case of Walt Kelly, the artist of a strip is creating "a sensually stimulating world" of which he is not a part—in this case, a cartoonist from Bridgeport, Connecticut, inventing a landscape in a Georgia swamp populated by talking animals[2]—what precisely is the reader being shown? Or, to borrow McCloud's words, what does the reader *see* and who is the reader invited to *be*?

In *Pogo*, the reader is presented with a northern cartoonist's vision of a magical, redemptive, often progressive landscape. Kelly's depiction of the Okefenokee Swamp appears to borrow almost unconsciously from the various discourses of a redemptive South made popular in the first half of the twentieth century. These discourses range from the pastoral images conjured by the Agrarians of the 1930s to the more political and socially transformative notions of southern destiny as defined by James McBride Dabbs and Martin Luther King, Jr. "Some scholars," writes Charles Reagan Wilson, "argue that southern literature and history have been used 'as sacramental acts,' intended by writers to counter the instability and chaos they perceive in the modern world" (Wilson 22; see also Wilson 31–35).[3] These are the messianic qualities Norman F. Hale describes when he argues that Pogo's "wisdom and humility" were originally embodied in Bumbazine. For Hale, Pogo's characteristics and his popularity are best understood by "tracing his development back to his truly humble beginnings as one of the 'disciples' of a little black Jesus!" (16). These twin ideas of a redemptive South and a messianic black humanity lead us to the second question suggested by McCloud's theories. What masks are Pogo's readers being asked to wear?

Based on Hale's argument, it might be argued that Bumbazine's "mask" is one that embodies, in Hale's words, qualities of "natural leadership" (9). Is Bumbazine's mask, then, the same as the "Black Mask of Humanity" Ralph Ellison examines in his famous essay on *Huckleberry Finn* (Ellison 42)? While this mask may have had its origin in the Enlightenment, it did not find its true shape until the era of the Romantic who was so "in revolt against the old moral authority" that he would "accept evil (a tragic attitude)" by "identifying himself with the 'noble slave'—who symbolized the darker, unknown potential side of his personality, that underground side, turgid with possibility, which might, if given a chance, toss a fistful of mud into the sky and create a 'shining star'" (Ellison 49). If Ellison's reading of Twain's Jim is applied to Pogo, the character's popularity might be understood as deriving from his moral authenticity—an authenticity tied to his blackness, a point Hale suggests but does not examine in all its implications. If a comic book or strip about a superhero, for example, provides its readers with the opportunity to wear the mask of limitless strength, power, and self-confidence, the mask available to Pogo's readers is one of compassion, justice, and freedom.

If Hale is correct—if Bumbazine and Pogo are messianic figures—they might also be examined in light of Toni Morrison's argument that "the Africanist narrative (that is, the story of a black person, the experience of being bound or rejected)" in American literature has been "a means of meditation—both safe and risky—on one's own humanity" (53). To return to the superhero analogy, if reading a Superman comic book grants you the power to imagine a greater physical self, reading *Pogo* would grant you the power to imagine a greater moral self. If Bumbazine was a "little black Jesus" and Pogo was his "disciple" and, later, his successor, then the Okefenokee itself possesses qualities of the "redemptive" South while at the same time providing a "playground for the imagination" as described by Toni Morrison. In this "playground," Morrison argues, the "dramatic polarity created by skin color" creates the possibility for "the projection of the not-me" (38)— that is, "a set of lines to *be*" (McCloud 43). Kelly's work points to a territory shared by McCloud's and Morrison's theories—how, for example, are we to read and understand the presence of non-white characters in comic book and comic strip narratives? While both McCloud and Morrison are useful in examining some of Bumbazine's earliest appearances, it is also important to examine Kelly's relationship to these characters and to the southern landscape he depicts in his work.[4]

The great irony at the heart of *Pogo*, as historian Eric Jarvis points out in an essay on Kelly's responses to the Civil Rights Movement, is that although the strip "was set in Georgia's Okefenokee Swamp and its tone was, therefore, necessarily Southern," Walt Kelly (1913–1973) was a "white liberal" from the northeast (Jarvis, "*Pogo* and the Issue of Race" 85). Born in Philadelphia, Kelly at age two moved with his family to Bridgeport, Connecticut (Kelly, "Autobiography" 9). As a student at Warren Harding High School in the 1920s, he became a reporter and cartoonist for the school newspaper. In a biography he wrote in the third person for his syndicate in the 1950s, Kelly described the influences that shaped his later career. Following his experiences at the newspaper he found himself "[s]ix years later" as a Disney animator "in Hollywood drawing mice (which is not the same as attracting mice, though there is truth in that thought also)" ("Autobiography" 9). During these formative years he and his fellow animators "turned out Snow White, Fantasia, Pinocchio, Dumbo, The Reluctant Dragon, and Baby Weems" ("Autobiography" 9). While his time at Disney had an impact on the elegance and whimsy of later work, his boyhood memories of Bridgeport, as Jarvis suggests, were equally significant to the development of *Pogo*. Issues of race, politics, and social justice, while cloaked in the idealized images of southern simplicity, good-humor, and hospitality, are in fact drawn from Kelly's New England boyhood (Jarvis, "*Pogo* and the Issue of Race" 85).[5] While Pogo might be set in the wetlands of Georgia, the basis of this imagined geography has a very different source—not the southern reaches of the United States, but southern New England. It appears Kelly found in idealized notions of the South a parallel to his own idealized memories of his childhood in Bridgeport.

As an example of the impact of Kelly's childhood in Bridgeport on his later political views, Jarvis points to an essay in the anthology *10 Ever-Lovin' Blue Eyed Years With Pogo* in which Kelly discussed "both his upbringing and his early opinions about ethnic and racial matters. He used his elementary school principal in Bridgeport as a rather nostalgic model of how society should approach these issues with 'gentility'" (Jarvis, "*Pogo* and the Issue of Race" 85). This emphasis on "gentility" is also expressed in an essay Kelly published in 1962 in the collection *Five Boyhoods*. In his evocation of the 1920s, Kelly describes a world just coming into being, a mixture of working and middle-class families filled with wonder over the automobile, the phonograph, the movies, and the radio. It is also a world still reeling from the chaos of World War I and uncertain of the glittering future promised by the wealth and recklessness of the Jazz Age. He and his elementary school classmates "were, to be blunt, sort of mercenaries. Not that we'd do anything for a buck, but it was almost everyone's belief that the value of an education could be measured in what it would bring you in dollars and cents. . . . Learning for its own sake and art for art's sake were not part of the general creed" (Kelly, *Five Boyhoods* 115). Perhaps this description of his boyhood explains Kelly's ambivalence towards his days as a Disney animator, which he described as "a jest really," as he worked with "1,500 other worthies" on the films that cemented the studio's reputation in the 1930s (Kelly, "Autobiography" 9). Kelly's reflections on the competing ideologies of "[l]earning for its own sake" and "art for art's sake," like the moral lessons of his childhood, found their way into *Pogo*. This contrast between art and commerce Kelly traced back to his childhood might explain the strip's appeal to scholars such as Walter Ong, who found in *Pogo* significant parallels to the modernist sensibility of writers including "James Joyce, Gertrude Stein, or E.E. Cummings" (99). Ong, however, was not convinced that Kelly had appropriated the literary techniques or ideologies of modernism consciously but had, instead, conjured a "habitat in which emerges something like automatic writing for the common man" (100). Ong's interest in the strip reflects the recognition Kelly's work received by other intellectuals and academics in the 1950s and 1960s.

Eric Jarvis argues that *Pogo* appealed most strongly to Kelly's fellow liberals in the 1950s. While the adventures of Pogo and his friends were enjoyed by readers of all ages, "[in the 1950s it] was seen not only as a whimsical strip with slapstick humour, but, also, as a vehicle for its creator, Walt Kelly, to vent his 'liberal' political views. For most readers the antics of Pogo's swamp animal characters were the reason for following the strip daily, but for others it became a barometer of liberal views in a conservative era" (Jarvis, "*Pogo* and the Issue of Race" 85). Kelly's caricatures of Senator Joseph McCarthy, Jarvis argues, "made it something of a beacon in a politically dark age" ("*Pogo* and the Issue of Race" 85).

Additionally, Kelly's popularity as a speaker on college campuses, documented in the posthumous collection *Phi Beta Pogo* edited by the cartoonist's widow Selby Kelly and Bill Crouch, Jr., brought him into contact with readers who found the literary antecedents of characters like Albert the Alligator, Churchy LaFemme, and Porky Pine in the pastoral tradition dating back to classical literature. Edward Mendelson, for example, located the strip in the same tradition as Virgil's *Eclogues* and Milton's "Lycidas." In a 1978 essay for *The Yale Review*, Mendelson argues for the strip's literary merits in a persuasive analysis of Kelly's devotion to the animal fable as a vehicle for wisdom and caricature: "In Kelly's pastoral, as in the classical and renaissance varieties, the rustics use their elaborately stylized language to speak about sophisticatedly urban issues. They write poems, suffer the pangs of unrequited love, and, for the most part, enjoy an innocence for which a reader feels nostalgia; while, at the same time, the pastoral artifice reminds him that such innocence has never existed outside of art" (16–17). In Mendelson's reading, the Okefenokee is a world in which figures like Senator Joseph McCarthy and, later in the life of the strip, J. Edgar Hoover, Spiro Agnew, and Richard Nixon, are always put in their proper place—exposed as fools, made harmless by the wit and compassion of Pogo and his friends.[6] Mendelson's reading of *Pogo* is echoed in the work of M. Thomas Inge, who describes *Pogo* as taking "the ancient form of the animal fable" (Inge 10) and in Norman Hale's book, where he argues that "Pogo is to the mid-twentieth century U.S. culture what Uncle Remus and Aesop's Fables were to other cultures: an animal-form representation" (7). All of these critics suggest the central role of Kelly's ideal South in *Pogo*.

As McCloud might suggest, the more abstract and iconic his drawings of Pogo became, the more freedom Kelly had to explore issues of race, politics, and culture. A realistic depiction of the Okefenokee or its inhabitants would have limited the scope of Kelly's moral imagination. As Kelly himself wrote in an essay for *Collier's* after visiting the Okefenokee Swamp in Georgia for the first time in 1955, "Friends who are cartoonists had often said to me: 'How can you draw a swamp if you've never been there?' Friends who *are* cartoonists knew better than to ask" (qtd. in Harvey 101–2). These questions of representation might be extended to Kelly's characters. If the setting of the strip is an idealized South, what qualities did Kelly choose to idealize in his characters?

Bumbazine, Pogo, and Albert the Alligator first appeared in "Albert Takes the Cake," published in *Animal Comics* #1 (dated December 1942/ January 1943; see Kelly, *Pogo and Albert* 5). According to Maggie Thompson,

Bumbazine's name is Kelly's play on *bombazine*, "a twill fabric with silk or rayon warp and wool filling, often dyed black to be used in mourning wear. Kelly loved odd, unusual, or funny-sounding words—words that could be played with" (8). While describing Pogo's "strange career" in his 1954 third-person biography, Kelly does not mention Bumbazine's central role in the early stories; rather, he offers several lighthearted reasons why Pogo found success not in comic books but as a comic strip character ("Autobiography" 9). The early Pogo's greatest flaw, Kelly jokes, was that the character "looked just like a possum" and lacked, as McCloud might argue, the more iconic, abstract, and child-like appearance of his later incarnation. Kelly provides other reasons why these early stories in *Animal Comics* and *Our Gang Comics* never achieved the popularity of the comic strip: "Cornering children when their parents were looking the other way, Kelly asked questions. The answers all added up to the same thing: 'That comic book didn't have no action in it. Nobody shot nobody. It was full of mice in red and blue pants. It stunk'" ("Autobiography" 9). However, both Eric Jarvis and Norman Hale argue that Kelly may have jettisoned Bumbazine in order to create a strip that would appeal to the wider audience available to newspaper comic strips.

By removing Bumbazine, Hale argues, Kelly had "removed the danger of raising these touchy issues" of black and white (7). Kelly explained that Bumbazine was dropped because "[b]eing human, he was not as believable as the animals" (qtd. in Jarvis, "Pogo and the Issue of Race" 86; see also Kelly, *Phi Beta Pogo* 22). However, Jarvis is more blunt is his assessment of these changes. While he is willing to suggest that Kelly had made "a wise move artistically," he also argues that this was "a politically wise move as well": "In the late 1940s a black central character who was portrayed in a positive light may possibly have been a difficult sell to editors or to the white reading public" (86). Of course, as Hale points out, one could argue that Bumbazine never really disappeared at all. Pogo not only became more human after Bumbazine was abandoned, but, from the perspective of both Hale and critic Denis Moore, he also became more southern.

What distinguished Bumbazine from the other characters in Kelly's early stories was, according to Hale, his ability to act as a "natural" leader (Hale 9). Hale argues:

> [Kelly's] characters, human and animal alike, represented neither highly educated people nor real animals, but something in between. "Natural" people. "Simple" people. . . . People who do indeed possess the "natural" kind of wisdom—that of knowing how to treat each other, how to get

along with each other, how to live on Earth—and for whom that is sufficient. (8)

Critic Denis Moore would equate what Hale calls "'natural' people" with the very best qualities of southern culture. In the estimation of both of these writers, Pogo and his swamp are southern because they are natural, and good, and real, the source of practical lessons on what is to be human. To borrow Hale's phrase, it is Bumbazine and Pogo's "natural" goodness that grants them the power to lead the diverse cast of creatures in the swamp and to rehabilitate those who lack the grace, compassion, and "gentility" to co-exist peacefully.

In "Playin' Possum: Pogo as the Compleat Southerner," Denis Moore argues that Pogo embodies the best, most forward-thinking qualities of "being Southern" (26). While Moore spends most of his 1981 article identifying fictional characters who could best carry Pogo's torch of empathy, inclusion, and good-natured social criticism into the 1980s (he draws parallels with *Doonesbury, Peanuts,* and *All in the Family*'s Archie Bunker until finally settling on Kermit the Frog; see Moore 29–30), he documents a number of qualities of the southern personality, only the best of which he attributes to Pogo: "xenophobia; gentleness, or at least some consciousness of manners; pride; a religiosity, which so often translates as both Protestant and narrow-minded; pronounced nationalism; and some combination of a sense of honor, a sense of humor, a sense of language, and a sense of place. Many respected observers have also noticed a tendency to enjoy fishing" (26; emphasis in original). For Moore, Pogo is a "compleat Southerner" because he rejects the more insidious qualities included on this list. Moore suggests that, at its most restorative, "being Southern" is synonymous with a Christ-like compassion and humility. According to Moore, Pogo possesses "a sense of humor, an awareness of the powers of language, [and] a pervasive hospitality" which are all qualities of the southerner: "We gaze at this list and at this possum a moment longer and we see list and critter merging into one simple adjective: 'gentle'" (27–28).

According to Hale, these are the same qualities once possessed by Bumbazine, who directed the animals in the swamp through his use of reason and because of his innate goodness (9). He could talk to and understand the animals because he had yet to be corrupted by the demands of society; in other words, he had yet to grow up, and was safe and secure in a world of childhood myth and fantasy played out in the world of the swamp, that world which, as Rod Giblett has pointed out, is "neither strictly land nor water" (3) but a space between the two; just as the swamp is a space that exists between the concrete and the fluid, Kelly's characters, as Hale rightly points out, take on "appearance and behavior [that] is 'in between' that of a real animal, with little or no intelligence, and that of a white-bearded professor" (8–9). Both Hale and Moore understand Pogo as an emblematic character who embodies the ideal of a "redemptive" South that grew in mythic status in the first half of the twentieth century (see Wilson 18–23).

This mythology of southern identity grew popular during the years in which Kelly created Bumbazine, Pogo, and his vision of the Okefenokee. It is almost as though Kelly, that son of southern New England, had borrowed a set of Utopian tropes from the southern Agrarians. As we have already seen in Walter Ong's criticism of Pogo, Kelly's work roughly coincides with the expressions of late Modernism as it made its slow progression to postmodernist trends in American literature in the 1950s and the 1960s. However, Kelly deploys characters, settings, and themes that would have been familiar to writers of the Southern Literary Renaissance, that period "from 1920 to 1950" which, as Charles Reagan Wilson describes, produced "a flowering of culture such as the South had never seen" (22). The literature of this period, Wilson stresses, was not limited in its interest or focus, however, to the South (22). The Agrarians of the 1930s, as Wilson points out, adapted one of the foundational tropes of American literature—American literature, that is, as celebrated and mythologized by Boston-based writers dating back to Longfellow and Emerson at the height of the American Renaissance. By the 1930s New England was no longer the home of a shining city on a hill; the South now became the home of this Utopian vision in the American literary imagination: "Instead of the New England city on the hill, the Agrarians, in effect, pictured a farm on a hill to be admired and copied" (Wilson 30). If *Pogo* is read from this perspective it might be added to the list of what Wilson describes as "nonsouthern attempts to market the South" along with the *Dukes of Hazzard* (Wilson 27). However, even in his earliest depictions of a Southern landscape in the pages of *Animal Comics*, Kelly's work is sympathetic and often endearing; Kelly rarely stoops to the buffoonery and simplistic stereotypes of the "good ol' boys" of 1980s television. There are a few notable exceptions, however, which will be examined later in this essay.

While the Agrarians sought redemption through a connection to the land, a connection believed to be no longer possible in the North, James McBride Dabbs and Martin Luther King, Jr., imagined a more radical "biracial South" whose struggle to resolve the conflicts between black and white could serve as a regenerative example for the nation and for the rest of the world (Wilson 31–34). For King, the Civil Rights Movement derived its hope and strength from the fertile territory of the South. As Wilson argues, "King's 'I Have Dream Speech' in 1963 portrayed a redemptive South that would be the scene for national salvation. . . . The region had been the center of black suffering and of flawed humanity, but ultimately the virtues of blacks and decent whites would lead to reconciliation" (32). As Wilson points out, the writings of James McBride Dabbs reinforce this concept of the South's potential for redemption and transformation, not only in terms of the Civil Rights struggle but also in relation to a nascent environmentalism which, by the end of the 1960s, had begun to take hold of the American imagination—due in no small part, it should be pointed out, to the critiques of pollution and environmental disaster in Kelly's later strips and in the final collection he published during his lifetime, *Pogo: We Have Met the Enemy and He Is Us*.[7] Read in the context of Dabbs's vision of the South's potential to transform the rest of the United States, Kelly's emphasis on protecting the environment is the logical conclusion of his strip, the destination to which these tropes were leading him from the strip's earliest days. For Dabbs, as Wilson describes, "the modern South had lessons to teach on the necessity of preserving the land and of ecological sanity. The southern experience at its best had nurtured an awareness of nature" (33).

The South's greatest contribution to Kelly's strip, then, must lie in these southern discourses—the myth or notion of a conflicted landscape whose failures have imbued it with a strength of character and a healthy resistance to the worst excesses of the North. While in the American imagination the South is the location of some of the nation's greatest violence and trauma— from the horrors of slavery to the modern, mechanized destruction of the Civil War—it is also, like the swamp itself, a place of refuge and healing. For Wilson, the South's greatest weakness is also its greatest source of strength: "As a people, Americans are notoriously ahistorical—looking toward the future, progressive, optimistic. But Southerners have a deep historical sense, which remains a national resource" (35). The human characters in the earliest Pogo and Albert stories reinforce the notion that Kelly had, consciously or not, adopted this vision of the South as a landscape filled with the potential for salvation. The landscape, of course, also provided him with the raw material for sight gags and slapstick comedy.

While in later years characters with a resemblance to human beings would appear in the strip only for grotesque, satirical effect (for example, in J. Edgar Hoover's appearances as a bizarre bulldog with a crew cut), Kelly featured humans other than Bumbazine in one of the earliest Pogo and Albert stories in *Animal Comics*. This story, simply titled "Albert the Alligator," is worth investigating in more detail not only for Kelly's depiction of human representatives of southern local color but also for its curious depiction of African American characters other than Bumbazine himself.[8] The plot of "Albert the Alligator" from *Animal Comics* #5 (Oct-Nov 1943) is as simple as its title. The story begins with Bumbazine in his role, just as Hale describes, as a leader to the animals in the swamp (see figure 3.1). As Pogo and the other animals call Bumbazine out for a picnic, he suggests they first take a swim, an idea that proves acceptable only to a collar-and-tie-wearing frog. A squirrel suggests they "just sit around and eat lunch after we go for as short a walk as possible," an idea which leaves their picnic vulnerable to Albert's always-scheming stomach (Kelly, *Pogo and Albert* 41). As Albert attempts to steal their lunch basket, he finds himself trapped in a hollow log. As he tries to escape, he knocks a hornet's nest from the branch of a tree. Now the entire swamp is angry with him—Bumbazine, the animals who were looking forward to their picnic and, most of all, the hornets, who accuse him of destroying their house. Insulted, Albert decides he will leave the swamp and what he calls his "fair-weather friends" to become "a successful man in the city" (44). To get to the city, he first heads to the railroad station, which introduces us to the other African American characters in the story. After a series of slapstick encounters with these characters, who are amazed with the "talkin' gator" (46), Albert hijacks a steam engine but within two chaotic pages has destroyed a wooden bridge while frightening most of the other citizens of the swamp. As the story closes, he has found his way back to his friends who ask him not to leave them because, as Pogo jokes, the swamp is "perty tame" without him (48).

As Maggie Thompson points out in her introduction to the first volume of the Eclipse Books series of *Pogo* reprints from the late 1980s, "these early stories" contain "the seeds of many themes Kelly used throughout his career," not the least of which is the fact "that from the very beginning Albert ate absolutely anything which intrigued him" (9). In addition to establishing Albert's relationship with the other creatures of the swamp, Kelly also cleverly introduces characters and concepts that would have been included for older, more sophisticated readers. Although *Animal Comics*, as Maggie Thompson observes, was marketed primarily to young readers, the stories contained jokes that would appeal to adults, perhaps the adults reading these stories to their children. According to Thompson, Kelly first created the characters and the setting for Oskar Lebeck "who was in the process of putting together a team of writers and artists whose genius was a major force behind the Golden Age of Funny-Animal Comics" in the early 1940s (8). The "concept"

3.1. From "Albert the Alligator," first published in *Animal Comics* #5 (October–November 1943). Reprinted in Walt Kelly, *The Complete Pogo Comics Volume 1: Pogo & Albert* (Eclipse Books, 1989). Copyright © Walt Kelly Estate.

3.2. From "Albert the Alligator," first published in *Animal Comics* #5 (October–November 1943). Reprinted in Walt Kelly, *The Complete Pogo Comics Volume 1: Pogo & Albert* (Eclipse Books, 1989). Copyright © Walt Kelly Estate.

of *Animal Comics*, Thompson suggests, also originated with Lebeck, who set out "to produce an anthology of adventure and humor stories suitable for young readers and attractive to adults" (8). This desire to appeal to old and young readers alike might explain the minstrel routine at the center of the story, as Albert tries to buy a ticket for "some big town—like Puddin' Bayou" (Kelly, *Pogo and Albert* 45). Other than Bumbazine, the other human characters in this story, black and white, are all stock figures that would have been familiar to Kelly's readers. The most fascinating of these stock characters are the men at the train depot, each of whom possesses qualities derived from the minstrel stage (see figure 3.2).

The cast of Kelly's minstrel routine are familiar; they possess wide, saucer-like eyes and absurdly round, thick lips. Once they have established that Albert is a "sho' 'nuff 'gator," a fight ensues (45–46). The train engineer pulls up to the station and asks, "Who owns this talkin' 'gator? I do b'leeve I'll buy him." The ticket office manager, however, immediately stakes his claim: "I saw him first. He b'longs to me!" The engineer leaves the train and begins to bargain with the clerk. Offering cash, he says, "Okay ... I'll pay yo' ten dollars an' I'll make a heap o' money showin' him off in N'Orleans." Before the clerk can respond, another character, who first witnessed the talking gator at the ticket window, interrupts: "Jes' a minute! I did sign-tiffic research on him! He's my 'gator!" A fight breaks out in the next panel as another character, dressed in suspenders and Zoot-suit-like striped yellow pants, enters with the warning, "Leggo my cousin and uncle, yo' unfriendly varmints!" (46). With his cigar and his umbrella, Albert stands apart from the fray and reminds the crowd, "Yo cain't buy me anyways. I isn't no dawg or hoss. I is a reg'lar hooman!" (46). The differences between Kelly's depiction of Bumbazine and the other human characters are intriguing. While in some of the earlier stories Kelly draws Bumbazine with the same wide eyes and thick lips as these characters, in "Albert the Alligator" Bumbazine looks like less like a caricature and more like a little boy. Bumbazine, like Albert, is "a reg'lar hooman," Kelly seems to suggest, because he avoids the corrupting influence of a "big town" like "N'Orleans." Contact with the outside world of trains, cities, and money brings chaos and confusion to the swamp, as Albert's failed attempt to hijack the train makes clear.

The introduction of money and commerce brings Albert's home into contact with the world beyond the swamp. The most stereotypical figures in the story are part of this world, as their greed leads them to acts of comic violence. The more they struggle with each other, the less "hooman" and the more stereotypical they become. As the engineer pulls out his cash and reveals his plan of turning Albert into a sideshow attraction in "N'Orleans" the swamp shifts from an abstract, comic playground to a location in the southern landscape. This landscape grows more detailed as the story winds its way to a conclusion and Albert hurdles off the tracks and into the swamp. Just before he finds himself "bust down de bridge" (48), he passes his other human neighbors (see Figure 3.2). The long, horizontal panel not only suggests the speed of the runaway train, but also provides Kelly with the space to populate this world in more detail. As two pigs look on, a corncob pipe-smoking black woman exclaims, "Land of livin'! De gov'mint sho messes things up these days!" (47). While she wears the clothes of countless other mammy figures from the popular culture of this era, she, like Bumbazine, lives a very different life than the engineer and the clerk. Outside the dull, violent world of commerce, she speaks as the only adult voice of reason in the story in her critique of the "gov'mint." While the other characters, including Albert, are eager to escape the swamp (at least for now), she is content, like Bumbazine and his friends, to take on the role of the observer and serve as the wise, wry commentator. Next to her house are two white neighbors; these two drunken, backwoods rustics are not the earthy, poetic spokesmen Edward Mendelson described, however. "Did you seed what I seed?" asks the first with his hands folded across his lap. His friend takes no notice of Albert and, raising a jug of what is presumably moonshine, responds, "Uh-huh—dis yere's pow'ful powerful" (47). In these scenes, Kelly employs each of these southern stereotypes for maximum comic effect. While the characters at the depot wear the clothes of the minstrel stage, these two men, with their beards, their swollen eyes, and their prominent bare feet, are depicted as harmless, ignorant, alcoholic hillbillies (how they managed to make their way from some Appalachian comic fantasy to the swamps of Georgia is not entirely clear). However, as the woman's speech suggests, the swamp is a safer, more magical place than the world of commerce and exploitation surrounding it. Even Albert, at the end of his failed attempt to leave the swamp, admits, "Nobody loves me—I is hounded all the time—but I'd rather be in the swamp than in the city!" (48). In the story's final two panels, Pogo and Bumbazine remind their friend he is home; his role in the swamp, as Pogo points out, after all, is to "pester us like a good feller" (48). To what extent, then, was Kelly merely employing preexisting tropes for comic effect? Or, as many critics have pointed out, did the liberal Kelly from the earliest moments in his career introduce characters who reversed or resisted the stereotypes of the era?

Fredrik Strömberg, Maggie Thompson, and Steve Thompson all frame their arguments in defense of Kelly's intentions in much the same fashion.

Each one suggests that while some of Kelly's images might no doubt be questionable or offensive to contemporary readers, he played an important role is bringing African American characters to a role of prominence in his early work (see Strömberg 93; Maggie Thompson 9; and Steve Thompson 11). While, as Maggie Thompson points out, "Some commentators have suggested that Kelly's Bumbazine (and, for that matter, the adult blacks shown) could be regarded as offensive," she argues that "Kelly treated *all* his characters even-handedly" by using all of them for comic effect. Like Hale and Strömberg, however, she suggests that Bumbazine "was probably the most intelligent, common-sense character in the swamps" (Thompson 9). To support her argument, she draws the reader's attention to Kelly's transformation of the Buckwheat character in *Our Gang Comics*: "Walt Kelly was, in fact, a pioneer in the use of blacks and females as equals in comic book stories: he made the Buckwheat character his own in the *Our Gang* stories, changing his name to 'Bucky' and demonstrating in story after story that Bucky was one of the bravest, most intelligent members of the gang" (Thompson 9; see also Steve Thompson 11).[9] While it is true that Bumbazine, with Pogo, often proves to be the most sensible character in these stories, the fact remains that Kelly employed a variety of images derived from the stereotypical iconography of his day. While in "Albert the Alligator" Bumbazine, like the old woman in the shack, keeps his distance from the characters at the station, and as a result looks less like a minstrel character and more like a child, he also appears with Pogo at the end of his first appearance, "Albert Takes the Cake," eating a giant slice of watermelon (Kelly, *Pogo and Albert* 15). If, as Hale and Moore have argued, Pogo embodies the best qualities of the South, it is worth examining how Pogo's southern qualities are linked to often contradictory depictions of blackness in these early stories.

Scott McCloud's brief reference to *Pogo* in *Understanding Comics* sheds light on why the character serves as such a fitting symbol for the abstract ideal of the mythic, redemptive South. In the second chapter of *Understanding Comics*, McCloud places Pogo Possum in the "Meaning" section of his Picture Plane along with other, in McCloud's words, "cartoony" characters including Osamu Tezuka's Astroboy, Crockett Johnson's Mister O'Malley, Carl Barks's Scrooge McDuck, and Pat Sullivan's Felix the Cat (McCloud 53). The other characters McCloud relates most directly to Pogo are Dave Sim's Cerebus and V.T. Hamlin's Alley Oop (53). Cartoonists whose work belongs in this corner of the diagram are, according to McCloud, most concerned with portraying "the beauty of ideas" (57). It is in this conceptual space, where "pictures are more abstracted from 'reality'" and therefore "require greater levels of perception, more like words" (49), that underground comix and funny animal comics collide: "Ironic that the two bastions of cartoony art," McCloud points out, "are underground and children's comics! Pretty far apart as genres go!" (56).[10] However, as McCloud points out, there are several cartoonists in both genres who deliberately mix abstract, iconic characters with realistic backgrounds—much as Walt Kelly did for the life of his strip.

The mixture of abstract figures with highly detailed backgrounds, according to McCloud, generates a potent cognitive experience for the reader. McCloud suggests an abstract or "cartoony" illustration increases "viewer-identification" (42). While this technique of mixing simple, almost child-like figures with complex, realistically rendered backgrounds is, according to McCloud, more common in European comics and Japanese manga, it is "a practical necessity" in animated films and, in American comics, as McCloud has argued, it is most common in underground comix and comics for children (43). What happens, however, when images of blackness are introduced into McCloud's theoretical framework? What experience, for example, is a white reader having while wearing the "mask" of a black, southern character such as Bumbazine? Or, to return to Kelly's often-quoted point that the animals in his strip were "more human" than the people, would it have been impossible for a wider, white readership to project their consciousness into a character such as Bumbazine, therefore requiring that the more abstract Pogo become the focus of the strip? Even Pogo's appearance, as Maggie Thompson describes, changed as he made his journey from comic book to comic strip from a more realistic, "ratty-looking" appearance to the more simple, iconic figure McCloud includes in his diagram (McCloud 53; Maggie Thompson 7; for one of Kelly's earliest drawings of Pogo, see the second panel of Figure 3.1; Pogo is the figure to the right of the panel calling the other animals to the picnic). While Kelly never worked in as minimalist a style as Charles Schulz, he utilized his training as an animator to suggest movement and emotion with the fewest possible strokes. At times, like other cartoonists of his generation, Kelly coupled the simplicity of his drawings with racial stereotypes to communicate meaning or to heighten comic effect. Does his use of these stereotypical images, however, blunt or contradict the liberal commentary Kelly introduced even at this early stage of the strip's development?

The images derived from minstrelsy in "Albert the Alligator" might be understood as serving the same function for Kelly as they did for popular performers dating back to Thomas Dartmouth Rice's Jim Crow performances in the 1830s. As music historian Charles Hamm reminds us, after all,

"Audiences did not laugh with Jim Crow, they laughed at him, at his dialect and dress and even movements" (121). Rice, like Kelly, was from the Northeast; the Jim Crow "caricature was devised and carried out by a native New Yorker, before an audience in a Northern city, and was described with obvious relish by a writer in a Northern journal *after the Civil War*" (Hamm 121; emphasis in the original).[11] The stock character of the comic Negro serves multiple purposes for Kelly. The characters at the train station in "Albert the Alligator" are comic types that would have been familiar to readers of *Animal Comics* in 1943. Therefore, they provide the cartoonist with an easy laugh, which does not require any comic setup of plot or prior characterization. This use of stock characters complicates McCloud's reading of certain comic characters as vessels for abstract ideas.[12] What idea, for example, is embodied by Kelly's train conductor? That of an ignorant but greedy opportunist? A sly Negro in a long line of trickster characters? Or could it be said that Kelly's depiction of Bumbazine as more realistic and "human" is itself an embedded critique of these minstrel-show images? Toni Morrison's comments on the impact of blackface minstrelsy and American literature are essential here, not only in removing the mask from "Albert the Alligator," but also in complicating McCloud's picture plane by introducing an "Africanist presence":

> Just as entertainers, through or by association with blackface, could render permissible topics that otherwise would have been taboo, so American writers were able to employ an imagined Africanist persona to articulate and imaginatively act out the forbidden in American culture. (66)

It should come as no surprise, then, that underground cartoonists would employ simple, abstract, child-like (or childish) images to critique everything from the sexual repression of the 1950s to the horrors of the Holocaust. Stock images or characters provide readers with the familiar and the comfortable, which, in the work of artists like Kelly, R. Crumb, and Art Spiegelman or more contemporary cartoonists such as John Porcellino or Carrie McNinch, are then transformed into the disturbing or the grotesque, usually for the purpose of, as Morrison suggests, confronting socially taboo topics. African American visual artists including Oscar Micheaux and Spike Lee have employed similar techniques by including blackface minstrel performances in their cinematic critiques of race and class divisions in the United States.[13] The danger of these images, however, lies in their denial of the experience of the black characters being portrayed.

In American literature of the nineteenth and early twentieth century, the presence of stock black characters was often, according to Morrison, a shortcut for characterization. Writers such as Ernest Hemingway, Morrison points out, will use a black or Africanist character for the purpose of "[e]conomy of stereotype. This allows the writer a quick and easy image without the responsibility of specificity, accuracy, or even narratively useful description" (Morrison 67). From this perspective, Kelly's black and white characters—with the important exception of Bumbazine—in "Albert the Alligator" are all examples of this economy of stereotype, the use of which opens a space for the critique of the urban, industrial culture which was so distasteful, for example, to the Agrarians. If blackness is associated with purity and "natural" goodness while the South, at its best, is a reminder of simpler, more noble times, Kelly employs Bumbazine/Pogo and the swamp itself in order, as Morrison would argue, to embody these ideas with little to no "specificity" or, geographically speaking, "accuracy" or "useful description."

In light of Morrison's arguments, the usefulness of Ralph Ellison's critique of *Huckleberry Finn* in an analysis of race in *Pogo* becomes clearer. Ellison argues that Huck's decision to steal Jim is a "pivotal moment" not only of the novel's plot but also, "by an ironic reversal, of American fiction" (48). This reversal, according to Ellison, has its roots in the Revolutionary era when blackness began to take on a symbolic quality in some sectors of the American imagination:

> It was later, when white men drew up a plan for a democratic way of life, that the Negro began to exert an influence upon America's moral consciousness. Gradually he was recognized as the human factor placed outside the democratic master plan, as a human "natural" resource who, so that white men could become more human, was elected to undergo a process of institutionalized dehumanization. (46)

Ellison argues that Jim is "not simply a slave" but "a symbol of humanity; in freeing Jim, Huck makes a bid to free himself of the conventionalized evil taken for civilization by the town" (49). Bumbazine and his successor Pogo, then, might be read not as representatives of some innate, "natural" human goodness, but as examples of the "'natural' resources" described by Ellison. One of the most striking examples of the "humanizing" impact Pogo has on the other characters in the strip—and therefore, by extension, perhaps, on Kelly's readers—can be found in his encounter with the Kluck Klams, a sequence collected in the 1966 collection *The Pogo Poop Book* (see figure 3.3).

3.3. From "The Kluck Klams" in Walt Kelly, *The Pogo Poop Book* (Simon and Schuster, 1966). Copyright © Walt Kelly Estate.

In this story, Pogo must use his redemptive powers to confront some of the most violent and destructive set of images associated with the South, those of the Ku Klux Klan.

As Eric Jarvis pointed out in his overview of Kelly's various responses to the Civil Rights movement, the cartoonist "was consistently opposed to secret political societies (such as the John Birch Society)" and "[o]n a number of occasions *Pogo* directed ridicule at the hooded figures of the Ku Klux Klan" ("Pogo and the Issue of Race" 87). Kelly also took issue with what he viewed as the extremism of the Nation of Islam by making "a type of connection he often resorted to in his political segments—the similarity in tactics between the radical right and the radical left" ("*Pogo* and the Issue of Race" 88). While, as Jarvis argues, Kelly presents Pogo as "the strip's voice of reason" in a sequence where the Possum lectures a group of ants who are members of "the Blue Muslins" (see Jarvis, "*Pogo* and the Issue of Race" 88 and *The Return of the Pogo* 127–29), it is the Kluck Klams sequence that displays Pogo's full poetic and messianic powers. Like Jim, Pogo has a humanizing effect on even the most lost, disembodied characters—in this case, two members of the Kluck Klams, a boy and his father.

The Pogo Poop Book from 1966 features a bright red cover dominated by the image of a white hooded figure. The cover copy informs us that the book includes the latest information on the Jack Acid Society—Kelly's parody of right-wing organizations such as the John Birch Society—and the "Kluck Klams." The centerpiece of the book is a story in which a small hooded figure approaches Pogo and exclaims, "Uncle Pogo! I *found* you.... I *found* you!" When Pogo asks the "young fella" to take off the sheet, the child responds, "No, my daddy won't let me ... we're Kluck Klams" (Kelly, *The Pogo Poop Book* 39) (see Figure 3.3). Behind the two figures is the lush imagery of the swamp—massive trees, birds, and stones. The child recounts his search for his father, and the constant rejections from the other animals. The lion, the bear, and the tiger all tell the hooded child to "Go away" because "you frighten my children!" (40). As the child runs deeper into the swamp, the cross-hatched backgrounds suddenly take on the appearance of Halloween ghosts and eyes appear in the knots of the live oak trees. The sounds of the animals and the trees, the child explains, are slowly replaced by "a great gibber of goblins" (43) and Kelly depicts a menagerie of ghastly creatures: bat-winged creatures, sharks, vultures, spotted snake eggs with stubby feet, huge chattering teeth, and a walking moonshine jug (or is it an inkwell?). Even these creatures, extras in an H. P. Lovecraft story animated by way of Disney, circle the child and exclaim, "Go away! Go away! You frighten our

3.4. From "The Kluck Klams" in Walt Kelly, *The Pogo Poop Book* (Simon and Schuster, 1966). Copyright © Walt Kelly Estate.

children!" (43). The horror of the scene reaches its climax after the child warns the creatures, "My Daddy told me always to be brave. You can't scare me!" The creatures find the child's father and then pull off his robes only to reveal "[t]here was nothing inside" (44). The child runs away from the terror of the scene, leaving behind the silhouettes of horned, prancing demons and his father's empty sheet.

For all his parodies of various right-wing political figures of the 1950s and 1960s, Kelly rarely conjures such bleak, unsettling images. Clearly there is an infection in the swamp; the "natural" balance Pogo embodies has been tipped in favor of alienation, confusion, and disillusionment. At the center of the destructive violence of the Kluck Klams there is nothing—no head, no heart, no soul, an empty space, a chilling absence. Pogo gently reminds the child all these things were a dream. Only Pogo knows where the child's father resides, and that place of emptiness and decay, like the image of the hooded child, strikes a note of realism in the story. Leaving the bizarre images of the dream pages behind, Pogo leads the child to his father: "Come on, son—is your home the old dark house?" Pogo asks. "How'd you ever guess?" asks the child as Kelly leads our eye to the next panel, which is filled with the ruin of a plantation house, its windows boarded and its facade overgrown with vines (45).

Pogo enters and tells the father the story of the child's nightmare. The father is a grotesque image—his back to the reader, he stands in his sheet and stares into a broken mirror covered in cobwebs (see figure 3.4). Two panels later the father tosses his sheet and that of the child to Pogo: "Take these and bury 'em!" commands the father (46). In the final long panel of the story, the child, in an echo of his encounter with Pogo at the start of the story, says, "Daddy! I found you!" A light casts shadows onto the grass beside the old mansion. "Looky, Pogo ... the ol' dark house got a *light* in it!" (46). As the story closes, Pogo begins to whistle and studies the child's now empty sheet. He drags the father's hood and sheet behind him. The evil presence that had flooded the swamp and the pages of the comic is now contained. In Pogo's world, the containment strategy is simple—after the telling of the story, the father realizes the error of his ways. We never see the father's face—is he an animal like the other citizens of Okefenokee Swamp? It is only through the telling of these stories that Kelly and his characters can locate the truth at the center of the emptiness. Meanwhile, the experience for the reader is one of shock. Even the caricatures of political figures so commonplace in the strip do not prepare the reader for the spectacle of panels in which Pogo sits beside hooded Klan members. Those juxtapositions of the hooded figures and the talking animals, the light and the shadow, the comic and the deadly serious, bring with them their own form of illumination. Images of hooded figures remind Pogo's readers that, after all, the Okefenokee is a swamp in the state of Georgia; it is not the Arcadia described by George Mendelson or the surrealist playground of Walter Ong.

Plantation houses are not exactly an uncommon sight in Pogo's world. In one of the sequences collected in *Pogo: We Have Met the Enemy and He Is Us*, Mole welcomes the Deacon to his home (see figure 3.5). Mole has just made a deal with Wiley Catt and the Fox. The two had kidnapped Hepzibah's nephew Humperdunk—not realizing, of course, that Humperdunk is a skunk and not the prized and allegedly valuable puppy they thought him to be. Upon first examining the little skunk and noticing his black and white stripes, Wiley Catt exclaims, "Dagnabbit! He been goin' to them dabslag integrated schools!" (Kelly, *We Have Met the Enemy* 70). No wiser than the two petty thieves, Mole begins treating Humperdunk like a puppy and decides to show off his new prize to the Deacon. Upon entering Mole's house, Deacon says, "You're the only one in the Swamp who maintains an old plantation mansion, Mole." The "mansion" is nothing like the broken-down home of the Kluck Klams. The one-room shack, with its rocking chair and sagging timbers, needs only one addition, according to Mole—a loyal companion. "Yes . . . in my twilight years I can enjoy the sweeping veranda . . . the vast vista . . . with a noble dog at my feet . . ." (87). Mole's "sweeping veranda" and "vast vista," however, consist of little more than the trees at the edge of the swamp. As the Deacon implies, Mole is an outsider, a relic of the past, distant from the other inhabitants of Okefenokee Swamp. Pogo himself does not appear in this sequence because the absurdity of Mole's claim is all too evident. His house is dilapidated; the "sweeping veranda" sags and threatens to collapse; his "dog" is a baby skunk. This subtle parody of "an old plantation mansion" raises some final questions about the role the Swamp itself played in the strip. It could be argued that the Okefenokee is just as much a central character as Pogo while, as McCloud might suggest, the realistically depicted backdrops of Kelly's strip are essential in providing readers with a "set of lines to *see*" (43) as they project their unconscious desires onto the blank screen of abstract characters like Pogo and Albert.

While a full reading of the significance of the Okefenokee is beyond the scope of this essay, it is important to consider the relationship between Pogo and his home.[14] If the Okefenokee is an "imagined geography," a vision of a southern swamp as depicted by a northerner, it is a geography with all the hallmarks of a carnival as outlined by Mikhail Bakhtin. Bakhtin's description

3.5. From "There's Nothing Like a Little Honesty" in Walt Kelly, *Pogo: We Have Met the Enemy and He Is Us* (Simon and Schuster, 1972). Copyright © Walt Kelly Estate.

of the work of Rabelais might also be employed to describe Kelly's work. Substitute *Kelly* or *Pogo* for *Rabelais* in the following passage and the strip's frequent ridicule of political figures of the 1950s and 1960s begins to take on the qualities of a medieval carnival: "Rabelais's images have a certain undestroyable nonofficial nature. No dogma, no authoritarianism, no narrowminded seriousness can coexist with Rabelaisian images; these images are opposed to all that is finished and polished, to all pomposity, to every readymade solution in the sphere of thought and world outlook" (Bakhtin 3). In *Pogo*, the swamp itself is a territory that opposes and ridicules the "finished," "polished," and "pompous."

Kelly's rendition of his swamp in all its beauty and complexity echoes David C. Miller's discussion of the reevaluation of wetlands present in some nineteenth-century American literature. This rehabilitation of the swamp as a place of transformation and discovery began, according to Miller, in "the 1850s [as] the swamp overcame, in the minds of many thoughtful Americans, its age-old stigma" (3). The European imagination, as Rodney Giblett points out, had for centuries produced works of art "satanising the swamp as part of their theologizing of the landscape: Dante by figuring one circle of hell as a slimy Stygian marsh, and Milton by troping Satan as a monstrous swamp serpent who is generated out of the slime of hell" (5). The swamp as demonic wasteland, of course, as Miller reminds us, persisted well into the twentieth century in multiple forms of popular media—as a landscape populated by other-dimensional elder gods and their subhuman (that is, non-white and non-Protestant) henchmen in the work of Lovecraft and his circle or as the doorway to psychotropic explosions of form and color in Alan Moore, John Totleben, and Steve Bissette's *Swamp Thing* stories of the 1980s. Like Kelly's *Pogo*, Moore's version of Len Wein and Berni Wright-son's 1970s swamp creature builds on the more nuanced vision of the swamp introduced in the mid-to-late nineteenth century. Miller's description of the physical elements of the swamp so appealing to writers and artists of the nineteenth century might be applied to Kelly's complex and beautiful renderings of the Okefenokee as well as to Moore's innovative depiction of the Swamp Thing's home in Louisiana:

> At the most visible levels of American culture, artists and writers discovered the distinctive "imagistic" features of the landscape: the arabesques of its vines and tendrils, the shifting patterns of light that played about its fastnesses, the surprising prospects offered at almost every step. This aestheticization of the swamp image revealed an ever-closer and more widespread engagement with the landscape in the years around the Civil War. . . . The immersion in the unknown which desert places had always represented came to be embraced by many as not only dangerous but also an exhilarating and self-renewing experience. (Miller 3)

This process of reflection and renewal is a hallmark of comic book swamp narratives. Much like Bram Stoker's *Dracula* (or Marv Wolfman's version of the character in the popular and long-running series *Tomb of Dracula*), Steve Gerber's Man-Thing stories written for Marvel in the 1970s, for example, focused attention on the creature's cast of characters rather than the creature himself. Those who come into contact with the creature find themselves undergoing sometimes violent physical or emotional transformations caused in part by the swamp itself, which, as Will Jacobs and Gerard Jones point out, Gerber described as a "nexus point" for "the very structure of reality" (Gerber qtd. in Jacobs and Jones 196). DC Comics' Swamp Thing, once the human scientist Alec Holland, spends most of his time brooding over his lost humanity like some moss-encrusted, bayou-dwelling version of the Incredible Hulk. The continued popularity of both characters suggests that the swamp for comic book readers holds the same hypnotic, multi-generational appeal as the fiend-ridden yet romantically compelling moors of Emily Brontë. What these other swamp narratives have in common with Kelly's work is an attempt to imagine the South as a location of transformation. Like *Pogo*, Moore's *Swamp Thing* stories and Gerber's *Man-Thing* narratives are almost always tales of redemption, either of the individual or of the community.

While many of the topical references in Kelly's *Pogo* might prove challenging for contemporary readers, especially those unfamiliar with images of perennial *Pogo* villains such as Spiro Agnew and J. Edgar Hoover, the strip remains a potent work of American comic strip art and a vital artifact of twentieth century American popular culture. While Kelly's rich imagination introduced us to a gallery of memorable characters, his two most evocative creations are Pogo the Possum and the Okefenokee Swamp. Pogo serves as a guide not just to the swamp, but also to American fantasies of race, identity, and geography. If Pogo is southern, then his southern identity is linked to his blackness, an identity associated with the purity of the outsider. Pogo's strength, however, is also his great weakness; his humanity, like that of Twain's Jim, is an abstract ideal, one that exists only in the redemptive southern landscape of Kelly's imagined geography.

While it would be inaccurate to argue that Kelly's strip provided his readers with simple escapism, even from the most complex problems of American politics, it cannot be denied that Kelly invented a world in which those problems could be debated, examined, and often resolved through comedy and laughter. If Pogo carried on the legacy of Bumbazine, it would perhaps be wise to read Kelly not only as a forerunner of the underground comix artists of the 1960s but also as the inheritor of the legacy of writers including Mark Twain and Charles Chesnutt—that is, as a social and cultural observer in the tradition of those late nineteenth-century local colorists. Just as those writers documented the changes taking place to the American landscape at the turn of the century, Kelly held up a mirror for readers seeking to validate their own best instincts and utopian social desires.

Notes

1. In *Orientalism,* Said argues that "there is no doubt that imaginative geography and history help the mind to intensify its own sense of itself by dramatizing the distance and difference between what is close to it and what is far away. This is no less true of the feelings we often have that we would be more 'at home' in the sixteenth century or in Tahiti" (55).

2. According to R. C. Harvey, Kelly made his first trip to Georgia's Okefenokee Swamp in 1955. The swamp's name derives from "an Indian word that means 'land of trembling earth'" (Harvey 101). After his first visit to the Okefenokee in January 1955, Kelly wrote an essay for *Collier's* in which he responded to those who had for years asked him how he could write about and draw a place he had never seen: "Some people said, 'If you go to the swamp, all your ideas may change. You will not find it the way you picture it, and you will be reduced to appearing on TV or going from door to door, selling sauerkraut and succotash" (see Harvey 101–2 and *Collier's* for April 29, 1955, pages 98–101). Harvey also includes the strip Kelly drew to accompany his essay, in which he, Pogo, and Albert walk through the swamp only to find a more realistically drawn possum in a cage.

3. For more detail on Charles Reagan Wilson's analysis of what he refers to as the development of "Southern Civil Religion" over the course of the twentieth century, see his book *Judgment and Grace in Dixie: Southern Faiths from Faulkner to Elvis* and his essay "The Burden of Southern Culture."

4. As of this writing in August 2010, the only Kelly stories readily available in new editions are his *Our Gang* stories from the early 1940s, edited by Steve Thompson and published by Fantagraphics. However, Fantagraphics has announced a new series of *Pogo* collections to be released beginning in late 2011. It would join Fantagraphics' other reprint series, including collections of Charles Schulz's *Peanuts* and Frank King's *Gasoline Alley,* as the definitive chronological collection of Kelly's strip. While the reprinting of Kelly's *Pogo* is just cause for celebration, I hope that Kelly's *Pogo* paperbacks also find their way back into print, as they include essays and stories Kelly created specifically for those collections. As Bill Blackbeard and Martin Williams point out in *The Smithsonian Collection of Newspaper Comics,* after all, "*Pogo* became the first comic strip to have its daily episodes reprinted virtually complete in book form, sequentially, year after year" (288). Having these original collections back in print would prove to be an invaluable resource for Kelly scholars and admirers. The posthumous scrapbook collections of Kelly's work edited by Selby Kelly and Bill Crouch, Jr., are also valuable resources for Kelly scholars. While these collections are no longer in print, inexpensive used copies can be found online. I would like to thank my student Deb Johann for providing me with copies of two of her father's beloved *Pogo* books, *Pogo* and *The Pogo Papers,* which provided the spark of inspiration for this essay.

5. Eric Jarvis's work on *Pogo* deserves special mention. While in this essay I have focused mainly on his arguments regarding Kelly and race as discussed in "The Comic Strip *Pogo* and the Issue of Race," his essays on Kelly in the context of the Cold War and Viet Nam provide a wealth of insights for contemporary Kelly scholars. References to his other essays on *Pogo* can be found in the Works Cited of this essay.

6. In a lecture presented at the Ohio State University in 1988, Bill Watterson suggested that Walt Kelly's *Pogo* and Charles Schulz's *Peanuts* might be read as narratives that emphasize the private/public duality defining American comics, and more generally, American culture as a

whole: "*Peanuts* explores the inner world of private insecurities and alienation, whereas *Pogo* explores the boisterous outer worlds of politics and interaction" (Watterson 10).

7. For more about Pogo's role in the first Earth Day in 1970, see Finis Dunaway, "Gas Masks, Pogo, and the Ecological Indian: Earth Day and the Visual Politics of American Environmentalism."

8. According to the Grand Comics Database, Bumbazine debuted in the first issue of *Animal Comics* dated December 1942/January 1943. He last appeared in *Animal Comics* #12 dated December 1944/January 1945. Between 1942 and 1945 he also appeared in issues 2, 3, 5, 8, 9, 10, and 11 of *Animal Comics* as well as in one story in *Our Gang Comics* #6 (July/August 1943). Since these original issues of *Animal Comics* and *Our Gang Comics* can be difficult to find and often prohibitively expensive, the best resource for Kelly's Bumbazine stories is *The Complete Pogo Comics* published in four volumes by Eclipse Books in 1989 and 1990. While the series is now out of print, copies can be found from libraries and from used booksellers online. The first Albert, Pogo, and Bumbazine story from *Animal Comics* #1, "Albert Takes the Cake," was also reprinted in Michael Barrier and Martin Williams's *A Smithsonian Book of Comic-Book Comics*. For more information on the Eclipse reprints, see cat yronwode's Eclipse Comics Index at http://www.luckymojo.com/comicswarehousew.html. For more information on Bumbazine's appearances from the Grand Comics Database, see http://www.comics.org/character/name/Bumbazine/sort/alpha/. Thanks are due to Dr. Gene Kannenberg, Jr., for his assistance in tracking down some of Bumbazine's appearances.

9. In his introduction to the first volume of Fantagraphics' recent series of *Our Gang* collections, Steve Thompson writes, "Walt Kelly was an early proponent of racial equality, both in his artwork and his personal life. In 1948, for instance, he provided artwork for a fundraising campaign to support the first interracial hospital in the country. In [*Our Gang Comics*], his portrayal of Buckwheat can only be defended on the basis of the conventions of the time. . . . It should also be noted that his use of black characters in other comic book work during the 1940s was against the common stereotypes, with art and dialogue that made [the African American characters] much more mainstream" (Thompson 9; see Steve Thompson, "Introduction to *Our Gang*," in Walt Kelly, *Walt Kelly's Our Gang* Volume 1).

10. Clay Geerdes explores Kelly's relationship to underground cartoonists of the 1960s and 1970s in "Pogo in the Underground" collected in *The Best of Pogo*. According to Geerdes, "Probably a handful of people, cartoonists among them, understand the many levels Kelly worked on in a single strip. He was to comics what William Faulkner was to the psychological novel" (91).

11. For more about blackface minstrelsy and its impact on American popular culture and, more specifically, on urban, white, working-class audiences of the nineteenth and early twentieth century, see the now-classic studies *The Wages of Whiteness* by David R. Roediger and Eric Lott, *Love and Theft*.

12. In Chapter 2 of *Comics and Sequential Art*, Will Eisner employs a Spirit story filled with stock ethnic characters to illustrate the effectiveness of comic stories that use images in place of words. This "pantomime," Eisner writes, "is an attempt to exploit imagery in the service of expression and narrative. The absence of any dialogue to reinforce action serves to demonstrate the viability of images drawn from common experience" (Eisner 16). These "images," however, include the Spirit's black sidekick Ebony and a host of other stock ethnic characters, including Middle Eastern, South Asian, and East Asian characters. As Morrison would argue, these are not so much "images drawn from common experience" as stock

characters who provide the cartoonist with an "economy of stereotype" substituted for characterization and "specificity" of place (67).

13. Micheaux includes a minstrel routine in one of his earliest sound films, *Ten Minutes to Live* (1932). For more on Micheaux, minstrelsy, and cinema, see Pearl Bowser and Louise Spence, *Writing Himself into History: Oscar Micheaux, His Silent Films, and His Audiences*. See also J. Ronald Green, *Straight Lick: The Cinema of Oscar Micheaux*. Lee examines the role of blackface minstrelsy in the history of American popular entertainment in *Bamboozled* (2000).

14. The role of the swamp in America literature has generated a number of useful books and critical essays. For more about the significance of the swamp in Pogo's world, see Tim Blackmore's essay "What a Picnic! Swamp Ecology in Walt Kelly's *Pogo*." For a discussion of Pogo, the Okefenokee, and Earth Day, see Finis Dunaway's "Gas Masks, *Pogo*, and the Ecological Indian: Earth Day and the Visual Politics of American Environmentalism." For recent studies of the symbolic significance of wetlands, see Anthony Wilson's *Shadow and Shelter: The Swamp in Southern Culture* and Rodney James Giblett's *Postmodern Wetlands: Culture, History, Ecology*. In a more general sense, Scott Romine's *The Real South: Southern Narrative in the Age of Cultural Reproduction* also takes up the issue of the real in southern literature, an issue both Wilson and Giblett address in their discussions of the depiction of swamps and wetlands in a variety of texts. For this essay, I have focused on David Miller's examination of the swamp in American literature as examined in his book *Dark Eden: The Swamp in Nineteenth-Century American Culture*.

Works Cited

Bakhtin, Mikhail. *Rabelais and His World*. Trans. Hélène Iswolsky. Bloomington: Indiana UP, 1984. Print.

Barrier, Michael Barrier and Martin Williams. *A Smithsonian Book of Comic-Book Comics*. Washington D.C. and New York: Smithsonian Institution Press and Harry N. Abrams, Inc., 1981. Print.

Blackbeard, Bill and Martin Williams. *The Smithsonian Collection of Newspaper Comics*. Washington D.C. and New York: Smithsonian Institution Press and Harry N. Abrams, Inc., 1977. Print.

Blackmore, Tim. "What a Picnic! Swamp Ecology in Walt Kelly's *Pogo*." *International Journal of Comic Art* 3.1 (Spring 2001). 38–58. Print.

Bowser, Pearl and Louise Spence. *Writing Himself into History: Oscar Micheaux, His Silent Films, and His Audiences*. New Brunswick: Rutgers UP, 2000. Print.

Duck, Leigh Anne. *The Nation's Region: Southern Modernism, Segregation, and U.S. Nationalism*. Athens: U of Georgia P, 2006. Print.

Dunaway, Finis. "Gas Masks, Pogo, and the Ecological Indian: Earth Day and the Visual Politics of American Environmentalism." *American Quarterly* 60:1 (2008): 67–99. Print.

Eclipse Comics Index. www.luckymojo.com/comicswarehouse.html. Web. 7 July 2010.

Eisner, Will. *Comics & Sequential Art*. Tamarac, Florida: Poorhouse Press, 1985. Print.

Ellison, Ralph. *Shadow & Act*. New York: Signet Books, 1964. Print.

Finis Dunaway's "Gas Masks, *Pogo*, and the Ecological Indian: Earth Day and the Visual Politics of American Environmentalism." *American Quarterly* 60.1 [March 2008], 67–99. Print.

Geerdes, Clay. "Pogo in the Underground." *The Best of Pogo*. By Walt Kelly. Eds. Mrs. Walt Kelly and Bill Crouch, Jr. New York: Fireside Books, 1982. 91–93. Print.

Giblett, Rodney James. *Postmodern Wetlands: Culture, History, Ecology*. Edinburgh: Edinburgh UP, 1996. Print.

The Grand Comics Database. www.comics.org. Web. 7 July 2010.

Green, J. Ronald. *Straight Lick: The Cinema of Oscar Micheaux*. Bloomington: Indiana UP, 2000. Print.

Hamm, Charles. *Yesterdays: Popular Song in America*. New York: Norton, 1979. Print.

Hale, Norman. *All Natural Pogo*. New York: Thinker's Books, 1991. Print.

Harvey, R.C. "Pogo Fest: for the Lore of Pogo." *Comics Journal*. February 2002. No. 241. 100–105. Print.

Inge, M. Thomas. *Comics as Culture*. Jackson: UP of Mississippi, 1990. Print.

Jacobs, Will and Gerard Jones. *The Comic Book Heroes from the Silver Age to the Present*. New York: Crown, 1985. Print.

Jarvis, Eric. "Censorship on the Comics Page: Walt Kelly's *Pogo* and American Political Culture in the Cold War Era." *Studies in Popular Culture*. 26.1 (2003): 1–13. Print.

——. "The Comic Strip Pogo and the Issue of Race." *Studies in American Culture*. xx1:2 (1998): 85–94. Print.

——. "The Comic Strip Pogo and Liberal Satire During the Viet Nam Era." *Popular Culture Review*. 16.1 (2005): 117–24. Print.

Kelly, Walt. "1920's." *Five Boyhoods*. Ed. Martin Kevin. New York: Doubleday, 1962. 79–116. Print.

——. "Autobiography, Circa 1955, Penned by Kelly for Syndicate PR Dept." *The Best of Pogo*. By Walt Kelly. Eds. Mrs. Walt Kelly and Bill Crouch, Jr. New York: Fireside Books, 1982. 9. Print.

——. *Phi Beta Pogo*. By Walt Kelly. Eds. Mrs. Walt Kelly and Bill Crouch, Jr. New York: Fireside Books, 1989. Print.

——. *The Pogo Papers*. New York: Simon and Schuster, 1953. Print.

——. *The Pogo Poop Book*. New York: Simon and Schuster, 1966. Print.

——. *The Complete Pogo Comics Volume 1: Pogo & Albert*. Forestville: Eclipse Books, 1989. Print.

——. *We Have Met the Enemy and He Is Us*. New York: Simon and Schuster, 1972.

Lott, Eric. *Love and Theft*. New York: Oxford UP, 1995. Print.

McCloud, Scott. *Understanding Comics: The Invisible Art*. New York: Harper Perennial, 1994. Print.

Mendelson, Edward. "Possum Pastoral." *Phi Beta Pogo*. Eds. Mrs. Walt Kelly and Bill Crouch, Jr. New York: Fireside Books, 1989. 15–20. Print.

Miller, David C. *Dark Eden: The Swamp in Nineteenth-Century American Culture*. Cambridge: Cambridge UP, 1989. Print.

Morrison, Toni. *Playing in the Dark: Whiteness and the Literary Imagination*. New York: Vintage, 1992. Print.

Moore, Denis. "Playin' Possum: Pogo as the Compleat Southerner." *American Humor: An Interdisciplinary Newsletter*. 8.2 (1981): 26–35. Print.

Ong, Walter J. "Bogey Sticks for Pogo Men." *Arguing Comics: Literary Masters on a Popular Medium*. Ed. Jeet Heer and Kent Worcester. Jackson: UP of Mississippi. 99–101. Print.

Roediger, David R. *The Wages of Whiteness*. New York: Verso, 1991. Print.

Said, Edward W. *Orientalism*. New York: Vintage Books, 1979. Print.

Strömberg, Fredrik. *Black Images in the Comics: A Visual History*. Seattle: Fantagraphics, 2003. Print.

Thompson, Maggie. "Let's Go Pogo." *The Complete Pogo Comics, Volume 1: Pogo & Albert*. By Walt Kelly. Forestville: Eclipse Books, 1989. 7–9. Print.

Thompson, Steve. "Introduction to Our Gang." *Walt Kelly's Our Gang* Volume 1. By Walt Kelly. Seattle: Fantagraphics, 2006. 8–11. Print.

Watterson, Bill. "Some Thoughts on Pogo and Comic Strips Today." *Phi Beta Pogo*. By Walt Kelly. Eds. Mrs. Walt Kelly and Bill Crouch, Jr. New York: Fireside Books, 1989. 10–14. Print.

Wilson, Charles Reagan. *Judgment & Grace in Dixie: Southern Faiths from Faulkner to Elvis*. Athens: University of Georgia P, 1995. Print.

———. "The Burden of Southern Culture." *Bridging Southern Cultures: An Interdisciplinary Approach*. Ed. John Lowe. Baton Rouge: Louisiana State UP, 2005. Print.

Southern Super-Patriots and United States Nationalism

Race, Region, and Nation in *Captain America*

—Brannon Costello

The concept of the superhero has been closely linked with a patriotic, even jingoistic, vision of the United States at least since Captain America socked Adolf Hitler on the cover of *Captain America* #1 in 1941. By the time the U.S. entered the war, Superman and his allies were swatting Japanese planes out of the sky and demolishing Nazi tanks. As comics historians such as Bradford Wright and William Savage have observed, superhero comics achieved a degree of cultural legitimacy during World War II by becoming an unofficial instrument of U.S. propaganda, promoting a view of America as democratic, virtuous, and unified (Wright 30–35, Savage 9–13). As Nicole Devarenne puts it, "from its inception *Captain America*, and the American superhero genre as a whole, [were] closely tied to a fantasy of heroic nationalism" (48). Although since the 1940s superhero comics have not consistently reflected such an optimistic view of the U.S., the association of the superhero with an idealized United States continues to be a dominant tendency in the genre.

Because of their history as emblems of national coherence, superheroes also serve as a productive site for investigations into the creation, maintenance, and sometimes disruption of national identity. Devarenne and others, including John Dittmer and Christian Steinmetz, have focused specifically on the role that Captain America has played in constructing the imagined community that is the United States of America. Steinmetz rightly argues that Captain America comics over the years have been "continually in the process of performing maintenance on the borders of imaginary national space" (191), yet it is crucial to remember that the nature of those boundaries, and of the work needed to maintain them, is not settled and stable.¹ This essay brings together an investigation of Captain America's role in constructing U.S. nationalism with a consideration of the role of the U.S. South as a region that both complicates and facilitates attempts to imagine the nation as a unified and coherent whole. Running through Marvel Comics' *Captain America* series from 1987 to 1989 (and with repercussions stretching into the early 1990s and beyond) the "Captain America No More" storyline[2] by writer Mark Gruenwald and several artists, including Kieron Dwyer, Tom Morgan, Dave Hunt, and Al Milgrom, chronicles what happens when the original Captain America, Steve Rogers—a son of New York and the New Deal—is replaced by a well-intentioned but reactionary and violent southerner, John Walker. In its depiction of Walker's irrational, violent tendencies and complicated relationship with his African American partner—the new "Bucky"—the story reveals and comments upon the ways in which the South's fraught reinscription into the national narrative in the 1980s inspired anxieties about how a nation with the South at the center, rather than the margins, might alter understandings of the United States as a whole. Reading Captain America in the context of southern studies thus not only complicates our understanding of how the character's adventures have constructed an ideal of U.S. nationalism but also offers a unique and intriguing perspective on the role of the South in the nation in the 1980s.

As many scholars in the field of southern studies have argued, narratives of southern exceptionalism have enabled what Barbara Ladd calls a "willed amnesia" central to the construction of U.S. nationhood; the South functions as a place where the U.S. imagines its un-American qualities are contained—a place both a part of, and apart from, the rest of the nation (1637). Malcolm X, well ahead of the game, famously remarked "Mississippi is anywhere in the United States south of the Canadian border" (qtd. in Nelson and Baker 231), a statement that urges a fundamental reconsideration of the effects and implications of such an amnesiac approach to the U.S. Of course, while the South often functions to carry the nation's burden of violence, racism, and depravity, it may also serve as a symbol of warmth, hospitality, and sustaining communal bonds. As Tara McPherson puts it, "The South . . . has long played a variety of roles within national mythmaking, alternating between (if not simultaneously representing) the moral other and the moral center of U.S. society, both keeper of its darkest secrets and former site of a 'grand yet lost' civilization, the site of both church bombings and good, old-fashioned family values" (17). Leigh Anne Duck observes that this ambivalence played a central role in formulations of U.S. nationalism in the early twentieth century, arguing that "the trope of the backward South comprised not only alarm at differences in economic

and cultural development but also celebration of communal forms of affiliation: the region was said to maintain social values that modernization was
purportedly eroding in the broader nation" (6).

In the 1960s and 1970s, leaders of business and industry both inside and
beyond the region attempted to have their banana pudding and eat it too in
their promotion of the ideal of the "Sunbelt": a modernized South friendly
to commercial interests, with none of the region's stereotypical negative
attributes and all of its positive ones. According to David Goldfield, the Sunbelt was characterized by its boosters as combining "racial progress" and
"unparalleled economic prosperity" (123–24), as a new South that stood for
"optimistic dynamism with flashing steel and gilded glass" (124). Yet beneath
the sunny rhetoric, he observes, the reality was more complicated: "The
South of the mid-1970s was a crazy-quilt of patches of prosperity zigzagging
between traditional areas of poverty, further bisected by pockets of growth
and snippets of new decay" (138).

On one hand, the Sunbelt-era South represented the darkest portions
of the nation's past; on the other, it represented a possible future for the
nation. Historians such as James Cobb argue that though many observers
welcomed what John Egerton called the "Americanization of Dixie," they
were considerably more anxious about "the southernization of America"—
about the ways in which the South began to play an ever more central role in
national culture and especially national politics. Cobb notes that a popular
magazine's 1976

> description of the South as the "New America" had seemed to suggest
> not only that the region's long run as the nation's "other" had finally
> come to an end but that a once ostracized Dixie might now actually
> show a stricken and uncertain nation how to rise above its divisions and
> doubts. Within a decade, however, many liberal observers were blaming
> the South's strong and still strengthening influence on national affairs
> for the emergence of what struck them as a very different "New Amer-
> ica," this one rigidly conservative and at times even reactionary, its rac-
> ism and intolerance, social indifference, and sometimes, its downright
> meanness, almost palpable. (318)

Drawing on the work of Edwin Yoder, Cobb cites examples such as "the
manipulation of the Willie Horton episode by Bush supporters in the 1988
campaign, Bush's veto of the Civil Rights Act of 1990, and his injection of
the minority quota controversy into the 1990 congressional election" as

evidence for the hypothesis that stirring up racial animosity to unite white voters across class lines, "once the subterfuge of choice among southern Democrats," had become a national strategy (319). Cobb is skeptical of placing too much emphasis on the South's role in the increasing prevalence of this political strategy, but he argues that the "Southernization of America" thesis was widespread among political and cultural pundits "as a convenient explanation/excuse for the sharply rightward shift in American politics and social attitudes. Southern white migrants to the North were singled out as the carriers of a contagion of grassroots racism, angry and intolerant religious fundamentalism, and the violent and misogynistic impulses that dominated country music" (319). However, McPherson argues that a romanticization of the South was at least as widespread as the demonization that Cobb describes. According to McPherson, the last two decades of the twentieth century were much akin to the last two decades of the nineteenth: in both eras, romanticized notions of the South served to facilitate national reconciliation after a period of conflict—but this reconciliation came with a cost. Writes McPherson,

> As the nation struggled to reconstitute itself after the Civil War, a consensual fantasy of the "grand old South" swept through white America, setting the stage for overturning the civil rights advances of the postwar moment. Similarly, certain nostalgic representations of the South during the 1980s were facilitated by (while also helping to sustain) a national political climate in which the rollback of the gains of the Civil Rights movement was both possible and sadly unsurprising. (17–18)

A crucial moment for the debate over the reinscription of region into nation was Ronald Reagan's notorious Neshoba County Fair speech in 1980. Reagan launched his presidential bid just a few miles from where the bodies of three civil rights workers, victims of one of the most notorious and highly publicized crimes of the 1960s, were buried in an earthen dam outside of Philadelphia, Mississippi. In this context, Reagan's rhetoric was striking. Without directly addressing the issue of racism, he instead, in language he had not used elsewhere on the stump, endorsed the doctrine of "states' rights"—the well-known euphemism for legal segregation and the extralegal apparatus that enforced it in the Jim Crow–era South. Reagan's speech was therefore double-voiced: on the one hand he offered a dog whistle to reactionaries who objected to integration and other social changes, and on the other, by couching his appeal in a rhetoric that avoided explicit mention of race, he made it possible for his supporters around the country to believe, or to convince themselves, that his comments were about an abstract principle of constitutional interpretation and not about race at all.

Reagan's famous attempt to negotiate the tension between nation and region—to appropriate the political power of the white South without having to tote the racist baggage that came with it, to both mark and elide the history of race in the U.S.—provides a useful frame for reading "Captain America No More." The story is a valuable site for understanding the evolving relationship between region and nation in the 1980s—an era in which, as Cobb and McPherson suggest, that relationship was particularly fraught and ambivalent. At a fundamental level, the story is about the complicated attempt to reimagine the South as part of the nation when the South has so long been seen as the epitome of everything the nation is not and, in many respects, should not be. As McPherson persuasively argues, popular forms such as television shows, films, and comic books of the era are a fertile ground for considering "the shifting registers of the representation of region, race, and place throughout this span of time, . . . [for] tracking the ways in which 'old' Souths were reconstituted at the moment of the South's modernization and continue to be reconstructed today" (2), and she finds that some of her objects of study evince "a hope that, with hard work and some new skills, we can spin feeling southern differently, encouraging a kind of affective mobility that moves beyond nostalgia, guilt, and white racial melancholia toward forms of reparation" (6). McPherson cites Will Shetterly and Vince Stone's comic book series *Captain Confederacy* (1986–1988, 1991–1992) as a particularly utopian text in this regard, one that "takes up the symbols of the South and imaginatively reconstructs them, shaking loose the stock figures, geographies, and temporalities of southernness" in order to "open up spaces for cross-racial alliance and antiracist identities" (145).

"Captain America No More" is considerably less utopian and considerably more ambivalent, at times seeming to offer a progressive alternative to the traditional dynamic of nation and region while simultaneously relying on racial and regional stereotypes that undermine the presentation of such alternatives. Yet by writing the South into the superhero genre, "Captain America No More" lays bare and to some extent critiques the process of forming a coherent national identity, raising questions about the deformations of history that the willed amnesia of nationhood requires and pointing toward alternative readings of U.S. history. Through its depiction of a southern Captain America and his relationship with his African American partner, the story both interrogates and sometimes reaffirms the traditional relationship between the South and the nation. Its representation of the South suggests both the possibility of a reimagined South that could play a central role in the nation and a lingering anxiety about what it might mean for the nation to set a southward course for the future. Ultimately, its grim conclusion sounds a cautionary note about the ways in which the South's reunion with the nation could be imagined in a way that would offer the illusion of progress but would in fact sustain regressive models of U.S. nationalism.

Gruenwald plants the seeds for this storyline as early as 1986 in issues featuring the original Captain America. In issues #321–322, Captain America clashes with an anti-nationalist terrorist organization known as ULTIMA-TUM; led by the fanatical Flag-Smasher, ULTIMATUM's aim "is to see all national boundaries erased . . . all symbols of separatism destroyed" (321:10). The story is significant for two closely connected reasons. First, Captain America is forced to kill an ULTIMATUM soldier with a submachine gun, an act which he believes tarnishes his "honor" because, he argues, "I never carry a gun. I have never taken another person's life" (322:4). This claim is remarkable for a character whose roots are in World War II, and it predictably inspired a return to a long-running conversation in the fan community about whether or not this claim, like others the character had made in the past, jibed with the character's established and likely history.[3] My aim here is not to wade into that debate, but simply to note that Gruenwald's Captain America is a representation of American innocence, someone who seems to believe that the nation's ideals can be fought for and won without excessive violence and certainly without bloodshed. As Jason Dittmer notes, even the fact that the character's main weapon is a shield "ma[kes] a very particular claim about America—that even its most powerful super-soldier was purely a defensive instrument of national policy" ("Retconning America" 39). Captain America's denial of ever having killed may even be read in the context of Ernest Renan's well-known formulation that amnesia about the violence that attends the foundation (and maintenance) of a nation is central to nationalism (Renan 11). Second, Captain America and Flag-Smasher have a lengthy dialogue about their competing ideals, with Captain America insisting that he does not represent the U.S. government but instead "the principles that America's politics, laws, and policies are based upon . . . freedom, justice, equality, opportunity" (322:17). This is a boilerplate Captain America pronouncement, but most interesting is how Gruenwald has Flag-Smasher respond: He asks why, then, Captain America does not call himself Captain Freedom or Captain Justice? Captain America replies, "I'd be glad to answer that for you right now, but I think I hear something. Yes. I see an aircraft!" (322:17). Flag-Smasher never gets his answer, but his question, and Captain America's inability to answer it, calls attention to a central problematic in Gruenwald's treatment of the character: the ideal of "America" he stands for is so divorced from the political, legal, and governmental institutions that allegedly generate and protect that ideal that it is not truly unique to the United States; yet he holds tight to an allegiance to the nation as a political entity for reasons he cannot articulate.

The character's appeal to an abstract notion of America is in line with Gruenwald's general direction for the character. Previous writers such as Roger Stern and J. M. DeMatteis had gone to great lengths to ground the character in a specific geographical and temporal context, playing up the conflict between his 1940s roots and his 1980s setting and grounding him in a richly imagined Brooklyn milieu. Gruenwald, by contrast, stripped that context away. As he put it in a 1988 interview, "I took away everything that made him Captain Manhattan or Captain Brooklyn Heights. I took away his Brooklyn Heights apartment so that his home could be America. I took away all the supporting characters that tied him to New York" (Zimmerman 9). Gruenwald instead focused on Captain America as a representative of ideals described in the series as "timeless" (327:17)—unmoored from and unaffected by history.[4]

Indeed, it is this conflict between timelessness and history that leads the original Captain America to give up his shield. In issue #332, a governmental Commission on Superhuman Affairs demands that he come to work for the United States in an official capacity. The commission frames its appeal by grounding the character in a specific historical moment, noting that he was created for specific political purposes by a specific politician. As one commissioner puts it, "According to official documents from the [Franklin Roosevelt] administration, the concept of using you as a symbol of fighting America originated in the president's office . . . . The uniform you now wear was designed and constructed by employees of the federal government as well. The very name 'Captain America' was a creation of some long-forgotten person on the federal payroll . . . . All of the terms you agreed to when you volunteered for Project: Rebirth are still legally binding" (332:7–8). Captain America rejects the Commission's offer, concerned that they would have him take part in political missions with which he might have moral qualms—assisting the Contras, for instance. Strikingly, despite the fact that his longtime girlfriend Bernie Rosenthal is a lawyer who encourages him to take his case to court, Captain America refuses—a further indication of the character's aversion to grounding his identity in law and history. By implication, even a court victory would be a failure because it would violate the notion of timelessness that Gruenwald has established as central to the character's understanding of his heroic role.

Steve Rogers's resignation as Captain America forces the commission to choose a successor, and they settle on John Walker, a flashy patriotic adventurer and sometime antagonist of Captain America known as the Super-Patriot. Walker bills himself as "the hero with his finger on the pulse of the eighties" (323:11). Yet despite the fact that Walker pitches himself as representing "the future" while Captain America represents "the past" (333:6), Walker hails from Custer's Grove, Georgia—from the region of the country typically associated with both the nation's dark past and its sustaining traditions. Walker's complicated temporality is central to Gruenwald's treatment of the relationship between region and nation, reflecting national ambivalence about "southernization" in the 1980s in ways that recall Duck's characterization of the imagined temporal discrepancy between nation and region during the 1930s. She argues, "southern traditionalism was increasingly seen as a threatening chronotype; no longer an effective container for the nation's disavowed antiliberalism, the trope of the backward South began to comprise an image of what the United States could become" (7). A southern Captain America implicitly challenges and complicates the familiar relationship between nation and region. While Steve Rogers, detached from history, embodies a fantasy of a liberal and modern nation that has replaced its history with a mythology of innocence, Walker is rooted in a time and place, and as Captain America, his adventures bring a history of violence and racism alleged to be contained in the South back into the nation at large.

The result of this complication is a series of stories—featuring a southern Captain America in service to the national government—that reflect and investigate anxiety over the place of the South in the nation. A central way in which Gruenwald and his artists suggest this anxiety is through the characterization of John Walker as unstable and barely in control of his superhuman body. Of course, idealized male bodies have always been central to the superhero genre, and in some cases the connection between masculinity and nationalism has been quite explicit. For instance, James Bucky Carter argues that Jack Kirby and Joe Simon's *Fighting American* comics of the 1950s demonstrated "how integrated notions of patriotism, nationality, the masculine body, and the other were within the American culture of the 1950s" (374), and Jason Dittmer states that depictions of Captain America in the early 1940s as physically desirable to women—friends and foes alike—"imbue[d] his representation of the nation as a particularly masculine one," yet his indifference to their desire or his own attractiveness "construct[ed] an image of America as a heroic nation without any selfish desire" ("Fighting for Home" 103). The nature of this connection varies across historical moments, and Susan Jeffords identifies a trend in which 1980s Hollywood action films reflect the masculinized, masterful, and heroic version of U.S. nationalism articulated in Ronald Reagan's public rhetoric. The visual icon of this ideal masculinity, the "hard body," is "the normative body that enveloped strength, labor, determination, loyalty and courage" (24). The "hard bodies" of such action stars as Bruce Willis and Sylvester Stallone were most often contrasted with "soft bodies," bodies that "contain[ed] sexually transmitted disease, immorality, illegal chemicals, 'laziness,' and endangered fetuses" (24). Jeffords asserts that

> the hardened bodies that emblematized Reaganism assisted citizens/ viewers in perceiving not simply those bodies but themselves as masterful, as in control of their environments (immediate or geopolitical), as dominating those around them (whether they be the soft bodies of other citizens or of enemies), and as able to resolve crises successfully (whether domestic or international in scope). Such bodies assist in the confirmation of this mastery by themselves refusing to be "messy" or "confusing," by having hard edges, determinate lines of action, and clear boundaries for their own decision-making. (26–27)

The hard body was usually heterosexual, male, and white, while the soft body "invariably belonged to a female and/or a person of color" (25). Yet, as Jeffords observed, implicit in the films of the era is a degree of ambivalence about the hard body, especially about what happens when the hard body is divorced from the disciplined mastery of its owner—when it lacks those "determinate lines of action" (105–6). Jeffords's framework nonetheless provides a useful model for understanding a key aspect of John Walker's characterization. In one sense, Walker is a perfect reflection of the masculine ideals of his time. Gruenwald describes him as "a harder edged, more Rambo-esque Captain America . . . because that seemed to be the temper of the times as I read it" (Ringenberg). But Walker's is an insufficiently disciplined hard body, an unnaturally and excessively hard body—powerful, male, and white, but also brutish and often driven by emotion. Through the depiction of Walker's lack of mastery over his lethal body, the text reflects classic stereotypes about the South and southern masculinity—stereotypes of southern men as savage, intemperate, and unintelligent, not yet fully civilized. The anxiety is not over Walker's use of violence to resolve conflicts—violence is inevitable in the superhero genre—but over his inability to regulate that violence properly.

Gruenwald implies the dangerous excess of Walker's body from the moment he first dons Captain America's costume: "Quite snug. Feels a bit strange," he remarks, a phrase that suggests his body is pressing against the boundaries of order and discipline for which his predecessor stood (333:17). As Walton notes, "his hulking frame visibly stretch[es] the Captain America costume to its limits" (169). Steve Rogers, who lacks superpowers, thwarts his foes through the calm and disciplined deployment of a body honed to the peak of human ability; by contrast, Walker, whose strength has been artificially enhanced, wreaks havoc with a body that often seems barely in his control, making himself a danger to friends and foes alike.[5] In an early outing as the Super-Patriot, he foils a would-be terrorist bomber mostly by luck, narrowly avoiding setting off a nuclear device in the process. Realizing his close call, he reflects, "What was I thinking of when I yanked on this platform? Guess I was so afraid he'd shoot me in the face, I forgot about this thing" (332:21). As an instructor tells him during training undertaken soon after he assumes the Captain America role, "If this training were real, pal, you'd've killed or grievously injured 17 people and died three times yourself . . . . You gotta learn to watch that strength of yours, kid. You keep throwing the shield harder'n you have to!" (334:7). His failure or inability to heed his instructor's advice leads to tragedy when he beats the dazed and weakened villain Professor Power to death in a blind rage (338:22). Although Walker's mastery of his hard body improves somewhat over time, his progress is undone after the death of his parents, an event that transforms him into a savage berserker. As one telepathic foe remarks, "He fights like a fiend—moves without thinking!" (346:25). Artists Dwyer and Milgrom frequently draw Walker's face obscured by shadow, his only visible feature the gleam of a maniacal grin (see for instance 346:24 and 347:23). As Matthew J. Costello notes, even when Walker realizes his actions are wrong, "he continues to be driven more by rage and violence than by reason and necessity" (173).

Walker's instability, his lack of control over his emotions and thus his body, is key to the other central way in which his characterization reflects anxiety about the southernization of America: his relationship with his African American partner, Lemar Hoskins, who takes on the identity of Captain America's sidekick, "Bucky." The original Bucky was, in traditional representations, an eager-to-please white teenager who idolized his mentor—an archetypal sidekick. The new Bucky is an adult African American man from Chicago. Although Hoskins is an adult as superhumanly strong as, and physically larger than, the new Captain America, he nevertheless squeezes into a faithful recreation of the original Bucky's uniform. The book almost immediately began receiving letters from outraged readers who noted that "buck" was a racist epithet and who pointed out the indignity of equating an adult black man with a white teenager. Gruenwald pleaded that he did not intend any offense and that he was not aware of the racial connotations of the new character's old name, and in later issues he addressed the issue directly, as will shortly be discussed.[6] It would be a mistake, however, to confuse Gruenwald's alleged ignorance of the racial connotations of "Buck" with a general indifference to race in the U.S. and to the function of race in regional/national narratives. As Gruenwald noted in a 1988 interview, his choice to create a southern Captain America was part of a larger project to explore antagonists whose conflicts with the original Captain America would reflect social and political issues in the contemporary United States (Zimmerman 7–16). Whatever Gruenwald's purpose, the work he produced with his artistic collaborators is rich with implication; if its reflections of anxieties of race, region, and nation are sometimes unintentional, they are no less worthy of study.

Although the name may have been chosen for its comic book legacy, it is nonetheless worth considering that "buck" is not simply a generic racial slur for any African American man, but connotes violence, danger, and sexuality. As Donald Bogle notes in *Toms, Coons, Mulattoes, Mammies, and Bucks: An Interpretive History of Blacks in American Films*, the "buck" figure in popular media dates back at least to *The Birth of a Nation*: "Bucks are always big, baadddd niggers, over-sexed and savage, violent and frenzied as they lust for white flesh" (13–14). Bogle goes on to note that the images of the "buck" proliferated in the cinema of the 1970s in movies such as *Sweet Sweetback's Baadasssss Song* and *Shaft*. These movies featured proactive black protagonists who "met violence with violence and triumphed over the corrupt white establishment" (235), men who were "menacing figures far different from the passive 'conciliatory' black types of the past" (242). If "buck" suggests threatening power, however, then "Bucky," with its juvenil-izing, familiar suffix, suggests the containment and deflation of that power. Bucky's visual design generates the same effect as his moniker. Although physically larger than the new Captain America and just as super-strong, he nonetheless looks faintly ridiculous in a dated costume designed for a teenaged white boy.[7]

Although the book pays lip service to the notion that Walker and Lemar are equal partners—rather than a hero and his sidekick—Lemar is generally portrayed as the more naïve, inexperienced member of the team, even despite Walker's own relative inexperience and his dangerous instability. Both the interracial pairing and the hierarchical relationship between the two ostensible peers have their roots in the larger pop cultural context of the era. The 1980s saw the rise of the interracial buddy cop movie, a genre that included such blockbusters as *48 Hours, Beverly Hills Cop*, and *Lethal Weapon*. Philippa Gates argues that cop dramas proliferated in the 1980s in part as a reaction to the denaturalization of assumed white male privilege, and interracial buddy cop films, "in response to the growing opportunities for African Americans and the apparent loss of white dominance[,] . . . negated the threat of this empowerment by placing an African American in the role of the hero's sidekick" (111). As Ed Guerrero puts it, "Hollywood has put what is left of the Black presence on the screen in the protective custody, so to speak, of a White lead or co-star, and therefore in conformity with dominant, White sensibilities and expectations of what Blacks should be like" (260). Gates further argues that while the conflict between the black and white protagonists' perspectives ostensibly serves as a way to expose and work through buried conflicts about race in the United States, "the concerns of race and class that are explored through the initial clash of the heroes are resolved through their eventual bonding, thus suppressing, rather than exposing, these issues as social problems" (111).

"Captain America No More" participates in this trend, but it also offers an intriguing variation: the terms by which their not-so-equal partnership is organized are reminiscent of racial codes associated with the nation's troubled racial history. By offering a return to the past in the guise of progress, the story exposes an anxiety about the viability of the South as the future of the nation. "Captain America No More" implicitly draws intriguing and troubling parallels between the superhero/sidekick relationship and the white patron/black servant relationship known as racial paternalism. One of the primary dynamics by which southern whites justified their domination of African Americans, racial paternalism was a system by which white southerners treated African Americans not simply as inferior but as childlike, as requiring the allegedly beneficent care of a white father figure. As southern historian Jack T. Kirby put it, paternalism "bound blacks to whites, apprenticed them not only as laborers but also as moral creatures" (16). Mississippi Delta planter William Alexander Percy described the relationship in his memoir *Lanterns on the Levee* as that of an older brother to "a younger brother, not adult, not disciplined, but tragic, pitiful, and lovable; act as his brother and be patient" (309). His familial metaphor at once seems to extend the possibility of advancement to African Americans while deferring their eventual adulthood to an unspecified future date. As I have written elsewhere,[8] the superhero sidekick and the African American in a paternalist culture share this condition of perpetual childhood: they train at the side of their heroic father-figures, learning their skills, techniques, methods, and perspectives, but, with some notable recent exceptions, they remain the sidekick, never aging into maturity and becoming superheroes in their own rights. The promise that they will one day grow up and fill their masters' shoes is rarely fulfilled, their adulthood endlessly deferred in a fantasy world where characters age incredibly slowly, if at all.[9]

Gruenwald and his artists represent this new Bucky and his relationship with his partner in ways that seem to echo racial paternalism. There is little difference in his attitude toward John Walker and in the original Bucky's toward Steve Rogers: he's eager to please, exuberant, a little reckless, and generally unburdened by the personal anxieties that weigh Walker down. He often praises his partner's prowess in battle or expresses envy at Walker's amazing shield. Figure 4.1, an image by Kieron Dwyer and Tom Morgan from issue #335, illustrates their relationship well: as Walker and Lemar prepare to embark on their first mission, a grinning Lemar, delighted that they have drawn what he believes is an easy assignment, gives his partner an exaggerated pat on the back, while Captain America looks away from him and worries about what complications might be in store (335:10). Although this new Captain America is a neophyte himself, he is still portrayed as his partner's wiser "older brother," to use Percy's language. For instance, in issue #338, Walker lectures Lemar on discipline, reminding him that their super-strength requires them to keep themselves in check in battle against normal opponents; Lemar's response is to drop the foe he has lifted high above his head with a comical "Aww—shucks!" (338:2). Later in the same issue, when Walker loses control and beats Professor Power to death, Lemar suggests that he has done the right thing, and Walker has to explain why he committed a wrong. The exchange, depicted in figure 4.2, is telling. Though Walker has demonstrated himself to be unstable, he is nonetheless positioned as the more morally sophisticated member of the team, guiding his partner to greater enlightenment. Note the similar composition of this and the previous image: Lemar's gaze is intently on Walker, while Walker looks away, a figure placement that emphasizes how the sidekick's concern for the hero is not reciprocated.

4.1. From *Captain America* #335 (November 1987). Written by Mark Gruenwald with art by Kieron Dwyer and Tom Morgan. Copyright © 2011 Marvel Entertainment, LLC and its subsidiaries.

4.2. From *Captain America* #338 (February 1988). Written by Mark Gruenwald with art by Kieron Dwyer and Tom Morgan. Copyright © 2011 Marvel Entertainment, LLC and its subsidiaries.

In many ways, then, Gruenwald and his artists' representation of the new Bucky confirms Marc Singer's argument that in superhero comics, "the handling of race is forever caught between the genre's most radical impulses and its most conservative ones" (110). Pairing a new, southern Captain America with an African American partner could potentially promote a progressive attitude toward race and suggest an alternative national/regional dynamic, yet the specific visual and verbal terms in which the relationship is represented paint a more troubling picture. By forcing an adult black man into the costume and identity of a white teenaged sidekick, the story suggests instead that national reunification might be facilitated by the appeal of a model of race relations associated with the southern past. The fantasy of racial paternalism as codified in the fiction of Thomas Nelson Page and other late nineteenth-century writers of the South was key to promoting reconciliation between nation and region, offering a sanitized and palatable version of southern race relations very different from that disseminated by abolitionists in the years before the Civil War. In many ways, the relationship between the new Captain America and Bucky seems to serve a similar purpose, providing a fantasy of southernness that, if it does not completely obscure the region's history of segregation and violence, offers a superficially progressive alternative that is in fact complicit in a deeply oppressive model of race relations.

The manner in which the team's relationship plays out in their early adventures further complicates the story's representation of race, region, and nation. Jeff Abernathy argues that one way the "national ambivalence over race" plays out in American literature is through depictions of failed interracial friendships in the South—beginning, of course, with Mark Twain's Huck and Jim. On the raft, they represent an ideal of interracial harmony, but once on shore, Huck betrays Jim and defers his escape so he can play with Tom Sawyer, a move Abernathy reads as suggestive of an anxiety about the interracial nature of American culture on the part of white Americans central to American literature and culture (Abernathy 6–7). This ambivalence comes through most clearly in Walker and Lemar's first mission, which sends them south to Walker's hometown of Custer's Grove, Georgia, and which requires that they temporarily put aside their camaraderie and pose as ideological foes. Their goal is to infiltrate the ranks of a right-wing paramilitary group known as the Watchdogs. From the beginning, their mission unsettles Walker. When a government official describes the Watchdogs as terrorists who "believe themselves to be arbiters of the public good" and who are "against pornography, sex education, abortion, the teaching of evolution," Walker reflects that he is against those things too, and when he arrives in Custer's Grove, he discovers that many of his old friends are members of the group (335:9).

Indeed, his affinity with the Watchdogs is central to their plan. He will pretend to be who he is, a concerned conservative citizen sympathetic to the Watchdog cause. The plan also calls for Lemar to pretend to be a talent scout for a men's magazine recruiting models for a nude pictorial. Strikingly, Lemar's first mission for the United States involves him playing up to another racist stereotype—that of the black pimp out to tempt white women down from their pedestals and into his bed. Here, Lemar plays the role of the "buck," with its associated danger and sexuality, but only as a ruse meant to serve the government's aims. As with his powerful body squeezed into a teenaged boy's costume, his safe performance of the "buck" suggests the containment of forces that might otherwise prove disruptive to white privilege.

Their plan requires Walker to feign outrage at Lemar's solicitation, landing Lemar in jail and attracting the attention of local Watchdog recruiters. All goes according to plan until, at Walker's initiation meeting, the Watchdogs announce their intent to lynch Lemar. As they prepare the noose, Walker wrestles with the proper course of action: break his cover and rescue his friend, or go along with the Watchdogs and count on Lemar's augmented neck muscles to save him—not a certainty, since Lemar has been drugged. In contrast to the calm, wise decision-making usually demonstrated by his predecessor, Walker struggles with paralysis; he has power, but he lacks the "determinate lines of action" that Jeffords described as essential to the idealized hard body. As Walker attempts to decide what to do, he convinces himself that perhaps the Commission has staged this whole mission: "Maybe they arranged for all this! Maybe this is a test! But if it is . . . what's the right answer? What's more important? Lemar's life or the mission? . . . It's like the Commission wants to know if I'm willing to risk a friend's life for the sake of a mission" (335:9). Artists Tom Morgan and Dave Hunt illustrate his anguish in a manner that suggests the inevitability of his eventual decision: as Walker wrestles with his options, Morgan and Hunt depict Walker from the neck up in series of tightening close-ups, with Lemar and his would-be lyncher reflected in the lenses of Walker's Watchdog helmet (see figure 4.3). The implications are clear: his perspective is literally framed by his Watchdog gear and figuratively framed by their values. His reverie broken by a Watchdog who ominously promises "plenty of lynchings in the months ahead," Walker elects to abandon his friend (335:19).

4.3. From *Captain America* #335 (November 1987). Written by Mark Gruenwald with art by Kieron Dwyer and Tom Moran. Copyright © 2011 Marvel Entertainment, LLC and its subsidiaries.

Thus, although the new Captain America and Bucky may stand, however problematically, for an ideal of a reconciled and racially inclusive America, Walker ultimately decides that in order to fulfill his duties as Captain America, he must betray Lemar, leaving him behind potentially to die in a terrifying form of ritualized racial violence. Notably, Walker leaves with the Watchdogs so that he can change into his Captain America uniform discreetly and bring the group down without jeopardizing his civilian identity. Thus, it is only his chosen solidarity with whiteness that allows this southerner to be Captain America, that allows his "American" and "southern" identities to coexist. Whether he is leaving in true or merely performed solidarity with the Watchdogs, the result is the same. In this he follows in the footsteps of Huck Finn and other southern characters who, as Abernathy puts it, "proclaim at once their whiteness and their Americanness, qualities [they often see] as one" (6).

This pattern repeats itself over the course of the next year of the series—perhaps surprisingly, given that after Lemar survives his lynching ordeal, he abandons the Bucky name and costume identity for the less demeaning identity of Battle Star. In issue #341, Lemar debuts his new name and costume, explaining that he petitioned the government to make the alteration after an African American prison guard he met on a mission explained the negative connotations of "Bucky" and told him, "You ask me, the government stuck you with that name to keep you in your place" (341:10). On one level, of course, this development reflects Gruenwald's acknowledgment of fan criticisms about the character, and over the next several issues, Battle Star begins to shed some of the lightheartedness, complacency, and submissiveness that had defined his characterization and drawn the ire of readers. Yet in some ways, his new assertiveness reflects a paternalist dynamic as well: in issue #344, Battle Star again plays the temperamental younger brother, smashing a telephone pole in anger over a new mission the government has given the pair, while Walker again plays the mature, older brother, attempting to calm him down (344:13). In general, the basic nature of Battle Star's relationship to Captain America does not alter. He remains the eager sidekick, still defined almost entirely by his concern for his partner's well being and by his loyalty to him.

In issue #347, Lemar's concern for Walker distracts him from the U.S. history exam he needs to take to belatedly earn his high school diploma (347:13–14). When Lemar offers to cover for Walker when he decides to go on a mission the government has forbidden, Walker dismisses his offer of assistance with a curt "Whatever" (345:9). Artists Dwyer and Al Milgrom depict this exchange in a panel tightly focused on Walker's eyes and furrowed brow, while Lemar's dialogue is contained in a word balloon whose point terminates in the far-right gutter of the page, a visual choice that underscores his marginality to Walker's goals and desires. As Walker withdraws further into himself, completely refusing to respond to his partner's jocular attempts to draw him into conversation, Lemar continues to fret about his mental health, thinking to himself, "I'm really worried for the guy, but there just doesn't seem to be anything he'll let me do to help him!" (348:15).

If Walker's dismissal of his partner's faithful devotion seems to conform to Abernathy's model of white protagonists who privilege connections among white people over those with their African American friends, the limitations of that model become clear during his next visit to the South in an adventure that weaves the threads of Walker's unstable, undisciplined body and racial betrayal. When Walker's parents are kidnapped by vengeful members of the Watchdogs, he takes off on his own and against the commission's orders, returning to Georgia to bargain for his parents' lives. Walker's sacrifice and betrayal of Lemar on his previous mission to Georgia served to allow his regional and national identities to co-exist, however uneasily. However, during the course of an unrelated mission, his identity has become public knowledge. Although Walker attempts to maintain the facade while in costume, referring to his parents as "the Walkers" and pretending not to know them, the Watchdogs easily see through the feeble ruse. Indeed, their refusal to heed Walker's imagined separation is revealed in this issue to be central to their ideology; they have no intention of playing Other to a national self. Instead, they see themselves not as southern separatists but as the only true Americans. They describe Walker not only as an "ally of indecency" but also as "the disgrace of the nation" (345:18).

Thus, the Watchdogs represent an even more extreme version of the anxiety that Walker embodies, an anxiety about an America in which the racial and political traditions associated with the South are no longer imagined to be contained on the periphery but are central instead, in which the reactionary South is not an aberration from the enlightened and liberal nation but instead the nation's very foundation. In this respect the Watchdogs further an ideology with roots in the Lost Cause mythology that emerged in the late nineteenth century and which continues to inform neo-Confederate ideology today. In this reading of history, southerners before the Civil War were the truest patriots of all, faithful to the nation until separated from it not by their own choosing but by northern treachery. As Cobb puts it, this mythology offered an image of "white southerners who had been scorned and persecuted by their countrymen for nothing more than their devout adherence to the most fundamental tenets of Americanism" (102).

As a traitor to this cause, Walker is condemned to the same punishment as Lemar: he will be lynched. Walker is initially paralyzed by indecision as to the best course of action, a stasis that underscores his inability to deploy his hard body in a masterful way. However, when he does act, his strategy is symbolically significant: he launches himself into the noose, jumping away from one group of Watchdogs and toward the guns of another. In one sense, his gesture suggests a solidarity with Lemar he had previously repudiated, a connection his thoughts make explicit: "They're planning to hang me—just like they tried with Lemar the first time we clashed! Lemar's augmented neck muscles enabled him to withstand strangulation! Hope mine will do the same!" (345:17). Further, it also represents a rejection of the values of the Watchdogs, with whom he had earlier identified, and of their understanding of the relationship between nation and region. Using his enhanced strength, Walker tears down a portion of the beam to which his noose is tied and uses it as an offensive weapon to incapacitate and even kill the Watchdogs. Yet his physical prowess is ultimately insufficient. He cannot destroy his foes fast enough to prevent their opening fire on his elderly parents, killing them instantly. This scene represents a failure to imagine a way of mediating the South's return to the nation. Although Walker's lynching leads him to identify with Lemar in a way that goes beyond the older brother/younger brother dichotomy of racial paternalism, that realization comes too late to help him save his parents' lives. While Walker does vanquish the Watchdogs, he proves unable to articulate any alternative to their understanding of region and nation. The issue's gruesome final panel—in which Walker, crazed by grief, cradles his bullet-riddled parents' bodies to him and converses with them as though they were alive (345:23)—returns us back to where we started: a place where the South figures in the national imagination primarily as a sentimental fantasy that obscures horrific violence.

Indeed, Gruenwald makes this delusion a central part of Walker's character. After being relieved of his duties as Captain America, Walker resurfaces as the USAgent, clad in a red, white, and black costume that Steve Rogers, calling himself simply "The Captain," had worn briefly during Walker's tenure as Captain America.[10] As part of his new role, Walker has adopted a new secret identity and cut off all ties with his past, including his friendship with Lemar, whom he pretends not to know, much to his friend's consternation. After the former partners come to blows over Walker's refusal to admit the truth, he finally admits his identity to Lemar in order to get his former partner to explain why he insists that his parents are dead—after all, he protests, he has been corresponding with them. After a trip to their graveside confirms Lemar's story, Walker confronts his government handler, who confesses that they altered his memory to make him a more effective soldier (380:26). When Walker demands that they restore his memories, they do so up to a point—but then alter them once more so that he believes that he asked for the original erasure himself (382:31). The implications about the motivation and method for the South's reconciliation with the nation are thus troubling: As the USAgent, Walker represents a South neither redeemed nor redeeming, but, rather, a South that continues in its traditional role, serving as a savage and violent force to which the nation can contrast its own enlightened nobility.

Gruenwald establishes this opposition in issue #350 in a telling image of Steve Rogers reclaiming his role as Captain America. After Walker's career as Cap was doomed by his inability to negotiate the suffocating pressures of U.S. history and racial politics, Rogers returns to the role free of these encumbrances: as seen in figure 4.4, he is depicted in a single full-page splash, floating in white space, free of any contextual markers, unburdened by history (350:45). Compare this image to those in figure 4.5 depicting the first time Walker dons the costume: a series of panels which fragment his body as he assembles his outfit piece by piece, followed by his complaint that the costume is "snug" (333:16).

4.4. From *Captain America* #350 (February 1989). Written by Mark Gruenwald with art by Kieron Dwyer and Al Milgrom. Copyright © 2011 Marvel Entertainment, LLC and its subsidiaries.

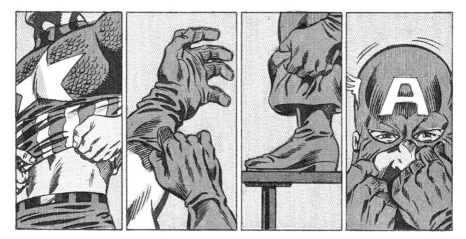

4.5. From *Captain America* #333 (September 1987). Written by Mark Gruenwald with art by Tom Morgan and Dave Hunt. Copyright © 2011 Marvel Entertainment, LLC and its subsidiaries.

Gruenwald further develops this contrast between the two characters in the way he defines their very different missions. As the USAgent, Walker works directly for the government and, in characteristically brutal fashion, deals with the darker aspects of American life that Captain America cannot or will not see, especially in terms of the government's complicity in various unethical or illegal schemes. This tension is suggested by his second-hand costume: though he is an official agent of the United States, he wears the garments of an *un*official, unsanctioned Captain America. The restored Steve Rogers promptly embarks upon a series of decidedly apolitical adventures, while in the very same issues the USAgent fights to save the life and work of Curtiss Jackson, a.k.a. the Power Broker, an underworld operator whose artificial strength-augmentation technology has been covertly adopted by the government in their quest to create the perfect killing machine (#358–362).

The implications of this new state of affairs are grim. Although the story, despite its problematic representations of race and reliance on regional stereotypes, seemed to offer the possibility of thinking beyond the familiar dynamic of the South as the nation's Other, its conclusion (to the extent that an open-ended serial can ever truly have a conclusion) does not realize that potential. Instead, that dynamic is made an explicit part of Walker's charge and is deliberately exploited by those with political interest in maintaining an illusion of the United States as timeless and idealized. In his slightly off-model costume, Walker resembles Captain America just enough to be mistaken for him from a distance; but up close, Walker's foes realize with horror that he does not share his more famous colleague's scruples or morals. The similarity-with-a-difference in costume and methods reifies the distinction between nation and region. Ultimately, the story suggests that the South never can be fully reunified with the nation—that there are too many with a vested interest in that separation, factions that will allow the South to be brought closer but must always keep it at arm's length, easily identifiable as Other in order to protect national innocence. Further, even this limited reunification is only made possible through the termination of Walker's friendship with Lemar, a fact that suggests that "racial betrayal," to use Abernathy's term, continues to be fundamental to a national identity that privileges whiteness.[11]

Gruenwald's "Captain America No More" and the stories that trace its aftermath offer a complex and sometimes vexing portrait of the relationship between the South and the nation in a critical historical moment, a time when the region's modernization and ever-more-central role in national life both provoked anxiety and offered the possibility of a productive reconceptualization of that relationship. Although the story ultimately proves too reliant on stereotypes and clichés about race and masculinity that perpetuate deeply entrenched ideas of the South to point any new way forward, it is nonetheless a valuable text both for comics scholars interested in superhero narratives and for southern studies scholars investigating how national anxieties about "southernization" played out in popular culture. Its focus on regional divisions within the imagined nation complicates the narrative of how Captain America, and perhaps the superhero generally, functions to maintain the borders of national identity. Further, it not only exposes the way in which the South continued to enable a willed amnesia about the nation's ills in the 1980s, but it also offers a cautionary depiction of how ostensibly progressive attempts at symbolic national reunification may have deeply reactionary implications.

Notes

1. Steinmetz's overview seeks to identify a broad trend, focusing only on the oldest and most recent Captain America comics. Robert Jewett and John Shelton Lawrence argue that, "As a typical embodiment of the American civil religion, offering regeneration of a helpless democratic society by selfless superheroism, Captain America stands squarely within the narrative tradition that can be traced back through earlier forms of American entertainment

of the biblical paradigms employed in the Indian captivity narratives" (35). As the sweep of their description suggests, Jewett and Lawrence are interested in Captain America as a broad concept. Such an approach is useful to a degree, but neglects the often radical differences in the character's depiction over the years as his adventures are chronicled by scores of writers and artists in distinct historical moments. Jason Dittmer has written most extensively on the role of Captain America in U.S. nationalism at various points in the nation's history; he argues in "Captain America's Empire" that the character serves to "connect the political projects of American nationalism, internal order, and foreign policy (all formulated at the national or global scale) with the scale of the individual, or the body. The character of Captain America connects these scales by literally embodying American identity, presenting a hero both of, and for, the nation" (627). While "Captain America's Empire" focuses on the role Captain America played in the era immediately after the 9/11 attacks, and other of Dittmer's essays focus on the character's role in the 1940s, 1950s, and 1960s, Dittmer does not deal with the era of the 1980s of interest to me here. See also Dubose and Matthew J. Costello.

2. Although the storyline as a whole has no formal title, I refer to it here and throughout using a common fan shorthand drawn from the cover of *Captain America* #332.

3. For a discussion of the history of this debate, see Phillip L. Cunningham, "Stevie's Got a Gun: Captain America and His Problematic Use of Lethal Force."

4. For a discussion of how different writers have handled the question of Captain America's "timeless" values over the years, see David Walton, "'Captain America Must Die': The Many Afterlives of Steve Rogers." Walton also reads the contrast between Steve Rogers and John Walker as one between timelessness and history, but his analysis of that contrast, a brief discussion in a longer piece, does not consider the role of race or region.

5. The question of whether the super-soldier serum that turned Steve Rogers from scrawny to strapping is an artificial enhancement was of interest to Gruenwald, who later in his run penned a story called "Streets of Poison," in which Steve Rogers must learn to be Captain America without the serum's rejuvenating abilities. For further discussion of this storyline, see Walton.

6. Gruenwald's fullest explanation can be found in his 1988 interview with Dwight Jon Zimmerman.

7. For a fuller discussion of the history of black characters in superhero comics, see Jeffrey Brown and Marc Singer.

8. See Brannon Costello, "Third Spaces and First Places: Jack Butler's *Jujitsu for Christ* and Hybridity in the U.S. South." *Mississippi Quarterly* 58 (2005): 613–38.

9. Exceptions to this rule have proliferated in the last few years, though it remains to be seen how many of these exceptions will become permanent. Worth noting is that the only major exception from the era of this story—DC Comics sidekick Kid Flash assuming his mentor's mantle and becoming the Flash—has recently been undone.

10. It is revealed that the Watchdogs and other groups that bedeviled Walker during his tenure as Captain America were secretly funded by the original Captain America's Nazi adversary, the Red Skull, as part of an attempt to discredit the very concept of Captain America and poison the U.S. from within. However, none of the Watchdogs or members of other groups were aware of the Red Skull's involvement, and it did not play a role in their mission or reaction to Walker; thus, I have not addressed it here.

11. A full consideration of the original Captain America's partnership with African American superhero the Falcon is beyond the scope of this essay, but it is worth noting that the Falcon's appearances in the comic in this period reinforce the distinction between Walker and Rogers. The Falcon sometimes takes the lead in his team-ups with an incognito Steve Rogers and his other partners, for instance in negotiating with police (#338), and when he exits the storyline (#345), he does so in order to take care of pressing concerns in his professional life as a social worker. Their friendship seems to lack the paternalism and racial betrayal at the heart of Walker and Lemar's relationship.

Works Cited

Abernathy, Jeff. *To Hell and Back: Race and Betrayal in the Southern Novel.* Athens: U of Georgia P, 2003. Print.

Baker, Houston A. and Dana D. Nelson. "Preface: Violence, the Body, and 'The South.'" *American Literature* 73 (2001): 231–44. Print.

Bogle, Donald. *Toms, Coons, Mulattoes, Mammies, and Bucks: An Interpretive History of Blacks in American Films.* 4th ed. New York: Continuum, 2002. Print.

Brown, Jeffrey. *Black Superheroes, Milestone Comics, and Their Fans.* Jackson: UP of Mississippi, 2001. Print.

Carter, James Bucky. "There'll Be Others: Fighting American, the Other, and Governing Bodies." *International Journal of Comic Art* 6.2 (2004): 364–75. Print.

Cobb, James C. *Away Down South: A History of Southern Identity.* Oxford: Oxford UP, 2005. Print.

Costello, Brannon. "Third Spaces and First Places: Jack Butler's *Jujitsu for Christ* and Hybridity in the U.S. South." *Mississippi Quarterly* 58 (2005): 613–38. Print.

Costello, Matthew J. *Secret Identity Crisis: Comic Books and the Unmasking of Cold War America.* New York: Continuum, 2009. Print.

Cunningham, Philip L. "Stevie's Got a Gun: Captain America and His Problematic Use of Lethal Force." *Captain America and the Struggle of the Superhero.* Ed. Robert G. Weiner. Jefferson, NC: McFarland, 2009. 176–89. Print.

Devarenne, Nicole. "A Language Heroically Commensurate with His Body: Nationalism, Fascism, and the Language of the Superhero Comic." *International Journal of Comic Art* 10.1 (2008): 48–54. Print.

Dittmer, Jason. "Captain America's Empire: Reflections on Identity, Popular Culture, and Post-9/11 Geopolitics." *Annals of the Association of American Geographers* 95.3 (2005): 626–43. Print.

———. "Fighting for Home: Masculinity and the Constitution of the Domestic in *Tales of Suspense* and *Captain America.*" *Heroes of Film, Comics, and American Culture: Essays on Real and Fictional Defenders of Home.* Jefferson, NC: McFarland, 2009. Ed. Lisa M. Detora. 96–116. Print.

———. "Retconning America: Captain America in the Wake of World War II and the McCarthy Hearings." *The Amazing Transforming Superhero! Essays on the Revision of Characters in Comic Books, Film and Television.* Jefferson, NC: McFarland, 2007. 33–51. Print.

Duck, Leigh Anne. *The Nation's Region: Southern Modernism, Segregation, and U.S. Nationalism*. Athens: U of Georgia P, 2006. Print.

Gates, Philippa. "Cop Action Films." *American Masculinities: A Historical Encyclopedia*. Ed. Bret E. Carroll. Thousand Oaks, CA: SAGE, 2003. 110–12. Print.

Goldfield, David R. *Promised Land: The South since 1945*. Wheeling, IL: Harlan Davidson, 1987. Print.

Guerrero, Ed. "The Black Image in Protective Custody: Hollywood's Biracial Buddy Films of the Eighties." *Black American Cinema*. Ed. Manthia Diawara. New York: Routledge, 1993. 237–46. Print.

Gruenwald, Mark (w), Paul Neary (a) and John Beatty (a). "Ultimatum!" *Captain America* #321 (September 1986). New York: Marvel Comics. Print.

———. "The Chasm." *Captain America* #322 (October 1986). New York: Marvel Comics. Print.

———. "Super-Patriot is Here." *Captain America* #323 (November 1986). New York: Marvel Comics. Print.

———. "Clashing Symbols." *Captain America* #327 (March 1987). New York: Marvel Comics. Print.

Gruenwald, Mark (w), Tom Morgan (p), and Bob McLeod (i). "The Choice." *Captain America* #332 (August 1987). New York: Marvel Comics. Print.

Gruenwald, Mark (w), Tom Morgan (p), and Dave Hunt (i). "The Replacement." *Captain America* #333 (September 1987). New York: Marvel Comics. Print.

———. "Basic Training." *Captain America* #334 (October 1987). New York: Marvel Comics. Print.

———. "Baptism of Fire." *Captain America* #335 (November 1987). New York: Marvel Comics. Print.

Gruenwald, Mark (w), Kieron Dwyer (p), and Tom Morgan (i). "Power Struggle." *Captain America* #338 (February 1988). New York: Marvel Comics. Print.

Gruenwald, Mark (w), Kieron Dwyer (p), and Al Milgrom (i). "Free Speech." *Captain America* #341 (May 1988). New York: Marvel Comics. 9–16. Print.

———. "Don't Tread on Me!" *Captain America* #344 (August 1988). New York: Marvel Comics. Print.

———. "Surrender." *Captain America* #345 (September 1988). New York: Marvel Comics. Print.

———. "Ambush!" *Captain America* #346 (October 1988). New York: Marvel Comics. Print.

———. "Vengeance." *Captain America* #347 (November 1988). New York: Marvel Comics. Print.

———. "Out of Commission." *Captain America* #348 (December 1988). New York: Marvel Comics. Print.

———. "Icecap." *Captain America* #349 (January 1989). New York: Marvel Comics. Print.

———. "Seeing Red." *Captain America* #350 (February 1989). New York: Marvel Comics. 1–45. Print.

Gruenwald, Mark (a), Mark Bagley (p), and Dan Panosian (i). "The Unremembered Past." *Captain America* #380 (December 1990). New York: Marvel Comics. 25–30. Print.

———. "Thanks for the Memories." *Captain America* #382 (February 1991). New York: Marvel Comics. 25–31. Print.

Jewett, Robert, and John Shelton Lawrence. *Captain America and the Crusade Against Evil: The Dilemma of Zealous Nationalism*. Grand Rapids, MI: Eerdmans, 2003. Print.

Kirby, Jack Temple. *The Countercultural South*. Athens: U of Georgia P, 1995. Print.

Ladd, Barbara. "Literary Studies: The Southern United States, 2005." *PMLA* 120 (2005): 1628–39. Print.

McPherson, Tara. *Reconstructing Dixie: Race, Gender, and Nostalgia in the Imagined South*. Durham: Duke UP, 2003. Print.

Percy, William Alexander. *Lanterns on the Levee: Recollections of a Planter's Son*. 1941. Baton Rouge: Louisiana State UP, 1973. Print.

Renan, Ernest. "What is a Nation?" Trans. Martin Thom. *Nation and Narration*. Ed. Homi K. Bhabha. New York: Routledge, 1990. 8–22. Print.

Ringenberg, Steve. "Interview with Mark Gruenwald." *Comic Art & Graffix Gallery Virtual Museum and Encyclopedia*. 1 August 2010. Print.

Singer, Marc. "'Black Skins' and White Masks: Comic Books and the Secret of Race." *African American Review* 36.1 (2002): 107–19. Print.

Steinmetz, Christian. "A Genealogy of Evil: Captain America vs. the Shadows of the National Imagined Community." *Captain America and the Struggle of the Superhero*. Ed. Robert G. Weiner. Jefferson, NC: McFarland, 2009. 190–203. Print.

Walton, David, "'Captain America Must Die': The Many Afterlives of Steve Rogers." *Captain America and the Struggle of the Superhero*. Ed. Robert G. Weiner. Jefferson, NC: McFarland, 2009. 160–75. Print.

Zimmerman, Dwight Jon. "Mark Gruenwald." Interview. *Comics Interview* 54 (1988): 5–26. Print.

"The Southern Thing"

Doug Marlette, Identity Consciousness, and the Commodification of the South

—Christopher Whitby

Kudzu's everywhere
It covers us from here to there
It's who we are, it's our destiny!
—*Kudzu: The Musical*

On Saturday July 21, 2007, the family of deceased editorial cartoonist Doug Nigel Marlette received another of many letters offering condolences on his passing and praise for the artist's sharp wit and ability to treat the most serious of issues with insight and humor. Before offering her final regards, Senator Hillary Rodham Clinton commented, "I always loved his contribution to our political dialogue, even if I wasn't always happy being a character in his cartoons!" (qtd. in Klein). Born December 6, 1949, in Greensboro, North Carolina, Marlette produced thousands of political cartoons, the nationally syndicated strip *Kudzu*, numerous cartoon anthologies (including *Faux Bubba: Bill and Hillary go to Washington*, a work concerning the aforementioned Senator and husband President Bill Clinton), and two novels, *The Bridge* and *Magic Time*. On July 10, 2007, Marlette was killed instantly when his Toyota pickup truck collided with a tree on a back road in Marshall County, Mississippi.

In an essay entitled "The Asterisk Southerner," Elizabeth Fortson Arroyo poses a question pertinent to Marlette's life and work: "What could be more Southern than to obsess about being Southern?" (qtd. in Cobb 287). Haunted by images of bigoted, lazy and backward southerners, Marlette commented,

> People often think of me as a "Southern" cartoonist, whatever that means. I have never sat down at the drawing board to chronicle the

folkways and mores of Dixie . . . but I am attracted to the issues of race, religion, and family that are so prevalent in that region. (*In Your Face* 50)

Discussing his attraction to cartoons, Marlette commented that they "pushed the boundaries of free speech by the very qualities that have endangered them: cartoons are hard to defend" ("Them Damn Pictures" 2). Using recognizable southern icons, many of which carried associations familiar to readers in the United States, Marlette's interests, concerns, and attacks were immediately presented to the viewer. The cartoons became Marlette's means of "confronting contradictions, pointing out the ironies and holding my own prism up to the light and looking at issues from my own perspective" (*Shred this Book* 6). As he put it elsewhere, "All of it is the same—Clinton, the Disneyfication of America—it is pushing things down people's throats, and there is a gag reflex. I embody the gag reflex" (Gross 18). For Marlette, Bill Clinton represented the debasement of southern ideas, the utilization of idealized southern identity for personal gain. While aware of the negative tropes within the common conception of the South, he wanted to ensure that the region was not being exploited as a means of superficially reasserting an identity, gaining power, or making money. Marlette critiqued this process through what he termed the "Faux Bubba" phenomenon, an issue that will be addressed later.

Through his strips, political and comical, Marlette juxtaposed personal ideas of what he believed society saw as the abhorrent "old" South—violent, racist, and backward-looking—with a progressive, and in his eyes redemptive, contemporary South. Published in 2002, Marlette's first novel, *The Bridge*, the tale of editorial cartoonist Pick Cantrell moving back to his southern home, demonstrates many parallels with his own life. Early in the text, central protagonist Pick is disciplined for a recent cartoon—a direct reference to the furor surrounding Marlette's image of the Pope adorned with a "No Women Priests" pin badge ("Controversial Cartoons"). Pick's employer refers to him as a "Cracker," conjuring up ideas of backwardness commonly associated with the South. Pick's response offers a succinct description of the anxieties Marlette experienced throughout his youth and cartooning career:

Yankees like Garvis still freely and without inhibition used insulting epithets for white Southerners like myself. Words like Cracker and Redneck flowed contemptuously from their lips with an impunity I found appalling, given the tenor of the times and the poverty, powerlessness, and marginalization of my people. (*The Bridge* 28)

Later, when conversing with a New York socialite, Pick reflects, "My southern drawl seemed to unnerve her ... every time I opened my mouth my IQ dropped below room temperature" (15). Marlette saw white southerners as marginalized in U.S. society due to assumptions that they were eternally on a lower social and economic level.

Marlette believed that had he "grown up in a different time, in a different place, I might have ended up drawing a cartoon strip about cats" (*In Your Face* 38). Using the idiosyncrasies of his southern upbringing as a starting point, this essay will address how Marlette's personal "southernness" manifests itself through his cartoon's visual iconography, both personal and cultural, and will examine how this "southernness" for Marlette is not merely an identity but an analytical lens through which to interpret national political, social, and religious climates. Marlette's work was especially concerned with an idea of solidarity between southern working classes, an idea based upon his lived experience in the South. He desired a widespread, sympathetic appreciation of inherited traditions as a means of producing a constructive and progressive future for the South. Marlette did not advocate a return to the South of the past, but he was also unwilling to watch those around him promote their notions of a modern South for personal gain. This essay considers the complicated nature of multiple local and national identities throughout Marlette's work alongside his own identification with competing images of the South. Paradoxically, however, while bemoaning the idealized constructions of those around him, he himself generates notions supporting an interpretation of the South he sees as identical with "reality." Like those he criticizes, his cartoons resonate with cultural codes constantly fetishized as a means of generating the solace of an identity imagined to be essential. By utilizing the icons of his putatively authentic South to lend authority to his perspective, Marlette seeks to use his cartoons to comprehend social upheaval and to advocate for a specific vision of what the South should become. My analysis is thus not concerned with whether or not Marlette's cartoons reflect a "real" or "authentic" South, but rather with, as Scott Romine puts it, "understanding how individuals and groups *use* these concepts in a region and age compelled by them" (10). In particular, I am interested in how Marlette's cartoons comment on how the South became a commodity utilized by a wider United States culture and the various uses to which that commodity was put.

Raised Southern Baptist, Marlette soon discovered the inconsistencies of a southern moral code that preached an ardent religious doctrine while violating the basic tenets of that doctrine on a daily basis. A southern baby boomer surrounded by the rhetoric of the segregationist South, Marlette drank from "whites only" fountains, sat at the front of buses where blacks were forced to sit in the back, and bore witness to the efforts of many southerners to maintain their region's supposedly glorious past. Journalist Michael Gross comments, "When the news broke about the 1954 Supreme Court decision in *Brown vs. Board of Education* . . . Marlette's family wasn't happy. 'These were troublemakers,' the 5-year-old was told" (2). Like many white southerners of his generation, Marlette struggled with multiple interpretations of the South. For the increasingly visible liberal youth movement of the sixties, the idea of a racist and politically reactionary South was problematic:

> My grandfather was part of that long-standing Southern populist tradition of identifying and sympathizing with the common man—as long as he is white and Christian. Perhaps the contradictions and ironies so vivid in the culture I was raised in brought out in me the satirist's rage and an impulse to "picture" those inconsistencies. (*In Your Face* 38)

Living in Laurel, Mississippi, home of Ku Klux Klan Grand Dragon Sam Bowers, Marlette witnessed the volatile interaction between racist white southerners and the burgeoning Civil Rights Movement. Greensboro, Marlette's birthplace, hosted early sit-ins putting pressure on governments to enforce racial equality, and his classmate's father was arrested in connection with the murder of Freedom Riders James Chaney, Andrew Goodman, and Michael Schwerner. Yet at age nine, surrounded by the hypocritical and moral injustices of segregation, he discovered *Mad Magazine*, which legitimized skepticism towards authority, highlighted the credibility gap between reality and what politicians and the nightly news proclaimed, and, most importantly, promoted the power of cartoons.

In 1966 on the naval base in Sanford, Florida, where his father was a hospital corpsman in the Marines, Marlette gained his first cartooning experience at the *Sanford Herald*. Later at Florida State University, he received his first editorial position working for the *Florida Flambeau*. In 1969, with the war in Vietnam raging, Marlette drew number ten in the draft, but applied, ultimately successfully, as a conscientious objector. This decision was not welcomed by family members. His father returned from the war shortly before his son's application for deference, and like the committee board

Marlette stood before, "found it hard to believe that I had picked up subversive notions like Love thine Enemy and Thou Shalt Not Kill at the First Baptist Sunday School" (*In Your Face* 32). Marlette secured his first major post in January 1972 with the *Charlotte Observer*, where he remained until 1987. Arriving shortly after the landmark *Swann vs. Board Of Education* legislation[1], his cartoons became "something of a symbol of the *Observer*'s commitment to Free Speech and its tolerance of unpopular ideas. Reneging on that would seriously damage that image" (*In Your Face* 40).

A phone call from Bob Kovach, newly appointed editor of the *Atlanta Journal-Constitution*, changed Marlette's life:

> One of Kovach's first moves was hiring me away from Charlotte . . . .
> He understood how strong an impact a cartoonist could have on readers . . . . That bringing in a cartoonist known for his, shall we say, controversial views would set the swashbuckling tone the paper needed.
> (*In Your Face* 44)

In the home of civil rights, Martin Luther King, and much of the great southern journalism of the sixties, Marlette and Kovach sought the creation of a great southern newspaper. Their partnership would result in a Pulitzer Prize in 1989 for a set of images concerning discriminatory bank practices.[2] Marlette's cartoon depicted a black couple requesting a mortgage and being told they would need to arrange a meeting with a loan officer. Unknown to them, but visible to the viewer, the advisor is dressed in a Klan outfit (*In Your Face* 45). While the door to the office is open, the couple cannot see in, even though they would have passed the door upon entry. The composition of the image demonstrated Marlette's cynicism regarding contrasts between Atlanta's New South idea of itself and the old-fashioned racism the banks were practicing—the city was open about its desires for racial equality and progress, but behind this surface progressivism was a society dominated by old racial hierarchies. Marlette felt this issue resonating throughout the idea of a post-civil rights South as a whole, and he saw cartooning as a way of articulating an alternative version of the South. In his 1988 collection *Shred This Book*, he states that cartoons "by their very nature challenge conventional thought. You will never see a good cartoon that says, 'Three cheers for the status quo!' or 'Hooray for the way things are!' Cartoons are a vehicle of attack" (*Shred This Book* 6).

While at first editor Kovach had been given free reign, the paper's owners became concerned that the free speech ethos of the paper was upsetting too many powerful people. Marlette commented that while Kovach was on his side, ensuring that his harder-hitting cartoons were printed, the pressure from above was too high. Eventually, following the newspaper's ploy of cutting budgets, relentlessly second-guessing his decisions, and pushing a *USA Today*-style format, Kovach quit (*In Your Face* 47). Marlette quit as well, but not before denouncing Kovach's ousting by staging a rally with his colleagues to air their grievances about what had taken place.

While initially known for his daily editorial cartoons, in 1981 Marlette began his long-running comic strip *Kudzu*, a work that celebrated "the values, humor, and original characters still to be found in rural America" (Herrick, Marlette, and Simpson, *Kudzu: The Musical* 2). In the imaginary sleepy southern village of Bypass, North Carolina, dreamer, poet, and central protagonist Kudzu Dubose, named after the famous flowering vine spread across the South, negotiates the landscape charged with the issues that influenced Marlette's formative years and which dominated his editorial cartooning; like Marlette, Kudzu is an adolescent living with the restrictions of his southern legacy and family.

Due to its publication in newspapers, *Kudzu*, like the majority of Marlette's editorial work, was predominantly black and white. Little attention is given to the background of images; it is the characters and their features that draw the reader's attention. Editorially, Marlette would usually include a single line of writing, if any, to add context. In *Kudzu*, however, the dialogue dominates the frame and is integral to character development. Rather than stand alone, the images in *Kudzu* depend on the dialogue to highlight the social, racial, and historical issues at play. Marlette's editorial images would feature a great deal more detail as their links to contemporary events and people required issues to be instantly recognizable. He stated, "I enjoy taking familiar symbols and clichés which have been trivialized and denuded of meaning and retooling their content and restoring their meaning by looking at them with new eyes" (*Shred This Book* 6). In terms of their readership, the audience for the two cartooning formats was very different. Whereas the editorial cartoons would have been read by an audience that cared deeply about political issues, Marlette saw the comic strip cutting across a broader class base. He commented:

With an editorial cartoon you have one chance, in a single frame, to tell your whole story; the punch line is immediate or not at all. In a comic strip there's more time to develop an idea. The situation can unfold a bit,

5.1. From *Kudzu*, by Doug Marlette. New York: Ballantine Books, 1992. Copyright © 1992 Doug Marlette.

and with dialogue, story telling, and timing, the idea can be set up and paid off. (*In Your Face* 80)

Kudzu had the freedom to build on subjects over numerous panels, sometimes spread across numerous weeks, to highlight the theme at hand. Consequently, the cartooning style of *Kudzu* is much simpler than that of the editorials. Due to the larger readership, the characters in *Kudzu* fit firmly into visual stereotypes and iconography, from the bespectacled, spotty, and nerdy Nasal to the cap-wearing good old boy Dub. Using these simple, recognizable stereotypes meant that certain assumptions would be made by the reader and allowed Marlette to contrast these with other ideas of southernness to illuminate issues he saw throughout the nation as a whole.

Dealing with the legacy of the southern past was central to Marlette's strip. As Jon Smith comments, "Like postwar Germany, the post-bellum, post-Reconstruction white south has had to deal with trauma and guilt" (76). One image noteworthy in this regard (see figure 5.1) is Marlette's presentation of Kudzu adorned in a Confederate Army uniform in front of a Confederate flag (*Kudzu* 19). In the image, the eye is drawn to the bold iconography of the flag, then to Kudzu in the forefront. Born in an era caught between idolization of the Lost Cause and the latest iteration of the New South, southerners like Marlette felt constantly defined by regional preconceptions. Like Kudzu in the cartoon, Marlette felt overwhelmed and overshadowed by the image of the South of the past; the fact that Kudzu's uniform is too large for him suggests how Marlette not only could not fit into the role and identity of the past but even felt overwhelmed by it. Marlette's cartoons were his means of facilitating a critique of this narrow definition of his regional identity through its juxtaposition with the qualities of virtue,

humor, and civility—the positive aspects of the South in popular conceptions—to construct a progressive direction and image for the South.

In a telling sequence, when Kudzu approaches Ida Mae, the "politically
correct, radically and ethically sensitive feminist" and states that he is "fine,"
she coarsely replies "shame on you" (*Even White Boys Get the Blues* 176).
Maurice, a young black southerner, tells the eponymous lead character that,
for Ida, Kudzu embodies all that is wrong with the twentieth century: "When
black is beautiful, you're white . . . when sister is powerful, you're male . . .
And on top of that, you're a Southerner! You're the wrong race, the wrong
gender, the wrong sexual preference, and you talk with the wrong accent!"
(*Even White Boys Get the Blues* 176). By positioning Ida Mae, Maurice, and
Kudzu alongside one another, Marlette presents the sexual, racial, and intellectual issues resonating throughout his formative years. In the climate in
which Marlette grew up, a period when the racist South was the skeleton
in the closet of American identity, for him, nothing was as abhorrent to the
nation as being a white southerner. The prevalence of these southern ideas
in popular culture and in the American mindset as a whole meant many
were unable to separate white southerners such as Marlette from these negative stereotypes, assuming the white South as a whole was complicit in the
racist and divisive South of the past.

Dub DuBose, Kudzu's uncle, represents the difficult considerations and
transitions that informed Marlette's cartooning ideas. Dub, "the Grand Old
Man of the Good Ol' Boys . . . as concrete as Kudzu is abstract, as anti-
intellectual, as stubborn and independent as Kudzu is reasonable and malleable," symbolizes, for Marlette, the conflict between the traditional view
of the South and the increasingly liberal youth movement (*In Your Face*
76). Always presented in simple, plain, stereotypically southern overalls
and trucker cap, as well as standing taller, wider, and larger in every way
than Kudzu, Dub represents the conservatism and masculine dominance
Marlette saw as characteristic of the previous generation. Even when bent
over working in his garage, Dub's accentuated size makes him tower over
Kudzu, suggesting that the view of the South that he represents continues
to dominate. Dub is Marlette's idea of a society that espouses a community spirit but is still entrenched in ambiguous racial and moral traditions.
Dub's mockery of Kudzu, informing the young protagonist of his belief that
"only little girls kept diaries," articulates the skepticism that Marlette's family,
like many sections of 1970s white southern society, had of this progressive
new generation reflecting upon and questioning pervasive southern ideals
(*Doublewide with a View* 99). Historically, the South has been recognized

as a predominantly patriarchal region. The image of the southern belle and the prevalence of conservative gender roles as a whole emphasized that the South was a region dominated by a restrictive, and to Marlette's generation, backward gender hierarchy. Dub's comments convey a society fearful of upsetting this gender relationship—Kudzu's reflection upon and criticisms of these inherited ideals is, for Dub, a sign he is jeopardizing the power and superiority this society possessed.

Marlette and Kudzu alike faced disbelief regarding their desires to venture north. Kudzu's mother swears, "no son of mine is going to float off in the haze and leaving his mama! Preacher Dunn, do you think it could be—hormones?" (*Kudzu: The Musical* 29). Mama, the "southern faded gentry to his father's redneck-cracker-trailer park gene pool," embodies Marlette's continuing ties to the traditional South (*In Your Face* 74). Unlike the southern belle image commonly associated with the South, "Mama" is presented as a stern-faced, harsh-looking woman dressed in her bedclothes and slippers. Panels show Kudzu receiving pager messages from Mama every time he desires to leave the South, creating what Maurice refers to as the "world's longest umbilical cord," to symbolize how youths such as Marlette were forever reminded of negative and restrictive southern identity constructs even upon leaving the region (*Even White Boys Get the Blues* 6).

Marlette's cartoons would continue to dissect the difficulties surrounding the reconstruction of a post–civil rights southern identity by addressing issues of memory, guilt, and commercial desire. Kudzu, Dub, Mama, and Maurice were vehicles for Marlette's investigation of his major theme—the discrepancies between a group's cultural practices and its idealized image of itself. Subjective perceptions and stereotypes interweave throughout Marlette's work, and *Kudzu* exemplifies the difficulties of isolating a "pure South," which, as Tara McPherson reminds us, does not exist. McPherson argues that the notion of a "true South" depends upon a "belief in an originary and pure southernness that is being 'sold out' and that exists (or once existed) in an untarnished relation to outside forces" (2). While Marlette felt his "Bubba Genes" were "stalked and assaulted, educated and refined, gentrified, and upwardly mobilized into submission"—a description that suggests that southernness is not only essential but biological—he himself struggled with the idea of southernness past and present (*Faux Bubba* 2). Marlette often replicated the pernicious tendency he attacked: the construction, implementation and perpetuation of an idealized, "pure" South. Marlette's exploration of the South rested on an uneasy relationship regarding his own authenticity; to adapt Scott Romine's language, by "pushing away from the tropes of the fake South, [he is] still using the South as a cartographic tool, a legend" (229).

No matter how far the road goes
It'll lead you back to us
Never be too far from home
—*Kudzu: The Musical*

For many, Jimmy Carter's election in 1976 signaled the emergence of an economically confident post-segregation South eager for national recognition; the imagery surrounding his victory was dominated by ideas of the Good Ol' Boy peanut farmer, family sentiments, devotion to God, and an opposition to expanding American materialism. The growing exposure of southern poor whites in political and popular culture seemed to suggest that formerly unequivocally derogatory terms were reimagined as signifiers of racial and cultural pride. Marlette's artistic output gathered momentum during the 1970s, a period in which assumptions regarding the South were challenged and his inclusion in a *Time* magazine article regarding Carter's New South would bring his work to a national audience.

Carter's success demonstrated that either he was not considered a typical southerner, or that the traditional interpretations of the South were being overshadowed by a "New" South in the minds of voters. Marlette drew Carter with an exaggerated smile in front of the White House, embracing a man who appears to be his brother, Billy Carter, as the stereotypical southerner in overalls (with a dumbfounded look upon his face) under the title "a role model 'first brother' even showed up in the white house" (*Doublewide with a View* 102). Carter's larger-than-life smile, with impeccable teeth, dominates the image (see figure 5.2). It seems Marlette is showing that the friendly, welcoming South, shown by the look on Carter's face, is key to victory. In many ways, the national embrace of Carter and the South he represented was an embrace of a superficial notion of the South, partly motivated by a desire to turn away from the civil rights controversies that had so dominated public life in the U.S. Cultural Historian Anthony Harkins highlights this emergence as "part of a general counter reaction to the social upheavals of the Civil Rights Movement, counterculture, and women's movement of the late 1960s and early 1970s" (211). Further, the New South of the 1970s and 80s emerged during a period when many saw southern peculiarities becoming increasingly centralized in mainstream American values and

A ROLE MODEL "FIRST BROTHER" EVEN SHOWED UP IN THE WHITE HOUSE...

5.2. From *Doublewide with a View*, by Doug Marlette. Atlanta: Longstreet Press, 1989. Copyright © 1989 Doug Marlette.

practices. Peter Applebome puts it this way: "Think of a place that's anti-government and fiercely individualistic, where race is a constant subtext to daily life . . . a place obsessed with states rights, as if it were the 1850's all over again. Such characteristics have always described the South. Somehow, they now describe the nation" (8). Likewise, the homogenization of America regions was seen by many to be leading to the nullification of the South as a peculiar region.[3] While the South became increasingly important politically, ideas of the region in terms of its moral contrasts with the North were challenged, with Vietnam and Watergate administering devastating blows to widely held myths of national invincibility.[4]

Marlette was well aware, however, that many southerners were still apprehensive about impersonal big cities, as seen in his cartoon of Kudzu expecting a warm welcome in New York but being held at gunpoint (*In Your Face* 47). He commented that "as a rule, southerners are suspicious of life in the big city. In fact, we are the best haters of New York City in the world, except perhaps for New Yorkers" (*In Your Face* 48). Set against a simple New York backdrop, Marlette contrasts the smiling face of Kudzu with the covered, harsh expression of the robber. The image conveys the belief of many southerners that the rest of the nation and the South were polar opposites in terms of attitudes; the South was community-oriented and open, whereas the north was driven by money and greed. Marlette, though, welcomed his move to the *New York Newsday* in 1989 as a challenge rather than an escape.

He would present his feelings in a cartoon of Kudzu drawing at an easel on the back of a stereotypically southern wagon under a sign leading the way to New York (*In Your Face* 48). This juxtaposition behind the image of himself as a southerner against the metropolis of the big city was integral to his work. He saw his movement from the South as a leap towards "energy, excitement and vitality . . . . The storm center of human achievement" (*In Your Face* 48).

His arrival gave him a feeling he had experienced before, though: "In the sixties the South was the nation's whipping boy . . . . However, over the last few years as the South has homogenized itself into the Sunbelt, it is slowly giving up the role of America's designated punching bag" (*In Your Face* 52). Crime, drugs, greed, and corruption, problems previously associated with the South, were now evident throughout the nation generally. Marlette's image of "The Big Apple" as a grenade with "race" written on the side addressed how issues he saw as a youth were evident nationally, ready to explode (*In Your Face* 51). James Cobb suggests that the peculiarity of defeat in war, "the exposure of racism as more than a Southern problem, and the national resurgence of political, social, and cultural conservatism" seemed to move the mainstream toward the South (8). Angry and sometimes violent opposition to busing and housing campaigns nationwide, along with George Wallace's success in presidential primaries above the Mason-Dixon, led Wallace to assert that large sections of the nation hated blacks, that they were all "Southerners."

As Joe Klein described it, "Doug's ability to offend—gracefully, brilliantly, effortlessly—went into overdrive when confronted by high-minded Dixie earnestness." Nowhere was this more evident than in Marlette's roasting of the "weekend Billy-bob" that appealed to a rehabilitated, post-civil rights southern aesthetic. In "Yuppies, Bubbas and the Politics of Culture," Catherine Bishir highlights Bubbas as individuals who drink "sweet iced tea so dark you can't see through it, or Wild Turkey and 7-UP. They often have girlfriends or wives with two first names . . . and a dog that rides in the back of a four wheel drive pickup" (8). The interplay between Souths "authentic" and fabricated led him to use the term "Faux Bubba," a term he would later use as the title of his 1993 collection regarding the election of Bill Clinton. Marlette believed that while many Americans could not claim legitimate ties to this southern image, they realized that employing its signifiers could be beneficial socially and politically. As regional differences slowly eroded, Marlette saw the gradual commodification of regionalism. Marlette's "Brief History of the Good Ol' Boy" timeline highlights American society's utilization of southern idiosyncrasies by addressing the "ethnic sub-class of culturally deprived white males known as Good Ol' Boys (Billybobbus-Rednexus). . . . Some had even been spotted as far North as Chi*cargo*" (*Faux Bubba* 6).

The image of archetypal southern shacks overshadowed by a quintessential New York skyscraper symbolized how he saw urban cities overshadowing southern ideas. The "good old boy" would diminish due to the rise of city and commercialism. This sketch forms part of a series in the collection *Doublewide with a View* centered on the rise, fall, and imminent departure of this breed of southerner. As well as anthropological images, including tales of bubbas becoming yuppies after "having their only tooth capped," Marlette presents a cultural timeline, titled "The Rise" in which he points out that "John Travolta's film homage *Urban Cowboy* ushered in 'Redneck Chic'" (*Doublewide with a View* 101). In this image Marlette depicts a smartly dressed individual in a suit wearing a cowboy hat to highlight the absurdity of southern tropes permeating into contemporary culture. The gentleman wears an ill-fitting suit, another suggestion that one idea cannot complement the other; the old South is struggling to align with the new South resonating throughout society.

Marlette intended to redeem the soul of the South. He was challenging the South of old to look at itself and objectively consider the issues hindering its development. Tara McPherson comments upon a similar interplay between multiple identities: "southern feelings are socially constructed but not determined. . . . We can draw on other traditions of white southern identity to counter the retreat into the past that buoys up a conservative white southernness" (246). In *Away Down South*, James Cobb also describes identity as being about the "*perception* of reality rather than reality itself[;] . . . identities [exist] not in isolation, but always in relation to other perceived oppositional identities" (3). Marlette's cartoons challenged hegemonic structures by comparing and contrasting multiple southern identities.

Marlette's reference to the sub-class and the good ol' boys adorned in work clothes and regional dialects highlights a South routinely lambasted by mainstream society. For Historian Lewis Killan, "the Southern accent was the primary identifying mark of the hillbilly, the term had a definite regional connotation. . . . Most important, it had a definite class connotation" (*White Southerners* 107). In "'*Who is and who ain't*' a genuine 'Good Ol' Boy,'" Marlette expresses his disdain for large sections of society adopting the Bubba image (*Doublewide with a View* 100). The image of a stereotypical yuppie chewing gum in faux hunting gear, proudly sporting his "authentic" southern cowboy hat, indicates the way Marlette saw higher classes adopting social signifiers of those below them to identify with a way of life to which they are not historically connected (*Faux Bubba* 14). Marlette saw southern culture, explicitly male, used to exploit a lack of identity within society. For Marlette, individuals such as Jerry Lewis, Mister Rogers and Clinton, or the Boardroom, Ultrasuede and County Club Crowd are "neither Bubbas nor Yuppies, though they can assume some of the behavior of each when it is appropriate" (Bishir 9).

Marlette juxtaposed his ideas of the "real" and "fake" South to bemoan the "faux rebels [who] express their dissidence in the politically correct slogans they mouth, organic foods they eat, vintage clothing they wear and the things they buy.... My generation thinks authenticity can be purchased like a historic home" (Schumaker). Continuing on from his image of the Faux Bubba mentioned earlier, Marlette presents a simple frame with a man holding an American Express card and the claim that "the new breed of privileged geek is reclaiming his masculinity the only way he knows how . . . Buying it!" (*Faux Bubba* 14). This strip demonstrates what Marlette saw as a lack in their lives, echoing the sentiments of Jon Smith, who argues that "the adoption of the pickup . . . in middle class southern white male culture reflects . . . an attempt to alleviate a bourgeois sense of having *no (masculine) identity at all*" (87, emphasis in original). Rather than showing an individual buying the goods, presenting instead only the hand and the exchange of currency, it can be seen as a comment that individuals were unaware of the meaning of their purchase. For Marlette, utilization of redneck terminology and Dixie iconography exemplified a subjective treatment of identity, in which lynching, racial, sexual and class exploitation were remnants left on the floor during the editing process. Marlette's images exemplify what Scott Romine highlights as "Nostalgia—utopianism with a backward glance—[that] functions as both a discrete industry and a diffuse cultural practice in a South whose past is almost uniformly undesirable" (*The Real South* 25). Although Marlette experienced emotional torment over his regional identity, he saw upwardly mobile white southerners consuming southern identity as quick as companies produced it. Marlette conveyed his anger at the way those who had once lambasted the South were now profiteering from it.

In *Kudzu*, Bypass's newest phenomenon, "Dial-a-Bubba,'" exemplified Marlette's growing fears about regional commodification (*Faux Bubba* 11). By picking up the phone and paying five dollars, callers could enjoy regional colloquialisms, including colorful exclamations such as "I'm fuller'n a tick! ... I been rode hard 'n' put up wet!" (*Faux Bubba* 7). Reverend Dunn, the local pastor with dubious moral groundings, criticizes Kudzu for his exploitation of such avenues. In the image Dub is under the hood of a car, most of his body obscured from view, emerging only to utter the words desired by callers, but even then he does not answer the phone—that task is left to Kudzu. His distancing, visually and physically, represents the shift from a real South to a fabricated, commodified, and for Marlette, fake, South. When told they would receive one hundred dollars for merely uttering the word "grits," though, Dunn's opinions change and he joins forces with the young entrepreneurs. The Reverend's quick transition highlights Marlette's belief that many sections of southern society were more than willing to sell their identity to the highest bidder, leaving no moral high ground from which to criticize the selling of the South. Marlette saw the "true" way as disappearing under the weight of high society's desires. Jon Smith suggests that "Southern or otherwise, when a bourgeois man who doesn't work with his hands affects a pickup truck or work boots, he generally expresses not an identity but a yearning for one" (83–84). Echoing Marlette's fear of a blinkered approach to southern history, Smith suggests that "as the South becomes more 'Americanized'—as identity becomes more and more structured as a lack to be filled by consumption—the paradoxical result may be the increasing commodity-fetishization of southernness itself" (83).

Marlette's belief in the death of an "authentic South" is presented through "Grits Aid," a series of strips in which southern luminaries such as Waylon Jennings and Willie Nelson, work a telethon to raise money to save the South. "Grits Aid" depicts Nasal and Kudzu utilizing tropes reminiscent of the liberal preservation movements of the 1970's such as badges and bumper stickers with slogans such as "Honk if your name is Bubba" and "Have you hugged a redneck today?" (*Doublewide with a View* 103). Cartoons depict stereotypes of those same movements he is parodying such as the hippies, and a feminist group announcing "what about good ol' girls? Er ... persons?" (*Doublewide with a View* 103). This latter cartoon demonstrates the gender dynamic still dominant in many southern narratives, the idea that saving the bubba similarly meant preserving conservative gender hierarchies.

Nasal and Kudzu's street campaign comes to nothing, however. Though every effort is made to ensure "Grits Aid" a success, the hoped-for, star-studded, and profitable climax of the drive is simply Maurice sitting in an empty auditorium playing blues songs, overshadowed by a large Confederate flag. In the panel, the three protagonists are eclipsed by the flag in the background, an image that suggests how, for Marlette, the new South will always be in the shadow of the old. Like Marlette, the failure of Kudzu and Nasal in their campaign to mediate a new image of an "authentic" and

5.3. From *Doublewide with a View*, by Doug Marlette.
Atlanta: Longstreet Press, 1989. Copyright © 1989
Doug Marlette.

culturally rich region leaves them "demoralized . . . their faith in humanity shattered" (*Doublewide with a View* 103). Their anger is representative of Marlette's frustration with stagnation throughout national politics and culture: society focused on an identity with no concept of accountability, a southern white identity divorced from context and history. Marlette's image echoes Jon Smith's statement that "far from liberating white southerners from, say, the alienation and homogeneity of northern U.S. culture, several clichés of white southern identity—the senses of community, place, and history—have more often tended to reinforce particularly crippling forms of narcissism" (77). For Marlette, this commodified southern image lacked any of the redemptive qualities promised by the end of legal segregation.

In one telling strip (see figure 5.3), Marlette portrays a line of tourists entering "Three Flags over Bypass," a reference to the Six Flags amusement park chain, proclaiming that they want to "see the last 'good ol' boy'" (*Doublewide with a View* 104.) There is no detail in the background of the panel; all we see are the tourists, Maurice selling tickets, and a sign for the park—no depth in the image or any specific views of the park. The image conveys, once again, Marlette's belief that the South is a commodity, a plaything for wider society. By using the analogy of the theme park, it presents the South as a disposable, purchasable, and instant source of gratification, a tool to convey what once was, but is now disappearing. A powerful strain in Marlette's *Kudzu* is lamentation that southern culture has become victim to a cultural lobotomy in which consumerism allowed individuals to pick and choose traits depending upon desire and cash flow.

Similarly, in his discussion of country music, John Egerton asks, "How much of that intimacy, that authenticity can be retained when the music goes uptown?" (206). Egerton's and Marlette's concerns were closely aligned. Marlette's "Fall of the Good Ol' Boy" strip suggests that cross-pollination with the North will lead to "urbanization, homogenization and other big words ending in 'ization. . . . [T]he region was transmuted into *gag* 'The Sunbelt'" (*Faux Bubba* 2). When the South went North, or "uptown," it was unable to remain true to itself and bowed to the dominant cultural demands, leading to what Marlette describes as "'Bubbacide'; the systematic extinction of the American Good Ol' Boy!" (*In Your Face* 45). Kudzu is shocked to discover an old tool shed from the previous generation:

Kudzu: Wow. It's like a lost civilization!
Uncle Dub: Yeah, and it's never gonna be that way again. (*Kudzu: The Musical* 62)

Rather than addressing identity as a fluid and shifting, even pragmatic construct, Marlette, like Kudzu and Dub, is deeply invested in the project of recovering and sustaining a "real" South. While Marlette may address the ways individuals use commodities to construct identities, he is rooted firmly in a model of identity as attached to place.

Marlette's work combines his affection for the traditional South as embodied in his nostalgia for his own past alongside his desires for southern progress. Presented as a hero of sorts, Kudzu is, for Marlette, an idea of "the Real South"—part of what Romine describes as the tendency by which, "in practice, the 'Real South' often turns out to be the one I desire . . . . [it is] a matter of getting *you* to accept my South, my heritage, my culture, and so forth as *authentic*" (14). Marlette's characters were an amalgamation of ideas of the South past and present, characters defined through a set of imagined relations to spaces and environments. The issue here, one addressed by Jon Smith, is "not the disappearance of the past but the appearance, through a multiplicity of media, of multiple pasts embedded in multiple places. There are so many of these pasts and places, in fact, that it is becoming possible to assemble an 'identity' self-consciously [so that] . . . we can expect to see from this new generation of middle-class southern whites a new attitude toward cultural coding" (94–95). Rather than regional reaffirmation, Marlette saw a symbolic re-appropriation weakening the South's distinctiveness. But in attempting to forestall this downward slide he attempted to make his constructed South the "real" South by adopting a personalized narrative. The plight of Nasal, Kudzu, and the "Grits Aid" campaign echoes the process Romine highlights when he states that "authenticity articulates a structure of desire and hence of absence" (4). It is through their desire to highlight the South in a society interested only in a superficial, commodified version of it that they become aware that society is ignoring the complexity of the region.

Once a honky, always a honky!
—**Marlette**, *Even White Boys Get the Blues*

The most common grounding of identity is that of a shared common past, real or imagined. James Cobb highlights the period following Civil Rights Movement as one of the most contradictory and unusual aspects of American history, with "the strong and apparently still strengthening inclination of Blacks in the South to identify themselves as Southerners" (128). Many African Americans returned to the South, where their ancestors had been sent as slaves, and in which they witnessed dehumanizing brutality. Seen as counter to the Black Power movements, this homecoming allowed African Americans to contemplate their heritage, pride, and strength—and to confront the hardships of urban life through assertion of their identity. Following the end of legal segregation, many white southerners struggled to deal with the new racial alignment, a structure where black citizens would theoretically experience equal standards of living. This interaction between whites and blacks would be central to *Kudzu*.

Marlette uses Nasal Lardbottom to address desires within the South to eradicate the derogatory stigma attached to "whiteness," or, if that proves impossible, to escape the category of southern whiteness altogether. The spotty, nerdy student and the "whitest boy at Bypass high" desperately attempts to be accepted as "hip" by black friend Maurice. Nasal, shown writing a letter to Santa, dreams of a "Non-white Christmas," writing to Santa asking for "a little pump and fake . . . a little shake and bake," a reference to his desire for skill at basketball, a sport seen as predominantly African American. Nasal attempts to construct a positive image of the region by "shedding the skin" of racial torment and violence (*Gone With the Kudzu* 41). An adolescent who "would give anything to be a righteous, jive-talking, high-fiving, soul brother," Nasal undertakes a "race lift" in an attempt to align culturally with black society (*Even White Boys Get the Blues* 55). With Nasal's

5.4. From *Even White Boys Get the Blues,* by
Doug Marlette. New York: Times Books,
1992. Copyright © 1992 Doug Marlette.

face covered in bandages while he practices basketball (see figure 5.4), Marlette critiques a society he saw appropriating aspects of black identity, especially in sport. The color of Nasal's skin is not evident, but his mask cannot
void past wrongs. John Egerton asserts, "Athletics may be doing as much to
influence racial attitudes in the United States as the emergence of economic
and political black power . . . . Even the most racist fans appear to accept,
however cheerfully, the lofty status of black heroes as well as white ones"
(178). Struggling to become "a brother," Nasal practices high-fives, proclaims
"my father took out a second mortgage to buy me a pair of Nikes!" and gets
the number 23 cut into his hair, a reference to basketball star Michael Jor-
dan. This signifies how, like southern identity, Marlette saw racial acceptance
built upon financially consumable icons (*Even White Boys Get the Blues* 53).
Before removing his "race change" bandages, onlookers exclaim "It can't be
Nasal . . . this dude dresses sharp . . . and he high-fives without hurting himself" (53). With Nasal's face covered, it is his actions, rather than his race, that
count. But when removing his bandages to complete his day as a "genuine,
authentic, full-fledged brother," the same Nasal is unveiled (55).

The failure of Nasal's race change illustrates Marlette's belief that while
sections of society hinted at progress, they were invested in an idealized,
subjective, and personal construction of race divorced from historical reality. By making race (or the South) a commodity rather than directly contem-
plating its complexities, many Americans misunderstood the issues at stake.

Marlette saw the dominant classes replaying the past to their own desires. Following the destabilization of the culture in the Civil Rights Era, white society scrambled for an identifiable history and culture not blighted by the shame of the southern past. As John Berger states, "a people or a class which is cut off from its own past is far less free to and act as a people or class than one that has been able to situate itself in history" (33). Through their fear of the present, Marlette saw individuals mystifying the past. Nasal's use of the term "Tarzan X" in the final strip of Marlette's *Even White Boys Get the Blues* indicates a lack of understating regarding the identity he attempts to utilize (186). By integrating the uncivilized Tarzan image with that of Malcolm X—a name taken to represent the nameless, voiceless African American—Nasal reveals his confusion about the issues at play. Marlette draws Maurice and Nasal between two panels, free of the borders of the standard comic strip. Free from the discussions of race in previous panels, Nasal finally exclaims, "King Kong! He was African, right?!" This misunderstanding leads Maurice to assert, "Once a honky, always a honky" (186). Like American society as a whole, Marlette shows how Nasal had attempted to free himself of old racial hierarchies, suggested by the lack of panel borders, but had returned to the stereotypes of old.

For Marlette, appropriation of southern ideas with dubious moral groundings was "the same dilemma that we moderate southerners faced when Klansmen burned crosses and terrorized Black Americans in the name of our Christ" ("Cartoon Fatwas" 3). He saw it as symptomatic of a time in which it was "hip" to be a southerner. David Blight suggests that the "power of denial can turn a lost war into a vibrant, necessary form of national chic" (347). The South remained a site upon which the trauma of slavery competed with the growth of what would become a booming nostalgia industry.

"I might as well have been getting a sex change operation," Marlette stated regarding the reaction of his friends and family to his move to New York (*In Your Face* 48). It took leaving the South for him to look at the South. He used cartooning to consider personal, social, and historical notions of individual, regional, and national identity. He was constantly struck with the feeling that he was out of place, dropped into an alien family and historical structure. Marlette's work not only attacked the excesses of contemporary society, but manipulated icons and stereotypes by juxtaposing them with his own "reality." Recognizing the necessity for viewers to connect with icons, Marlette conveyed his version of the South alongside what he believed to be the debased and commodified South of contemporary society. Marlette's cartoons exemplified how "The South" became a site of negotiation and navigation. As Romine states, "we may come to different Souths, but neither will be solid in fact or in practice. In fact, we may dwell in alternative realities or simulations" (236). Marlette stated, "Cartoons distort and reflect reality like fun-house mirrors, and if we are not too insistent upon literal representation and doctrinal purity, we can sometimes catch them in a glimpse of some hidden truth about ourselves" (*Shred This Book* 158). Ultimately, Marlette used his cartoons to prompt southerners to remind themselves of where they had been and how a more complex understanding of their past could serve as a foundation for future development.

Notes

1. The ruling supported busing as a remedy for the *de facto* segregation of public schools.

2. Bill Dedman's prize-winning "The Color of Money," which utilized Marlette's images, highlighted biased mortgage lending within middle-income Atlanta neighborhoods.

3. This phenomenon is contemplated extensively in John Egerton's landmark text *The Americanization of Dixie*.

4. Population shift into the South and West between 1970 and 1990 saw the number of residents in the eleven states of the Old Confederacy growing by 40 percent, equating to 40 million people, twice the national growth rate, influencing the South's political power. The eleven Confederate states, plus Oklahoma and Kentucky, now elected 137 of the 435 seats in the House of Representatives, 17 more than in 1960 (Applebome, "Dixie Rising" 9). By 1990, if a candidate won the southern states, only one third of the nation's remaining votes would be necessary to win.

Works Cited

Applebome, Peter. *Dixie Rising: How the South is Shaping American Values, Politics and Culture*. New York: Harcourt, 1996. Print.

Berger, John. *Ways of Seeing*. London: Penguin, 1972. Print.

Bishir, Catherine W. "Yuppies, Bubbas, and the Politics of Culture." *Perspectives in Vernacular Architecture* 3 (1989): 8–15. Print.

Blight, David. "Southerners Don't Lie, They Just Remember Big." *Where These Memories Grow: History, Memory, and Southern Identity*. Ed. Fitzhugh Brundage. Chapel Hill: U of North Carolina P, 2000. 347–51. Print.

Cobb, James C. *Away Down South: A History of Southern Identity*. New York: Oxford UP, 2005. Print.

Cooper, William J., and Thomas E. Terrill. *The American South: A History*. 3rd ed. New York: McGraw-Hill, 2002. Print.

Egerton, John. *The Americanization of Dixie*. New York: Harper and Row, 1974. Print.

Gross, Michael. "Doug Marlette." 9 April 2009. Web. www.mgross.com/uploaded/Marlettecut.doc.

Harkins, Anthony. *Hillbilly: A Cultural Icon*. Oxford: Oxford UP, 2004. Print.

Herrick, Jack, Doug Marlette, and Simpson Bland. *Kudzu: The Musical*. New York: Samuel French, 1999. Print.

Killan, Lewis. *White Southerners*. Amherst: U of Massachusetts P, 1985. Print.

Klein, Joe. "In Memorium . . . and a Touch of Class." *Time*. 15 July 2007. Web. www.time-blog.com/swampland/2007/07/in_memoriumand_a_touch_of_clas.html. 14 February 2008.

Marlette, Doug. *The Bridge*. New York: Harper Collins, 2002. Print.

——. "Cartoon Fatwas." *The Brook: News about Stony Brook University*. Web. www.dougmarlette.com/pages/brookfall.pdf. 9 April 2009.

——. "Controversial Cartoons." Web. http://www.dougmarlette.com/pages/controvtoons.html. 8 April 2010.

——. "A Conversation with Doug Marlette." http://www.harpercollins.com/author/authorExtra.aspx?authorID=20524&isbn13=9780060505219&displayType=bookinterview. Web. 9 April 2009.

——. *Doublewide with a View*. Atlanta: Longstreet Press, 1989. Print.

——. *Even White Boys Get the Blues*. New York: Times Books, 1992. Print.

——. *Faux Bubba: Bill and Hillary Go To Washington*. New York: Times Books, 1993. Print.

——. *Gone With the Kudzu*. Nashville: Rutledge Hill Press, 1995. Print.

——. *In Your Face: A Cartoonist at Work*. Boston: Houghton Mifflin, 1991. Print.

——. *Kudzu*. New York: Ballantine, 1992. Print.

——. *Shred this Book: The Scandalous Cartoons of Doug Marlette*. Atlanta: Peachtree, 1988. Print.

——. "Them Damn Pictures." *Nieman Report*, Winter 2004. Web. http://www.dougmarlette.com/pages/neiman. 2 September 2009.

McCloud, Scott. *Understanding Comics: The Invisible Art*. New York: Harper Perennial, 1994. Print.

McPherson, Tara. *Reconstructing Dixie: Race, Gender and Nostalgia in the Imagined South*. Durham: Duke UP, 2003. Print.

Romine, Scott. *The Real South: Southern Narrative in the Age of Cultural Reproduction*. Baton Rouge: Louisiana State UP, 2008. Print.

Schumaker, Kirsty. "The Marlette Mystique." *Metro Magazine*. Web. http://dougmarlette.com/pages/mystique.html. 9 April 2009.

Smith, John. "Southern Culture on the Skids: Punk, Retro, Narcissism, and the Burden of Southern History." *South to a New Place: Region, Literature, Culture*. Ed Suzanne Jones and Sharon Monteith. Baton Rouge: Louisiana State UP, 2003. 76–95. Print.

II.

Emancipation and Civil Rights Resistance

Drawing the Unspeakable

Kyle Baker's Slave Narrative

—Conseula Francis

Even a cursory reading of Kyle Baker's *Nat Turner* (serialized from 2005–2007 and collected in 2008) reveals two things. First, the story is incredibly violent. Nearly every page features a gruesome act of graphic violence, or, at the very least, some consequence of violence. Second, in telling the story of Turner's life up to and including his infamous 1831 slave insurrection, Baker seems to, as critic Marc Singer suggests, attempt to "jazz up slavery with chases and fight scenes and huge Frank Miller heroes who battle dozens of guys in silhouette" ("Kyle Baker"). For some readers these features might mark *Nat Turner* as a failure. Indeed, Singer worries that the "real impulse behind *Nat Turner* is not historical documentation or assessment but simply the vicarious pleasure of revenge." I would argue, however, that it is precisely these troubling aspects of *Nat Turner* that make the book so compelling.

In the introduction to the collected edition of *Nat Turner*, artist and writer Kyle Baker explains how he came to create a comic book version of Turner's life. Having encountered Turner's name and story over and over again in books, in paragraphs no longer "than a few sentences mentioning the name, the date, and that [his rebellion] was important," Baker became curious (6). "Who was this man who was important enough to be mentioned in *all* the history books, yet is never spoken about at length?" (original emphasis). In other words, who is this man we know without actually knowing? What is this story we pass on from generation to generation without actually telling it? What accounts for the gaps in the popular narrative surrounding Turner? Baker attempts to answer these questions about Turner and his story using the comics form.

Rather than drawing on the now considerable body of historical and creative work devoted to Turner and his raid,[1] Baker instead uses the 1831 *The Confessions of Nat Turner* by Thomas Gray as the text of his book. Albert

Stone suggests we read the published *Confessions* with caution. Thomas Gray, a "white lawyer and slaveholder," published a document that is "part dictation, part paraphrase of Turner, and part editorial by Gray" (166). We cannot take for granted that these final words of Nat Turner come to us as Turner intended. Yet, and here again Stone is instructive, Gray is a "prime source of information and ideology associated with Nat Turner's life and the revolt." I treat Turner's *Confessions* in this essay the same way Baker does in his book, as the "prime source" of information on Turner, and as closest to how Turner is perceived in the popular imagination. I hope to show, though, how Baker's comic highlights the insufficiency of that information. Though *Confessions* provides almost all of the text in Baker's story, his art carries the narrative weight of the story. And while Baker does nothing to sugarcoat the violence of Turner's 1831 raid on the people of Southampton County, Virginia (the deaths of 55 men, women, and children are presented as exactly what they are—grisly and violent), he uses the comics form to contextualize that violence. Turner's actions become, then, not the actions of a lone, crazed individual. Instead, they are part and parcel of the horrifically violent institution of slavery.

While Baker does not label his narrative as a corrective, it certainly functions that way. Baker's comic book gives context and flesh to this influential figure in American and African American history whose story is often, ironically, relegated to "just a few sentences." He also gives voice to the silences in the traditional slave narrative. The form of the traditional slave narrative, most often political pieces serving very particular ideological purposes, cannot adequately express the physical and psychological violence of slavery. Yet, it is this very violence that is the "unspeakable thing unspoken," to borrow a phrase from Toni Morrison, that gives those narratives power. Baker's narrative calls attention to this paradox by juxtaposing the emotionless, detached 1831 *Confessions* with provocative, disturbing, almost completely wordless images. These images not only provide an unflinching look at the horror and violence of slavery; they also force the reader to consider what it really means for a man—a living, breathing, feeling, thinking man—to be treated as property. Baker's *Nat Turner*, ultimately, is able to tell the story that the enslaved man himself could not.

I argue that Baker reconsiders the basic rhetorical premises of the slave narrative with *Nat Turner*. That reinvention is most clear when we consider how traditional slave narratives work. In particular, it is useful to note that the very thing that makes nineteenth-century slave narratives effective rhetorical tools in the fight against slavery also creates the very gaps Baker's comic book aims to fill. Arguably, nineteenth-century slave narratives, "autobiographical narratives of former slaves" (Andrews 667), served the function of gaining white sympathy for and participation in the abolitionist movement. The autobiographical form, focusing as it did on the details of an individual life, worked to humanize a group of people to an audience often doubtful of black humanity. This task required particular rhetorical strategies and resulted in specific narrative gaps. Taking Frederick Douglass's 1845 *Narrative of the Life of Frederick Douglass, An American Slave, Written By Himself* and Harriet Jacobs's 1861 *Incidents in the Life of a Slave Girl*, as examples of the form, I hope to demonstrate the narrative gaps Baker's narrative fills.

The prefatory matter in the nineteenth-century slave narratives, typically letters and testimonials from respected and respectable white men and women attesting to the character of the narrative's author and the veracity of his or her tale, serve to put readers at ease. The testimonials assure readers that their time will not be wasted nor will their sensibilities be assaulted, at least not unduly. Lydia Maria Child, writing as editor of Jacobs's narrative, tells readers,

I am well aware that many will accuse me of indecorum for presenting these pages to the public; for the experiences of this intelligent and much-injured woman belong to a class which some call delicate subjects, and others indelicate. *This peculiar phase of Slavery has generally been veiled*; but the public ought to be made acquainted with its monstrous features, and *I willingly take responsibility of presenting them with the veil withdrawn.* (my emphasis, 337–38)

"Yes", Child seems to say to readers, "I know the tale of sexual degradation you are about to read is beyond the pale, but the female's experience of slavery is just as important to our understanding of the institution as the male's experience. I accept responsibility for any injury to delicate sensibilities." She accepts responsibility because, as a white woman, it is hers to accept. Jacobs, a black woman and a former slave, cannot really accept it because she is not a member of bourgeois polite society. She is not, in the end, part of the "public" who might be offended.

And because she, and Douglass and other enslaved people who escaped bondage, are not part of this "public," their word means very little. The prefatory material aims to attest to the importance of the narratives, but they also exist to counter readers' doubts about the plausibility of the stories making the rounds in abolitionist circles. William Lloyd Garrison writes, in a letter that introduces Douglass's narrative,

[Northerners] do not deny that the slaves are held as property; but that terrible fact seems to convey to their minds no idea of injustice, exposure to outrage, or savage barbarity. Tell them of cruel scourgings, of mutilations and brandings, of scenes of pollution and blood, of the banishment of all light and knowledge, and they affect to be greatly indignant at such enormous exaggerations, such wholesale misstatements, such abominable libels on the character of the southern planters. (250)

Garrison's words surely challenge readers to step up to the moral plate with regards to slavery. They also, though, suggest that these same readers need much convincing. Writers like Jacobs and Douglass were always writing against the belief that they could not be trusted to tell the truth about slavery. This meant, of course, that they couldn't tell the truth about slavery, at least not the whole truth. If the goal of the slave narratives was to gain the sympathy of white readers, then the authors of slave narratives needed to be strategic about which details they offered and which they held back. James Olney, in "'I Was Born': Slave Narratives, Their Status as Autobiography and as Literature" (1985), calls nineteenth-century slave narratives "autobiographical performance" (149). He writes, the "autobiography may be understood as a recollective/narrative act in which the writer, from a certain point in his life—the present—looks back over the events of that life and recounts them in such a way as to show how that history has led to this present state of being." In other words, authors carefully construct the "I" in slave narratives, not to depict an accurate picture of the enslaved person's life, but rather to depict a "patterned significance," a significance meant to move nineteenth-century readers. In practice this means finding significance in those experiences and events that represent what Penny Tucker calls an "achievement of respectability through literacy, literary eloquence, and reason" (140). In short, nineteenth-century slave narratives do not ask readers to look fully at slavery; instead they ask readers to look at respectability achieved despite slavery. Turner's own nineteenth-century narrative, with its emotionless, detached, unapologetic description of unspeakable violence, fails this respectability test at every turn.

And, if we follow Singer's interpretation, *Nat Turner* fails the morality test as well. Nineteenth-century readers needed to recognize the respectability of the slave narratives' authors so they could, in turn, cede these authors the moral high ground. The abolitionist argument against slavery was largely a moral one, and those making the argument had to demonstrate strict adherence to that morality, particularly the part that eschewed violence and sought no revenge. It is difficult to overstate the effect this has had on our popular narratives of slavery and responses to racial injustice. We assume and demand that the enslaved/oppressed demonstrate their moral superiority at every turn, primarily through denouncing violence. Thus, Malcolm X and Nat Turner survive in our popular memory as violent disturbers of the peace and underminers of a worthy cause, while Martin Luther King, Jr. has practically become the patron saint of the U.S. And figures like Denmark Vesey are held up as examples of the dangers of black violence, despite the fact that his planned 1822 slave insurrection never materialized.

The example of Vesey is useful here to demonstrate the legacy of the respectability/morality required by the nineteenth-century slave narratives. In Charleston, South Carolina, the site of Vesey's failed insurrection—and the home of the still visible responses to that failed insurrection in the forms of barbed bars gracing the tops of gates of homes dating from the era—local organizers have joined with the municipal government to erect a memorial to Vesey in a public park (ironically, this park adjoins The Citadel, the military college that came into existence as part of Charleston's efforts to contain possible black violence). The planned memorial has at least as many detractors as supporters, and the source of contention seems to be the morality, the moral rightness, of Vesey's actions. Despite the utter failure of his plan to kill as many Charlestonians as possible and escape with others to Haiti,[2] Vesey is still treated by many as a murderer. As a commenter to a local newspaper, in response to the local government donating $40,000 to the memorial fund, stated:

WHY? Why would anyone want to erect a statue of a murderer? This is CRAZY to use tax payer money to honor someone who tried to kill as many people as possible during his day. A statue to honor great people such as MLK, GW Carver, etc. would be the thing to do and money well spent! If Denmark was a great man he would have tried to gain his freedom without harm to others. Great people overcome great obstacles, MLK, Clarence Thomas, and I could go on and on on all the great African Americans who played by the rules, and overcame hatred, and made a HUGE difference in our lives! NO to "I have to kill everyone in my path VESEY." (Comments)

I don't mean to suggest that Singer wants to confine Turner to the margins of history as the commenter seems to want to do with Vesey. However, Singer's wish that *Nat Turner* "had the courage to judge or condemn its hero as easily as it praises him" suggests a longing for the same kind of moral certainty, one in which lashing out violently against a pervasive system of dehumanizing and degrading oppression is always wrong. In occupying the moral center, authors of nineteenth-century slave narratives make a powerful, compelling argument. In refusing that morality, in embracing ambiguity instead, *Nat Turner* dares to revise the slave narrative.

And again, it is the descriptions of violence that seem to set these narratives apart. If you are making common cause with readers by virtue of your shared notions of morality and respectability, then you can't risk troubling that alliance with anything immoral or disrespectful. The trick authors of slave narrative have to learn, a trick that Turner makes no use of at all in his *Confessions* (in part, certainly, because Gray's rhetorical goals are markedly different than Douglass's and Jacobs's), is how to write about violence using code and metaphor. Jacobs's tale of sexual humiliation is important in this regard, particularly because Jacobs is not raped by her master, Dr. James Norcom. Her sexual degradation and humiliation is real and deeply felt, to be sure, but functions primarily as a *metaphor* for all the different sorts of degradations and humiliations suffered by female slaves. In the chapter titled "The Trials of Girlhood," Jacobs writes of turning fifteen, "a sad epoch in the life of a slave girl" (360):

> No matter whether the slave girl be as black as ebony or as fair as her mistress. In either case, there is no shadow of law to protect her from insult, from violence, or even from death; all these are inflicted by fiends who bear the shape of men. . . . She will become prematurely knowing in evil things. Soon she will learn to tremble when she hears her master's footfall. She will be compelled to realize that she is no longer a child. If God has bestowed beauty upon her, it will prove her greatest curse. That which commands admiration in the white woman only hastens the degradation of the female slave. (361–62)

While Jacobs learns to "tremble when she hears" Norcom's footsteps because he whispers "foul words" in her ear (361) and threatens to move her away from the watching eye of her grandmother, her description of the "trials of girlhood" certainly suggests considerably more violence and abuse than this. Again, I argue, she speaks in code here, lest she offend the delicate sensibilities of her readers more than necessary. Her descriptions of Nor-com's advances substitute for the many other sexual abuses and humiliations suffered by enslaved people. Her narrative, however, cannot dwell in these abuses because ultimately her story is about her triumph over them and the possibility of triumph for other enslaved women, if only Jacobs's readers will pick up the fight. Douglass's famous fight with the slave breaker Edward Covey functions in much the same way. The fight, literally a fight for his humanity (his victory means that "however long [he] might remain a slave in form, the day had passed forever when [he] could be a slave in fact" [299]), stands in for the routine physical violence of slavery. While Douglass's story is the epitome of respectability achieved through "literacy, literary eloquence, and reason," it is set against a backdrop of cruelty and violence and unspeakable horror.

Ultimately, Olney argues, a certain sameness permeates the nineteenth-century slave narratives. He calls them a "sequential narrative" that fit into a preformed "mold with regular depressions here and equally regular prominences there—virtually obligatory figures, scenes, turns of phrase, observances, and authentications" (151). I argue that this mold achieves its rhetorical end, gaining white sympathy, in part by coding violence and focusing narrative attention elsewhere. The 1831 *Confessions* gives us no shield from the brutality of Turner's rebellion, and Baker's challenge is to make effective narrative use of that violence. While some readers might look to the religious rhetoric in the *Confessions* as a suggestion of divinely sanctioned violence, I maintain that without the trappings of the traditional slave narratives (particularly the prefatory matter attesting to the respectability/morality of the narrative's author), Turner's religious convictions come off as crazed rather than as prophetic. It is only when coupled with Baker's narrative images that Turner's prophecy, and the violence that ensues, takes on righteous weight.

I argue that the comics form is central to this project. Baker calls comic books a "visual medium" that demands artists choose "a subject with opportunities for compelling graphics" (6). For Baker, Turner's story has the added benefit of being filled with "action and suspense" and Turner himself seems to possess "superhuman abilities." In short, Baker suggests, in addition to being a significant chapter in American history, Turner's life story is also all the stuff of which comic books are made. More interesting for our purposes, though, is *how* comics are made.

Countering Scott McCloud's commonly accepted definition of comics as "juxtaposed pictorial and other images in deliberate sequence" (8), R. C.

Harvey posits that the "blending" of visual and verbal content, rather than sequencing, is at the heart of how comics "work" (25). I am relying on two of Harvey's ideas in my reading of *Nat Turner*. The first is his notion that the interdependence of words and pictures creates an "economy of expression." Baker's narrative is a skillful blending of words and pictures, in this instance Baker's art and Turner's words from the 1831 *Confessions*. Baker's black, white, and gray images contain almost no words, aside from the occasional sound effect, and we get only brief excerpts from Turner's narrative. The book is, in many respects, incredibly sparse, but the interdependence of the verbal and visual elements and the economical use of each, creates quite a powerful story. I also find Harvey useful because of an idea he borrows from Judith Yaross Lee. Lee argues that the defining feature of *New Yorker* "gag cartoons" is the "ironic relations between image and text" (qtd. in Harvey 32). In other words, Harvey writes, comics achieve meaning because "words and pictures blend to achieve a meaning neither is capable of alone without the other."

Baker's images, by themselves, tell a particularly gruesome and heartbreaking story. The scenes of slavery he paints are, at times, difficult to look at. But they alone cannot tell Turner's story, cannot fill in the gaps that exist in those "few sentences mentioning the name, the date, and that it was important." Similarly, history has shown us that the story Gray tells us in *Confessions* also cannot communicate the full story. Baker's use of the comics form, his bringing together of narrative images (not merely illustrative ones) with Turner's words, gives a "complete" picture of Turner's life, while also calling into question the very notion that we can ever know Turner's "complete" story. The "ironic" relationship between the words and pictures allows Turner's slave narrative to convey meaning differently than it does alone.

Baker's story opens with a facsimile of the frontispiece of the original edition of the 1831 *The Confessions of Nat Turner*. From this frontispiece we learn that these confessions were "fully and voluntarily" made while Turner was in jail awaiting trial (I pause here to remind the reader again that I am fully aware of the problematic nature of the 1831 *Confessions*. I am, however, treating that text as Baker does, namely as the source from which this story comes). We are also promised lists of the "Whites who were Murdered" and the "Negroes brought before the Court of Southhampton and there sentenced" (10). This facsimile gives the suggestion that the images we are about to see, indeed, the images on the facing page, are part of the narrative related by Turner to Gray in 1831. It reads as if Baker may be simply illustrating the 1831 text.

In truth, though, Baker does anything but. *Confessions* begins as nineteenth-century slave narratives typically do, with an account of Nat Turner's birth. "I was thirty-one years of age the second of October last," Turner tells Gray, "and born the property of Benjamin Turner, of this county" (Gray). He proceeds quickly through his life to the events of the rebellion, the details of which take up the vast majority of *Confessions*. Baker's version of the story begins more ambiguously.

Baker's story is verbally silent for the first twenty-five pages. The first page of four panels depicts an open-air market in Africa (11). The streets are filled with people, men and women, young and old alike, going about the business of their daily lives. The third panel features a close-up of a young man smiling flirtatiously at a young woman featured in the last panel of the page. She is beautiful—large, wide eyes, exquisite cheekbones, full lips. We do not know this yet, but this woman is Turner's mother and it is her story we will follow for most of Book 1, "Home."

The flirtation continues for a few more panels but is abruptly interrupted by a wordless shout from a man on the street. Everyone looks to where he is pointing to see black men with guns on horses racing toward them (13). It is then that the reader realizes that what she is reading is the story of the capture of a group of Africans for sale into slavery. Baker uses closure particularly well here. McCloud defines closure as the action or information communicated in the gutter, i.e., the space between comics panels. For McCloud closure is crucial because only a fraction of the action in any given comic occurs on the page. The reader, according to McCloud, has to supply the missing action (68–69). Nothing other than the knowledge of the Atlantic slave trade that she brings with her to this book tells the reader that what Baker depicts here is something profoundly more horrible than an inter-tribe quarrel or war. The reader participates in making meaning here. Baker adds to the horror with a graphic depiction of the violence that accompanies trafficking in humans: a close-up of a bullet penetrating the head of an elderly man (16), several other men in various stages of being felled by bullets, and a young boy dead on the ground next to his overturned basket of market goods (17). Everyone screams in terror as the horses and gunmen drive on.

The violence takes a turn when we see the beautiful young woman from the first page come to the rescue of a young boy (18–23). For some readers the physical impossibility of the young woman's actions remind them too much of the over-the-top feats that fill the pages of superhero comics. Such feats, the argument goes, have no place in such a serious and "real" story.

But it is precisely in this kind of hyperbolic imagery that Baker comes closest to recreating the sentimentality of nineteenth-century slave narratives. Again, the narratives are "autobiographical performance," not just a recitation of the events of a person's life. And that performance is a sentimental one meant to appeal directly to the emotions, to tug at the heartstrings.

Baker's depiction of the pursuit and capture of Turner's mother, in all of its derring-do excess, works the same way. Turner's mother picks the young boy up, races through the jungle, hides in trees, manages to shoot one of the slave catchers, and ensures the boy's freedom. She, however, is not so lucky. Coming to a cliff and facing the choice of turning around and giving herself over to slave catchers, or throwing herself over the edge to certain death, our heroine makes the only choice she can, the choice the reader is urging her to make. Page 27 features two panels (see figure 6.1). The first is a close-up of the woman's face, steely with resolve as she prepares to jump. The second is a long shot of her graceful fall, her head held high and arms outstretched, ready to embrace death. This is the first of a number of moments when Baker's art makes us feel the horror of slavery, really makes us root for truly horrific things (like this woman's suicide, for instance) because we know how horrible New World slavery will be. Again, Baker makes great use of closure here. The violence we see on the page is always in the context of the knowledge we have of the violence we don't see.

As a result, the woman's failure to escape packs a particular rhetorical punch. Page 28 features a single panel that takes up the entire page. We see only our heroine's legs and feet, straight up in the air as she descends to her death. A slave catcher's lasso encircles one of these legs and we next see our heroine in an iron collar, shackled to a line of Africans, marching tearfully through the jungle, presumably to the coast to be transported to the Americas (29). She encounters dead bodies, skeletons, and skulls. She is shaved and yanked about on her chain. She is stripped naked, and when she fights back, she is nearly shot by the first white man we see in the book (30–36). Only after all of this, only after twenty-five pages, do we finally get text (other than the occasional "boom" sound effect to indicate gun fire) in the narrative. Baker includes an excerpt from *Twenty Years of an African Slaver*, the journals of an actual slaver, Theodore Canot (see figure 6.2). "The head of every male and female is neatly shaved; and if the cargo belongs to several owners, each man's brand is impressed on the body of his respective Negro. . . . They are entirely stripped, so that women as well as men go out of Africa as they came into it—naked" (36). Coming as they do after twenty-five pages of wordless images, Baker positions Canot's words to provide some context for those images, to

6.1. From *Nat Turner*, by Kyle Baker. New York: Harry N. Abrams, 2008. Copyright © 2008 Kyle Baker.

FROM THE MEMOIR OF CAPTAIN THEODORE CANOT:
TWENTY YEARS OF AN AFRICAN SLAVER

"The head of every male and female is neatly shaved; and, if the cargo belongs to several owners, each man's brand is impressed on the body of his respective negro.... They are entirely stripped, so that women as well as men go out of Africa as they came into it—naked."

6.2. From *Nat Turner*, by Kyle Baker. New York: Harry N. Abrams, 2008. Copyright © 2008 Kyle Baker.

help us make sense of what they mean. If Harvey and Lee are right about the "ironic relation" between words and images, then Canot's words help the images mean something they don't by themselves.

Yet the greatest narrative shift comes not in our understanding of the images, but instead in our understanding of Canot's text. The journals of men like Canot make up part of the historical record of slavery, help to provide the kind of knowledge of slavery that the reader brings to this book. Blending these words with Baker's images, making them interdependent for meaning on these images, shows the profound inadequacy of those words (and perhaps the inadequacy of the historical record generally, and maybe even the inadequacy of Baker's text). Canot's excerpt does not come close to adequately expressing the horror we have just witnessed, nor the horror depicted in the next four panels as the beautiful, brave African woman we have followed for twenty-five pages is forced to the ground and branded like an animal. Canot's words increase our horror because it becomes evident that this woman's story—her pain and horror and grief and humiliation— have been invisible in the historical record.

I've lingered on this opening sequence because it so nicely illustrates how the entire book will work. In telling Nat Turner's story, Baker begins long before Turner's birth in the U.S. Baker suggests two things by doing this. First, in Turner's story are the stories of all those in enslaved in the institution. He brings Turner's narrative closer to traditional slave narratives in doing this, in making Turner's individual story larger than the individual. And second, Baker suggests we cannot even begin to fill in the narrative gaps of Turner's story with our knowledge of the historical record because the historical record can only hint at the horror and violence of that story. For twenty-five pages we see people shoved and trampled and shot and stripped and shaved and branded and killed, all without comment. The violence happens without words to explain it. There is no narrative respite from the horror. There is only unrelenting fear and pain and beauty broken. And when the words do finally come, in all their inadequacy, they throw into stark relief the tragedy we've already experienced. The comics form, with its economy of expression, I argue, allows Baker to deliver a small treatise on all that is missing from our cultural narrative surrounding slavery. And that's just the first twenty-five pages.

Early in *Confessions*, Turner relates an event from his childhood that "made an indelible impression on my mind, and laid the groundwork of that enthusiasm which has terminated so fatally to many, both white and black and for which I am about to atone at the gallows" (Gray). Turner refers here to the first of the "visions" he will have throughout his life, visions that lead him to believe that God calls him to rebel against the institution of slavery. While Gray's text does not offer any details about this event, Baker's story uses the event to introduce Turner.

After the young African woman is shaved and branded, we next see her in the bowels of a slave ship, shackled and lying amongst hundreds of other captives. The subsequent panels depict a baby being born among feces, a woman dying and a rat feeding on her corpse, and sharks hungrily circling the ship, all while our heroine watches in shock and terror. When the ship reaches its destination, the dead are thrown overboard and the unruly are beaten (40–47).

It is here that Baker shifts our attention from the story of the woman we've been following from the beginning to another, the woman who has given birth on the ship. As the madness of the slave trade erupts around her, she clutches her baby to her chest protectively. Over several pages (47–49) we see her weigh her options, the same options our heroine weighed as she stood on that cliff. The difference, though, is that the young mother is making a choice for her child—should she allow him to be taken into the unspeakable horror she knows awaits (and it is significant that she as yet has no experience of slavery—the preamble to the actual institution has provided her enough of a preview of its unrelenting cruelty), or should she do what is necessary to save him from that fate? Over the next five pages (51–55) we watch as the mother rushes away from the guard and tosses her baby overboard to the waiting jaws of a shark. A sailor manages to catch the baby just before he falls into the shark's open mouth, but the mother bites the sailor and he drops the baby. The baby is free, and once again Baker puts us in the position of applauding something awful.

Only after all this do we finally meet Turner and hear his words. Page 57 features a young Turner, surrounded by a group of other children, relating the story of this baby, all while a pair of shocked women looks on. In his own words he tells us that at three or four years of age he told the other children "something which my mother, overhearing, said it had happened before I was born." A picture of the baby descending into the mouth of the shark appears above his head. This caused people to say in "my hearing, I surely would be a prophet, as the Lord had shown me things that had happened before my birth" (57).

Some readers might question whether the events of Book 1 are true or why Baker includes details not in the 1831 *Confessions*. I would answer that the factuality of Turner's mother's life, as depicted by Baker, is beside the point. The point is that Baker uses the comics form, the interdependence of verbal and visual elements, to highlight the ways *Confessions* fails to tell us what we want to know, and perhaps fail to tell us Turner's actual story. We want Turner to tell us what compels a man to carry out the kind of unspeakable violence that resulted in the deaths of 55 white men, women, and children. We suspect that slavery can drive a man to such actions, but Turner's words, as related by Gray and speaking of prophecies and visions, gives us no sense that this is true. The form Turner speaks in, the slave narrative (not to mention the jailhouse confession), cannot tell the full story of slavery or of Turner's life. Slave narratives intend to move sympathetic whites to action.

Confessions does not ask for sympathy, or even for our understanding. In them Turner merely recites the facts as he knows them. By wedding Turner's words to pictures, images constructed out of his knowledge of slavery (the bibliography included in the collected edition indicates that Baker consulted several primary and secondary documents in addition to the 1831 *Confessions*), Baker gives the *Confessions* context, grants Turner a human complexity that the popular narrative about him has erased. In Baker's story the Turner we first meet is not a man guilty of the premeditated murder of 55 people. Instead the Turner we first meet is a young boy, "three or four years old," whose head is full of the memories of his mother's home, and all that the institution of slavery has done to destroy that home and its people. The visions, then, that he receives from the Lord are not idle prophetic chatter or the hallucinations of a crazed man. Instead they are a lifelong preparation for war.

Book 2 of *Nat Turner*, "Education," depends more heavily on *Confessions*, particularly in its second half. In the middle of Book 2 Turner's words tell us that though the focus of his "restless, inquisitive and observant mind" was mostly religion, "there was nothing that I saw or heard of to which my attention was not directed" (85). Book 2, then, stands as a litany of all the things Turner might have noticed, including the torture of enslaved people (whipping, pouring salt into wounds, cutting off of hands), children being fed from pig troughs, punishment for reading, singing and communicating with other enslaved people, fathers fleeing in the night, children encouraging fathers to run, and enslaved people pretending to be ignorant to appease suspicious whites (75–89). Again, Baker suggests through his art that Turner's story is the story of many more people than just Turner, and that his words can only convey their meaning fully when we know those stories.

Halfway through Book 2 *Nat Turner* focuses more closely on Turner himself, though, again, the events presented in Baker's story are not in *Confessions*. At one point, after communication with The Spirit, Turner runs away and eludes capture for thirty days. Eventually, however, he returns of his own accord, stating that the "Spirit appeared to me and said I had my wishes directed to the things of the world, and not to the kingdom of Heaven, and that I should return to the service of my earthly master. . . . And the Negroes found fault, and murmured against me saying that if they had my sense they would not serve any master in the world" (96). Again, Turner's words are a matter of fact, an entry in the historical record. He offers little more than what happened—he ran away, God told him to come back, other black people thought he was crazy—and little in the way of what it might have felt like to be free and to willingly return to the chains of slavery. Baker's images that accompany these words fill in many of the blanks.

Alongside a panel depicting blacks' astonishment at Turner's return are two more panels, a close-up and then a long shot, showing a heartfelt reunion between Turner and his mother (96). The next page shows Turner meeting, then marrying an enslaved woman, and his mother rejoicing at the union. Turner doesn't return simply to his "earthly" master. He also, more importantly, returns to a family and a community. Baker presents these human connections as more important than even Turner's prophetic visions by the prominence of their presence in this story. Turner may have been communicating with God, Baker suggests (and, indeed, nothing in *Nat Turner* encourages us to doubt Turner's prophetic visions), but he was also living a life that included the love and affection of and connection with other people. Baker suggests that Turner is being driven by more than his faith in God.

Over the next four pages Baker depicts the breakup of Turner's family through the sale of his wife and children. A particularly poignant panel (101) (see figure 6.3) shows Turner's mother standing over the stick figure drawings his children have made in the dirt floor of his now empty cabin. Only then does Baker gives us an extended quote from *Confessions*. Stretching over the next two pages (102–3), Turner describes his vision of "white spirits and black spirits engaged in battle" (see figure 6.4). Turner withdraws from the "intercourse of [his] fellow servants" to better comprehend what God is telling him.

> I sought more than ever to obtain true holiness before the great day of judgment should appear and then I began to receive the true knowledge of faith. And from the first steps of righteousness until the last, was I made perfect; and the Holy Ghost was with me, and said "Behold me as I stand in the Heavens"—and I looked and saw the forms of man in

6.3. From *Nat Turner*, by Kyle Baker. New York: Harry N. Abrams, 2008. Copyright © 2008 Kyle Baker.

6.4. From *Nat Turner*, by Kyle Baker. New York: Harry N. Abrams, 2008. Copyright © 2008 Kyle Baker.

different attitudes—and there were lights in the sky to which the children of darkness gave other names than what they really were—for they were the lights of the Saviour's hands, stretched forth from east to west, even as they were extended on the cross on Calvary for the redemption of sinners. And I wondered greatly at the meaning thereof—and shortly afterward, while laboring in the field, I discovered drops of blood on the corn as though it were dew from heaven—and I communicated it to many, both black and white in the neighborhood. (102–3)

Because this is the most we have heard Turner speak at once so far in the book, the effect is overwhelming. We are suddenly as overpowered by Turner's words as he is overtaken by these visions and words from God. The image, too, overwhelms, stretching horizontally as it does over two pages and taking up about two-thirds of those pages. Baker depicts Turner with his fists upraised and his mouth open in a roar, while all around him a storm rages. Taken together, the words and the images on these two pages show a man caught up in the awesomeness of God, and surely this is true. Turner's own words suggest he is in constant awe at being chosen as one of God's prophets. Yet, these words and images do not stand alone. They come immediately after the harrowing sequence of Turner's wife and children being sold away from him. The reader, then, can not help but read the storm as also a reflection of Turner's anger and despair. Again, while Baker does nothing in this story to discount Turner's claims to prophetic powers, he nonetheless takes great pains to place those powers into the body and mind of a man who feels deeply all the atrocities of slavery. Turner may indeed rededicate himself to a Spirit that will eventually call him to revolt, but that rededication occurs after his life and spirit are devastated by slavery.

Pages 104–5 conclude Book 2 and show Turner after his rededication to the Lord. "'And on the 12th of May, 1826, I heard a loud noise in the Heavens, and the Spirit instantly appeared to me and said the Serpent was loosened and Christ had laid down the yoke he had borne for the sins of men, and that I should take it on and fight against the Serpent, for the time was fast approaching when the first should be made last and the last should be first'" (104). The angry passion in his eyes as he preaches the Word to fellow blacks reflects the anger in his eyes we saw earlier (100) when he contemplates the intact white family that forces the separation and destruction of his own. Baker connects the two events—the passion of his fury and the passion of his faith—in this image.

The scene continues on the facing page. The Holy Bible is our focal point, appearing in the middle of the page in Turner's outstretched hand, surrounded by the raised fists of those listening. The Bible, and, by extension, Turner and his preaching, are ominous and threatening in this scene. Here Turner isn't merely executing the work of God—he is harnessing the wrath of God and the frustration of his people to rain down justice on the unjust. However much Turner's words may have been read as the ramblings of a crazed man before, in Baker's comic book, they can no longer be read this way. Regardless of whether or not we believe in Turner's visions, Baker's art allows us, commands us, to believe in his pain, grief, and righteous anger. We also believe he has it well within in his power to wield that anger as a weapon. In his preface Baker tells us that "Turner was a lousy fighter, an inept swordsman, and most of the people he tried to kill didn't die by his hand. His sole strength was his superior brain. He became a leader of men because he had developed his mind by reading" (7). Baker's story fills the gaps of the popular narrative with a picture of a man ready to do what was necessary to right the wrongs of slavery.

By the time we get to Book 3, "Freedom," we are well prepared for the violence of Turner's raid. We are prepared not just because we started the

6.5. From *Nat Turner*, by Kyle Baker. New York: Harry N. Abrams, 2008. Copyright © 2008 Kyle Baker.

story knowing how it ends, but also because Baker's version of this story suggests that it can have no other end. Of all the books, "Freedom" relies the most heavily on Turner's words, with passages from *Confessions* appearing on nearly every page. Baker's images depict exactly what Turner's words describe—the grisly, violent deaths of white men, women, and children at the hands of black men. To call this section of the narrative horrific is an understatement. It is in this section, though, that Baker is most successful at revising the slave narrative. "Freedom" allows Turner's words to do what traditional nineteenth-century slave narratives do most effectively—argue for black humanity—precisely by not shying away from the topic those narratives do not easily contain—violence.

The first images of "freedom" are ominous. Baker uses closure effectively here, relying on readers' knowledge of events to come to build tension. A black man works at splitting wood in the yard of a large plantation house. A young white boy plays near him, chasing chickens (107). The young boy pauses in his play to wave at the black man, whose name, we will soon learn, is Will (see figure 6.5). The boy's smiling face is in the background, while Will's large axe takes up the foreground (108). The last image on this page is a close-up of Will smiling and waving at the boy (and the reader), though the smile seems more sinister than friendly. In just a few pages Will uses this same axe to kill this boy.

Turner's description of their plan follows this sinister opening scene:

> It was quickly agreed we should commence at home (Mr. J. Travis's) on that night, and until we had armed and equipped ourselves and gathered sufficient force, neither age not sex was to be spared, (which was invariably adhered to). We remained at the feast until about two hours in the night, when we went to the house and found Austin; they all went to the cider press and drank, except myself. On returning to the house, Hank went to the door with an axe, for the purpose of breaking it open, as we knew we were strong enough to murder the family, if they were awakened by the noise; but reflectively that it might create an alarm in the neighborhood, we determined to enter the house secretly, and murder them whilst sleeping. (112)

Turner's words alone are damning. He is planning to kill people in their sleep. The words encourage no sympathy whatsoever in the reader. But, of course, they are not meant to. Turner has come to the end of his life. His death is certain. He has no reason to hope for mercy, nor is it clear he wants any, even if offered. Turner doesn't intend, as do Douglass and Jacobs, to gain support of white readers. He seems intent only on reciting the facts as he knows them. Nor does the recorder of these facts, Thomas Gray, seem particularly motivated by abolitionist zeal, or perhaps, even by the desire to record Turner's words accurately. As a result, the image of Turner and his followers, as described above, is one of a band of drunken, half-crazed men, haphazardly and gleefully embarking on a barely thought-out campaign of murder. Turner's words do very little to explain what motivates the others to join him (though, at one point in *Confessions* Turner, surprised at seeing him, asks Will why he has joined. Will responds that "his life was worth no more than others, and his liberty as dear to him" [Gray]). They do very little to counter the image of him from the popular narrative—a cold-blooded murderer. But Turner's words do not stand alone here.

Baker's art does not let us turn away from the violence of Turner's raid. When Turner enters his master's bedroom (113), the scene is chilling. Travis and his wife sleep peacefully in their bed, appearing in soft focus in the panel background. The gleaming axe in Turner's clenched fist pauses in the foreground. Turner's words—"'it was then observed that I must spill the first blood'"—suggest that the deaths of the Travises are more for ritual effect than anything else. The look in Turner's eyes as he delivers the blow (114) is positively crazed. Alas, he delivers a wholly ineffectual blow and we are witness to the bloodied Travis and his terrified wife awaking to find themselves surrounded by several black men intent on murder.

Will steps in to finish the job and "laid [Travis] dead with a blow of his axe, and Mrs. Travis shared the same fate" (115). It is a grisly, chilling scene. It pales, however, in comparison to the following panels depicting, in succession: a black man tracking bloody footprints on the floor as he clutches a bloody axe, a group of black men with axes and covered in blood, another woman's bloodied body on the floor, and, finally, a white woman's bloodied arm hanging in death off the side of a bed over the decapitated body of a white man (116–17). "The murder of this family, five in number, was the work of a moment" Turner's words tell us (117). There are no euphemisms, no rhetorical niceties to hide behind. Baker forces the reader to look directly at what it would mean, what it would *look like*, to kill 55 men, women, and children, with axes and swords and clubs, in their sleep. Importantly, however, Baker first spends 100 pages focusing that same unflinching gaze on the institution of slavery and the violence and destruction it inflicts. Turner's violence is not an aberration, then. It is a consequence of slavery.

Before the men can move on to the next house they remember the Travis family consists of six, not five, members—they have forgotten the baby. As they consider what should be done, Turner remembers the sale of his wife and children, the destruction of his own family, depicted by a visual replay of that scene from Book 2 (120). The reader remembers, too, the pain and grief and anger—grief that can never really be healed. Again, this is a detail Baker offers that doesn't appear in *Confessions*. But like the story of Turner's mother in Book 1, the story of Turner's family rings true. It hardly matters, really, whether or not these "invented" events happened in Turner's life. They happened often enough in the lives of enslaved black men and women as to be rendered true here. Turner's story becomes the story of all enslaved people, their stories are the story of the whole institution.

Consequently, the death of the Travis baby in Book 3 was written all the way back in Book 1 when Turner's mother's suicide attempt to escape slavery is thwarted by that slaver's rope around her ankle. Lest we think of Turner's murderous campaign as simply that, or as simply the work of the Lord (as Gray's emotionless, detached text suggests), Baker reminds us that Turner is much more than this. He isn't simply, or even primarily, a prophet of the Lord, or a man on a mission. Turner is also, perhaps most importantly, an enslaved man who has suffered immeasurably at the hands of slavery. Baker reminds us that we can never understand Turner's story or the deaths of those 55 men, women, and children by only reading the *Confessions* or consulting the official historical record. History records Turner as a religious fanatic whose murder spree results in the deaths of innocents. Baker, through the skillful use of the comics form, acknowledges Turner, and, implicitly, other enslaved men and women, as complex, thinking, feeling, human beings. However horrible the violence in "Freedom" may be, and, to be sure, it is nothing but horrible, Baker's *Nat Turner* never lets us forget that this violence is a direct result of the original violence of slavery.

And, yet, *Nat Turner* is not without its ambiguities. The black men who join Turner on his raid are depicted by Baker as monstrous and gleeful in their rampage. They are not handsome, thoughtful, faithful men moved to action by pain and grief. Instead they are thoughtless thugs out for drunken revenge. And the white man who discovers the plot and organizes to stop it is depicted as handsome and rightfully appalled at the destructions he sees before him (154–59). Going back to Singer's concern that *Nat Turner* seems to lack a moral center, I would argue that Baker achieves exactly the right ambiguous tone in the story. How should we judge the man who lashes out violently against the system that has degraded and dehumanized him, that stole his father from him, that stole his family away? How much do we sympathize with his desire to break the system that broke him? When is violence driven by righteous anger and when does it become reckless revenge? How violent does slavery have to become before violence is a justifiably appropriate response? However much Baker's story champions Turner (and it certainly does), it also never lets us forget that the violence he commits, even if understandable and inevitable, is also, finally, wrong.[3]

To speak fully and often of Turner's story is to attend to the physical, mental, sexual, and emotional violence that might drive someone like Turner to embark on a campaign of murder. Baker's narrative highlights the narrative insufficiency of *Confessions*. That text's detailing of the prophecies driving Turner to his rebellion is unsatisfactory as an explanation of that rebellion. Baker's additions, not just in content and plot, but also the images that help Turner's words mean differently, paint a picture of the very real human cost of chattel slavery as practiced in the U.S. That cost includes not only the unnamed African who dies aboard the slave ship and the baby thrown overboard to the sharks, but also Turner's relationships with his mother, father, wife, and children, and the lives of those killed during his rebellion. Baker's slave narrative completes the picture merely sketched in draft in the 1831 *Confessions*, thus providing us a satisfying, if morally ambiguous, explanation for why Turner might want to bring down the wrath of God on the institution of slavery.

Notes

1. See Mary Kemp Davis's *Nat Turner Before the Bar of Judgment: Fictional Treatments of the Southhampton Slave Insurrection* (1999), Scot French's *The Rebellious Slave: Nat Turner in American Memory* (2004), Kenneth S. Greenberg's *Nat Turner: A Slave Rebellion in History and Memory* (2004), and Stephen B. Oates's *The Fires of Jubilee: Nat Turner's Fierce Rebellion* (1975) for analysis and narratives of the raid. See also Robert Hayden's poem "The Ballad of Nat Turner" (1962), the still-debated William Styron novel *The Confessions of Nat Turner* (1967), and the Independent Lens film *Nat Turner: A Troublesome Property* (2004).

2. Recently historian Michael Johnson argued there is little evidence to suggest that the Vesey plot ever existed. Instead, Johnson, asserts, then Charleston mayor James Hamilton, Jr., used the fabricated plot for political gain. Johnson's argument caused quite the stir in historical circles and, like the claim that Olaudah Equiano was born in South Carolina and not in Africa as his narrative claims, continues to create sharp divides among African Americanists. See "Denmark Vesey and his Co-Conspirators" in *William and Mary Quarterly* (October 2001) and the responses in "The Making of a Slave Conspiracy, Part 2" in *William and Mary Quarterly* (January 2002).

3. While reading *Nat Turner* as a "Frank Miller comic in slave-narrative drag," as Marc Singer does, might seem compelling for some, the pulp hero trappings of the book are its least interesting parts. Turner comes off, at times, as a superhuman badass out to vanquish his evil foes and in the comic's original run, Baker's tongue-in-cheek promotional materials attempted to reach superhero comic book readers who favored violence and adventure with promises of "a harrowing manhunt! Hair breadth escapes! A spine tingling capture!" Ultimately, though, the book thwarts any expectations that such language may have raised of vicarious violence typical of many pulp genres, given that Turner orchestrates the cold-blooded murder of 55 people, women and children included, but it succeeds, however, in telling us a new, compelling story of slavery.

Works Cited

Andrews, William L. "Slave Narrative." *The Oxford Companion of African American Literature.* Ed. William L. Andrews, Frances Smith Foster, and Trudier Harris. New York: Oxford UP, 1997. 667–70. Print.

Baker, Kyle. *Nat Turner.* New York: Harry N. Abrams, Inc., 2008. Print.

Comments. "Denmark Vesey memorial plans move forward." Tenisha Waldo. 5 September 2007. *postandcourier.com.* Post and Courier.com. Web. 5 August 2010.

Douglass, Frederick. *Narrative of the Life of Frederick Douglass, An American Slave, Written By Himself.* [1845] *The Classic Slave Narratives.* Ed. Henry Louis Gates, Jr. New York: Prentice Hall, 1987. 243–331. Print.

Gray, Thomas. *The Confessions of Nat Turner.* 1831. *pbs.org.* PBS Online. Web. 1 February 2010.

Harvey, R. C. "How Comics Came to Be." *A Comics Studies Reader.* Ed. Jeet Heer and Kent Worcester. Jackson, MS: UP of Mississippi, 2009. Print.

Jacobs, Harriet. *Incidents in the Life of a Slave Girl.* [1861] *The Classic Slave Narratives.* Ed. Henry Louis Gates, Jr. New York: Prentice Hall, 1987. 333–513. Print.

Johnson, Michael P., "Denmark Vesey and His Co-Conspirators." *The William and Mary Quarterly* 58.4 (2001): 915–76. Print.

McCloud, Scott. *Understanding Comics.* New York: Harper Collins, 1993. Print.

Olney, James. "'I Was Born': Slave Narratives, Their Status as Autobiography and as Literature." *The Slave's Narrative.* Ed. Charles T. Davis and Henry Louis Gates, Jr. Oxford: Oxford, UP, 1985. Print.

Singer, Marc. "Week 8: Kyle Baker, Nat Turner." 3 March 2010. *notthebeastmaster.typepad.com.* I Am NOT the Beastmaster Blog. Web. 5 August 2010.

Stone, Albert. "*The Confessions of Nat Turner.*" *The Oxford Companion of African American Literature.* Ed. William L. Andrews, Frances Smith Foster, and Trudier Harris. New York: Oxford UP, 1997. 166. Print.

Tucker, Penny. "Traumatic Traces: Slave Narratives, Post-traumatic Stress, and the Limits of Resistance." *Representing Minorities: Studies in Literature and Criticism.* Ed. Larbi Touaf and Soumia Boutkhil. Cambridge: Cambridge Scholars Publishing, 2006. 139–49. Print.

"Black and White and Read All Over"

Representing Race in Mat Johnson and
Warren Pleece's *Incognegro: A Graphic Mystery*

—Tim Caron

At the conclusion of his essay on Spike Lee's film, *Bamboozled*, visual culture theorist W. J. T. Mitchell meditates on the literal meaning of the phrase "the color line," a term which, he points out, is "something of an oxymoron" if it is taken literally. As he says,

> Color is, in traditional pictorial aesthetics and epistemology, the "secondary" characteristic—evanescent, superficial, and subjective—in relation to the "primary quality" of line, which connotes the real, tangible features of an object, and which is *the central feature of the stereotype and caricature as linear figures.* Color cannot be delineated or touched, we suppose; it only appears to the eye—and not to all eyes, or to all eyes in the same way. (308, emphasis added)

This is the crucial paradox of racial categories Mat Johnson and Warren Pleece have inscribed into the pages of their collaboration, *Incognegro: A Graphic Mystery*—the color line, as with the attendant concepts about race that it seeks to police, is both unreal and deadly real. It is a metaphorical construct with lethal ramifications. *Incognegro* perfectly exemplifies one aspect of Mitchell's critical insight: Johnson and Pleece ably demonstrate the consequences in store for those who cross these subjective lines of color.

If, as Mitchell suggests, color can be said to exist only in the eye of the beholder, what more powerful way for Johnson and Pleece to intervene into the history of racist representations of African Americans in comics than by eliminating all color from their book? How better to destabilize the white South's attempts to "read" categories of black and white in the physiognomy of its citizens than by limiting all of their creative responses to black marks on white paper? How better to destabilize received notions about the obviousness of visual codes of race than by creating a black character whose racial identity is fluid and dynamic? As the light-skinned hero of *Incognegro*, Zane Pinchback, says to his darker-complexioned twin brother, Alonzo, once they have safely made it to Harlem: "Identity is open-ended. Why have just one?" (129). In "erasing" color from their text, Johnson and Pleece seek not to eradicate racial categories but to wrestle with the racialized representations of African Americans in the comics medium—for to place a word, a concept, or a literary text "under erasure" is to actually draw attention to it, forcing us wrestle with an abiding absence. What then is remarkable about Mat Johnson and Warren Pleece's collaboration on their graphic mystery is the way in which it struggles mightily to render visually the artificiality of racial categories.

"physiognomic signs of ethnicity"

Art Spiegelman asserts in "Dirty Little Comics," his introduction to the anthology *Tijuana Bibles: Art and Wit in America's Forbidden Funnies, 1930s-1950s*, that "since cartoons are a visual sign language, the stereotype is the basic building block of all cartoon art" (8). While certainly not condoning these types of racist stereotypes so common in American cartooning, Spiegelman's insight goes a long way in explaining the persistence and power of these types of demeaning representations in American comics.[1] Johnson and Pleece's *Incognegro* is a most curious intervention into the ongoing conversation about visual representations of race in comics because these collaborators adopt an approach radically different from the way in which most mainstream comics explore this question. Johnson and Pleece's work is not a direct response to or rebuttal against the myriad racist caricatures to be found in the work of various cartooning giants, such as Winsor McCay, Frank King, or R. Crumb; nor is *Incognegro* an expression of black masculine power commonly found in comic book superheroes such as the Black Panther, Black Lightning, the Falcon, or a host of other heroes that cropped up in the 1960s and '70s; nor is *Incognegro* self-consciously attempting to present an African American historical figure, such as Kyle Baker's *Nat Turner*, or Ho Che Anderson's *King*, or an African American folk hero, such as Derek McCulloch's *Stagger Lee*, to a broader reading audience. Rather, Johnson and Pleece take as their subject the very act of representing race. Within the comics medium, Johnson and Pleece have created figures that allow us to study the visual and verbal representations of race as they exist alongside one another on the printed page, for it is in the interplay of words and images that meaning is created in the comics medium.[2]

In their collaboration, Johnson and Pleece ask much the same question art historian Michael D. Harris asks in *Colored Pictures: Race and Visual Representation*: "what does blackness look like?" (10). The title, *Incognegro: A Graphic Mystery*, is instructive in seeking an answer to this question: the etymology of the term "graphic" hearkens back to the ancient Greek term, *graphikos*, and can refer to either writing or drawing. In *Incognegro*, Johnson's script and Pleece's black and white line drawings work in harmony to plumb the mystery of racial representation because Zane is not simply described as being light complexioned; rather, he's drawn without any of what Spiegelman, in his essay, "Little Orphan Annie's Eyeballs," refers to as the "physiognomic signs of ethnicity" (18) commonly used to render a comic book character as black. This essay, then, is an investigation into the subtle ways in which race is—and is not—written and drawn onto the pages of *Incognegro*, a work rendered in monochromatic drawings but that still has the ability to convey to its readers exactly which characters (other than our protagonist, Zane) are placed into the racial categories of "black" and "white" by a white southern culture desperate to construct fixed, stable racial categories.

". . . amplification through simplification. . ."

In order to better appreciate what these collaborators are attempting in the depiction of race as a "graphic mystery," it is helpful to explore how meaning is generated in the comics medium, particularly how racial identity is rendered. There is probably no better place to begin in considering the relationship between form and meaning in the comics medium than Scott McCloud's influential work, *Understanding Comics*. In seeking to account for comics' power, McCloud describes "cartooning as a form of amplification through simplification." McCloud expounds on this idea, going on to say, "When we abstract an image through cartooning, we're not so much eliminating details as we are focusing on specific details. By stripping down an image to its essential 'meaning,' an artist can amplify that meaning in a way that realistic art can't" (30). McCloud's theories about how comics generate meaning seem to be heavily indebted to comics legend Will Eisner and his ideas about the role of stereotypes in the comics medium, particularly as they are laid out in *Graphic Storytelling and Visual Narrative*, his textbook for fledgling graphic artists. Characterizing them as an "accursed necessity" (11), Eisner considered stereotypes to be the very building blocks of the art form. While taking pains to provide the etymology of the word stereotype ("The actual word comes from the method used to mold duplicate plates in letterpress printing"), Eisner explains his view that stereotypes are indispensable to the comics medium:

> Comic book art deals with recognizable reproductions of human conduct. Its drawings are a mirror reflection, and depend on the reader's stored memory of experience to visualize an idea or process quickly. This makes necessary the simplification of images into repeatable symbols. Ergo, stereotypes.[3] (11)

Eisner's explanation of the preponderance of stereotypes in American comics has the tidy organization of a syllogism, making it difficult to deny either his major premise, that comics readers rely upon experience to "process" a work, or his minor premise about the necessity of easily "repeatable" images. Despite this neat rhetorical maneuver, Eisner is not oblivious to the potential misuse and abuse of a comics-creating practice grounded in stereotypes, for as he acknowledges, "stereotype has a bad reputation not only because it implies banality but because of its use as a weapon of propaganda or racism" (11). However, for Eisner the possible benefits outweighed the potential drawbacks.[4] These potential drawbacks should not be glossed over too quickly, though, especially for comics readers who are sensitive to issues of race as they are manifested in such a strongly visual medium. In the words of Derek Parker Royal, comics readers should understand the implications of the views of comics creators such as Eisner because:

> In comics and graphic art there is always the all-too-real danger of negative stereotype and caricature, which strips others of any unique identity and dehumanizes by means of reductive iconography—the big noses, the bug eyes, the buck teeth and the generally deformed features that have historically composed our visual discourse of the Other. (8)

Royal's short list of racist iconography common to American cartooning and comics is certainly not exhaustive, but it is striking when one realizes that these same distortive techniques have been used to malign African Americans, Hispanics, and Asian Americans. Comics artists have recycled these misrepresentations, only altering skin tones and hair textures, to represent nearly every major American ethnic group.

McCloud, in turn, "amplifies" Eisner's own views regarding stereotypes and produces a theory with profound implications for our understanding of racial representations in American comics, for what has been traditionally "amplified" in the comics representations of African Americans? Typically, it has been those perceived signifiers of racial difference that allow us to make authoritative claims about racial identity. These types of visual distinctions are vital to Western art because they serve to bolster ideas about race everyone is supposed to "know." As Nicholas Mirzoeff points out, "The definition of the Other as wholly different from the Self was, of course, haunted by anxiety that difference was more apparent than real. It was therefore crucial that difference should not only be known but visible" (17). This anxiety over racial difference and how it might not be manifested did, indeed, haunt the white South. While the widespread belief that a single drop of black blood was sufficient to render one black made policing the color line easier in some respects, the so-called "one drop rule" still allowed for some people of mixed ancestry to "pass" as white. The white South responded, of course, with a type of hyper-vigilance, for the latent characteristics of "blackness" might be lying dormant in any ostensibly white citizen, just waiting to manifest in some uncivilized fashion. To allay these racial anxieties, and to reinforce the notion that the racial Other was visibly identifiable, the white South held all the more dearly to a steadfast faith in the physiognomic signs of racial difference.

Taken together, McCloud and Mirzoeff's insights go a long way in explaining the abiding endurance of racist iconography in American comics. With the help of McCloud and Mirzoeff's assessments, we can begin to see how white comics creators have "amplified" those physical features of African Americans that, to them, signify the most important and expressive differences between whites and blacks. While the comics medium specializes in the rendering of interior states of characters, such as anger, joy, love, pride, or frustration, through the representation of their given physicality, it is now clear that comics have also attempted to render the inner "blackness" of African Americans as well, such as the alleged docility, mischievous child-like behavior, and/or hyper-sexuality often ascribed to them. However, American comics have succeeded much more frequently only in cataloging the most superficial of physiognomic features. What readers of American comics have received, for the most part, are shallow caricatures rather than animated characters.[5]

"Able to pass for a Nordic in the blink of an eye!"

Incognegro opens with Johnson and Pleece's deliberate attempt to short-circuit these types of shallow caricatures by creating an African American protagonist who is light enough to pass for white. Following in the line of such black literary ancestors (as Ralph Ellison might use the term) as James Weldon Johnson, Walter White, and Nella Larsen, Mat Johnson tells the story of a young, ambitious, light-complexioned African American male, Zane Pinchback, who lives in Harlem during the 1930s. While Zane, unlike many characters who inhabit contemporary comics, is not a superhero *per se*, he does have an alter ego: as "Incognegro," he uses his fair skin to investigate and report on lynching in the U.S. South for a large Northern newspaper, the *New Holland Herald*. As Zane's friend, Carl, quips early on in the novel: "My buddy Zane. The high yellow super negro! Able to pass for a Nordic in the blink of an eye" (10).

When the novel opens, Zane's editor sends him to Mississippi on his latest mission as Incognegro. However, this time, the victim of the soon-to-transpire lynching is Zane's twin brother, the darker complexioned Alonzo Pinchback. Zane's foppish friend, Carl, eager to prove his manhood both to himself and his beautiful fiancée, decides to tag along on this dangerous mission. Once the two men arrive in Tupelo, Mississippi, they take advantage of their light skin to mix among the town's white citizens to gather evidence proving Alonzo's innocence. The two men then split up: Zane endures a series of violent encounters with moonshiners and an in-bred family of poor whites as he collects evidence to free his brother, while Carl tries to ingratiate himself among the white citizens of Tupelo by pretending to be an Englishman interested in buying property in the area. Through the violent encounters, Zane collects the evidence necessary to prove his brother is innocent of killing a white woman. However, Carl's true racial identity is soon discovered by a one-eyed Klansman who believes that Carl, not Zane, is the undercover reporter Incognegro who has interfered with his lynching campaign in the past. Zane prevents his brother's lynching, but is powerless to stop the Klansman, with the aid of a mob composed of the town's men, women, and children, from lynching Carl.

Zane is not the only character passing as a white male, however. Central to the plot complications that unfold in the course of Zane's investigations, which Johnson characterizes as a "noir thriller" (Lorah, "Mat Johnson on *Incognegro*"), is the discovery that the woman whom Alonzo is accused of murdering, Michaela Mathers, his white lover and partner in the moonshine business, is, in fact, alive. The woman discovered at the still and whose face was disfigured beyond recognition was the town's deputy sheriff, Francis Jefferson-White, who had been passing as a white male. While complimentary notices and laudatory reviews of *Incognegro* in newspapers such as the *New York Times*, the *Seattle Times*, and the *San Francisco Chronicle* all dwell upon Zane's act of racial passing, this example of gender passing receives no attention at all. Perhaps this is a result of many of the marketing features of the book, including a photo of the light-complexioned Johnson on the cover and a brief "Author's Note" that precedes the actual text of the book in which Johnson explains how his own multiracial identity led him to write *Incognegro*.

These extra-diegetic elements appear to have had a profound influence on *Incognegro*'s reception, marking this graphic novel as a "race book" to the virtual exclusion of other thematic concerns such as gender, a concern that in some ways is just as central to the book. In this brief "Author's Note," Johnson recounts what it was like growing up as a "black boy who looked white." In an effort to transform his "ethnic appearance" into an "asset instead of a burden," Johnson, along with a light-skinned cousin who has "half black/half Jewish," would play in his neighborhood, "pretending to be race spies in the war against white supremacy." One can easily imagine little white boys, with blue or red bath towels tied around their necks, running around this same neighborhood, pretending to be Batman or Superman, while Johnson's mixed ancestry inspired him to fantasize about other types of secret or dual identities. Johnson's own experiences as a light-complexioned African American male clearly inspired him in composing *Incognegro*, for he, like his literary creation, is light-skinned enough to pass: ". . . people who meet me know that ethnically I'm black, but I look very white" (Lorah, "Mat Johnson on *Incognegro*").

The birth of his twins in 2005 provided further impetus for the book's emphasis upon external racial signifiers. Like the brothers in *Incognegro*, Johnson describes his own children in his "Author's Note" as "two people with the exact same ethnic lineage destined to be viewed differently only because of genetic randomness," words that could just as easily describe the twin brothers of *Incognegro*, Zane and Alonzo Pinchback. In a curious omission, Johnson does not mention the sex of the twins, leaving us wondering if the children are boys or girls. Similarly, there is a strange silence regarding gender in discussions and early reviews of the book, especially considering the fact that within the pages of *Incognegro* the gender passing of Francis is just as sensational, if not quite as disruptive to the status quo, as the passing of Zane and Carl as white males. When Francis's secret is discovered, Zane's accomplice asks, "Why would a woman do something crazy like that?," to which Zane responds, "Right. No sense. Who would pretend to be a white man in this world? What could be the possible advantage of that?"[6]

". . . our own proper regard for the scene"

If nothing else, one must grant that Johnson and Pleece are at least very consistent in their focus upon race to the exclusion of gender—and the manner in which race and gender are often inextricably intertwined—for this focus runs throughout the text of *Incognegro* as the book both opens and closes with splash pages devoted to exploring the ways in which race is so sinisterly encoded in American culture. The book opens with a splash page that, to use the very telling language of graphic narratives, "bleeds" to the edges of the page (see figure 7.1). A black man is shown being lynched by a white mob that is portrayed as simultaneously brutal in the violence directed at its black victim and celebratory in the performance of this ritual that will further strengthen the communal ties of this white Southern community. The reader is afforded a bird's-eye-view of the opening tableau, a scene all too painfully familiar to anyone knowledgeable with the history of southern race relations. Pleece's opening image manages to simultaneously evoke both the viciousness and the banality of spectacle lynching. Notice, for instance, the telling detail of the mother who is smiling serenely at her young daughter in the middle foreground of the illustration, as if the lynching exists only so that she may dispense some benevolent lesson about the necessity of maintaining strict racial purity.

Pleece's visual representations of the spectacle of lynching within the pages of *Incognegro* are among the most powerful images in the entire book, and most of the visual impact of this opening splash page is derived from the illustration's uncanny similarity to one of the nation's most shameful photographic genres, the lynching photograph. Pleece's clear lines and his skillful use of shading to render depth of field lends a kind of photo-realism to this haunting image, and the reader cannot help but make connections between this illustration and lynch photographs. In fact, a photographer is seen entering into the panel in the lower left-hand corner, serving as a grim reminder that while fewer lynchings occurred as the twentieth century progressed, lynching became increasingly "choreographed," and photography was increasingly incorporated into that deadly choreography in order to

7.1. From *Incognegro: A Graphic Mystery*, by Mat Johnson and Warren Pleece. New York: DC Comics, 2008. © Mat Johnson and Warren Pleece.

provide a warning to African Americans that similar acts of violence could occur in the future (Smith 14). Perhaps the most common element in the grisly genre of lynch photography is a visual trope that is among the oldest structuring devices in all of photography, and Pleece carefully places just such a figure close to the visual center of the splash page: a figure pointing to the lynch victim. As Anthony Lee astutely observes in his "Introduction" to *Lynching Photographs*, such a figure is a "surrogate" for the viewer of the lynch photograph whose function it is to "cue our own proper regard of the scene," (6) and the "proper regard" would, of course, be an unwavering sense of racial solidarity for the photograph's original white audience. In fact, Shawn Smith maintains that "the photograph functions *as an extension* of the pointing man's commanding gesture, his demand to look. The image is made for the murderers, to represent their point of view" (12, emphasis added). Despite Pleece's evocation of prior lynch photographs in this opening illustration, there is one glaring difference between this opening splash page and most lynch photographs, namely that the lynch victim in the splash page is still alive, a key variation that allows Pleece to draw upon the terrible power of lynch photography without replicating the genre's racist intent. Lynch photographs were almost always taken of the mob's victims post mortem in order to express white authority over black bodies. The fact that Pleece renders the victim of the lynching in the moments before the mutilation and murder elicits sympathy for him from the reader.

It is the comics medium itself, though, that cues the reader that Pleece's drawing is meant not to celebrate racial violence but to combat it, for it is in the blending of Pleece's drawing and Johnson's words that the exploration of racial representation begins in earnest. While the graphic image of the first page is so violent as to resist the neat borders of the graphic novel's typical framing device of panels, the accompanying first-person voice that opens the story is contained within caption boxes placed across the top of the page. The tension between the image spilling across the page and the clipped, measured voice of the speaker is telling. Our as yet unidentified narrator provides both a national and a personal context for the story about to unfold: "Between 1889 and 1918, 2,522 negroes were murdered by lynch mobs in America. That we know of. Now, since the beginning of the '30s, most of the white papers don't even consider it news. To them, another nigger dead is not a story. So my job is to make it one. That's all" (7).

Text and image function together here to quickly orient the reader as to the manner in which Johnson and Pleece will be exploring the indeterminacy of race in the pages of *Incognegro*. As readers, we bring with us a knowledge of and familiarity with the racial motivations for most lynchings, and this familiarity allows us to surmise the racial identity of the lynch victim. His skin tones are no darker or lighter than the crowd tormenting him, but his position at the center of a lynch mob in conjunction with the unknown speaker's determination not to let this latest racial murder go unremarked instantly marks the victim's racial status as black. However, while the racial identity of the man being lynched is signaled both by the text and the opening image, the racial identity of the speaker on this opening page can only be surmised. Over the next two pages, the reader watches the lynching victim suffer the ritual brutalities common to spectacle lynchings:

> The main event . . . began with a period of mutilation—often including emasculation—and torture to extract confessions and entertain the crowd, and built to a climax of slow burning, hanging, and/or shooting to complete the killing. The finale consisted of frenzied souvenir gathering and display of the body and the collected parts. (Hale 204)

Nearly every element of this gruesome catalog is rendered in the opening scene of *Incognegro*, and Johnson and Pleece highlight key elements of the lynch ritual, such as the celebratory atmosphere among the white crowd (several men are drinking and passing flasks and bottles), the taking of souvenir photos, and the claiming of "trophies" from the lynched victim. Slowly, the reader discovers that what we are witnessing is narrated by a figure who is actually in attendance at the event being described, a figure mingling among the crowd, pretending to be the photographer's assistant in order to collect names and addresses of the men in the lynch mob. The narrative surprise that Johnson and Pleece have dealt us in slowly revealing that the photographer's assistant is really an undercover reporter is quickly surpassed by a second discovery (see figure 7.2). Someone interrupts Zane's narrative to ask, "How do you keep them from discovering you?", and he playfully responds, "That I'm a journalist?" We then turn the page to discover what has been hidden in plain sight in the opening pages of the novel: "No, that you're really a Negro," his listener responds (9–10).

Suddenly, we then realize that the figure who has been delivering the "voice over" narration of the opening pages and the figure we've seen collecting names and addresses among the lynch crowd are the same person: Zane is telling, via flashback, his friends in Harlem of his close escape. The splash page on which his identity is revealed shows that the only thing that distinguishes Zane from the rest of the crowd is how he is dressed. He

7.2. From *Incognegro: A Graphic Mystery*, by Mat Johnson and Warren Pleece. New York: DC Comics, 2008. © Mat Johnson and Warren Pleece.

simply looks more dressed up than the other men at the lynching. The narrative punch delivered in this passage is one that only the comics medium can deliver because text and image work powerfully here to challenge not just the racist attitudes behind spectacle lynching; rather, the very categories of race themselves are challenged.

As historian Grace Hale reminds us, lynching not only served as extralegal enforcements to the practice of segregation but were themselves the ultimate expression of segregated space in southern culture, for "only whites, whether they endorsed the violence or not, could experience the 'amusement' of a black man being [lynched]" (205). The assembled white crowd takes it as an article of faith that all members of the crowd are also white. What is remarkable in this opening sequence is how Johnson and Pleece manipulate our commonly held notion that images are more stable than words. What we learn, though, is that images, the things we see with our eyes, can be just as indeterminate as language. Understanding that visibility is the most common basis for discussions of racial difference, Pleece's depictions of Zane play with the semantic slippage that exists both in language

7.3. From *Incognegro: A Graphic Mystery*, by Mat Johnson and Warren Pleece. New York: DC Comics, 2008. © Mat Johnson and Warren Pleece.

and in pictures. When we first see Zane, it is among a white lynch mob, and he appears sympathetic to their cause; therefore, we place him into a fixed and stable racial category.

In addition to this lynch scene that opens *Incognegro*, Johnson and Pleece depict another later in the text. Despite their best efforts, Zane and Josiah Ryder, a local man recruited to help Zane in his investigations, are unable to prevent the townspeople from lynching Zane's friend, Carl. The splash pages depicting this gruesome violence contain many of the same constituent elements—a hooded Klansman, mothers, and curious children, all levels of the

7.4. From *Incognegro: A Graphic Mystery*, by Mat Johnson and Warren Pleece. New York: DC Comics, 2008. © Mat Johnson and Warren Pleece.

social strata attend the event—but the two parallel pages create slightly different emotional responses in the reader (see figure 7.3). For example, Pleece draws both lynchings from the same slightly elevated perspective, suggesting that the viewer is removed from the mobs committing this heinous act. The perspective allows the viewer to gain a critical and moral distance from the lynching, thus ensuring that readers do not share the murderous attitudes of the crowd.

Another similarity between the two splash pages is the central figure of the tree that serves as the improvised scaffold for the victim. Not only is this detail historically accurate, as many lynch victims' bodies were displayed in trees, but Pleece's rendering of the tree resonates with associations of strength and stability, suggesting that the white South's racial attitudes are nourished by the blood of African Americans. Furthermore, the crowds at both lynchings are equally celebratory, as each mob treats the occasion as something of a carnival, complete with alcohol and picnic-style food vendors.

Most striking of all, though, about this second lynching scene is Pleece's heavy use of shading and darkness to create an even more ominous tone for the lynching of Zane's friend, Carl. The first lynching is shocking because it unexpectedly opens the book, but the emotional stakes of the second one have been raised considerably because of the reader's attachment to the victim. Whereas the first scene startles the reader into a consideration of the practice of spectacle lynching, the second such incident reminds the reader of the humanity of both the lynch victim and the members of the African American communities who were frequently unable to save loved ones— sons, brothers, husbands, friends—from the hands of murdering lynch mobs. This reminder is made all the stronger a few pages later when we simultaneously see Carl actually suspended from the tree and Zane's emotional response to the loss of his friend (see figure 7.4).

Pleece's drawing style occasionally lacks detail and nuance, causing some of his drawings of human faces to remain rather flat and emotionless, but his "close-ups" here of Zane's face clearly express the anguish, anger, and frustration at his inability to save his friend. Visually linking the two panels within the larger splash page is the figure of Carl himself, and his broken body pressures the central focal point of the page in order to create sympathy for Carl in the reader. If, as Jacqueline Goldsby maintains, "lynching photographs figure the dead as signs of pure abjection who radiate no thought, no speech, no action, no will" (231), then Pleece's drawing succeeds in re-humanizing the lynch victim. By rendering Carl and the nameless man lynched at the beginning of *Incognegro* at all stages of the lynch ritual, what Goldsby describes as the "scopic aggression" (231) of lynch photography is mitigated in Pleece's line drawing, and his artwork instead reminds us that these men did indeed possess thought, speech, action, and will.

". . . visually codified representations"

Of course, not every African American character in Johnson and Pleece's graphic novel has Zane Pinchback's ability to pass for white. While sleuthing around Tupelo, Zane is aided by a man named Josiah Ryder. Ryder agrees to help Zane because Zane saves Ryder's son from a sure beating at the hands of a gang of angry white youths. To repay Zane's kindness, Ryder agrees to help with the investigation, providing Zane with transportation and the reader with important exposition throughout the narrative. Ryder's function in the text is that of the "native informant" common to the private eye genre of noir detective fiction, the informed local who provides necessary information to both the questing detective and the reader about the particular time and place in which the detective is conducting his investigation.

Perhaps most importantly of all, the juxtaposition of Zane and Ryder provides the reader with an opportunity to compare Ryder's racialized depiction, both in language and in images, throughout the novel with Zane's representation. As Marc Singer points out in "'Black Skins' and White Masks: Comic Books and the Secret of Race," "comics rely upon visually codified representations in which characters are continually reduced to their appearances" in order to convey information about a character's racial identity (107). That is precisely the case with Ryder, only I would add that his blackness is rendered both visually and verbally.

On the one hand, Johnson and Pleece have collaborated wonderfully to fully utilize the comics medium to destabilize our received notions of racial identity by creating Zane Pinchback, a comics character who is ethnically African American but who is rendered with none of the medium's standard visual tropes of blackness. On the other hand, the writer-artist duo must clearly indicate the racial status of black characters, like Ryder, who are not light enough to pass for white. In the "Introduction" to the 2007 issue of *MELUS* devoted to graphic narratives and multi-ethnic literature, "Coloring America: Muti-Ethnic Engagements with Graphic Narrative," Derek Royal maintains that the medium of graphic narrative is incredibly well-suited to explore issues of racial and ethnic identity precisely because the medium "foreground[s the] relational perspective between and among individual subjects. Such visual strategies are an essential component of multi-ethnic graphic narrative, writing that by its very nature relies upon themes of cultural context and contingency to generate meaning" (10). Just as comics, in general, relies upon the reader's involvement to fill in the spaces between the panels, *Incognegro* relies upon the reader's ability to shuttle between various depictions of racial representation in order to discover that racial categories are sometimes easily recognizable, but other times, they are neither as fixed nor as stable as one might have imagined.

The challenge, of course, is to present to the readers of *Incognegro* an African American character immediately recognizable as black without relying upon the distorting and destructive visual stereotypes used to represent African Americans in comics within the confines of a monochromatic book in which no character's skin color is depicted. That stereotypes are often considered the very building blocks of the comics medium by leading theoreticians and creators as Spiegelman, Eisner, and to a lesser degree, McCloud, comes as no surprise if one accepts the claim made by some literary and art critics that stereotypes—and the act of stereotyping itself—are actually necessary to our day-to-day functioning in the world. For instance, in his investigation into stereotypes in the Western literary tradition, *Difference and Pathology: Stereotypes of Sexuality, Race, and Madness*, Sander L. Gilman asserts that "everyone creates stereotypes. We cannot function in the world without them" (16). Echoing this view of the utility of stereotyping is the Dutch art critic and historian, Jan Nederveen Pieterse who, in his exploration of visual representations of Africans in Western art, *White on Black: Images of Africa and Blacks in Western Popular Culture*, explains that "in cognitive psychology, stereotypes are taken to be schemas or sets which play a part in cognition, perception, memory, and communication. Stereotypes are based on simplification and generalization, or the denial of individuality; they can be either negative or positive" (11).

Gilman and Pieterse acknowledge, however, in their work on stereotypes the fact that "no stereotypes have had more horrifying translations into social policy than those of 'race.' Tied to the prestige of nineteenth-century science, the idea of racial difference in the twentieth century became the means for manipulating and eventually destroying entire groups" (Gilman 129). Given the pernicious uses for which racialized stereotypical visual representations have been employed, the challenge is then to find an expressive visual language capable of rendering African Americans in a neutral or positive manner, a "visual shorthand for representing African Americans . . . [that] depends on the presence of a recognizable, stylized black physiognomy" (Harris 218).

Johnson and Pleece's success in creating this "visual shorthand" can be measured by examining the principle techniques they have used to render Ryder's blackness, both visually and linguistically. Take the images of him, for example, that we see in the scene in which Ryder and Zane search Francis's cabin for clues to her whereabouts. I chose this scene for analysis because it so aptly demonstrates the complexities of rendering race and because it provides numerous opportunities for juxtaposing the visual and verbal depictions of Zane and Ryder as they share nearly all of the panels on the page. Ryder is drawn with many of the physiognomic signs of racial difference, to borrow Spiegelman's phrase again, such as a broad nose and full lips, yet Pleece's realistic drawing style allows him to depict these features in a straightforward style that does not tend toward exaggeration or distortion. These are not the "visual signifiers of discredited blackness" used throughout the nineteenth and twentieth centuries as "indicators of degenerative mental and moral qualities" (Harris 29, 30). Rather, these are presented in the pages of *Incognegro* as the recognizable manifestations of racial difference without placing value judgments upon them.

Since, as Harris points out, physical traits that have come to be "defined as racial," such as "dark skin, woolly hair texture, full lips, and broad noses," (29, 30) all too often carry negative associations with them in American visual culture, the challenge faced by Pleece as a visual artist was to find—or create—some means of signaling Ryder's racial category in a neutral fashion. The technique Pleece settles upon is an intriguing one: throughout *Incognegro*, Pleece strains to depict Ryder in deep shadows in order to emphasize his "blackness," a technique used to mixed results in this scene. The top panel on page 101 provides a good example of this technique. Behind the figures of Ryder and Zane, we see a lantern, providing light for the interior of the cabin. Placed behind the two men, the lantern's light should cause deep shadows to fall across both of their faces, but only Ryder's face is heavily shaded. Pleece's shading technique is used in every image of Ryder throughout the book, in fact. Further emphasizing Ryder's racial status is Johnson's rendering of his speech in the southern vernacular. "I takes it you ain't never been married?", Ryder says after Zane explains how he believed that the sheriff's wife would be too timid to shoot him with a shotgun. When one compares Ryder's speech with Zane's northern inflections, little doubt remains in the reader's mind as to the presumed racial identities that the white South would assign to the two men.

If Pleece's insistence upon depicting Ryder in deep shade and shadows, even on a brightly lit day, strains our credulity, a greater danger exists in the way Ryder's speech is rendered, because passages like these come dangerously close to lapsing into the old, stereotyped representations of race that are all too common in the history of American visual culture, for as Harris reminds us, "images devised to construct a concept of blacks in the nineteenth century in support of racist ideology were commonly accompanied by correlative language, whether to describe blacks or to represent them through dialogue" (5). Whereas Johnson and Pleece mean to suggest a particular context for Ryder through their depiction of him, what they conjure up instead is the long history of distortive representations of African Americans in American popular culture in which ungrammatical speech is considered "talking black." Harris lists a variety of methods that black artists have used in their attempts to neutralize racist depictions of African Americans, such as "inversion," "recontextualization," and "reappropriation," all of which are attempts to invest racist misrepresentations with new meanings and messages. In the passage under consideration, it seems as if Johnson and Pleece are attempting to "reappropriate" racialized visual and verbal discourse, to take certain hurtful techniques used to render blackness visible in American culture and create neutral meanings for them. Such a strategy is fraught with danger, however, for as Harris asks, "can the application of a veneer of new interpretations overcome the subconscious impact of an image? Are these strategies truly effective or merely diversionary chimera?" (191). In other words, in attempting to counter racist depictions, Johnson and Pleece run the risk of actually reinforcing the very racial attitudes their work purports to oppose, for verbal and visual texts consistently defy their creators' attempts to control them. By utilizing stereotypes in order to dismantle that very type of stereotypical and uncritical sort of thinking about race, Johnson and Pleece run the considerable risk of unintentionally invoking the very ideas that they are working so hard to controvert.

". . . a tangible substance and a boundary . . ."

While Ryder's racial identity is fixed, Zane's is fluid. Perhaps the most intriguing sequence in the entire book occurs early on as Zane prepares to travel down south as Incognegro, and Johnson and Pleece reveal the transformation ritual that Zane performs (see figure 7.5). Besides removing some of the body from his wavy hair, Zane's transformation from black to white is attitudinal, not physical. In a remarkable two-page sequence of the novel, we witness Zane's movement—literally—from black to white. If, as Zane tells us, "race is a strategy. The rest is just people acting. Playing roles" (19), then his light complexion allows him to simply leave "black" Harlem for "white" Manhattan on the twentieth century's Underground Railroad: the subway. Amidst the greater freedom of the North, Zane can simply refuse to occupy the racially segregated "space" to which darker-skinned African Americans have been marginalized.

7.5. From *Incognegro: A Graphic Mystery*, by Mat Johnson and Warren Pleece. New York: DC Comics, 2008. © Mat Johnson and Warren Pleece.

Just before we see him take his journey across the color line, we see Zane staring at himself in a mirror as he becomes Incognegro, but what he sees reflected there are not only images of himself but images from the nation's racist heritage. In Pleece's drawings in these panels, Zane becomes the literal embodiment of the nation, for in two of the panels on this page are superimposed drawings that visually emblematize the country's complicated racial history. In the top right panel, the mirror allows Zane to look into the past, and what he sees is an image of "the southern tradition nobody likes to talk about. Slavery. Rape. Hypocrisy" (19). In the very next panel, Zane's figure is rendered in exactly the same attitude; however, what has changed is the image superimposed in the mirror over his reflection. He is now looking at the American flag, and Zane thinks to himself, "Since white America refuses to see its past, they can't really see me too well, either" (19). Here, Johnson and Pleece create a couple of startling visual metaphors in this sequence: Zane, in one panel, is looking into the nation's history, and as a man of mixed ancestry himself, he is literally looking into his own past. This fusion of individual and national history is rendered even more powerfully when Johnson and Pleece collapse the distance between the registers of national and personal history when they create the visual metonym of representing the American flag literally on top of Zane. In this moment, Zane becomes the unacknowledged but literal embodiment of America's racist past.

The pages accompanying the verbal and visual description of Zane adopting his Incognegro persona are among the most powerful in the entire book, reminiscent of the meditations on race and nationhood from the opening and closing pages of Ellison's *Invisible Man*. Johnson and Pleece have blended text and image beautifully in these pages, crafting a dense, lyrical passage that rivals one of the nation's great works of imaginative literature in its deft and nuanced exploration of race and politics. Graphic narratives, at their very best, recognize the false dichotomy between those who see the world as a text and those who see it as a picture, between those who privilege either spectatorship or reading over the other.[7] Rather, the highest achievements in the comics medium present a world view to their readers in which one is impossible without the other. *Incognegro* rewards concentrated critical attention because it succeeds in raising important questions about the representations of race in America.

Notes

1. Spiegelman himself has been at the center of many controversies regarding comics and racial representation over the past few decades. Consider, for instance, his own *New Yorker* magazine cover of a black woman and a Hasidic man kissing; his numerous public comments on cartoon representations of Muslim figures; and his own work on *Maus*, which provides a visual counter-argument to Nazi propaganda that equated Jews with vermin such as rats and his reappropriation of those visual codes of representation.

2. For the purposes of this paper, I am siding with R. C. Harvey in his ongoing debate with Scott McCloud about how meaning is generated in comics. Simply put, McCloud believes that meaning in comics is generated through the juxtaposition of sequenced images,

while Harvey maintains that comics' meaning resides in what he calls the "visual/verbal interplay." For more on this fascinating, and good-natured, argument, see Harvey's chapter, "The Aesthetics of the Comics: A Preamble Through History and Form" in his *The Art of the Funnies: An Aesthetic History* and McCloud's seminal work, *Understanding Comics*.

3. See W. J. T. Mitchell's *What Do Pictures Want?: The Lives and Loves of Images* for a similar viewpoint about the inevitability of stereotypes: "We all know that stereotypes are bad, false images that prevent us from truly seeing other people. We also know that stereotypes are, at a minimum, a *necessary* evil, that we could not make sense of or recognize objects or other people without the capacity to form images that allow us to distinguish one thing from another, one person from another, one class of thing from another" (296).

4. See Jeremy Dauber's excellent "Comic Books, Tragic Stories: Will Eisner's American Jewish History" for an analysis of the role of stereotypes in Eisner's work. While focused solely upon Eisner's long career, Dauber's essay is instructive for anyone interested in the topic of racial representation in American comics. Of particular interest is Dauber's exploration of Eisner's reliance upon racial stereotypes in his drawing of Ebony, the African American sidekick of *The Spirit* during the magazine's run in the 1940s, and Eisner's later regret over the stereotyped figure's representation.

5. Fredrik Strömberg catalogs a number of these characters in *Black Images in the Comics: A Visual History* from titles such as Winsor McCay's *Little Nemo in Slumberland*, T. C. McClure's *Sambo and His Funny Noises*, Hergé's *Tintin in the Congo*, and Frank O. King's *Gasoline Alley* as well as popular figures such as Eisner's Ebony White and Crumb's Angelfood McSpade.

6. Francis's "passing" as a white male and her subsequent love affair with the sheriff has, within the pages of the novel, a curious analog in the figure Michaela Mathers and her relationship with Alonzo Pinchback. While she has not crossed the gender line to live as a man as Francis has, Michaela does exhibit several traditionally masculine behaviors such as wearing pants, running an illegal still in the woods, and chewing tobacco. As Judith Halberstam notes in *Female Masculinity*, women defy gender conventions for several reasons: female masculinity can result from "the excesses of male supremacy," or it can be a "unique form of social rebellion;" female masculinity can signal "sexual alterity," or it can mark "heterosexual variation;" and female masculinity "marks the place of pathology" or it can represent "the healthful alternative to what are considered the histrionics of conventional feminities" (9).

7. See Nicholas Mirzoeff's *An Introduction to Visual Culture* for discussion of these two competing views within the critical discourse of the humanities. Mirzoeff persuasively argues that "even literary studies have been forced to conclude that the world-as-a-text has been replaced by the world-as-a-picture. Such world-pictures cannot be purely visual, but by the same token, the visual disrupts and challenges any attempt to define culture in purely linguistic terms" (7).

Works Cited

Dauber, Jeremy. "Comic Books, Tragic Stories: Will Eisner's American Jewish History." *AJS Review* 30.2 (2006): 277–304. Print.

Eisner, Will. *Graphic Storytelling and Visual Narrative*. New York: Norton, 2008. Print.

Gilman, Sander L. *Difference and Pathology: Stereotypes of Sexuality, Race, and Madness*. Ithaca: Cornell UP, 1985. Print.

Goldsby, Jacqueline. *A Spectacular Secret: Lynching in American Life and Literature*. U of Chicago P, 2006. Print.

Gustines, George Gene. "Black and White and Graphic All Over: A 1930s Tale of Race, Passing and Pain." *New York Times*. March 3, 2008. Web.

Halberstam, Judith. *Female Maculinity*. Duke UP, 1998. Print.

Hale, Grace Elizabeth. *Making Whiteness: The Culture of Segregation in the South, 1890–1940*. New York: Vintage, 1999. Print.

Harris, Michael D. *Colored Pictures: Race and Visual Representation*. Chapel Hill: U of North Carolina P, 2003. Print.

Harvey, R. C. *The Art of the Funnies: An Aesthetic History*. Jackson: UP of Mississippi, 1994. Print.

Johnson, Mat and Warren Pleece. *Incognegro: A Graphic Mystery*. New York: DC Comics, 2008. Print.

Lee, Anthony W. "Introduction." *Lynching Photographs*. Ed. Anthony W. Lee. Berkeley: U of California P, 2007. 1–9. Print.

Lorah, Michael C. "Mat Johnson on *Incognegro*." Newsarama. Web.

McCloud, Scott. *Understanding Comics: The Invisible Art*. New York: Harper Perennial, 1994. Print.

Mirzoeff, Nicholas. *An Introduction to Visual Culture*. New York: Routledge, 1999. Print.

Mitchell, W. J. T. *What Do Pictures Want?: The Lives and Loves of Images*. Chicago: U of Chicago P, 2005. Print.

———. *Bodyscape: Art, Modernity, and the Ideal Figure*. New York: Routledge, 1995. Print.

Pieterse, Jan Nederveen. *White on Black: Images of Africa and Blacks in Western Popular Culture*. New Have: Yale UP, 1992. Print.

Royal, Derek Parker. "Introduction: Coloring America: Multi-Ethnic Engagements with Graphic Narrative." *MELUS*. 32.3 (2007): 7–22. Print.

Shawl, Nisi. "*Incognegro*: Black, white, and injustice all over." *Seattle Times*. March 8, 2008. Web.

Smith, Shawn Michelle. "The Evidence of Lynching Photographs." *Lynching Photographs*. Ed. Anthony W. Lee. Berkeley: U of California P, 2007. Print.

Singer, Marc. "'Black Skins' and White Masks: Comic Books and the Secret of Race." *African American Review* 36.1 (2002): 107–19. Print.

Solomon, Charles. "Review: Johnson goes 'Incognegro.'" *San Francisco Chronicle*. March 1, 2008. Web.

Spiegelman, Art. "Those Dirty Little Comics." *Tijuana Bibles: Art and Wit in America's Forbidden Funnies, 1930s-1950s*. Ed. Bob Adelman. New York: Simon & Schuster, 1997. Print.

———. "Little Orphan Annie's Eyeballs." *Comix, Essays, Graphics, and Scraps*. New York: Raw Books, 1999. Print.

Strömberg, Fredrik. *Black Images in the Comics: A Visual History*. Seattle: Fantagraphics, 2003. Print.

Everybody's Graphic Protest Novel

Stuck Rubber Baby and the Anxieties of Racial Difference

—Gary Richards

In any number of ways, *Stuck Rubber Baby*, Howard Cruse's 1995 graphic novel, is a mesmerizing text that broke new ground, particularly with its unique marriage of genre and content. A gay cartoonist who, since the 1970s, has created such iconographic series as *Barefootz* and *Wendel*, Cruse again deploys the graphic form in *Stuck Rubber Baby* to explore a set of tensions surrounding the racial and sexual politics of the Deep South in the 1960s.[1] To do so, via something of an updating of Huckleberry Finn and Scout Finch, Cruse creates as narrator and central protagonist Toland Polk, an apparently middle-aged white man now displaced from the South whose reminiscences delineate his youth in the fictional Clayfield, a major southern city based on Birmingham. (For understandable artistic, personal, and even, one suspects, legal reasons, Cruse adamantly begins commentary appended to the novel by asserting that "*Stuck Rubber Baby* is a work of fiction, not autobiography. Its characters are inventions of mine, and Clayfield is a make-believe city" [213]; however, he immediately clarifies, "That said, it's doubtful I'd have been moved to write or draw this graphic novel if I hadn't come of age in Birmingham, Alabama, during the early '60s" [213].)[2]

As Toland recounts his southern childhood and early adulthood in the Kennedy era, he foregrounds his hesitant, vexed radicalization to liberal political activity during the Civil Rights Movement. The process's starting point, Toland emphasizes, is one saturated with white racism within both his particular household and the broader cultural spheres of the post-World War II decades. The evolution subsequently includes his gradual introduction to political activism and its array of practitioners, his residual disinterest in and distance from this world, and ultimately his anxious immersion into a cycle of politicized violence that results in a series of martyred individuals.

Intricate though this narrative already is, Cruse provocatively complicates Toland's identity—and southern history—by weaving into these reminiscences the protagonist's equally anxious negotiations of sexual identity. These elements include his recurring early moments of homoeroticism that most typically remain unacknowledged until much later; his largely abortive attempts as an adult to enact heterosexuality, ones that nevertheless lead to the birth of his daughter, the baby tangentially conceived because of the defective condom of the novel's title; and his adult sexual experimentation with other men. These negotiations culminate, as suggested through the frame narration's brief glimpses of Toland's current same-sex partnership, in his full acceptance of gay identity.

With this unique focus, Cruse not only boldly takes the graphic novel into largely uncharted territory but also simultaneously positions his text within at least two established sub-genres of southern literary production and calls attention to the absences within those sub-genres. On the one hand, *Stuck Rubber Baby* exemplifies what southern intellectual historian Fred Hobson has termed the "white southern racial conversion narrative." In *But Now I See*, he argues that this form arose in the 1940s and, through the autobiographical works of Lillian Smith, Katharine Du Pre Lumpkin, James McBride Dabbs, Willie Morris, and others, became a codified sub-genre that persisted throughout the twentieth century. All these persons, Hobson clarifies, penned "works in which the authors, all products of and willing participants in a harsh, segregated society, confess racial wrongdoings and are 'converted,' in varying degrees, from racism to something approaching racial enlightenment" (2). Drawing upon but significantly revising a long tradition of religious narratives, these works centralize "a recognition and confession of the writer's own sins and the announced need for redemption, as well as a description of the writer's radical transformation—a sort of secular salvation" (4).

This trajectory is precisely that of the anxiously "redeemed" Toland, who confesses his transgressions both within the narrative—"And I'm talking about the really frightening words that all the habits of a lifetime were screaming at me to hold back and leave unsaid" (193)—and, more important, through the narrative itself. Indeed, the first page of the novel features Toland's face dominating the other panels, bleeding to the page's edges, and staring somberly and squarely at readers, all elements that underscore the importance of the telling of the narrative about to be recited. Here and throughout the novel, Cruse has Toland conspicuously foreground the narrative as the evidential document and thus rehearse Hobson's point that "the writing of a conversion narrative is, to a great extent, the final proof of that conversion—the equivalent of testifying" (4). Moreover, although Toland is a fictional representation, as Cruse carefully denotes, his story is one strongly inflected by autobiography, and even this autobiography links Cruse, the son of a Baptist minister, to the racial conversion narrative with its biblical cadences and Protestant antecedents.

On the other hand, with its attention to sexuality equal to its attention to race, *Stuck Rubber Baby* is also squarely within the sub-genre of the "coming-out novel," that specialized subset of the *Bildungsroman* that centralizes a character's sexual coming-of-age in ways that vary from mythic hetero-normativity. These novels, like the autobiographies discussed by Hobson, follow a set trajectory, moving with only slight variation from unawareness to anxiety to acceptance. Here, however, instead of racial identity, the youthful protagonist negotiates her or his emergent homosexual, bisexual, or otherwise culturally deviant sexual identity, ultimately arriving at not so much redemption for past transgressions as insight and celebration. Although the most famous of these novels, such as E. M. Forster's *Maurice* and Edmund White's *A Boy's Own Story*, are removed from southern United States culture, the region has produced any number of these fictional narratives, with Truman Capote's *Other Voices, Other Rooms* infamously instigating the regional manifestation that has continued through Rita Mae Brown's *Rubyfruit Jungle*, Ben Neihart's *Hey, Joe*, and, some might argue, Dorothy Allison's *Bastard Out of Carolina*.

As suggested earlier, Cruse has Toland follow the coming-out novel's anxious progression toward an eventual acceptance of his homosexuality. Like Forster and Capote, among others, Cruse goes so far as to sentimentalize this acceptance and its rewards. Forster famously declares of Maurice's romanticized fate, "A happy ending was imperative. I shouldn't have bothered to write otherwise. I was determined that in fiction anyway two men should fall in love and remain in it for the ever and ever that fiction allows, and in this sense Maurice and Alec still roam the greenwood" (250), and Capote has Joel Knox ultimately find in the cross-dressing Randolph a reassuring model for performing gender and sexuality: "She beckoned to him, shining and silver, and he knew he must go: unafraid, not hesitating, he paused only at the garden's edge where, as though he'd forgotten something, he stopped and looked back at the bloomless, descending blue, at the boy he had left behind" (231). As if similarly to reassure that coming out is worth its attendant anxieties, Cruse offers a parallel reward to Toland in his partner and their idealized upscale urban domesticity, complete with reassuring images of food preparation (96), terms of endearment (135), and displays of physical intimacy (207). Moreover, the unnamed same-sex partner consistently works to facilitate Toland's therapeutic repetition of the narrative. At times, the partner does so by offering leavening lightness. "This part of the story always kills me" (60), he interjects when Toland narrates his engagement in heterosex. "Tsk, tsk! What are we to do with these thin-skinned patriarchs?" (167), the partner quips when the gay Sammy Noone confronts his dictatorial father within Toland's recounted tale. However, when Toland needs to be comforted rather than teased during this ritual, the partner silently offers bolstering physicality, holding Toland's hand and embracing his shoulders when he recounts Sammy's lynching (179). Cruse's text may even be among the most anxiety-allaying within this subgenre since, whereas readers must wait until the ends of the novels to learn of Maurice's and Joel's consoling fates, Cruse introduces the partner's stabilizing presence in the first pages of *Stuck Rubber Baby* and has him briefly but regularly punctuate the rest of the text, thus consistently reminding readers that, although Toland's trauma may never be fully quarantined to the past, the present includes a gratifying gay relationship that facilitates the negotiation of that trauma.

By fusing these two sub-genres—the white southern racial conversion narrative and the coming-out novel—*Stuck Rubber Baby* not only becomes significantly more complex but also implicitly critiques these sub-genres for their recurring silences regarding the other's preoccupations: the racial conversion narrative's general silence about sexuality and homosexuality in particular, and the white-authored coming-out novel's general silence about racial bias and privilege. Hobson addresses the former in *But Now I See*, convincingly delineating the cultural politics that prevented Lillian Smith from writing openly about her lesbian sexuality during the mid-twentieth century, and offering that "her sexual identity was a major factor—just how major she herself perhaps did not fully recognize—in the making of Smith as a bold *racial* commentator" (22). And yet, despite this informing trace of the sexual within the racial, Smith's autobiographical writings, like those of the other figures whom Hobson scrutinizes, nevertheless remain largely silent on homosexuality. Likewise, the cited southern coming-out novels often minimize their white protagonists' racial awareness. Capote's Joel Knox, for instance, may dramatically evolve in his negotiations of gender and sexuality, but his relationships with Zoo and other African Americans remain largely static and problematically racist, with Zoo being a near reinscription of the mammy figure. If these coming-out novels do overtly address white racism and racial privilege, as Allison does in chapter six of *Bastard Out of Carolina*, the effort often seems forced, heavy-handed, even obligatory. When Bone internally dissects her cousin Grey's racist actions and attitudes toward the African Americans living next to his family's apartment—"I couldn't say what I was thinking, couldn't say, 'That [black] child is prettier than you'" (84)—the matter of Bone's ostensibly enlightened racial identity seems largely and reassuringly resolved, and Allison rarely returns to it. Once readers encounter a text like *Stuck Rubber Baby* that features a protagonist's simultaneous negotiations of race and sexuality, the silences and muted articulations of the two discrete sub-genres seem all the more apparent.

This is not to say, however, that *Stuck Rubber Baby* is the first—much less only—southern text to fuse these sub-genres and/or their preoccupations. Cruse's work may well be the first graphic novel to do so in significant ways, but for decades other southern novels and autobiographies have grappled to represent the simultaneous negotiations of these axes of identity. At precisely the historical moment depicted in *Stuck Rubber Baby*, the early 1960s, Carson McCullers attempted, though with disappointing results, to craft in Jester Clane, the protagonist of her novel *Clock Without Hands*, a character whose coming out as gay is interwoven with his dawning liberal consciousness regarding race and racial injustice. Somewhat later and certainly not surprisingly, black gay, lesbian, and bisexual southern novelists like Alice Walker and Randall Kenan offered protagonists such as Celie from *The Color Purple* and Horace Cross from *A Visitation of Spirits* for whom race and homosexuality (and/or homoeroticism) are of equal importance. Finally, a spate of autobiographical writings by contemporary European Americans has, with varying emphases, fused these sub-genres: Florence King's *Confessions of a Failed Southern Lady*; Mab Segrest's *Memoir of a Race Traitor*, especially when read in tandem with the essays of *My Mama's Dead Squirrel*; and, most recently, Kevin Sessums's *Mississippi Sissy*, to name but a few.

What makes *Stuck Rubber Baby* unique and therefore even more significant within this grouping is its graphic form, a form that inherently complicates the codified processes of prose novel reading and that has proved extraordinarily appealing to contemporary readers. Like the best graphic novels, Cruse's is an engagingly drawn text, where page after page subtly evinces the careful interplay of form and content. Consider, for instance, when Toland first meets Sammy Noone, the flamboyantly gay musician who is friend to Toland's housemate Mavis. Although Toland, when forced to categorize his sexual orientation during his recruitment physical, has briefly acknowledged to himself the cryptic homoerotic feelings and activities of

8.1. From *Stuck Rubber Baby*, by Howard Cruse. New York: Paradox Press, 1995. Copyright © 1995 Howard Cruse.

his childhood, he largely manages to keep his resolution to squelch these feelings and what they may signify: "By the time Clayfield Stadium came into view, I'd decided that this homo stuff had to get nipped right in the bud! So I set about doing just that. And pretty successfully, too, as best I could judge" (10). When Sammy's aggressive, almost instantaneous flirtations with Toland—casually caressing his face, declaring his eyes "too soulful!" (15)—threaten to violate this resolve, Cruse structures the panels, shown in figure 8.1, to violate in turn their otherwise neatly regular organization: the panel where Sammy touches Toland—and only this one—bleeds to the bottom of the page and draws readers' eyes directly to the erotically charged contact of male bodies. Here, then, in both the novel's form and thematic content, male same-sex intimacy quite literally exceeds the borders of propriety.[3]

Similarly sophisticated visual images, rife with symbolic function, punctuate the rest of the novel. When the police raid Clayfield's main gay bar, The Rhombus, and thus implicitly threaten the gay and lesbian revelers with imprisonment (45), Cruse organizes the panels so that, when viewed as a whole, the white gutters replicate the regularly spaced bars of a jail cell, a technique he again deploys to similar effect when police question Toland after Sammy's lynching (182–83). Likewise, although less subtly, Cruse represents Toland's traumatic memories of the lynching (178) with dark fragmented images that defy any neat pattern of organization or respect for marginal integrity. The precariousness of Toland's mastery of this trauma is suggested when he offers his public recital of the lynching at Sammy's memorial service, shown in figure 8.2. Cruse depicts the disciplined beginnings of Toland's address—"winding my way fairly articulately through the anecdotes I'd mapped out in my head beforehand" (190)—within a regularized rectangular panel, but, as he loses control of his emotions, Cruse increasingly fragments and distorts the images to mirror Toland's anxiety: sizes of panels vary widely, frames cede regular right angles, panels tilt, and margins relentlessly grow compromised. Moreover, Cruse imagines Toland's body within these panels as fragmenting before readers' eyes. The first image of the page offers this body as a near-unified whole, although the wafting smoke does compromise this corporeal unity, figuratively cutting Toland off at the knees. By the second row, however, as the symbolic irregularities of form proliferate, Toland emerges only as a series of dismembered individualized body parts: an ear, a set of knuckles, a magnified nose and mouth. To horrific effect, Cruise literalizes this fragmentation of Toland's body in the final image, eradicating his torso and limbs altogether and offering a violently exploding skull that replicates the image the teenage Toland projects for himself after seeing graphic photos of Emmett Till (2).

8.2. From *Stuck Rubber Baby*, by Howard Cruse. New York: Paradox Press, 1995. Copyright © 1995 Howard Cruse.

This interplay of graphic artistry and provocative subject matter has rightly garnered *Stuck Rubber Baby* significant praise, and most critics have agreed with Tony Kushner, who, in his 1995 introduction to the novel, deems Cruse "a pioneer in the field of lesbian and gay comics, an important participant in the underground comics movement, and in my opinion one of the most talented artists ever to work in the form" (iii). Like Cruse, a gay man who eventually relocated to New York from the South of his childhood, Kushner is perhaps expectedly biased toward this particular project, having been one of the crucial sponsors during its four-year completion, as Cruse clarifies on his website. Moreover, as suggested by plays such as *Angels in America, Homebody/Kabul,* and *Caroline, or Change,* a musical interrogating the same moment of southern history as *Stuck Rubber Baby,* Kushner has been a consistent champion of overtly politicized art, especially from gay perspectives, and therefore approvingly notes that Cruse's novel is a heavily politicized one: "It articulates a crying need for solidarity, it performs the crucial function of remembering, for the queer community, how essential to the birth of our politics of liberation the civil rights movement was" (iv). And yet even reviewers without these shared personal and ideological investments have celebrated *Stuck Rubber Baby*'s achievement, noting, for instance, the work's length, complexity, and thematic coherence. A testimony to the novel's importance and popularity is the reissue by DC Comics' Paradox Press in June of 2010, complete with a new introduction by acclaimed fellow cartoonist and memoirist Alison Bechdel as well as a second wave of positive reviews. Blogger Michael C. Lorah, for instance, offers that this "oft-neglected stepchild . . . deserves far better" than its first reissue only at its fifteenth anniversary. "In case you're wondering, it holds up very well," he asserts. "The book is just as good, perhaps better, than any comic you've ever read." Writing for *Lambda Literary,* Cathy Camper fully concurs: "*Stuck Rubber Baby*'s depth of characterization, setting, psychological insight, and history make it a perfect example of how a graphic novel is not simply a compilation of cartoons. This reprinting calls attention to the masterpiece it is, not only in queer literature, but also as an exemplary work in the graphic novel genre, one that deserves to stand as a model of the form for young cartoonists straight and gay."

And yet, especially when placed within the contexts of broader southern literary production, *Stuck Rubber Baby* ultimately reveals itself as a text distinctly limited in its imaginings of southern race and sexuality. Always prone to melodrama, the novel seems to emerge from a guilt-infused white perspective that, in its efforts to interrogate and indict the dominant culture of the 1960s South for its racism and homophobia, consistently romanticizes the region's black culture, crafting a set of idealized African Americans who, in their near-perfection, ironically lose validity as characters in a novel ostensibly committed to representing historical reality. As Harper Lee's *To Kill a Mockingbird* and others of its ilk remind, Cruse is not alone in crafting a text with this troubling white investment in idealized black culture, but his depictions often seem particularly maladroit and perhaps even anachronistic, coming as late as they do in the century.

In Cruse's novel, whites consistently emerge as overtly racist, politely or benignly racist, or ineffectual in their support of the Civil Rights Movement, whereas blacks emerge as models of efficient protest and paragons of racial tolerance. The same holds true for black sexual tolerance. Although African American homophobia has been vigorously debated, especially regarding its extent and virulence relative to that of European-American culture, a critical strain has persistently indicted black prejudice in this arena. During the emergence of academic black feminism, Barbara Smith notably spotlighted a commonplace African American presumption that "[h]omosexuality is a white problem or even a 'white disease'" and chastised, "This attitude is much too prevalent among people of color. Individuals who are militantly opposed to racism in all its forms still find lesbianism and male homosexuality something to snicker about or, worse, to despise" (101). Likewise, James Baldwin, tagged by homophobic discourse as "Martin Luther Queen," raised similar concerns within his fiction and other writings. Even more so than Smith or Baldwin, however, Randall Kenan has repeatedly indicted black homophobia within specifically southern settings, whether in the rabid sermons of the Reverend Barden in *A Visitation of Spirits*, which deem homosexuality unnatural and "unclean" (79), or in the mundane cultural investments of Maggie MacGowan Williams in "The Foundations of the Earth," which deter her when "called on to realign her thinking about men and women, and men and man, and even women and women. Together . . . the way Adam and Eve were meant to be together" (63). In contrast, Cruse conspicuously removes all traces of black homophobia and has the black community—and he does present it as a unified, solitary one—affirm gay existence in virtually all forms. In contrast, white homophobia circulates with both great freedom and the intent to punish and seclude, as does white gay racism.

Consider first Cruse's idealization of his African American characters' multiple tolerances—racial, sexual, and otherwise. He evinces little of the complexity and subtlety demanded by Eve Sedgwick, who two decades ago described the process of coming to the "long, painful realization, *not* that all oppressions are congruent, but that they are *differently* structured and so must intersect in complex embodiments" (33). Each category of identity is thus "likely to be in a unique indicative relation to certain distinctive nodes of cultural organization" (33). Cruse insists, however, that all minoritized identities are similarly structured, having Les Pepper, one of the novel's most valorized characters, overtly articulate the parallel inherent immutabilities of both racial and sexual identity in a rather shopworn rhetorical move: "Martin Luther King himself could walk up an' say to me, 'Les, you gotta quit bein' gay!' . . . An' I'd say to him, 'Sure thing, Dr. King—just as soon as you stop bein' Negro!" (48). Cruse in turn depicts the black community's tolerances as concomitant and mutually constitutive and underscores the tolerance of racial otherness as an enviable starting point.

For all their justified critique of dominant white culture, African American characters remain to a person distanced from separatist positions and instead welcome racial integration, warmly embracing whites, for instance, within the black-led civil protest movement, as symbolized when the white character Ginger visits the black character Sledge's home, "a visit that left everybody feeling like they'd all been reared in the same cradle" (51). The few concerns among African Americans that do emerge associated with white presences are quickly dismissed. When Raeburn scrutinizes Toland on his first visit to the predominantly black political gatherings at the Melody Motel, asking other African Americans, "Jus' how many of our trade secrets're you two givin' away to this stranger here?" (26), the others roundly chastise Raeburn, who confesses, "Don't get shook up, man—I'm only joshin'!" (27). Although these characterizations and plots crucially structure Toland's first-person narration, they do not seem to reflect his specific biases, which, within the relayed narrative, are largely detached from and somewhat skeptical of African American culture; rather, these investments appear to be primarily those of Cruse as the writer/artist.

Given his commitment to concomitant tolerances, Cruse depicts this black community to be equally at ease with homosexuality, not only tolerating to it but at times embracing and even celebrating multiple manifestations of it within racialized contexts: individual gays of both races, such as Sammy Noone and Les Pepper; intraracial lesbian couples, such as Marge and Effie; and interracial gay couples, such as Les and Toland. Moreover, this community welcomes even the most flamboyantly transgressive elements associated with mid-twentieth-century homosexual identity, such as overt violations of gender normativity. For instance, Cruse not only centralizes Esmereldus as a drag performer but highlights his accompanying camp discourse, replete with gender switching, as when he articulates his diva worship of Anna Dellyne Pepper: "Ol' Esmereldus hasn't given up on her! This queen's gonna hear 'Secret in the Air' from the lady's lips one more time or die tryin'!" (47). Likewise, just as Esmo is metaphorically embraced by the community, so too is the inescapably gay Sammy physically embraced by Dinah, the Noones' African American maid: "Mister Sammy! I don't believe what I'm seein'! You come here right this minute an' give me a hug!" (160).

This community likewise tolerates explicit bodily enactments of homosexual desire, and Esmo can publicly articulate without censure what approaches hypersexuality. "Thank God the moon isn't full tonight! I get such unseemly nocturnal desires when moons are full" (81), he offers, only to be teased, "As if Miss Esmereldus wasn't in heat 365 days a year!" (81). This openness even persists outside the bar-centered subculture that gives rise to this banter. When Les takes Toland to the Melody Motel for their sexual tryst, Toland notes, "From the way the Melody's security guards and desk clerks acted, I gathered it wasn't that unusual for Les to wheel into the motel at odd hours with a male companion in tow. In fact, they lobbed a key at us without even asking for paperwork, which I thought was gracious of 'em" (137). The sexual nature of the same-sex rendezvous thus seems an unproblematic open secret, even when enacted by an interracial pair.

Because of this widespread openness, members of this black culture—homosexual and otherwise—can and do move among markedly differing social arenas with incredible fluidity, unlike these persons' white counterparts. For instance, with the placidity encoded in her name, Mabel Lake moves from playing hymns on the organ at her church on Sundays to playing Broadway show tunes from *The Music Man* and *The Pajama Game* at gay enclaves like The Rhombus and Alleysax on the weekends, unlike Sammy, who is fired from his position as the Episcopal organist. "Mabel covers all bases," Toland learns on his first visit to The Rhombus. "She plays for sinners on Saturdays, an' for God an' Rev. Pepper on Sunday mornings" (42). Les, son of the Reverend Harland Pepper, similarly displays this fluid movement among cultural arenas that one might expect to be mutually exclusive. On the night of the racially motivated bombing of the Melody Hotel, Toland marvels, "Les stayed at his daddy's beck and call. I was impressed at how a partyboy from The Rhombus could turn into a perfect preacher's kid at the flick of a switch" (106).

Les's role in the novel, however, is far more central and romanticized—in multiple senses—than merely embodying this fluid social movement. He is the crucial figure who engineers Toland's first fully acknowledged sexual interaction with another man, an idealized session that rivals those that

Forster allots to Maurice and Scudder. During this extended sequence, Les remains a model of concerned attentiveness, consistently attuned to Toland's levels of anxieties and, much like his adult partner within the novel's framing narrative, acting so as to alleviate those anxieties when they threaten to incapacitate Toland. When Les's invitation to dance at Alleysax—"C'mon, baby. Let's do the scary thing" (136)—does indeed prove too frightening to Toland in its public nature, Les orchestrates the private tryst at the Melody that proves as melodic as the motel's name and the rain falling outside the window. "And then we made love" (138), Toland dreamily reminisces. "Afterwards I was lost in such a mood of contentment . . ." (138). Moreover, through Les's deft guidance, the night evolves into a reassuring sexual mentorship, and, although the love-struck Toland cannot initially understand Les's gentle analysis of gay promiscuity, the meanings eventually become clear to the novice performer of homosex: "I was sitting in some musty office waiting for a job interview . . . when all of a sudden various neurons from assorted sectors of my brain opened fire on each other . . . And I knew that Les was right: I wasn't in love with him. Not him in particular!" (151). Instead of becoming a partner or even a routine sexual companion, Les metamorphoses into a trusted friend who reemerges to insist that he accompany and provide emotional support to Toland when he journeys to visit his daughter "for the first and last time" (200) before she is put up for adoption: "When I confided to Les what the trip was for, he decided I should have company on the drive" (200).

Les is not alone in these supportive endeavors, as Cruse imagines an extensive coterie of African Americans to ably assist in Toland's sexual mentorship. This starts almost immediately, with Mabel's depiction as an oracular source of knowledge for the perplexed white boy. On his first visit to The Rhombus, when Mabel is petitioned to resume her music after the police raid, she hisses with maternal protectiveness, "Hush up, Clyde! I'm explainin' stuff! These children are new!" (45). Marge and Effie are similarly scripted. After reactionary locals lynch the gay organist Sammy Noone for his sexual and racial transgressions, his family gives "him about as inconspicuous a funeral up in Ridgeline as they could manage and still have it be in a church" (184). In contrast, the pair of black lesbians, along with Mabel, not only decides to "throw a party at Alleysax where we could all remember Sammy—and say goodbye to him—together" (184) but also shepherds the meditative Toland into the ultimately redemptive ceremony in which he publically articulates his homosexuality: "It was good that I let Marge herd me inside to hear the kids sing" (186).

8.3. From *Stuck Rubber Baby*, by Howard Cruse. New York: Paradox Press, 1995. Copyright © 1995 Howard Cruse.

In the juxtaposition of these memorial services, Cruse also manipulates form to reinforce the ideological thrust of his content, as shown in figure 8.3. Relegated to the upper left corner—and thus the periphery—of the page, the church where Sammy's formal funeral is held stands in eerie isolation outside an individualized panel, virtually devoid of human presences and significantly surrounded by a sterile sea of whiteness on the page, presumably a negative comment on the white culture that would worship within the represented space (184). In contrast, the representation of Alleysax, drawn to be roughly triple the size of the church, is positioned at the center of the page within an expansive panel where a perfect semicircle provides a serene dome for the image. Gone are the rigidity and brittleness of the previous image, since detailed crosshatching and stippling create warmly reassuring patterns of multi-toned darkened areas for the African American nightclub. Moreover, there is virtually no pure white space left within the panel, a parallel to the club's integrated clientele. Finally, a flurry of activity from a multitude of people fills the space, marking Alleysax as teeming with life, whereas the hearse and cross that overshadow the humans in the previous image emphasize absence and death. At almost every point, Cruse's juxtaposed panels shore up a gulf between a desolate, cold, white cultural space and a vibrant, reassuring black one.

A key presence within Toland's emotional performance at the memorial at Alleysax is yet another African American, Shiloh, who, as the scarred survivor of the racially motivated bombing of the Melody, physically jars Toland from his set remarks and into his fraught public articulation of his role in Sammy's death. Shiloh's tortured black body conjures Sammy's tortured queer body and forces Toland to struggle with the relation of his closetedness to Sammy's murder-inducing openness. When the boundaries begin to blur—"Why was Toland lying flat in the dirt by The Wheelery's back steps, unconscious but alive . . . and why was I, Sammy Noone, suddenly ten galaxies away?" (192)—Toland anxiously pronounces his own queerness, knowing "I'd find understanding in Shiloh's eyes" (193). Marked by "a ferocious fire" that rips though Toland's "neck like the claws of an animal" (192), this charged moment of "conversion" parallels those delineated by Hobson but now centralizes sexual identity instead of racial identity.

Empowering as this coterie of black individuals is, it is Cruse's idealization of the African American family in Harland and Anna Dellyne Pepper, Les's parents, that proves most sustaining in Toland's sexual acknowledgment and maturation. This depiction quite literally becomes a matter of black and white for Cruse, since he crafts the novel to be virtually devoid of cohesive, supportive white families. Toland's parents, mildly racist faux-intellectuals, and Sammy's mother are dead, and Toland's sister, Melanie, is in an ill-fated childless marriage to the bigoted homophobe Orley, who rants about Sammy, "Life don't get much more farcical that this, sugar lamb! [. . .] A degenerate queer on the public airwaves castin' aspersions on an officer of the law!" (114). With even less subtlety, especially in his naming, Cruse offers Sammy's father, the "loathsome throwback" Cuthel Noone (124). This largely reprehensible figure is not only estranged from his son because, according to Sammy, Cuthel Noone "hates the fact that once upon some enchanted evening he was screwing my lovely mom an' a silly little fairy sperm came wiggling out of his big, butch dick" (125), but also paralyzed "so bad off he can't arch his eyebrow without a forklift!" (125), evincing heavy-handed symbolism worthy of McCullers's *Clock Without Hands*. The form of the pages devoted to the proper white southern home symbolized by the Noone mansion (164–66), shown in figure 8.4, reinforces the horror that Cruse grants this space. Here, as an increasingly magnified image of the paralyzed patriarch provides a background that bleeds to the pages' edges, individual panels in the foreground and speech balloons assume no orderly organization and instead vary wildly in size, distractingly overlap, and are interspersed with tilting historical documents, such as postcards and photographs. The result is a sustained chaos that works to thwart any ease in reading these pages and thus to mark white patriarchy as anxiety-inducing.

Within this context of absent or horrific white nuclear families, the Peppers shine all the brighter as beacons of familial acceptance and support. As Les jokes to Toland, everyone in the Pepper household knows and accepts his assigned role while acknowledging and respecting others': "Papa's the preacher in the family an' I'm the faggot" (48). But Harland Pepper's respect for sexual otherness extends well beyond his own family, manifesting so extensively that he even apologies for disrupting Esmo's drag performance after the bombing of the Melody: "I'm sorry to have interrupted things here, but there's been a terrible tragedy this evenin'" (105). Cruse has the reverend emerge as a model of human warmth and forgiveness throughout the novel and never more so than when consulting with Toland on that same night of the bombing. His arm clasping the white boy's shoulder, the minister interacts with such paternal openness that Toland willingly casts the black man as a surrogate father and guiltily confesses, "I do recall a fleeting wish I had that my daddy could've been more like Harland Pepper" (111). Cruse underscores this simultaneously interracial and intergenerational harmony by repeatedly superimposing the faces of the two characters and reassuringly regularizing the panels for these four pages (108–11), presenting three orderly rows that vary only slightly in the panels' sizes, just enough to retain

8.4. From *Stuck Rubber Baby*, by Howard Cruse. New York: Paradox Press, 1995. Copyright © 1995 Howard Cruse.

visual interest and to escape the previously mentioned monotony associated with incarceration. This particular image of Harland Pepper, struggling to extend understanding and forgiveness to Mabel Lake's momentarily violent acts and literally embracing a young white man, haunts Toland throughout the rest of the novel, especially when his former brother-in-law confesses his role in Sammy's death. Upon hearing Orley's revelation, Toland chastises himself in hindsight for coldly rejecting the man: "The dude was angling for forgiveness, for Christ's sake! Harland Pepper would've at least offered some generosity of spirit!" (199).

The most idealized figure, however, is Anna Dellyne, the former singer turned dutiful minister's wife to Harland Pepper whose music has justly grown mythic in its abilities to soothe and restore: "Anna Dellyne was sitting on the edge of Shiloh's bed, lovingly singing one of her old-time songs for him. His eyes were closed. Who could tell if he was even hearing her? The audience in the doorway, though, was totally rapt" (131). Even for non-gay characters, she functions as a sympathetic role model, such as to Ginger, who seeks to replicate the older woman's independent early career: "Anna Dellyne talks about how much it meant to her to be on her own in New York when she was startin' her career" (128). Much to Toland's dismay, Ginger so invests in Anna Dellyne's friendship that she replaces him as Ginger's privileged confidante. "That's when a white rage swelled up inside of me," Toland says of Ginger when she is struggling with abortion and adoption. "She'd talked it all over with Anna Dellyne . . . even before she'd said anything to me!" (129).[4] But Cruse even more closely ties Anna Dellyne to the nurture and support of gay men and their subcultures, her son included. "Mama knows," Les tells Toland when he sees Anna Dellyne at Alleysax. "It's cool. She's always had 'sissyboy' friends" (47). The standard within her repertoire of songs is "Secret in the Air," the repeated lyrics of which serve as bookends for the novel and are preoccupied with the anxiety of closetedness: "Somethin' tells me there's a Secret in the Air . . . Nods and whispers among my sisters here and there . . . Awkward pauses . . . Eyes averted . . . Little warnings oddly worded . . . Can the truth be all that hard to bear? . . . Hell is livin' with a Secret in the . . . " (16, 189).

As a result of this personal history of homophilic investments, it is Anna Dellyne who attends to Sammy when he is beaten at the protest—"I'm gonna find somebody who'll get you to a doctor, sugar" (72)—and pointedly nudges Toland to accept his homosexuality through her extended anecdote regarding her friend Shelby, who, "bless his heart, was as gay as a peacock!" (132). His closetedness, Anna Dellyne patiently explains to Toland, proved

8.5. From *Stuck Rubber Baby*, by Howard Cruse. New York: Paradox Press, 1995. Copyright © 1995 Howard Cruse.

emotionally disastrous: "An' the crazy thing was, everybody respected Shelby when he was gay, but I can't think of a soul who liked him much when he was straight!" (133). Here again Cruse has a valorized character affirm the reassuring immutability of sexual identity. Shelby "wasn't geared toward bein' straight," Anna Dellyne opines. "To put it bluntly, Shelby bein' straight bordered on the ludicrous! Bein' gay, on the other hand, had always come natural to him" (133).

The final pages of *Stuck Rubber Baby* complete this idealization of the Peppers, who ultimately emerge as fully accepting surrogate parents for the orphaned Toland. Indeed, Cruse succumbs to clichéd didacticism here, having Anna Dellyne impart a final instruction to the hapless white boy. While looking up at flying birds, she instructs Toland:

Just come over here to the house now an' again when you've got time to kill. We'll come out on the stoop an' you can watch me sing for those birds in the yard! They don't come to review me for the newspapers! They don't cluster up in chairs to stare at me! An' they don't expect me to be anybody besides who I naturally am! Be like them, honey, an' I'll sing for you whenever you like. (205)

Through the telling of the narrative years later, Toland imaginatively arrives at precisely this psychic location, presumably again and again with each rehearsal of the tale in sync with the playing of Anna Dellyne's album. At this moment, shown in figure 8.5, the maternal black figure sings and consoles within Toland's memory, erasing in the penultimate panel the chill of winter, as denoted at the far left, and replacing it with the lush pastoral space of the African American South, an image so expansive that the single panel swells and bleeds to fill two pages (208–9).

With these manifold interrelated idealizations of African American culture, Cruse hazards at least two risks. The first is quite simply the misrepresentation of the complexity with which southern African Americans have assumed homophobic, homophilic, and/or neutral stances regarding homosexuality. Although, as mentioned, any number of scholarly assessments and creative works have sought to theorize and document this complexity of late, few surpass in balance and specificity E. Patrick Johnson's series of oral histories collected and published as *Sweet Tea: Black Gay Men of the South*. Highly skeptical of blanketing indictments of southern black homophobia, Johnson dutifully works to debunk the myth that "the black community (as if there is only one!) is more homophobic than white communities" (94), highlighting within the interviews and their introductory commentary the various ways that black gay southerners have in actuality often encountered the acceptance suggested in Cruse's novel. However, Johnson also refuses to ignore the strains of homophobia that have circulated or have begun to circulate of late in these enclaves, pointing, for instance, to the fact that "[b]lack religious leaders in particular are siding with white antigay conservatives in a way heretofore unseen in the black church—an institution that would, as one of my informants put it, 'shut down if all of the sissies exited'" (14). Unlike Cruse, Johnson states flatly from a position within these communities, "Most of the black people I know hold or express homophobic views, including members of my own family" (94), but then uses this acknowledgment to theorize in provocative ways how, for instance, "notions of black respectability manifest internalized homophobia" (15). These are the complexities erased by Cruse in his ostensibly supportive representation of southern African Americans

The second problematic aspect of these images is the presumably unintentional repositioning of African Americans into subservient roles to European Americans. Granted, these black figures may no longer be lacing Scarlett for the Wilkeses' ball, relieving Huck of his night shifts on the raft, or driving the bellowing Benjy past the Confederate statue, but Cruse's African

Americans are still almost without variation deployed in the caretaking of white identity—and white queer identity in particular—even as they actively seek racial equality within the protests of the Civil Rights Era. Although whites are consistently depicted here as flawed by racism, internalized and externalized homophobia, and indecision, and blacks are depicted as empowered agents of change, free from destructive biases, Cruse's narrative ironically channels this empowerment to the recuperation of healthy white identity. Virtually every black character—Dinah, Mabel, Marge, Effie, Shiloh, and especially Harland, Anna Dellyne, and Les Pepper—gains his or her most lasting stature within the novel through the mentoring of the white gay Toland Polk. If, as then-First Lady Hillary Rodham Clinton reminded a year after the publication of *Stuck Rubber Baby* in her citation of the African proverb that it takes a village to raise a child, Cruse perhaps unwittingly suggests through his novel that is takes a village of black folks to raise a white homosexual in the U.S. South. Readers thus stand to leave this otherwise engaging, even thrilling contribution to southern literary production with the gnawing anxiety that Cruse's novel, within its specific context of the Freedom Summer of 1964, ultimately cedes only limited freedom to African Americans.

For Cruse, however, these risks were and remain clearly worth taking. In recent interviews associated with the 2010 reissue of *Stuck Rubber Baby*, he has reminded of at least three historical moments of insurgent racism in the U.S. that he sees as interrelated: the civil rights era, when Cruse was himself becoming increasingly attuned to southern racial injustice; the Reagan era of the 1980s, when the ideas for his novel were germinating; and the current era of a backlash against a Barack Obama White House, when the novel is being reintroduced to the reading public. For Cruse, these latter two moments and their defining reemergences of racism demand a return to the images, narratives, and politics of the civil rights era, even if this return, like *Stuck Rubber Baby*, potentially oversimplifies the complexities of the previous time. He clarifies that three decades ago, "Reaganites were busy making veiled racism respectable again during the '80s. This was a big motivation for me to express my outrage about that by paying tribute to the movement's genuine heroes." Likewise, in the same conversation with interviewer Alonso Duralde, Cruse implies that in the current moment, "with what's been happening lately with the Tea Party and Rand Paul and the Arizona anti-immigrant law," it is imperative to return to these same "genuine heroes." His contemporary graphic protest novel no doubt features many of the same problematic aspects as those of *Uncle Tom's Cabin* and *Native Son* that so famously nettled James Baldwin a half-century ago, but, for Howard Cruse and no doubt others, at moments of insurgent racism, literary propaganda like *Stuck Rubber Baby* stands to retain its usefulness and power.

Notes

1. For greater biographical detail on Cruse, see www.howardcruse.com.

2. Although Cruse largely fictionalizes the civil rights-era South in the novel, he incontrovertibly fixes the historical setting through allusions to specific biographical figures: U.S. President John F. Kennedy (1); Emmett Till, the African American boy murdered in Mississippi in 1955 (2); civil rights leader Martin Luther King, Jr. (48); and James Chaney, Andrew Goodman, and Michael Schwerner, the trio of civil rights workers murdered in Mississippi in 1964 (201).

Cruse has also repeatedly clarified the specific autobiographical elements, offering, for instance, in an interview with Alonso Duralde: "The only literally autobiographical part was me/Toland getting our girlfriends pregnant in the course of trying to be straight. There are many other small moments, too. The draft induction pretty much happened to me. But many things in the book were made up or are my versions of other people's experiences."

3. Although Cruse does not consistently have all bleeds function in this fashion, the "excesses" of homoeroticism designated in this fashion recur systematically throughout the novel. The opening page of Chapter 18, for instance, features only two bleeds, both of which centralize queer content: an image of Sal Mineo, the actor from *Rebel without a Cause* who fuels Toland's homoerotic desires; and Toland's gratifying memory of sex with Les Pepper (151). To underscore the disruptiveness of this desire even further, Cruse also conspicuously tilts these two panels within a pattern of right angles.

4. Toland's anger at Anna Dellyne reminds just how distanced this white character and his biases are from Cruse and his as the writer/artist. At precisely the moment that Toland is most critical of African American culture, Cruse emphatically depicts it as sagaciously comforting.

Works Cited

Allison, Dorothy. *Bastard Out of Carolina*. 1992. New York: Plume, 1993. Print.

Camper, Cathy. Rev. of *Stuck Rubber Baby*. By Howard Cruse. *Lambda Literary*. 26 Jul 2010. Web. 12 August 2010.

Capote, Truman. *Other Voices, Other Rooms*. 1948. New York: Vintage, 1975. Print.

Cruse, Howard. *Howard Cruse Central*. Web. 12 Aug 2010. http://www.howardcruse.com/.

———. *Stuck Rubber Baby*. New York: Paradox Press, 1995. Print.

Duralde, Alonso. "Howard Cruse Talks 'Stuck Rubber Baby' and the Resurgence of Racism." *Queer Sighted*. 2 Jun 2010. Web. 12 August 2010.

Forster, E. M. *Maurice*. 1971. New York: Norton, 1987. Print.

Hobson, Fred. *But Now I See: The White Southern Racial Conversion Narrative.* Baton Rouge: Louisiana State UP, 1999. Print.

Johnson, E. Patrick. *Sweet Tea: Black Gay Men of the South.* Chapel Hill: U of North Carolina P, 2008. Print.

Kenan, Randall. "The Foundations of the Earth." *Let the Dead Bury Their Dead.* San Diego, New York, and London: Harcourt Brace, 1992. 49–72. Print.

———. *A Visitation of Spirits.* 1989. New York: Vintage, 2000. Print.

Kushner, Tony. Introduction. *Stuck Rubber Baby.* By Howard Cruse. New York: Paradox Press, 1995. i-iv. Print.

Lorah, Michael C. Rev. of *Stuck Rubber Baby.* By Howard Cruse. *Newsarama.com.* 8 Jul 2010. Web. 12 August 2010.

Sedgwick, Eve Kosofsky. *Epistemology of the Closet.* Berkeley and Los Angeles: U of California P, 1990. Print.

Smith, Barbara. "Homophobia: Why Bring It Up?" *The Lesbian and Gay Studies Reader.* Ed. Henry Abelove, Michèle Aina Barale, and David M. Halperin. New York and London: Routledge, 1993. 99–102. Print.

III.

The Horrors of the South

Of Slaves and Other Swamp Things

Black Southern History as Comic Book Horror

—Qiana J. Whitted

> Where I was before I came here, that place is real. It's never going away. Even if the whole farm—every tree and grass blade of it dies. The picture is still there and what's more, if you go there—you who never was there—if you go there and stand in the place where it was, it will happen again; it will be there for you, waiting for you.
> **—*Beloved,*** Toni Morrison

Of the many captivating changes that British comic book writer Alan Moore brought to his run on the DC Comics *Swamp Thing* series from 1984–1987, two are especially significant. He began by reconceptualizing the character's physiological structure as sentient plant matter, rather than as the mutated and monstrous human being first developed by Len Wein and Berni Wrightson in 1971.[1] All that was left of biochemist Alec Holland after the bio-restorative formula explosion plunged him into the swamp slime was *consciousness*; Moore revealed that the creature was little more than living vegetation in the shape of a man, one whose "humanity" operated like phantom limbs on a mossy, hulking frame. With this transformation, Moore's Swamp Thing could move freely about his environment by willfully allowing his body to die and reanimate anywhere plants thrive. Swamp Thing, while still an aberrant presence among his human neighbors, developed a more interdependent relationship with the land and became a deeply compassionate guardian of the Green.

Even as Moore altered Swamp Thing's form to make him more versatile, mobile, and intellectually complex, a second major modification fixed the character more firmly in space and time by establishing the comic's setting in and around present-day Houma, Louisiana. After determining "which swamps he was the Thing of," Moore told interviewer George Khoury that he researched the area's history and culture as well as its geographic features, "so that I could *use* the location, so that I could get interesting images or atmospheres from it" (Khoury 88). The results of Moore's research are vividly manifested through the artistic style of Stephen Bissette who, along with other artists including John Totleben, Alfredo Alcala, and Ron Randall, brought a darker, more intricate realism to the series.[2] It is through these collaborative efforts to convey the regional "atmospheres" of *Swamp Thing* that we see a more focused engagement with United States southern history and its landscape of horrors, including storylines that grapple with the region's legacy of slavery.

This essay takes a closer look at Moore's depiction of the South and the manner in which *Swamp Thing* comments upon social and cultural histories of racial oppression. My analysis will focus, in particular, on two issues from the "American Gothic" story arc that employ well-known comic book horror tropes to illustrate a tale of vengeful slaves and unrepentant masters: "Southern Change" (#41) and "Strange Fruit" (#42). These issues, published in 1985, adapt many of the formal and aesthetic qualities of early horror comics, yet my reading also connects the ideological thrust of *Swamp Thing*'s zombie tale with the post-civil rights era development of the "postmodern slave narrative"—a literary sub-genre similarly concerned with issues of historical recovery, cultural rebirth, and identity formation.[3] I maintain, for instance, that the concept of "rememory" that Toni Morrison develops in her 1988 novel, *Beloved*, is useful in framing an experiential understanding of the present as being physically and psychologically inscribed with traces of the past. Described by Caroline Rody as a trope that "postulates the interconnectedness of minds, past and present," rememory is used as both a verb and a noun in Morrison's novel to convey the lasting materiality of thoughts and emotional resonances. In *Beloved*, the main character regards places as entities stratified with "thought pictures" that, once formed by a person or an event, endure with an affective potency that can be perceived by others.[4]

These interminable "thought pictures" of rememory can also describe the way southern history is understood in *Swamp Thing*. Rather than simply exhuming the inarticulate monsters of *Tales from the Crypt*, Moore and Bissette complicate the discourse of zombification and spiritual possession to foreground a trauma that reaches beyond the grave. What is especially significant about Moore's unearthing of the past in "Southern Change" and "Strange Fruit," I argue, is the way in which the no-longer-human body of Swamp Thing is juxtaposed against the dehumanization of the enslaved blacks on the Robertaland Plantation. They, too, are objectified and physically bound to the land, and as their restless bones push up through the earth, they also clamor for freedom: "Freedom from this blighted soil, where buried grievances have poisoned the roots of the world and all its cultures. Freedom from these tainted lands that bear such sour fruit" ("Strange Fruit" 42:3). To be sure, Alec Holland's past as a white American scientist never included generations of forced slave labor. Still, the subtle narrative correlations that Moore employs to heighten Swamp Thing's encounter with the South ultimately furnish the material horrors of black enslavement with psychological resonance. Multiple codes of signification in the slave uprising coalesce around the discourses of nature, moral reciprocity, and memory that are central to *Swamp Thing*.

In his new form, as protector of the land and its residents, Swamp Thing must do more than empathize with the plight of the enslaved; his charge is to end the cycle of pain and injustice that will free the victimized blacks and allow them to rest in peace. His decision to destroy the Louisiana plantation in a fire that consumes most of the undead slaves reaffirms the idea of the southern past as a riotous, uncontrolled growth that must not be allowed to thrive in the present. Swamp Thing's experience demonstrates that like a stubborn weed, history's evils will be continually rehearsed—literally, in this case, by a TV crew using Robertaland to film a new southern soap opera—until the old growth is burned out. Such dangers are further manifest through anxieties over zombification, where "to succumb is to become, and once you have become a zombie, self is lost irrevocably to the other" (Boon 35). The comic makes creative use of metaphors of enslavement in zombie folklore to convey larger fears about the monstrous clamoring of history. As a result, while the story presupposes the importance of remembering the past, the conclusion's anti-pastoral uprooting also warns against the dangers of being consumed (and enslaved) by it.

My reading of *Swamp Thing* seeks to contribute to emerging conversations in African American cultural and literary studies about racial representation in modern American comics. The last decade has seen a preponderance of critically acclaimed comics that explore African American history and legend in an effort to *demystify*—to expose misconceptions and reveal new dimensions of black subjectivity. In works such as *Nat Turner* by Kyle Baker and *King: A Comics Biography of Martin Luther King, Jr.* by Ho Che Anderson, the comics medium doubles as an archive for the creative exploration of key moments, figures, and evolving ideologies.[5] The push toward realism is understandable given the way black people and other ethnic groups have often fared on the comics page. From indecipherable buffoons and minstrels to the infantilized primitives of jungle comics, black comic book characters have been utilized as projections of white fears and fantasies since the Depression Era. Comics that seek to represent the inner lives of black men and women in a more nuanced and visually complex manner help to counter prevailing racial stereotypes while depicting a view of the past that will set the record straight. In his essay, "Drawing on History in Recent African American Graphic Novels," Michael Chaney provides a cogent analysis of how texts like Anderson's *King* seek "to discover or invent a usable history" for African Americans through the comics medium (199). Yet even as the storytelling strategies in more comics cross genres and experiment with narrative and aesthetic innovations, their representations are largely mimetic, tethered to an understanding of coherent historical realities and often affirmed by "authenticating documents" (prefatory material, primary sources, bibliographies) appended to the comic.[6]

Swamp Thing's evocative departure from these trends begins with its adaptation of fantasy and horror conventions. Moore and Bissette employ what literary critic Timothy A. Spaulding describes as a "non-mimetic approach to slavery" that foregrounds the supernatural and otherworldly, fracturing space and time in a way that dismantles totalizing narratives of history in a manner not unlike novels such as *Flight to Canada* by Ishmael Reed (1976), *Kindred* by Octavia Butler (1979), *Middle Passage* by Charles Johnson (1990), and more recently, Edward P. Jones's *The Known World* (2003). At the same time, the relationship of "Southern Change" and "Strange Fruit" to the well-established *Swamp Thing* series offers an alternate mode of written and visual authentication, one that uses a fictitious monster and his physiological connection to the South as a conceptual metaphor for material and spiritual reconciliation. Readers are thusly urged to piece together intertextual historical, cultural, and artistic codes in order to effectively interpret the visual and verbal sequences of supernatural fantasy.

Bolstered by these claims, it is my hope that the strengths and weaknesses of *Swamp Thing*'s engagement with African American history can also serve as a framework for evaluating creative offspring such as the serial comic *Bayou* by Jeremy Love that advance the themes of Moore's postmodern slave narrative. Certainly, the mini-series *Hellblazer: Papa Midnite* by Mat Johnson and Tony Akins provides another, more direct connection with *Swamp Thing* and offers a northern view of black enslavement that complements Moore's bayou stories.[7] I am more interested, however, in how Love's swamp tale reimagines the grotesque landscape of southern horror and folklore in ways that allow for a more fully realized African American perspective, one in which the South's "duality of attraction and repulsion" is ever-present and inescapable (Harris 2).

American Gothic

The zombie uprising on the Louisiana plantation in "Southern Change" and "Strange Fruit" is best understood in the larger context of the "American Gothic" storyline in *Saga of the Swamp Thing* from 1985–1986. Described by Moore as "an odyssey through American horror," the series pays homage to the way Wein and Wrightson reformulated "stock cliché horror formats" in the original *Swamp Thing* by placing classic monsters such as werewolves, vampires, and zombies in contemporary contexts. Moore justified his choices by stating that, "if they could be made relevant to the world in which the readers existed, symbolic of things bigger than just another vampire story, another werewolf story, then that could yield rewards" (Khoury 93). The prelude to Moore's horror odyssey is "The Nukeface Papers" (#35–36) in which a traveling hobo, contaminated by the toxic chemicals from a Pennsylvania nuclear power plant, ends up fatally poisoning Swamp Thing with a touch of his hand. Having tracked the factory's waste dumping scheme to Louisiana, Nukeface's radioactive presence affects local residents, school children, and a pregnant woman's unborn baby, and yet the narrative makes clear that the story's villain is also a *victim*—a product of American corporate greed and carelessness. Bissette depicts a modern wasteland strewn with newspaper clippings that enumerate the human collateral damage of acid spills, gas leaks, and other hazardous waste accidents. Against such nameless forces, Swamp Thing, a plant elemental, is forced to find a new way to thrive and to safeguard his home and his loved ones.

Thus, "American Gothic" begins with a post-mortem Swamp Thing struggling to understand his regenerative powers. In his mind, Alec Holland's memories, his cognitive energies and desires, persist as the tangle of vines and earth that was once his "body" disintegrates completely. With the help of the British sorcerer and occult detective John Constantine, Swamp Thing acquires mastery over "instant transport" abilities and learns how to seek out a new corporeal home by sending his mind "out into . . . the Green" (36:18). Constantine's larger motive, however, is to enlist Swamp Thing's help in quelling the sudden increase of nightmarish eruptions across the country: underwater vampires in Illinois, werewolves in Maine, and zombies in Louisiana. As with his depiction of Nukeface, Moore conveys the circumstances of each monster's existence so as to invite Swamp Thing's empathy and in turn, the reader's understanding. In the issues "Still Waters" (#38) and "Fish Story" (#39), we meet vampires of the Midwest that had mutated and formed an underwater community after being trapped by Swamp Thing's own attempt to cleanse the town of the fanged creatures two years earlier.[8]

Moore exploits the contrast between the grisly images of the vampire's parasitic craving for blood and the voice of their domestic yearnings: "Why must we be destroyed? We asked for so very little . . . Only a home that we could call our own [. . .] and a safe place to raise our children" (39:19).

Likewise, in "The Curse" (#40), the werewolfism of a housewife underscores the collective silencing and denigration of women. The controversial issue places the werewolf folk legend—with its central icon of the moon—in concert with the main character's menstrual cycle. Citing the antiquated tradition of isolating "tainted" women during their menses in the tale of the "Red Lodge," the story follows a woman similarly alienated by the objectifying delusions of pornography, sanitary napkins ads, and a society in which "the Red Lodge is everywhere" (40:17). Swamp Thing arrives in the New England town just as the wife has transformed into a werewolf and is lashing out at her abusive husband in a suicidal rampage. At the end of the comic, when the werewolf has transformed back into a woman, Swamp Thing is the one who lifts her body to its final resting place beneath the moon. Stories such as "The Curse" ultimately reveal that Swamp Thing's strength lies in his compassion; he uses force defensively and each time he is poisoned, eaten, burned, or killed, the solutions to these problems lie in the creative use of his own body as an instrument of release. Ironically his heroism is misunderstood by the scene's bystanders who see him only as a monster—the "it" that must be cast out: "Oh, God, it's got a woman! Why doesn't somebody do something?" (40:22). The onlookers' fears in Maine extend to Swamp Thing's return to the South where he moves, reluctantly and regretfully, from the liminal spaces of the swamp land to a Louisiana plantation's heart of darkness.[9] The "American Gothic" story arc, with its emphasis on Swamp Thing's character development, aids in what Charles Hatfield refers to as "the invocation of learned competencies" (135) that will allow readers to decode the approaching analogies between the title character and the undead slaves in "Strange Fruit."

Cultural Scripts

Interestingly enough, Swamp Thing has encountered the ghosts of slavery before in Wein and Wrightson's original *Swamp Thing* run. In issue #10 from 1974, Swamp Thing saves the life of "Auntie" Bellum, an elderly black woman. She tells him the story of Black Jubal, a proud slave whose spirit came back from the dead to take his revenge on a sadistic master for sexually abusing

9.1. From *Saga of the Swamp Thing* #41 (October 1985). Written by Alan Moore with art by Stephen Bissette and John Totleben. Copyright © 1985 DC Comics.

an enslaved woman named Elsbeth. Soon after hearing the tale, Swamp Thing is ambushed in a nearby graveyard by his nemesis Anton Arcane, who threatens to steal and possess his body. Arcane boasts of his plans to enslave humanity and declares himself "the undisputed master of the world!" (10:15). With each reference to slavery, the graveyard winds become a "muffled cry of outrage and despair" until, in the climactic moment, Black Jubal and his cohort materialize from the spirit world to help Swamp Thing escape. The next morning Swamp Thing goes looking for the old woman and finds only Auntie Bellum's crumbling tombstone engraved with her full name: Elsbeth Bellum. While the title of the issue—"The Man Who Would Not Die"—presumably refers to Arcane's synthetic resurrection, an alternative reading of the title confers heroic manhood and spiritual immortality upon Black Jubal and underscores his determination to prevent *any* creature in *any* time from being enslaved as a "thing." Moore and Bissette expand upon the model established by Wein and Wrightson by highlighting the existential implications of Swamp Thing's being and by unearthing a toxic maze of oppression and violence in the South that is "concealed beneath the world's skin" like restless bones in a graveyard (41:15) (see figure 9.1).

"Southern Change" opens with a flashback to 1842 in which the plantation's white owner, Wesley Jackson, has just ordered the flaying of an enslaved black man for becoming romantically involved with his wife. Over a century later in the swamps outside present-day Houma, we find Swamp Thing and Abby ruminating over the frailties of human nature as a TV crew has set up their cameras at this same plantation to film a new soap opera with celebrity stars and a cast of local black residents as slaves. Abby remarks on the irony: "So, like, all these descendants of liberated slaves are earning good money by becoming slaves again!" (41:4). Over the course of a few weeks—notably, on days marked by Voodoo ceremonies and feasts—the actors on the set become possessed by the restless ghosts of the area until the night of the climactic "zombie walk" when the plantation slaves rise up from their graves to take deadly revenge on the master that executed them before being killed himself.

In his discussion of an earlier *Swamp Thing* storyline that involved incest, Moore joked, "No offense intended to any Southern readers down there, of course; I realize that these comics stereotypes must wear thin after a while" (Khoury 90). The same could be said of the stock characterizations in "Southern Change." Comics stereotypes and generalizations about the South abound in the story, yet the self-referential absurdity of the TV show—along with other popular culture references to *Gone With the Wind* and Jimi Hendrix's song "Voodoo Child"—also help to complicate these

9.2. From *Saga of the Swamp Thing* #41 (October 1985). Written by Alan Moore with art by Stephen Bissette and John Totleben. Copyright © 1985 DC Comics.

regional simplifications. No only do the actors and their indulgent squabbles call attention to the performative nature of southern racial politics, but the soap opera's frivolous approach to its historical subject also suggests a modern disregard for the profound psychic consequences of enslavement. The celebrities behave as if their status, professional training, and modern experience will distance them from their antebellum "characters." Once the actors assume their roles however, they become spiritually inhabited by the past: the black actor, Billy Carlton, who expresses resentment and anger over "this Stepin' Fetchit stuff" (41:9), ends up kneeling and cowering like his enslaved counterpart, while Richard Deal, the sympathetic liberal white actor who once complained that "thinking like a racist is so difficult" (41:13), transforms into Wesley Jackson in an instant.

Consider how in figure 9.2 the show's script, rolled up in Deal's hand in one panel, becomes in the next a whip—an instrument of force that acts as a metonym for a different kind of cultural "script" in which the roles of black and white southerners are defined by socially constructed racial hierarchies and institutional economies of power and production. Moore places these cyclical patterns of racial violence and oppression in concert with a discourse of tainted rebirth—of people and communities, of landscapes and spaces. Like the postmodern slave narrative, the *Swamp Thing* story assumes control of the historical record by employing "elements of the fantastic to occupy the past, the present, and in some cases, the future simultaneously" (Spaulding 5). The show's director, unaware that the actors are possessed, praises Carlton for improvising new lines, not realizing that he and his counterparts are following a script that has already been written into the collective "rememory" of the region. In other scenes, the shift between present and past is more understated; for instance, Carlton's transformation is indicated only by the way his shirt changes color from yellow to white (41:10–11). Deal's eyes shift from blue to brown (42:13). The local black residents who are hired to work on the film are also affected as they abandon their duties to begin silently preparing ceremonial offerings on the plantation grounds (41:16). This temporal schism is further marked in the comic narrative by parallel and mirrored images including the distorted reflection of Robertaland in the pond surrounding the plantation (41:9).

Visual codes such as these demonstrate the way in which the narrative's subtext is further communicated by the form, artistic style, and design of *Swamp Thing*. Bissette frames the episode in measured, symmetrical panel arrangements in keeping with the cyclical nature of the plot and the dialectical tensions between past and present, life and death. By contrast, in and around Robertaland, the plantation's gothic atmospheres are conveyed through overlapping panels that are often set at odd, unsteady angles (like tombstones) to intensify the temporal layers within a single moment. Indeed, time is set by a different calendar in "Southern Change"—through date stamps that alert the reader to Afro-Haitian ceremonies from July's *Feast of Papaogou* to August's *Mystere L'Orient* and through the intricate pictorial marginalia of Voodoo symbols, sacred animals, and somber black faces and skulls that surround each section. At times, the racial primitivism suggested by the artistic team's depiction of Voodoo appears at odds with Moore's efforts to reshape the cultural trope. Consider, for instance, the cover art of issue #41 that depicts an image of Swamp Thing as a small, mossy Voodoo doll stabbed with pins. Clutching the doll is a black hand with sharp, yellowed fingernails and a crude bracelet of teeth around the wrist. It is an image that does not correspond to the events within the story itself—not unusual in comic books where the cover art is illustrated separately—yet the Afro-Haitian iconography, rendered as a "frightening projection of white cultural fears and obsessions" (Rossetti 146), shapes the reader's first encounter with the narrative nonetheless.

Indeed, the cover is the gateway to the "clash and collaboration of different codes of signification" comics readers are compelled to parse in order to extract meaning from the work (Hatfield 41). Part of the knowledge base Moore and Bissette draw upon is the fraught history of Voodoo and zombification in horror comics since the 1940s, iconic images that were used to convey the hidden, racialized terrors lurking within the "everyman." With titles like "Voodoo Death" and "Drawn and Quartered," series such as the popular *Tales from the Crypt* often followed naïve white Americans to Haiti where they stumble across midnight rituals of "chanting, screaming natives" in the jungle (*Tales from the Crypt* 23:2) and seek out witch doctors to purchase Voodoo talismans. These earlier horror comics emphasized the soulrobbing power of possession as well as the dangers of using "black magic" to circumvent societal norms and moral codes. Stories like "Voodoo Death" brought the primitive mysticism of jungle comics to the suburban homes and city streets of post-WWII America and used the threat of zombification to underscore fears of an internalized Other.

Decades after the Comics Code and its prohibitions against the "walking dead" led to the demise of series such as *Tales from the Crypt*, *Swamp Thing*'s Len Wein wrote stories featuring Brother Voodoo for Marvel's *Strange Tales* and *Tales from the Zombie*. These and other 1970s comics employed horror tropes in a manner similar to popular "zombie apocalypse" films such as George A. Romero's *Night of the Living Dead* (1968). As mindless hordes of decaying human beings, the incoherent mobs in these stories are intent only on destruction. In her study of Romero's work, Kim Paffenroth points out that zombies "straddle the line between living and dead" in a way that precludes survivors from grieving and moving on (12). Humans are forced to battle the animated corpses in these stories in order to remain alive and keep from becoming zombies themselves. Any apparent resemblance between the slow-moving dead in *Swamp Thing* and Romero's malevolent mobs (or the soulless "Zuvembies"[10] of Marvel Comics) aids in the expression of a familiar horror aesthetic, much like the Voodoo doll cover art.

But just as Charles Chesnutt relied on his nineteenth-century audience's knowledge of Uncle Remus tales to distinguish his own post-bellum narratives of slavery in *The Conjure Woman*,[11] so too are the monsters in "American Gothic" distinguished through the reworking of horror formulas that, as Bissette has stated, aim to "shatter the old 'EC Comics' mold" (Weiland). At times the zombies in *Swamp Thing* appear to lack a sense of consciousness, but in other instances they think and discern. They seek justice, rather than the kind of manipulation suggested by the image of Swamp Thing as a Voodoo doll. Moreover, the comic's visual and verbal elements work together to break down what Kevin Alexander Boon refers to as the dialect of "the human self and the monstrous other" by unearthing the interior lives and longings of the slaves in the story (34).[12] By definition, of course, zombies *are* enslaved creatures, controlled corpses that have not been permitted to rest. Yet Moore's zombies are bound not merely to a single master named Wesley Jackson, but also to a vicious master narrative—what Swamp Thing refers to as "emotions . . . so fierce and caustic . . . that they burned their imprint into the soil itself" (42:5).

Return of the Repressed

What, then, can we learn from Moore's adaptation of zombie horror in relation to cultural scripts of racial oppression and violence in *Swamp Thing*? Spaulding has argued that postmodern slave narratives such as Morrison's *Beloved* "reject realism," in part, as a way of conveying "a political act of narration designed to reshape our view of slavery and its impact on our cultural condition" (3–4). In "Southern Change," the same kind of historical defamiliarization is initiated through the first panel of Moore's story in which the reader, entombed in darkness, is repositioned from the perspective of the dead. "What do the dead people think about?" the narrator asks, and later as the images move up through the earth and into a view of the plantation: ". . . and which voices are the loudest?" (41:1). Readers knowledgeable of EC Comics-style horror may already be familiar with this kind of heightened identification with the monstrous Other. Yet Moore tempers this narrative strategy with a more empathetic transference, not unlike the memorable cross-racial twist in the last panel of the *Weird Fantasy* tale, "Judgment Day."[13]

The technique is revisited at the start of "Strange Fruit"—with its nod to the anti-lynching song—when we are placed inside a coffin with a skeleton that is unable to "sleep." Readers follow the corpse as it rises from the grave in a two-page spread, sliced by vertical panels as shown in figure 9.3. In this pivotal scene, enslaved beings rise and reunite in an alternate history of the American South, "the history of courageous resistance and love and the expressive cultural practices of the slave community" (Rushdy 139). Skeleton lovers kiss, while others lift decomposed children into the air in jubilation. The narrator observes:

After the first exuberance of the resurrection had abated, they quietly discussed what they wanted to do most, now that they were alive again.

9.3. From *Saga of the Swamp Thing* #42 (November 1985). Written by Alan Moore with art by Stephen Bissette, John Totleben, and Ron Randall. Copyright © 1985 DC Comics.

Some wanted a job, and a home, and a right to vote. Some of the women wanted new clothes and some of the men joked about that. As always, there was an unimaginative majority who only wanted revenge ... but they all wanted liberty, that much was unanimous. (42:3)

These black men and women may be the "strange" fruit of the title, but as with his modification of vampires and werewolves, Moore's so-called zombies resist the dehumanization of the monster trope by voicing familial affections, speaking "quietly," and joking about new clothes. They embrace one another after emerging from their coffins and exhibit enough reason in these moments to deliberate upon their next step. Indeed, to the extent that the gratuitous violence of multi-ethnic zombie mobs has been used to signify "the senseless brutality of racism, a hideous punishment for its continued presence in our supposedly 'civilized' society" (Paffenroth 18), the behavior of the zombies in *Swamp Thing* also underscores the image of black Americans as desiring subjects in their never-ending struggle for liberation. In these moments, Moore opens up a space for a different kind of script—what Rushdy, quoting James C. Scott, refers to as "the 'hidden transcripts' of resistance to be found in those subordinated experiences of enslaved peoples" (227). As history's repressed victims return, it is *their* voices that are the loudest. Just as Swamp Thing's body of plant matter—the "*not* Alec Holland"—becomes an unexpected province of humanity, so are the Robertaland slaves more than decomposing monsters, more than objectified flesh. The brutality of the past prevents them from cultivating similar powers of "instant transport" however, leaving them spiritually bound to the earth without the ability to pass on.

It is important to note that Swamp Thing models a mutually productive relationship with the land and the life cycles of the natural world throughout the story. Early in the narrative he lifts a dying bird from the ground and whispers to the creature, "just let go . . . of the flesh . . . of the pain" before crushing its remains into his own body. He reassures Abby that he only wants to "absorb its riches . . . as it decays. . . . Death . . . shall nourish life . . . and nothing . . . shall be wasted" (41:12). The brief scene underscores the extent to which the idea of death as nourishment for the living is actually turned on its head in Robertaland's old slave graveyard. As the zombie walk comes to a halt at the steps of the mansion, time and space collapse, and one of the black men declares:

> The pain . . . cannot remain in the past . . . or hidden beneath the soil. . . . That which is buried . . . is not gone. That which is planted . . . will grow . . . [. . .] We want our freedom . . . and if freedom is not given . . . then we must all . . . repeat this night . . . of pain and suffering until freedom comes . . . even if that takes forever . . . . (42:14–15)

The hallucinating actor, whose flesh Wesley Jackson now inhabits, raises a shotgun to replay the massacre of 1842 once again. Swamp Thing steps in the path of the gun and with the words, "I will not . . . allow . . . this evil . . . to continue!" uses his own body as kindling to destroy the house and burn out the roots of a "bad tree" (42:18). The image recalls the banishment of the parasitic ghost woman in *Beloved* whose embodiment of the past was prevented from making a home among the living. As one outraged neighbor in Morrison's novel reflects: "The future was sunset; the past something to leave behind. And if it didn't stay behind, well, you might have to stomp it out. Slave life; freed life—every day was a test and a trial. . . . Nobody needed a grown-up evil sitting at the table with a grudge" (Morrison 257).

The same logic drives Swamp Thing's decision to destroy the "grown-up evil" at the southern estate. In Swamp Thing's first encounter with slave ghosts, Black Jubal rescued him; now in Moore's version, his body's "liberating flame" frees the enslaved men and women. Zombie tales have often depicted the undead as being afraid of fire, yet in their first and last willful act, many of the walking cadavers "embrace" the flame as freedom in an ironic reversal of southern lynching practices. And as Robertaland burns, Swamp Thing makes a personal connection: "The fire consumes me," he reflects, "For an instant . . . I recall . . . another man . . . who burned. His fear . . . his suffering . . . welling up from my borrowed memory . . . Holland" (42:18). Shortly after the blaze, amidst the blackened timber and bones, emerges the thrilling "SLUPP GWIP PWOC" of green shoots pushing up through the ground and taking shape as the reconstituted Swamp Thing (42:19).

As stated previously, the stories in the "American Gothic" thread develop alongside Swamp Thing's growing realization of his own abilities as a creature of the Green. The first time Swamp Thing reincarnates himself, after being poisoned by Nukeface, he struggles to come to terms with an identity that is divided between physical states: Man and vegetable. Human and nonhuman. Living and dead. "I . . . am. But . . . where am I? What . . . am I? The soil about me . . . rich and wet . . . half-swallowing me. I recognize . . . its texture. I . . . am in . . . the swamp. I am . . . the swamp thing. How strange . . . I thought that I . . . was dead" (37:2). His hybridized existence is not merely a common characteristic of monsters from the mythological Minotaur to the modern horror film zombie (Paffenroth 7), but also a living manifestation of how such divisions can be productively negotiated. In "Southern Change" and "Strange Fruit," Moore's fictitious creature—a monster whose flesh is literally composed of the roots and plant growth of the South—models the process of Duboisian "double-consciousness" through which African American slaves and their descendants are compelled to see themselves by an oppressive social and economic system. The intergenerational legacy of black suffering surfaces again and again like Holland's "borrowed memory" to inform and overshadow the newfound potential of the present. As Swamp Thing straddles the boundaries of declarative subject ("I am") and object ("the Swamp *Thing*"), his reality parallels the possibilities and limitations of the slave's condition.

Oddly enough, this parallel may explain why one of the zombies refuses the cleansing flames of the plantation and finds comfort in a movie-theater ticketing booth in a town in Arkansas called "Springville." Speaking with the same stilted dialogue that Swamp Thing uses, the black man delights in the free popcorn and asks, "This . . . is my box and my own . . . little window?" (42:23). Could it be that just as the Swamp Thing finds comfort in returning to his home in the swamp, the dislocated zombie is reassured by the confinement of a brand-new "box" surrounded by Hollywood monsters and the familiar "scripts" of Voodoo horror films? How are we to reconcile the irony and humor of this closing scene that juxtaposes the movie posters of *Night of the Living Dead*[14] with the mournful face of a discombobulated elderly black man in the window? There are places where the narrative suffers from not devoting more energy to developing individual African American characters and this epilogue, I would argue, is one of them. Moore, himself, has called the zombie issues "his least favorite," saying only that "nobody's fault but mine—I didn't do a very good job" (Khoury 93). Perhaps the conclusion's inconsistencies in tone and character development are part of the reason why.

Likewise, despite the poignancy and richness of the collective black voices that rise from the grave in *Swamp Thing*, the *living* African American characters remain exasperatingly one-dimensional, adhering far too closely to stereotypical images of the angry black militant and the mammy figure. When one of Abby's co-workers, a heavy-set, dark-skinned cook named Alice, encounters her dead father among the zombie mob, she does not rejoice, but collapses in tears over how she feels "all ugly and old" (42:11). The black actor Billy Carlton—who seems to speak only in angry platitudes when he is not snorting cocaine—is rendered incoherent and terror-stricken by the end of the tale. If we recall Swamp Thing's understanding of "buried mazes" beneath the earth that "still determine the paths . . . of those who walk above" (41:15), then one might argue that characters like Billy and Alice are among those destined to remain trapped and broken wanderers. Such is the all-consuming power of the master narrative that enslaves generation after generation. Spaulding reminds us that, "far from the romanticized notion of individuality, postmodern slave narratives depict freedom as contested and wrought with conflict" (21). Likewise, the careless naiveté of Abby's remark in the aftermath—"They'll block out what happened here and get on with their lives. They'll be okay" (42:19)—serves to reinforce the provisional nature of Swamp Thing's efforts. In light of Moore's strangely unresolved ending, one can't help but wonder if there is any land below the Mason-Dixon Line not touched by "old and cherished horrors" (42:11).

Blood and Beauty in Jeremy Love's *Bayou*

Of *Swamp Thing*, artist Stephen Bissette has said that "if we named any of the best horror comics from any particular era, they're drawing from earlier work. Part of this is the fact that the more resonant archetypes are always re-embraced and reinvented to suit a new generation's needs" (Weiland). Such is also the case with *Bayou*, a serial comic by writer and artist Jeremy Love that re-embraces and reinvents the archetypes of black southern folklore in a way that deftly advances the themes of Alan Moore's postmodern slave narrative. The comic debuted in 2007 through Zuda Comics, the webcomics division of DC Comics, and was the first Zuda publication to make the transition from the web to print in 2009. While *Swamp Thing* summons forth the southern past through a zombie netherworld, *Bayou* constructs a rich parallel reality where talking bloodhounds wear the hats of the Confederacy, Brer Rabbit works on a chain gang, and the dead guide a young black girl named Lee Wagstaff on a journey through the Jim Crow looking-glass. Love's aesthetic choices are particularly attentive to the paradox of pleasure and pain that distinguishes the Deep South, once characterized by James Baldwin as "the great, vast, brooding, welcoming and bloodstained land, beautiful enough to astonish and break the heart" (qtd. in Harris 2). Representations of racial violence and terror unfold alongside an appreciation for black southern culture and networks of community.

Lee's companion is the title character, a blues-singing monster named Bayou, who aids her in a quest to rescue a young white friend and save her own father from the lynch rope. Bayou's immense stature, gentle manner, and green skin connect him to hybrid monsters like Swamp Thing whose physiology acts as an extension of their natural surroundings. Both creatures draw on their inextricable relationship with the land as they shift grudgingly from observer to plot participant. Love's "black" swamp thing is considerably more implicated in Lee's mission, however; helping the young girl means defying the oppressive power structures of "Dixie," an alternate world in the comic "formed from the blood, war, and strife that plagued the South" (Arrant). There are even indications in the early issues that Bayou was once enslaved and forcibly separated from his own children, given that a fear of their master—Dixie's unseen "Bossman" General Bog—hinders his every action. At one point, Bayou laments his decision to involve himself in Lee's problems and in response she, arms thrown wide, shouts back:

> *You kiddin' me!* You a damn fool and I'm sick of your whining! I'm the little girl, I'm the one that should be whining and crying, not you! Look at you! You a big ol' monster with arms like tree trunks! You can whup just about anything in the whole wide world! Watchoo got to be cared of some Bossman fo? If I was big as you, I'd be the Bossman! (1:149)

Bayou's knowledge of the area, his brawn, and even his skill in hoodoo magic are an asset to Lee, but it is clear that what he lacks is her audacity and courage—however untested it may be—to see Bog's master narrative for the calculated invention it is. Their exchange reveals the enduring psychological wounds of racial oppression that, in keeping with the non-mimetic speculation of postmodern slave narrative, seem to mar even the mythical potential of black folk legend. Why else, the narrative seems to ask, would "a big ol' monster with arms like tree trucks" have a back covered with scars and whip marks?

In turn, *Bayou* draws the reader into a fictitious Mississippi town during the 1930s by drawing on a set of intertextual codes and character-driven allusions that depart substantially from Moore's modification of zombie horror in *Swamp Thing*. Patrick Morgan's coloring and Love's artwork—which initially resemble a children's cartoon with warm tones, simple iconography, and traditional panel arrangements—diverge meaningfully from the story's darker themes. In an interview, Love remarks upon his investment in the comic as an act of recuperation:

> I've always been interested in the mythology of America. The South, in particular, seems like a haunted place. You have this region that is covered with blood, but produces so much beauty. I never really felt connected to African mythology until I started reading Joel Chandler Harris's Uncle Remus tales. Seeing how elements of African mythology were interwoven with American folklore was the spark. What led me to the Uncle Remus tales was Disney's *Song of the South*, a film I've always had mixed feelings about. I felt I as an African American creator could reclaim that mythology. (Arrant)

What results is a kind of blues comics pastiche, not unlike the prose of Zora Neale Hurston or the mixed-media collages of Romare Bearden that juxtapose "blood" and "beauty" by merging incidents such as the murder of Emmett Till with African and Greek mythology, "Uncle Remus" tales by Joel Chandler Harris, and Lewis Carroll's *Alice in Wonderland*. Few reviewers explicitly acknowledge a kinship between *Bayou* and *Swamp Thing*; nevertheless, I maintain that the pioneering horror series also offers an attractive interpretive framework for Love's work. Understanding Moore and Bissette's strategies in the comics medium allows us to better assess how *Bayou* amplifies the horrors of the commonplace through the fantastic, personifies southern landscapes, and invokes the legacy of African American struggle through spatial and temporal rifts of "rememory." While *Bayou* does not take place during the antebellum era, it follows the lead of other postmodern slave narratives in furnishing "a political act of narration designed to reshape our view of slavery and its impact on our cultural condition" (Spaulding 4).

The politics of *Bayou* emanate, of course, from a preoccupation with place. Of special interest to Love are the social and psychological meanings attached to negotiated spaces and borders in places such as segregated facilities of Charon, Mississippi, or the delta land on which the sharecropper Calvin Wagstaff and his daughter live and work (but will never own). As Trudier Harris notes, "mental shackles control black bodies as aggressively as did legal sanctions in the South. In history and literature, therefore, the physical space of the South combines with the psychological implications of being on southern territory" (4). Even in the parallel reality, the comic's swamp creature is trapped in a maze of boundaries—Bayou insists the woods in Dixie aren't "safe" (1:95), but laments that the Bossman won't allow him to leave the swamp (1:112). The complications of space extend also to the murdered body of Lee's friend, a young black boy named Billy Glass whose death sets the narrative plot in motion. Later in the story, the reader is relocated behind the cruel, lifeless frame of a lynching postcard to see young Billy in the spirit world, refusing to part with the body he once inhabited as it is mutilated and abandoned in the Yazoo River. "It's my body!" Billy screams, "I ain't leavin' it to rot in the bayou!" (2:73). In this scene, which resonates keenly with Swamp Thing's meditations on the cycle of life and death, *Bayou*'s angel/ancestor figure, Mother Sista, consoles Billy by reminding him: "Honey, that body is just a vessel. If you cling to it, bad things will happen" (2:74).

However it is Love's heroine, Lee Wagstaff—uniquely endowed with the ability to access haunted places—who is situated at the center of *Bayou*. Lee remarks early on, "the Bayou is a bad place. Ain't nuthin' good ever happened around there" (1:4). Indeed, before Billy's body was dumped there, Lee's

9.4. From *Bayou*, by Jeremy Love. New York: DC Comics, 2009. Copyright © Gettosake.

mother drowned when a storm washed her into the river. Her best friend Lily goes missing after being gobbled up by a monster named Cotton-Eyed Joe that emerges from its depths. The swamp mud forms tiny hands to grab Lily's feet, while butterflies and ladybugs begin to consume her flesh, but Lee somehow manages to pass in and out of the Bayou unharmed (1:40). When her father has been falsely accused of kidnapping Lily, Lee marches past the town's Confederate monument to the sheriff's office where a gathered crowd of angry white men glare, spit, and wait for nightfall. Most importantly, Lee is gifted with a kind of second sight and appears to be the only human who can see Billy's spectral aspect, glowing with amber-colored wings. With Billy's help she continues to fearlessly negotiate unsafe spaces in her search for Lily and discovers the vast interdependency between the town of Charon and the surreal landscapes of Dixie. "What we do here makes a difference to our fleshly brother and sisters," Mother Sista divulges to Billy. "We can throw their world in chaos if we do battle here. . . . That Girl comin' done changed everything" (2:79–80).

Lee dissolves an even greater boundary after she is fatally injured in a forest trap and brought back to life by Bayou's blood and folk healing. In the

9.5. From *Bayou*, by Jeremy Love. New York: DC Comics, 2009. Copyright © Gettosake.

purgatorial state shown in figure 9.4, she learns of her own death from Billy. But after being told that monster's life-saving hoodoo won't last, she asks Billy how much more time she has on earth:

> "Few days at best."
> "Daddy and Lily . . ."
> "HA HA HA You got a few days to live and all you can think about is some damn white girl. Whatta bunch of horse s%$*!"
> "Hush Billy Glass! If you woulda learnt to watch your mouth I wouldn't ta had to fish you out that water!"
> "That ain't right to say Lee. Ain't right at all. What them peckerwoods did to me was horrible. Just horrible. And they finna do the same to your Daddy if'n you don't get your black a#@ movin'!" (1:108)

Lee is not a zombie and she is not quite the walking dead. But she is a kind of threshold figure that embodies the liminality of the postmodern black subject in her ability to bridge the literal and the allegorical (there is even some indication that Lee's special abilities may stem from the mysteries surrounding her deceased mother, a sultry blues woman nicknamed "Tar Baby" whose full identity has not yet been revealed). Lee is armed both with a shotgun and a child's doll; she doesn't think twice about wringing a chicken's neck for dinner (1:24) and boosting Brer Rabbit's leg irons (2:85), but she feels self-conscious about what Mrs. Rabbit calls the "nappy mess" of hair on her head (2:21). In her traveling sack, Lee carries the ax of an ancestor descended from runaway slaves and Choctaw Indians as a kind of talisman, while the spelling of her name signals the famous leader of the Confederate Armies in the Civil War (1:51).

History intrudes further into Lee's present through breathless moments of "rememory" that are not quite dreams or flashbacks, but material traces of the past. In the haunting scene shown in figure 9.5, Lee stumbles through the woods into a cluster of trees sagging with the lynched bodies of half a dozen black men and women in various stages of decomposition (1:48). Golden butterflies and mosquitoes at dusk frame the interplay of life and death in a single splash panel. Man and nature converge, as the gnarled roots of a tree in the foreground resemble fingers and knuckles, while the feet of the dead body in the center of the panel appear to be rooted in the soil. It is clear that what Lee has stumbled upon is not a single moment, but a temporal disloca-tion of borrowed memories not unlike the overlapping panels of "Southern Change." A chorus of unattributed voices calling her name intensifies the visual convergence. And Lee is not the only one whose actions are guided by someone else's "thought pictures" in the story. In other scenes, Bayou strug-gles with flashbacks of his own in which he sees a young African girl named Nandi and a pair of children with shackles around their necks speaking in Lee's voice (1:114, 140).

Such visual and verbal codes allow *Bayou* to signify southern history not merely as a series of cultural scripts as *Swamp Thing* suggests, but as a microcosm of competing fictions the reader is forced to negotiate. A staged lynching photograph, inflammatory newspaper accounts of Billy's so-called assault, and Calvin Wagstaff's crimes—even the crude police sketch of Lee's father—are all exposed as cruel inventions and tall tales (1:77). On the other hand, in *Bayou*'s parallel world, we encounter "real-life" trickster rabbits that frequent juke joints, greedy Golliwogs, and a villain disguised as a flock of carnivorous "Jim Crows" (1:130). This is how Love defamilarizes traditional representations of history, by bringing such fictional characters and their mythical exploits to life in the hyperrealistic setting of Dixie even as their actions underscore the age-old power structures (and survival strategies) that drive mid-century American racial politics.

So we might read Lee's quest to find Brer Rabbit and confront General Bog, then, as a journey *into* master narrative, through the totalizing story once used as the taproot of American chattel slavery and maintained to control men like her father after Emancipation. Recall Swamp Thing's observation of the crumbling Louisiana plantation in "Strange Fruit": "And even though . . . its design is long since buried . . . It still guides the footsteps . . . of those who tread . . . the world above" (42:5). Lee and Bayou retrace Dixie's "buried mazes," breaking down one precarious boundary after the next and unraveling the authoritative fictions of southern oppression. And in one ironic twist, the young protagonist is confronted with just how fragile and indeterminate the stories that shape her worldview can be. "I sprung you from that chain gang cuz' I needs yo' help," Lee explains to Brer Rabbit after finally catching up with him later in the series (2:96). The anti-climactic exchange proceeds as follows:

> "Lost my best friend and if I don't find her . . . my daddy will die. I now seein' you keep all the stories in dis wide world. I was thinking you can dig up a story out yo' noggin that tells you where my friend is."
> "HA HA HA HA! You, Ha Ha Ha, you fools came all the way here on the count of my stories? HA HA HA!! I lost dem stories in a dice game in Nawlins to Brer Fox!"(2:97)

Like *Swamp Thing* three decades earlier, *Bayou* effectively challenges the notion of the South as a closed, unified narrative by manipulating the representation of African American history and memory through speculative genres. These comics put forth a reading of the past as a place in which "its boundaries are fluid and provisional, its meaning plural and in play, circulating through the conscious and unconscious intentions of the writer, the reader, and culture" (Geyh xxii). Further manifestations of this open, fraught textuality can be found in hybrid identities of creatures like Swamp Thing, Bayou, the zombie mobs of the Robertaland Plantation, and even the protean child, Lee Wagstaff. Through these characters, the postmodern slave narrative's struggle to reclaim the past, to explore the turmoil between the Self and the Other, and to unveil the deep consequences of an interdependent world are given new life in horror and fantasy comics.

Notes

1. In his introduction to the trade paperback collection, *Swamp Thing: Dark Genesis*, writer Len Wein discusses the creative origin of the Swamp Thing character as he first appeared in DC's *House of Secrets* #92 and later in his own titled series. The issues written

by Alan Moore as part of the second run were titled *Saga of the Swamp Thing* from #21–#45. With issues #46, the series reverted back to its original title, *Swamp Thing*.

2. Bissette and Totleben joined the series in 1983, a year before Moore was brought on as writer.

3. By using A. Timothy Spaulding's term, "postmodern slave narrative," my conceptual framework highlights contemporary texts that experiment with form, narrative voice, genre, and other "postmodern aesthetics and politics" in a manner that differs from "neo-slave narratives" that revisit the conventions of antebellum slave autobiography more closely (Spaulding 1–4).

4. As Rody explains, for the main character of Morrison's *Beloved* "a 'rememory' (an individual experience) hangs around as a 'picture' that can enter another's 'rememory' (the part of the brain that 'rememories') and complicates consciousness and identity" (Rody 110). In the oft-quoted scene from the novel, Sethe tells her daughter:

> "Some things go. Pass on. Some things just stay. I used to think it was my rememory. You know. Some things you forget. Other things you never do. But it's not. Places, places are still there. If a house burns down, it's gone, but the place—the picture of it—stays, and not just in my rememory, but out there, in the world. Someday you be walking down the road and your hear something or see something going on. So clear. And you think it's you thinking it up. A thought picture. But no. It's when you bump into a rememory that belongs to someone else." (Morrison 35–36)

5. Other recent publications include *The Original Johnson* by Trevor Von Eeden (2010), *Incognegro: A Graphic Mystery* by Mat Johnson and Warren Pleece (2008), *Satchel Paige: Striking Out Jim Crow* by James Sturm and Rich Tommaso (2007), *Stagger Lee* by Derek McCulloch and Shepherd Hendrix (2006), and *Bluesman* by Rob Vollmar and Pablo G. Callejo (2006–2008).

6. My allusion to "authenticating documents" mindfully connects the strategies of the aforementioned comic book creators to the rhetorical methods of the antebellum slave narrative, a genre that, as critics such as Robert Stepto and William Andrews point out, seeks to counter notions of black dehumanization through persuasive "fictions of factual representation" (Hayden White qtd. in Andrews 16). For more analysis on how a comic like Kyle Baker's *Nat Turner* adapts and revises slave narrative conventions, see Conseula Francis's essay in this collection.

7. Papa Midnite, New York kingpin and Voodoo practitioner, is an associate of John Constantine, the character who was first introduced in *Swamp Thing* and later evolved into his own series, *Hellblazer*. Other recent black comics that experiment with fantasy, horror, and speculative fiction and parody include *The Hole: Consumer Culture* by Damian Duffy and John Jennings, and *Birth of a Nation: A Comic Novel* by Aaron McGruder, Reginald Hudlin, and Kyle Baker.

8. The Rosewood Vampires make their first appearance in *Saga of the Swamp Thing* #3, "A Town Has Turned to Blood."

9. Although the events I examine in "Southern Change" and "Strange Fruit" do not occur in the swamp surrounding Houma, it is important to acknowledge the role this terrain plays in establishing the foundation of Swamp Thing's uncommon strength. In his analysis of Walt Kelly's *Pogo* in this collection, Brian Cremins suggests that the "imagined geography" of the

swamp facilitates the exploration of alternate realities and serves as a province for more fluid psychosocial boundaries as well. Without question, Moore capitalizes on the dialectic of risk and renewal that the swamp symbolizes throughout his time with the series and in his development of the Swamp Thing character.

10. "Zuvembies" was the term favored by Marvel Comics to circumvent the Comics Code's prohibition against zombies and other monsters.

11. Obviously, the circumstances under which Chesnutt wrote as one of the first major African American authors to capture the attention of the white-controlled publishing industry were vastly different than for Moore in the 1980s. Yet the comparison is useful for the ways in which Chesnutt took advantage of the popular conventions of southern local color fiction to subtly condemn the system of oppression that served as slavery's foundation. As Richard Brodhead notes in his introduction to *The Conjure Woman and Other Conjure Tales*, "All is compliance, so far as the surface appears of these stories goes. Nevertheless Chesnutt makes his adopted form carry other messages than it had in other hands—messages always obliquely conveyed behind an elaborate show of conformity" (Chesnutt 6).

12. Boon makes a crucial distinction between zombies and the walking dead, noting that "the reanimated dead are not proper zombies unless they lose some essential quality of self" (36). Nevertheless, my insistence on the term and discursive framework of the zombie is purposeful, not simply because Moore refers to the comic as a "zombie tale" but because I assert that the historical reality of American slavery and oppression, the act of reducing humans to chattel labor suggests an analogous loss of an "essential quality of self" that the story seeks to recover.

13. In *Weird Fantasy* #18 (1953) by Al Feldstein and Joe Orlando, an American astronaut refuses to allow Cybrinia, the Planet of Mechanical Life, membership in the Earth's Great Galactic Republic because of the orange robots' practice of segregating and oppressing their blue counterparts. It isn't until the last panel—when the astronaut removes his helmet—that the reader discovers that Earth's representative is a black man whose dignified expression and professional responsibility demonstrates the progress humankind has made in the future.

14. During the controversy over an earlier issue of *Swamp Thing* that was rejected by the CMAA's Comics Code (#29), artist Stephen Bissette has noted that he sent editor Karen Berger clippings of zombie movie ads to convince her of the pervasiveness of the walking dead in popular entertainment (Weiland). The appearance of these movie posters in "Strange Fruit" not only normalizes the actual appearance of the walking dead in his story, but also marks the artistic limitations within the comics industry during the early 1980s.

Works Cited

Anderson, Ho Che. *King: A Comics Biography of Martin Luther King, Jr.* Seattle: Fantagraphic Books, 2005. Print.

Andrews, Williams. *To Tell a Free Story: The First Century of Afro-American Autobiography, 1760–1865.* Urbana: U of Illinois P, 1986. Print.

Arrant, Chris. "Born on the Bayou: Jeremy Love Talks Zuda, Bayou." *Newsarama.* October 25, 2007. Web. http://forum.newsarama.com/showthread.php?t=134214

Baker, Kyle. *Nat Turner.* New York: Abrams, 2008. Print.

Boon, Kevin Alexander. "Ontological Anxiety Made Flesh: The Zombie in Literature, Film, and Culture." *Monsters and the Monstrous: Myths and Metaphors of Enduring Evil.* Ed. Niall Scott. Amsterdam: Rodopi B.V., 2007. 33–43. Print.

Butler, Octavia. *Kindred.* New York: Doubleday, 1979. Print.

Chaney, Michael. "Drawing on History in Recent African American Graphic Novels," *MELUS* 32.3 (2007): 175–200. Print.

Chesnutt, Charles. *The Conjure Woman and Other Conjure Tales.* 1899. Durham: Duke UP, 1993. Print.

Craig, Johnny. "Voodoo Death!" *Tales from the Crypt.* 23:7. (1951). New York: EC Comics. Print.

Duffy, Damian (w) and John Jennings (a). *The Hole: Consumer Culture.* Chicago: Front Forty Press, 2008. Print.

Eeden, Trevor Von. *The Original Johnson.* IDW Publishing, 2010. Print.

Feldstein, Al (w) and Joe Orlando (a). "Judgment Day!" *Weird Fantasy* #18 (1953). New York: EC Comics. Print.

Geyh, Paula and Fred G. Leebron, Andrew Levy, ed. *Postmodern American Fiction: A Norton Anthology.* New York: W.W. Norton, 1988. Print.

Harris, Trudier. *The Scary Mason-Dixon Line: African American Writers and the South.* Baton Rouge: Louisiana State UP, 2009. Print.

Hatfield, Charles. *Alternative Comics: An Emerging Literature.* Jackson: UP of Mississippi, 2005. Print.

Johnson, Charles. *Middle Passage.* New York: Scribner, 1998. Print.

Johnson, Mat (w) and Tony Akins (a). *Hellblazer: Papa Midnight.* New York: Vertigo, 2006. Print.

Johnson, Mat (w) and Warren Pleece (a). *Incognegro: A Graphic Mystery.* New York: Vertigo, 2008. Print.

Jones, Edward P. *The Known World.* New York: Amistad, 2003. Print.

Khoury, George. *The Extraordinary Works of Alan Moore.* Raleigh, NC: TwoMorrows Publishing, 2008. Print.

Love, Jeremy. *Bayou.* Zuda Comics, 2007–2010. Web. https://comics.comixology.com/#/series/2632

——. *Bayou.* Vol. 1. New York: DC Comics, 2009. Print.

——. *Bayou.* Vol. 2. New York: DC Comics, 2010. Print.

McCulloch, Derek (w) and Shepherd Hendrix (a). *Stagger Lee.* New York: Image Comics, 2006. Print.

McGruder, Aaron and Reginald Hudlin (w) and Kyle Baker (a). *Birth of a Nation: A Comic Novel.* New York: Crown Publishers, 2004. Print.

Moore, Alan (w), Stephen Bissette and John Totleben (a). "The Nukeface Papers, Part 1." *Swamp Thing* #35. (April 1985). New York: DC Comics. Print.

——. "The Nukeface Papers, Part 2." *Swamp Thing* #36 (May 1985). New York: DC Comics. Print.

Moore, Alan (w), Stan Woch and John Totleben (a). "Still Waters." *Swamp Thing* #38 (July 1985). New York: DC Comics. Print.

Moore, Alan (w), Stephen Bissette and John Totleben (a). "Fish Story." *Swamp Thing* #39 (August 1985). New York: DC Comics. Print.

——. "The Curse." *Swamp Thing* #40 (September 1985). New York: DC Comics. Print.

Moore, Alan (w), Stephen Bissette and Alfredo Alcala (a). "Southern Change." *Swamp Thing* #41 (October 1985). New York: DC Comics. Print.

Moore, Alan (w), Stephen Bissette, John Totleben, and Ron Randall (a). "Strange Fruit." *Swamp Thing* #42 (November 1985). New York: DC Comics. Print.

Morrison, Toni. *Beloved*. New York: Knopf, 1987. Print.

Paffenroth, Kim. *Gospel of the Living Dead: George Romero's Visions of Hell on Earth*. Waco, TX: Baylor UP, 2006. Print.

Pasko, Martin (w) and Tom Yeates (a). "A Town Has Turned to Blood." *Saga of the Swamp Thing* #3 (July 1982). New York: DC Comics. Print.

Reed, Ishmael. *Flight to Canada*. New York: Simon & Schuster, 1976. Print.

Rody, Caroline. "Toni Morrison's *Beloved*: History, 'Rememory,' and a 'Clamor for a Kiss.'" *American Literary History* 7.1 (1995): 92–119. Print.

Rossetti, Gina. *Imagining the Primitive in Naturalist and Modernist Literature*. Columbia: University of Missouri Press, 2006. Print.

Rushdy, Ashraf H. A. *Neo-Slave Narratives: Studies in the Social Logic of a Literary Form*. New York: Oxford UP, 1999. Print.

Spaulding, A. Timothy. *Re-Forming the Past: History, The Fantastic, and the Postmodern Slave Narrative*. Columbus: Ohio State UP, 2005. Print.

Stepto, Robert. *From Behind the Veil: A Study of Afro-American Narration*. Urbana: U of Illinois P, 1979. Print.

Sturm, James (w) and Rich Tommaso (a). *Satchel Paige: Striking Out Jim Crow*. New York: Hyperion, 2007. Print.

Vollmar, Rob (w) and Pablo G. Callejo (a). *Bluesman*. New York: ComicsLit, 2006. Print.

Weiland, Jonah. "A Horrific View of Comics: A Chat With Stephen Bissette." *Comic Book Resources*, 29 October 2003. Web. http://www.comicbookresources.com /?page=article&id=2792

Wein, Len. "Introduction." *Swamp Thing: Dark Genesis*. New York: DC Comics, 1991. Print.

Wein, Len and Berni Wrightston. "The Man Who Would Not Die." *Swamp Thing* #10 (May–June 1974). New York: DC Comics. Print.

Crooked Appalachia

The Laughter of the Melungeon Witches in
Mike Mignola's *Hellboy: The Crooked Man*

—Joseph Michael Sommers

To accurately discuss the Melungeons, a group once identified by Library of Congress researchers as the largest "little race" of miscegenated[1] people in the 1960s (Pollitzer 722), or even to discuss the accuracy of Mike Mignola's representations of them in his 2008 comic book mini-series *Hellboy: The Crooked Man*, is a daunting task. The Melungeons are a people somewhat shrouded in mystery, mythology, and, until recently, a history composed more of reportage and conjecture than of rigorous anthropological or ethnographic investigation. Wayne Winkler offers the most succinct and generally agreed-upon definition of the Melungeon people as a group whose cultural and ethnic makeup is composed of a complicated and indeed contested constellation of races and ethnicities, including whites, African Americans, and local indigenous tribes who lived along a geographic and cultural partitioning of the Virginia and Tennessee borders near the Cumberland Gap ("About"). But to describe them so neatly forecloses discussion of the vexed nature of the historical treatment and scholarship concerning the Melungeon people that Mignola's work, the focus of this investigation, participates in. As such, a brief examination of the historical record is in order.

In a piece composed for the *Geographical Review* in 1952, Edward T. Price assessed the state of the Melungeons and their public reception from the perspective of his day, age, and location: "To some people [Melungeon] is only a general derogatory term to be bestowed on anyone who momentarily arouses their antagonism. [For others], the Melungeons have had to fill the place of the bogeyman in holding children in the straight and narrow path" (256). Toward this last point, Price then quotes from what he tells us are remarks in S. M. Burnett's 1889 *American Anthropologist* account, remarks that stand as an ominous warning to those same children Price indicates were likely scurrying under their bed linens as he, at that very moment, typed the word "Melungeon." That lengthy quotation Price attributed to Burnett: "The Melungeons will get you!"

Winkler, in the 2004 piece cited earlier, even recapitulates the quotation in his narrative. Interestingly enough, Burnett never wrote these words. However, this misattribution was not due, necessarily, to any inflammatory journalistic malfeasance on Price's part—that is to say, unless one considers dramatic understatement a form of journalistic malfeasance. Burnett's actual nineteenth-century reflection on the Melungeon people reads as follows:

> I first heard at my father's knee as a child in the mountains of Eastern Tennessee, and the name had such a ponderous and inhuman sound[2] as to associate them in my mind with the giants and ogres of the wonder tales I listened to in the winter evenings before the crackling logs in the wide-mouth fireplace. And when I chanced to waken in the night and the fire had died down on the hearth, and the wind swept with a demoniac shriek and terrifying roar around and through the house, rattling the windows and the loose clapboards on the roof, I shrank under the bedclothes trembling with a fear that was almost an expectation that one of these huge creatures would come down the chimney with a rush, seize me with his dragon-like arms, and carry me off to his cave in the mountains, there to devour me piecemeal. (347)

Rather than accuse Price of filtering his journalism through derisive remarks such as Burnett's or of even attacking these Appalachian people as mythological monsters haunting the mountains, I note that Price simply chose to represent the group somewhat metonymically as a bogeyman of legend as opposed to accusing the over 15,000[3] people who identified themselves as Melungeon in the 1950s of human dismemberment and cannibalism. A kinder representation, by comparison, yet a representation still deeply troubled.

Fifty years later, it would appear that Mignola does not afford the Melungeons the same courtesy. In the second issue of *The Crooked Man*, a three-issue mini-series set in Virginia's Appalachia in 1958, Hellboy has a short discussion with Tom Ferrell, a local man who shares his adventure, about the Melungeons—specifically, about the supposed Melungeon witches and the history of their relationship to the locals—as they pass near a coal mine en route to burying Tom's recently deceased father.

Tom: The Melungion[4] witches.

Hellboy: The who?

Tom: Melungions. Supposed to be descended from the settlers who disappeared at Roanoke Island .... There's all kinds of crazy stories about them. (2:5)

They continue:

Tom: They're supposed to be a special kinda evil. They were never around here much—not till the big cave-in of '02. My pa used to tell me about it. A hundred men got trapped down there, and for a day and a night the air was fulla them Melungions, flyin up here and down into that mine. Pa says there was some screaming down there for a while, then nothing. He figured those witches went down there to eat those fellas.

Hellboy: I hate that kind of crap.

Tom: And he never heard tell of any of those witches comin back up out of there again. (2:5–6)

In Mignola's defense, not to represent the Melungeons as something monstrous and insidious somewhat undercuts their potential to be the antagonists for Hellboy, the protagonist of the series and the "World's Greatest Paranormal Investigator," who also happens to be the harbinger of the Biblical Apocalypse. His true name, *Anung un Rama*, literally translates to, "[he] upon whose brow is set a crown of fire," and he is destined, some believe, to bring about the destruction of humankind. While he cannot be readily classified as anti-heroic, it is difficult to go too far into discussion of Hellboy without mentioning that he was brought to Earth in an attempt to destroy it. However, one could argue that Mignola has Tom simply participate in that same discourse of myth, rumor, and legend and that he only recapitulates to Hellboy, much like Burnett, the yarns spun to him by his father when he was a boy. That would be reasonable, perhaps, if the universe Mignola constructs throughout *Hellboy* was not one where "history, mythology, horror tropes and good-old fashioned storytelling [are woven together with] threads of historical reality shot through with references to books, folklore, theology [etc.]" (Yolen). Likewise, Richard Corben, the artistic collaborator on *Crooked Man*, does not seem to offer any critical perspective on Tom's description of the Melungeons when he depicts the rotting, wailing, semi-nude, and feral-looking Melungeon witches directly below the

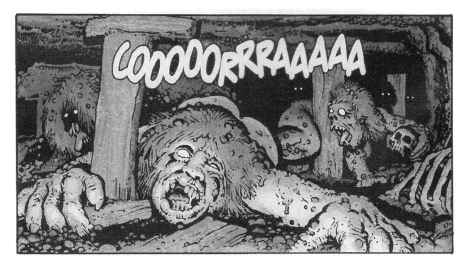

10.1. From *Hellboy: The Crooked Man* #2 (August 2008). Written by Mike Mignola with art by Richard Corben. Copyright © 2008 Michael Mignola.

aforementioned dialogue in a panel washed in sepia-tones of dirty browns and moldering greens (see figure 10.1). And although Hellboy, here only 14 years old, could be read as dismissing Tom's story as "crap," given what he has already seen in his two years working for the Bureau of Paranormal Research and Defense, he likely plays the line, like the threat, straight and with concern.

As a recent critique has noted, while Mignola by no means turns all of the characters in *The Crooked Man* into "inbred, hillbilly stereotypes," he does, potentially, participate in perpetuating "a negative and pernicious stereotype" of mountainous residents of southern Appalachia in the 1950s (Professor Fury). These comments rejoin a glowing evaluation from Don MacPherson, who lauds *The Crooked Man* as a stylized "organic [and] exaggerated" presentation of the Melungeons "as twisted, distorted figures, as physically warped as the corruption that lies beneath the surface" ("Eye on Comics"). These two evaluations of the same material are diametrically opposed, and there would seem to be no middle ground between them. However, what I hope to add to the conversation about this text comes by way of possible explanation of Mignola's motivations and accomplishments and of exculpation of Mignola from charges of racial stereotyping or egregious misrepresentation of a historical Melungeon people. I offer a reading that instead suggests that *The Crooked Man* undermines and refutes these stereotypes by situating them in a complex narrative of history, myth, and memory and by giving a voice to a people long silenced in official histories.

As Winkler notes, the Melungeons generally resented the token interest taken in their people due to the sensationalistic and hegemonic construction of their heritage by popular outsider newsprint and magazine journalism ("About"). Yet, in Mignola's recent construction of the Melungeons in *The Crooked Man*, he plays directly with and into those popular accounts, constructing a tale of *accused* cannibalistic Melungeon witches who terrorize Virginian locals only to be ultimately defeated by Hellboy and Tom. Mignola's *The Crooked Man* allows the Melungeons to laugh at their portrayal in the Bakhtinian sense of the term. In this case, laughter is a sort of "parod[ic] double" that does not "undermine" the "people and things" thought to be laughed *at* (Morson and Emerson 434; Bakhtin, *Dialogic Imagination* 71), but instead, allows ridicule to reverberate *in all directions*, in this case, even back at the source of the original ridicule. As such, Mignola exposes the ridicule of the Melungeons in late-nineteenth- and early twentieth-century depictions by using the same discourse conventions of the original journalistic misrepresentation, making the reader uncomfortably complicit with the earlier consumers of such fictions while freeing the Melungeons from that era's singular and limiting interpretation of them.

Mignola appropriates the reportage of slanted popular local color journalism about the Melungeons prevalent through the mid-twentieth century and continues this usage in the construction of his character, Hellboy, a construction that centers on an idea of examining the interstitial narratives formed in an interplay of history, religion, mythology, and other discourses through the lens of popular narratives. In the case of *The Crooked Man*, I will argue that Mignola chronotopically[5] constructs a still very young and somewhat naïve Hellboy amongst the Virginia mountain people in an effort to appropriate the late nineteenth- and early twentieth-century outsider gaze upon the Melungeons. I will examine the voices and active discourses constructed in *Crooked Man* (both within the period and contemporarily) as they are used by Mignola to create the concept of a growing, learning Hellboy who, at this point along his chronology, is still learning the trade that will eventually lead him to become the "World's Greatest Paranormal Investigator." As such, Corben and Mignola's creation of the Melungeons within the comic accurately recovers the misconceptions evident within the time period in an effort to create the Bakhtinian laughter necessary in our time period for both a dilettante Hellboy to begin his maturation into the role with which the reader is familiar as well as to let the comic reader view the grotesque misrepresentation of a maligned people through the period-appropriate eyes of the youthful protagonist.

A History of Misrepresentation:
Seeing the Melungeons through the eyes of "the white"

I take and use the terminology of the spectator here from Burnett's piece, where he writes, "In the course of time, however, I came to learn these creatures with the awe-inspiring name were people somewhat like ourselves . . . the white" (347). My undertaking here is not to account for the many different explanations of historical antecedents of the Melungeons, but, rather, to address the possible polygenesis of the manifold mythological and legendary attributes that feed into Mignola's construction of them in *The Crooked Man*. As David Steven Cohen notes, "History and legend are two different uses of the past. They should not be confused with each other or with the past itself. The past is what actually happened; history and legend are what is written and traditionally said, respectively, about the past" (260). Few would disagree. Problematically, as Cohen notes in his consideration of the Ramapo Mountain People, a group similar to the Melungeons based in New York and New Jersey, the difference between history and legend is quite "elusive," to say the least (260). Part of that mystery is due to the dissemination and cultivation of some of the oldest myths surrounding the origins of the Melungeon people.

When speaking of the idea of the "Vanishing South," a concept to which the Melungeons' history certainly belongs, George Tindall expands the conversation to note that the very idea of "the South" as a consumer product of the newspaper and journal trade has always been vanishing, or, as he puts it, it "has a long and honored tradition" of disappearing (3–4). He notes that by the mid-twentieth century, in particular, the "distinctiveness" of the South seemed "doomed" to the eyes of the northerner, causing it to appear to be a treasure in the process of becoming lost (4). As such, northern reporters clamored to it in an effort to record as much as possible before the South fell off the map entirely, making it, in Tindall's mind, a prime site of commodification for the northern reporter, who wrote stories about his sojourn into the "hillbilly" culture "out in the boondocks" (4).

More to the point, the Melungeons have fascinated local color journalists, mythologists, and secondhand cultural anthropologists, northern and southern alike, since the first recorded speculations about their origins as descendants of the lost Roanoke Island colony who intermarried with the Croatoans in 1590 (Winkler, *Walking* 38; Allen 653; Ball 1). Not to be confined to a single origin story, however, others have also suggested a Portuguese ancestry, (Ball ix) or Spanish, or Moroccan, or Guinean, among others (Ball 23–40; Allen 651). Even stories of pirates and shipwrecked sailors have found their way into the legend of the Melungeons' beginnings (Elder 33–34).

To say such polygeneity might frustrate an anthropologist would be an understatement equivalent to Price's earlier remarks, but some have grown so frustrated as to simply imply the Melungeon people are raceless. The Melungeons' identity, from an ethnographic view of the South, is one of perpetual loss, absence, and, of course, mystery. They do have a common geographic epicenter in Hancock Country, Tennessee, even if that too was, in part, constructed for them by spurious accounts by local reporters for the newspapers.[6] Yet, the element common to all accounts is that the Melungeons are "self-perpetuating," a quality largely brought about due to their being "mixed-racial isolates" (Beale 704). This exotic history spurred on the interests of both local and northern readerships (Schrift 107).

Calvin Beale, who composed a 1957 study on what he then termed "tri-racial isolates" (704), is an important figure in much of the scholarship concerning the Melungeons. His 1972 article brings to the forefront the issue of "race," a term that frustrates Wayne Winkler, a contemporary authority on Melungeon history and a Melungeon himself, as he argues that "America has had an unhealthy obsession with race and the notion of 'purity,'" and that this obsession "is why Melungeons and other mixed-race people were subjected to sometimes-harsh legal sanctions and isolation" (xii). Beale draws from an 1891 account published in the *Boston Arena* by Will Allen Drumgoole:

> In about 1890, a young Tennessee woman asked a state legislator, "Please tell me what is a Malungeon?" "A Malungeon" said he, "isn't a nigger, and he isn't an Indian, and he isn't a Whiteman. God only knows what he is. I should call him a Democrat, only he always votes the Republican ticket." (*Walking* 705)

As Beale notes, that young woman was Drumgoole herself[7], and her account was consistent with the racial attitudes of the day. It also helped form and foment the racial and ideological profile of the Melungeons from that point forward. She certainly did not serve them well as a public relations specialist:

[The Melungeons] became a living terror; sweeping down upon [the people of the foot hills], stealing their cattle, their provisions, their very clothing, and household furniture.

[The Melungeons] became shiftless, idle, thieving, and defiant of all law . . . . After the breaking out of the [Civil] War . . . the greater number remained with their [brandy] stills, to pillage and plunder among the helpless women and children.

Their mountains became a terror to travelers; and not until within the last half decade has it been regarded as safe to cross Malungeon territory.[8] (qtd. in Winkler 271)

Deplorable, inaccurate, degrading, ignorant: any of these terms could be used to describe the Drumgoole account, and all would have been accurate even by the standards of the day. Further into the account, however, is a short passage of interest to the construction of the Melungeons in 2008:

They believe in witchcraft, "yarbs," and more than one "charmer" may be found among them. They will "rub away" a wart for ten cents, and one old squaw assured me she had some "blood beads" the "wair bounter heal all manner o' blood ailments." (qtd. in Winkler 275)

The Melungeon people were accomplished herbalists who employed, in Elizabeth Hirschman's terms, "folk medicine" (141), and were "never far removed from *animism*," or following the lunar calendar (142). This should not come as a surprise. As has been copiously noted, the Melungeons believed in messages that could travel on the wind, primitive astrology, numerology, divination through the "reading" of entrails, ghosts, and other spectral phenomena—and believed that witches *did*, in fact, exist (Hirschman 142–43). Admittedly, Hirschmann also writes, this was before they converted to monotheistic Christianity; as another prominent critic writes, "Historically, Melungeons were Baptist" (Elder 108).

However, there does seem to be a peculiar hint of plausibility to the admittedly untrained journalistic account Drumgoole provided of exotic spiritual and religious rituals within the Melungeon community. Granted, her use of these traditions and rituals was exploitative, and, in the 1800s, that manner of journalistic narrative may have been permitted or even encouraged. One would think that the "politics of heritage" (Schrift 106), in which tracing one's bloodline and other such rumor-mongering seems to supersede anything remotely connected to journalistic integrity or fact-finding, would not have been part of the mid-twentieth century scholarship that stressed objective description. And yet such approaches persist:

> Folks left [the Melungeons] alone because they were so wild and devil-fired and queer and witchy. If a man was fool enough to go into Melungeon country and if he come back without being shot, he was just sure to wizen and perish away with some ailment nobody could name. Folks said terrible things went on, blood drinking and devil worship and carryings-on that would freeze a good Christian's spinal bone. (Berry 60)

The account is Brewton Berry's, and it was published in 1963's *Almost White*. It is not a renegade piece of academia; in fact, the accounts of a plural Melungeon history fraught with error continued well into the twentieth century. In these accounts come tales discussing witchcraft, devil-worship, and lethal spell casting, all topics that Mignola addresses in *The Crooked Man*. Popular journalism was no less sensational; in the same year as the Berry account the *Tennessean Magazine* published reports of "Melungeon grannies scrambling across the hills on special occasion to observe secret rites over the graves—'speaking in unknown tongues'" (Ivey 97). A few years later, in 1970, the *San Francisco Examiner & Chronicle* reprinted Berry's remarks in a piece entitled "Mystery of the Melungeons" focusing primarily on witchy business and devil worship (Ivey 97). Most chroniclers attribute this mid-century renaissance of interest in Melungeon ritual and practice to one particular locus of dissemination, a *Saturday Evening Post* piece from 1947 entitled "Sons of the Legend." In this story, William Worden wrote of these "strange people" (28) who have lived "brooding on their mountainside" since the Civil War (128). Worden warns his readers how locals enforce discipline by uttering an oft-repeated refrain to their children to "Act purty or the Malungeons'll get ya," once again reinforcing the notion of Melungeons as bogeymen that colors so much of their history (128).

The stories took root. Katherine Vande Brake's seminal study *How They Shine: Melungeon Characters in The Fiction of Appalachia* goes to great lengths to document the mid-century misrepresentation of the Melungeons in fictive accounts. One of particular interest details the small collection of stories in *God Bless the Devil!: Liars' Bench Tales*, a 1940 collection of stories republished in 1985. The editors of the republished volume quietly and angrily pronounced the volume to be replete with "hoax" accounts constituting little more than "nonsense," "fantasy," and "fakelore"[9] (137). The editors of *God Bless The Devil!* go to great length to make the point that fakelore—that is, inaccurate, likely fabricated, folklore—pervades Melungeon history and is particularly erroneous even compared to the already vexed accounts. Calling it a "product of its time," Charles Wolfe goes on to explain that stories such as those where "Old Horny," another appellation for the devil, consorts with local Melungeon women as part of their inculcation into witchcraft (qtd. in Vande Brake 142) drew upon already popular miscast accounts of Melungeon "herb lore" (146) to propagate an "art" consumable to the "everyday working class citizen" (138). Wolfe sublimates his response politely. Vande Brake does not. Referring to the re-retelling of Melungeon tales through fiction as a "tampering" with already spurious accounts and field work (138), she declares these "witchy" accounts in the work of popular writers such as Sharyn McCrumb and Virginia Hamilton to be outright bastardization and "myth," and she indicates that these accounts state that,

> Melungeons can hex people so that they die, [citing] on good authority ("folks") the awful religious practices that the Melungeons allegedly practice. Blood drinking and devil worship have long been associated with witches; sons and daughters of the devil might conceivably do such things. (146–47)

One critic ultimately sums up the popular work surrounding the Melungeons. In her section labeled "The Problem of Secondary Sources," Melanie Lou Sovine notes that, while firsthand accounts are rare and secondary accounts are almost totally unreliable, without the secondhand sources provided by local journalists and crooked mid-century depictions by anthropologists and scholars relying on that secondary material, discussion of the Melungeons would be "nonexistent" (31). As such, "stereotypes" and "biases" occupy the place of scholarship (35), and they are both incongruent with each other and "unreliable" (36). And yet, as she notes, these errors occupy the historical record of the Melungeons until the end of the twentieth century. Accurate or not (mostly not), this is the cultural history of the Melungeon people for the rest of America.

Laughing at Misrepresentation:
Mike Mignola's *Hellboy* through Mikhail Bakhtin

Mike Mignola is not an uncelebrated artist and writer. In fact, *The Crooked Man* took home the 2009 Will Eisner award for Best Limited Comic Book

Series. Authors and critics alike have reflected that praise, with luminaries such as Alan Moore stating that:

> *Hellboy*'s greatest and least-obvious accomplishment [is] in crafting work as good *as the work that inspired it* really was, but in the more demanding task of crafting work as good as everyone *remembers* the original being. . . . It's not enough to merely reproduce the past. Instead, we have to blend it artfully with how we see things now and with our visions for the future. ("Introduction," emphasis added)

I highlight certain of Moore's words to credit him with first noticing that Mignola constructs his narrative for Hellboy around an idea of situating the character within established popular notions of known history. His work on *Hellboy* has been labeled as both "pulp" (Weiner 12; Gianni) and "pop" (Bloch). As such, Mignola's *Hellboy* is couched in a sort of parodic discourse, both valorizing and quietly mocking, of the narratives that inspired it. Mignola tells the story of *Hellboy* in analeptic and paraleptic time and space. In other words, *Hellboy*'s narrative is told by bracketing the character between two historical points (May 9, 1994, where we first meet "Red," and December 23, 1944, when he is brought to Earth) and then constructing the larger arch-narrative through the telling of side- and back-stories out of chronological order. The effect created is one of an expanding mythology told in episodic, though non-linear, time.

Mignola takes this approach in an effort to demystify the delicate situation of celebrating his half-demonic protagonist[10] by diffusing his *Hellboy* universe with elements of Hellboy's interaction in an otherwise established "real" history where the citizenry is quite at ease with him due largely to his coverage by the popular press of the period. As Tom Ferrell tells Hellboy in *Crooked Man* #1, "I heard of you, you know. Recognized you right off. Saw a picture of you in *Life* magazine some years back" (1:5). Generally, a large, crimson-skinned demon (complete with cloven hooves, a tail, and horns [which he does file off]) might shock everyday people in Mignola's world, but it is rarely even commented upon as unusual. As figure 10.2 indicates, Tom is at ease with Hellboy, and he even refers to the picture of a young Hellboy in *Life* as "cute . . . like a little monkey" (1:5).

This mention of Hellboy in popular journals of the period is not coincidental. Mignola creates Hellboy as a piece of walking modern mythology who mingles in and out of established history. In *The Crooked Man*, his placement in the remote mountainous regions of Virginia presents him as a walking piece of outsider mythos to the locals within the book. And, if

* THREE-YEAR-OLD HELLBOY APPEARED IN THE MAY 1948 ISSUE.

10.2. From *Hellboy: The Crooked Man* #1 (July 2008). Written by Mike Mignola with art by Richard Corben. Copyright © 2008 Michael Mignola.

one considers that Tom Ferrell can only account for him through knowledge gleaned from *Life*, Hellboy seems to parody the plight of the Melungeon witches tormenting him and Tom.[11] That is to say, just as the Melungeon witches are a strange piece of walking—haunting, really—mythology, known only to northerners as represented in published reports, so Hellboy, a visitor here, is a strange piece of outsider mythos to these locals who, despite the oddities surrounding them, are not accustomed to having a demon's progeny walking amongst them, let alone helping them with their troubles. Strangely, however, the Virginian mountain people do not fear him. They welcome him with hospitality and civility, hoping he and his peculiar connection to the demonic can help with their local witch problem (2:2).

While Bakhtin did not write on visual narratives or the graphic novel as we know them today, he did characterize novels as being inspired by a "laughing truth" that leads to generic parody (Morson and Emerson 433). According to Bakhtinian critics, this is the place in writing where "values become ritualistic, collective and generalizable" (Morson and Emerson 433), particularly for parodic discourse built from what Bakhtin calls laughter. Though the formative discussion on laughter is contained in Bakhtin's *Rabelais and His World*, two of the long essays comprising *The Dialogic Imagination*, "From the Prehistory of Novelistic Discourse" and "Forms of Time and of the Chronotope," explain both what laughter is and how it can function in something like a comic book. Laughter, for Bakhtin, is just that: "ridiculing . . . another's direct discourse" (*Dialogic Imagination* 50); in Mignola's case, "direct," can translate to "dominant," in the sense the term is used in contemporary theoretical circles. However, it is what is being laughed at that illustrates laughter's potency for revolution in the novel. It is Bakhtin's opinion that laughter, or ridicule, allows for the lower classes or oppressed citizenry an opportunity to ridicule the oppressive or dominant discourses that the novel subverts through its poly- and hetero-vocality. That is to say, the oppressive tyranny of the established traditions (established through supposed historical accounts and supposed unbiased journalism) be damned: *Hellboy* allows for the voices of the oppressed to finally be heard on the record.

For Bakhtin, when those under oppression (for my purposes, the Melungeon people) are allowed voice, to speak for and as themselves by representation in the comic, they corrupt the power of the dominant discourse that had monologically directed the oppression through one uniform, "straightforward" voice (in this case the uniform voice of journalism) (Bakhtin, *Dialogic Imagination* 52). What is described here, though, is not necessarily found in the novel as we generally accept it; Bakhtin does not find the usage of laughter, as such, in his era to be as liberating as he would like. To the contrary, he tends to find it to be focused in one direction, "*at* people and things," as opposed to allowing those people to laugh back at the entrenched establishment (Morson and Emerson 434). Yet, in pre-novelistic discourses, such as the "folkloric and semi-folkloric" ones (Bakhtin, *Dialogic Imagination* 158), the laughter of those deemed to be "grotesque" (Bakhtin, *Dialogic Imagination* 158) was allowed to be heard. And with that laughter came the power of the "destruction of the old picture of the world and the positive construction of a new picture" where both worldviews are "indissolubly interwoven with each other" (Bakhtin, *Dialogic Imagination* 169).

Thus, the goal is not the disestablishment of the prior dominant discourse of tyrannical viewpoints. Instead, the tyranny is held up to the voices of the impoverished and forced into a public, dialogical conversation so that the audience can make a more nuanced and complex assessment of those once viewed only by the terms of a monological tyranny. Mignola provides the reader of *The Crooked Man* with such an opportunity, using the special circumstances surrounding *Hellboy*'s somewhat novelistic/somewhat folkloric narrative, to liberate the Melungeons from their historical prison and to laugh at centuries of oppression. However, it is crucial to note that it is *an opportunity* to liberate the Melungeons from this monological view. It is not a promise, and it cannot be an order.

For, as Bakhtin writes in *Rabelais and His World*, Rabelais's writings were linked to "popular characters" and accounts and were particularly "nonliterary" in that they did not conform to established and sanctioned guidelines for folkloric discourse (2, 5–6). To the contrary, his writings celebrated the "blasphemous rather than the adoring," "the coarse, dirty, and rampantly physical . . . image of the folk . . . diametrically opposed to those celebrated" by the establishment—then, the Soviet establishment (Holquist xix). Rather, this "comic literature"—here, meaning imbued with the ability to parody and laugh at the entrenched dogma of the sanctioned discourses—"was infused with the carnival spirit and made wide use of carnival forms and *images*" (italics mine, *Rabelais* 13). The grotesque images, as also depicted in Mignola's work on *Hellboy*, are often exaggerated but bound to a "positive, assertive character" who frees the oppressed from the tyranny of the sanctioned discourse while still acknowledging *all* elements of the greater narrative as an "indivisible whole" that must be shown in order to be laughed at (*Rabelais* 19).

In other words, from Bakhtin's perspective, for the parody to "liberat[e] the object from the power of language in which it had become entangled as if in a net," the entirety of the net must be presented (*Dialogic Imagination* 60). Bakhtin argues that for the oppressed to be able to laugh, they must face their oppressor in order to engage the parody by virtue of an enforced conversation in print. For this type of parody "can generate true heroes who are heroic precisely because they contain more possibilities for growth and change" from the established and sanctioned discourses (Morson and Emerson 434). Thus, if approached from the Bakhtinian notions of laughter, Mignola's *Hellboy* cannot and will not change the historical reality of the treatment of the Melungeon in the time period under examination. However, it can provide "new perspectives" and a "freedom of interpretive choice" long withheld from both the reader and the Melungeons, provided Mignola presents the reader with "concrete facts," a more complete account, of the representations he wishes to parody (Morson and Emerson 435). Mignola cannot change the history of this treatment, but, as Bakhtin writes, he can allow the contemporary reader the opportunity to act as "witness and the judge" of local color journalists and scholars who provide the background for his parody (qtd. in Morson and Emerson 435).

The investigation may now directly address the Melungeons' representation in *The Crooked Man* to investigate Mignola's parodic use of local color accounts and oral representations to see if he allows the witches an opportunity to laugh at the oppressive treatment of hundreds of years of misrepresentation and mythologization. I use the term "witches," as that is how they are first referenced[12] by Tom; however, I should qualify my own remarks to look at how the *Melungeons* stand at the forefront of this debate. The two primary antagonists are immediately recognizable as Melungeon: Jeremiah "Miser" Witkins, the titular "Crooked Man," and Effie Kolb, the witch who seduces Tom as a young boy into witchcraft. As both Hirschman and Brent Kennedy observe, the surnames Kolb and Witkins are both bastardizations of established Virginian Melungeon names, Cole and Wilkins, respectively (Hirschman 150; Kennedy 172, 174). Further, the Crooked Man's noted appellation, Miser, holds a peculiarly double-voiced significance for Mignola's efforts: first, it is a further bastardization of one of the most common and recognized Melungeon names "Mizer" (Kennedy 172), while, second, it establishes that Witkins was, in life, a miser. Tom tells Hellboy, "Folks always said that [Witkins] was only good for two things—causin trouble and makin money from it. An that's what got him hanged in the end. But that chief devil in Hell sent him back—to hoard souls now, stead of gold" (1:13). As the Drumgoole account makes clear, the popular conception of the Melungeons held them as likely to be thieves as they were pirates. In a different account,

Kennedy presents the widely known story of the Melungeon "BrandyJack" Mullins, a convicted counterfeiter and renowned worker in silver (19). Pat Elder corroborates the story to note that the Melungeons in folklore were often connected with the lost silver mines of Jonathan Swift (120).

While versions of the story differ, one that Elder recounts holds that the Melungeons usurped the mines as part of the "supposed counterfeiting of silver dollars" (121). In *The Crooked Man*, Witkins is portrayed as coveting brownish-dirty coins in both his life and afterlife, but, when he is ultimately defeated by Tom and Hellboy through the use of Tom's lucky witchbone, his plenty is exposed to be "the souls he'd got hold of over the years" (*Crooked Man* 3:23). The implications in both cases are relatively clear: Witkins, a man crooked both in his transactions in life and in his posture in death (from being resurrected after being hanged), is Melungeon; Effie[13], his servant, and a woman capable of witchcraft (she can fly and is shown to transform Tom's father into and from a desiccated horse [1:19–20]) is as well.

Witkins and Effie are formidable and frightening opponents, but they are not quite the horrors that Cora Fisher imagined. While one will recall Tom and Hellboy's discussion of the Melungeon witches as they pass a coal mine and the ensuing graphic depiction of moldering bodies writhing underneath them, at no time do these depictions of witches conclusively enter into the events of the main narrative. Cora, the young woman who "took up with some of those women from back up the mountain" (1:17), believes that she can hear them calling out her name from the mines beneath them, but, as Hellboy and Tom tell her, these witches should not have any power during the daylight hours (2:7). Admittedly, the sky has turned black and Tom believes that they are now operating on "The Devil's time," but a few panels later, it is shown that Effie and Witkins have been manipulating Cora in an effort to make Tom use his lucky witchbone (2:15). Tom crafted the object when he was a child using a technique Effie taught him, but he has only now used it. This gesture, in his mind and Effie's, now makes him the property of the miserly Crooked Man. He has used his witch powers and must pay the devil his due. As Effie says, "That's right, Tommy. He gave you that power and you finally used it. If he didn't own you before he sure as hell owns you now" (2:15). The panels illustrating Cora's visions of the moldering witches, whom only she can hear, appear to be little more than a green-tinted hallucination meant to terrify her, but it is Effie and The Crooked Man who cause her to transform into a variety of Lovecraftian insects and beasties in an effort to trick Tom into using his bone. Witkins and Kolb play into the legends Tom recounts to Hellboy and makes them real inside Cora's mind. She believes

10.3. From *Hellboy: The Crooked Man* #1 (July 2008). Written by Mike Mignola with art by Richard Corben. Copyright © 2008 Michael Mignola.

the Melungeons are *gonna get* her, but they are not the rotting grotesques she imagines are in the mines. They are the Crooked Man and his servant.

As she departs, Effie Kolb laughs at Tom. It is the second time she has done so. Initially, she laughs at him as he discovers the squalid horse she has been riding is actually Tom's father, who is only transfigured long enough for Tom to recognize him, and for him to help Tom realize that he turned into a horse as punishment for Tom for leaving Virginia. Tom says, "He's dead. She done this cause a me" (1:21). Admittedly, Effie has fooled them twice: once to trick Tom into using his wishbone and, secondly, to laugh at the pain he caused his father by leaving. While it may seem cruel, Tom has actually done wrong by both her and the Crooked Man.

He recalls to Hellboy a firsthand narrative of how he came to acquire the power of his lucky witchbone. Tom claims knowledge of Effie's witchy ways even when they were children: "Effie was a witch, an she got me all turned around, got me to thinking maybe I should be a witch too. All that talk about havin power over other folk . . . I dunno, she made it sound pretty good" (1:11). What that account does not tell you, but Corben's art reveals, was that Effie made it sound pretty good by approaching a then fifteen-year-old Tom naked, admittedly, a Tom "with no more sense than a sack fulla nails" (1:10), and seducing him (see figure 10.3).

Tom does acquire powers, but when Witkins, gnarled and crooked now as the Devil's emissary, came for his soul in repayment, Tom reneged upon the arrangement: "Let me tell ya, [Hellboy], one look at him scared all the bad thoughts right out of me" (1:14). While Effie is by no means without error, it is Tom's cupidity and sexual desire that lead him into debt with the Devil's merchant. He claims that Effie got him all turned around, but he also easily admits: "I knew right off she was nothin but trouble, but, well . . . I was fifteen" (1:11). As a result of his reneging on their arrangement, his father suffered miserably, and Tom leaves out of complete self-interest and preservation: "I just kept runnin. Didn't say goodbye to my ma an pa . . . . I didn't care where I was goin" (1:14). Though one can say Effie laughs at Tom for any of a variety of malicious reasons, one must also acknowledge that Effie may simply resent him for running off. Twenty years later, when they are reunited over the Crooked Man's arrangement with Cora, she greets him cordially with a hello and a warning to stay out of Cora's business when he has not even concluded his business with Witkins. Kolb is a witch, and Witkins possesses her soul in this narrative. She has absolutely no choice but to follow his commands, or her punishment will be most severe (3:23–24).

Tom understands this situation and takes it reasonably stoically. He realizes that his "penance" for his crimes is to have to bury his own father for the "foolishness of [his] youth" (2:2). Hellboy, on the other hand, does not take the news so well. In this narrative, Hellboy occupies the reader's position (and vice versa): relatively unaware of what is transpiring, reactive, and inexperienced in this local situation, trying to piece the story together while

Tom does the real detective work. In fact, given that Hellboy is actually the son of a demon and a witch (a fact of which he is not yet aware) being dragged into a fight with a set of witches supposedly spawned from the devil, Mignola creates a delightful bit of irony for Hellboy and the reader who likely does not realize his or her own complicity in reading another account of Melungeon witchcraft. In fact, the readers, like Hellboy, need not be aware of their own complicity in a long-standing tradition of mistake. The reader is not the one who needs to laugh; rather, it is the textual Melungeons who need to expose the naiveté of those consuming this text. As the main narrative of *The Crooked Man* is not an interactive textual experience where real participants might communicate with one another, Hellboy cheerfully stands in for us and takes the bulk of the beating.

As the comic's hero, Hellboy really should not operate as the comic's foil, but, as our surrogate in the conversation, he must bear witness to Tom's paying for his foolishness by allowing the Melungeons their laugh. Mignola alleviates this tension through a relatively simple and brilliant maneuver. As *Hellboy*, the comic, is told out of chronological order, he places this event at a moment when Hellboy is young and immature. At this point in Helboy's history, he does not, as yet, understand his greater role on Earth. This is actually depicted in *Crooked Man* #2 when Tom asks Hellboy if he understands his own burden yet. Hellboy responds with uncertainty:

Hellboy: I guess.
Tom: You don't feel it yet.
Hellboy: Guess not.
Cora: You will. (2)

Cora's warning to Hellboy seems somewhat ominous, but the reader of *Hellboy* is more than aware of Hellboy's larger role in the potential destruction of the planet. It is a moment of laughter in which the audience understands that Hellboy is unaware of his own destiny that has already been seen in the greater corpus of thirty-plus comics in the *Hellboy* series. But Mignola also depicts Hellboy, who, as the protagonist of his own comic, stands in as the character to whom the reading audience connects most strongly (Russell 43), as a foolish surrogate for an audience taking advantage of the Melungeons' mythological history. The contemporary reading audience, through Hellboy, is put in the place of earlier generations of readers who uncritically consumed warped accounts of Melungeon life, finding them grotesque, disgusting, and laughable. Now, the Melungeons get an opportunity to laugh at and ridicule those who once ridiculed them. Witkins, the Devil's emissary, as he puts it to Tom, "had a deal" with the people he took advantage of, Melungeon or otherwise, and Witkins tells him, "you still gotta pay for it" (3:1). Witkins is speaking to Tom and Hellboy, both outsiders to the Melungeons, but the argument applies to the reader as well. In order to tell this story, Mignola makes use of the tropes and schemes of witchcraft and various touch points of Melungeon legend. He uses the histories written by the crooked, bankrupt journalism of myth and legend in order to tell a story about how the Melungeons were taken advantage of by a Crooked Man because, to liberate in a Bakhtinian sense, he can only present a more complete account. Direct revision is just as totalitarian as the initial oppression the book seeks to expose. The Crooked Man in question could just as easily be seen as a metonymy of a crooked collection of histories taking advantage of the Melungeons.

Of course, we must remember that, as with Effie, the Crooked Man is not the most positive representation of the Melungeons and is consistent with the worst misreading of their legend. But he does get some opportunity to laugh at the misperceptions of Melungeons, specifically their connections with witchcraft and Christianity. Seemingly drawing straight from the Drumgoole and Berry accounts shown earlier, the sheer terror inspired by Witkins's presence as a cursed Melungeon seems to be enough to unite African Americans and whites (and demons) in a geographical area still divided along color lines during the period. When Hellboy and Tom take up sanctuary in the large, white, dilapidated church pastored by the African American Reverend Watts, they believe themselves to be safe because they have found sanctuary on consecrated land. Watts claims, "Their magic don't work here day or night" (2:21). With considerable confidence, Witkins rejoins that comment telepathically, smugly stating, "You think that's true, Tommy?" (2:21). Witkins thus challenges this particular church's status as a literal and metaphorical sanctuary. Corben illustrates the church as a white edifice whose best days are long behind it, now in complete disrepair, led by a priest without a congregation. Watts seems to believe that God will operate as his trump card in this battle, and, yet, whether due to some overconfidence in his own powers or the overt hypocrisy of the moment, Witkins remains unimpressed: "Let him go, [Watts] . . . I ain't afraid of [Hellboy]. And I SURE as Hell ain't afraid of you" (2: 22–23).

Standing at the edge of the church grounds with a coterie of witch allies (gnarled and bent old women whose power, if any, is ambiguous, and who are far from the moldering terrors of Cora's imagination), the Crooked Man

10.4. From *Hellboy: The Crooked Man* #3 (September 2008). Written by Mike Mignola with art by Richard Corben. Copyright © 2008 Michael Mignola.

challenges Watts's authority and exposes him to be something of a fraud himself. Witkins tells Watts, "Can't help but notice the sad state of that old church. It's a shame.... She looks like she might fall down any time" (3: 5–6). This ominous claim is a damning critique of a faith that seems to be failing. And indeed, Witkins's powers cause the church to fall. The white paint chips away; the mortar crumbles and The Crooked Man exposes the sanctuary as little more than a shack figuratively and literally built upon shaky foundations. Mignola and Corben illustrate this point as Witkins, during battle with Hellboy and Tom, reanimates several of the church's former parishioners

10.5. From *Hellboy: The Crooked Man* #3 (September 2008). Written by Mike Mignola with art by Richard Corben. Copyright © 2008 Michael Mignola.

from the church graveyard, congregants who would have likely shunned the Melungeons and their supposed depravity. Yet, they are depicted just as desiccated and ripe with decay, utterly grotesque in their zombie-like state, as the Melungeon witches who had earlier called out to Cora. The critique is subtle but certainly seems to undermine simple dichotomies of Melungeon corruption versus non-Melungeon purity as, below the ground, everyone suffers the same putrefaction—and, as Witkins and the witches reveal, Watts's parishioners were hardly models of rectitude when they were above the ground, either: "There's Abel Jacobs who beat his wife," one witch remarks; "And Nate Greene who stole from the government," says another (3:9).

Witkins offers the blind, old priest enough wealth to restore the church from the "sad state" it is in, and when Watts declines, Witkins shows Watts exactly how flimsy a sanctuary it is by using his power and restoring the preacher's youth and sight so that he might enjoy the money he has offered a bit more. And while Watts claims that he came "fairly by my years and ... afflictions" (7) and that he does not want the Devil's gifts, Corben illustrates him to be hypocritical, tempted by his newfound youth and potency. This becomes particularly apparent when Witkins produces a young woman for his new eyes to gaze upon, reminding Watts that he once had "a weakness for the pretty girls" (3:8). When the young woman requests a kiss from the priest, his piety begins to crumble as his restored vigor, her beauty, and his moral beliefs come into direct conflict with each other in front of the reader, who can see his defenses melting away before their very eyes. Unfortunately, the joke is on Watts: just as they are about to embrace, Witkins turns the young lady back into a grotesque corpse who still entreats affection from Watts (see figures 10.4 and 10.5).

The Crooked Man takes advantage of the folklore and superstitions that Watts, Hellboy, and Tom all believe in to demonstrate the extent of his power. He shows them to all to be fools before his power as he mocks Watts's claims, not setting foot on church ground but instead causing supernatural events to occur on church property and within the church itself. The knowledge of the Melungeons in which Watts and Tom were so secure has proven to be inadequate and incomplete, and Witkins's rampage emphasizes the dire consequences of investing in such a simple view of the Melungeons. Watts, so proud and defiant before, used his faith in his beliefs as a sword against Witkins; now, he cowers before the awesome power of the Crooked Man, praying that God might take his sight away from him (3:11). Tom, essentially, gives up: "I'm done for" (3:1).

As one might suspect, an immature Hellboy responds to being made to look foolish the only way he can: with threats of violence. The Crooked Man responds in kind by again illustrating that the church offers him no protection by magically shooting the churchyard's fence pickets through Hellboy, much to the enjoyment of the women surrounding him (3:4). Ultimately, in order to defeat him, Hellboy is forced out of the failed sanctuary into a direct confrontation with the Crooked Man, and he is successful. Yet, in order to defeat him, Hellboy must utilize the power of the Melungeons and rectify it—in fact, sanctify it: Watts transforms the Tom's witchbone through the power of the Holy Spirit and uses it to burn a cross into the shovel that Hellboy uses to defeat Witkins (3:15–16). Metaphorically, Mignola forces both Hellboy and the reader to take stock of their knowledge of the Melugeons and think about them in a *slightly* different way. As depicted by Mignola and Corben, Hellboy and his allies are forced to hold the Melungeons up to the light, at the safety of arm's length, and make them less abhorrent by mixing something from their own sphere (The Holy Spirit) into something from the Melungeons' sphere in order to transform the witchbone into a weapon for good (3:15–16). Even in overall defeat, this is a slight victory for the Melungeons, as this reconciliation between factions forces Hellboy to meet Witkins on his own terms, breaking down the artificial binary between Melungeons and non-Melungeons.

It might be seen as something of a pyrrhic victory for the Melungeons to only be able to laugh at their oppressors in yet another representation of themselves as being depicted as strange, exotic, and foreign, but there is something to be said for Mignola taking the time to make the reader confront those representations. Although the dominant narrative seems to have reasserted itself at the story's close, that narrative has been revealed as deeply flawed, not truly accounting for the type and extent of Witkins's power and, perhaps by extension, for the complexity of the Melungeons in general. Further, Mignola includes something denied them in most popular representations: the possibility of reconciliation and reintegration into the larger community. Tom, Watts, and Hellboy are not the only inhabitants of the dilapidated church. Cora's ghost, thought to be totally beholden to the Melungeons, is there as well; she warned Watts to prepare for their arrival. Watts says that "the Devil might've got her body but he didn't get her soul. Lord be praised for his little mercies" (2:18). Cora rejoins with an unheard "Amen" (2:18).

The same might be said for *The Crooked Man* in its entirety. It cannot undo decades and centuries of journalistic mistake. It can, however, make the reader look squarely at the history and challenge it. Alan Moore once wrote of *Hellboy*, "There seems to be some new scent in the air [here]: a sense of new and different possibilities; new ways for us to interact with History" ("Introduction"). Yet, it is a good question to pose as to why Mignola simply does not seize the opportunity in *Hellboy* to confront directly a history of monological journalism hell-bent, pun intended, on appropriating an historical misreading of the Melungeon people for commercial or exploitative ends. It is even fair to openly wonder if Mignola, not unlike Drumgoole, does the same thing in *The Crooked Man* (this essay could not be a *fair* Bakhtinian reading of laughter if it was not directly open to that interpretation).

However, I would suggest that for Mignola to create a dialogue with history as he does with *Hellboy*, he would have to do so in a manner that allows for inquiry, not didacticism or pedantry. *Hellboy* has always existed as a story between the margins of history; it is a narrative that seemingly has always been part of our history, but Hellboy's interactions with it are intentionally veiled from the public and interstitial. Hellboy acts, and is often a catalyst, for elements in an established history, our history, but his story has always fallen between the spaces of recorded history. *Hellboy* fills in the absent accounts and occluded entries in the historical record to provide a more complete picture of Mignola's representation of our world, pockmarks and all. As such, *The Crooked Man* is almost a perfect metonym for picking up and continuing the Melungeon conversation that had also fallen into the cracks of history. However, Mignola does not suggest that his work exculpates, or even seeks to exculpate, history of any crime or damage, but he does suggest that *Hellboy* may open the door to new manners of exploration of and discussion with it. Perhaps that is a good enough starting point for reentry into the Melungeons' story. With any luck, it becomes a trend.

Notes

1. To be accurate to Pollitzer's piece, he identifies them as most others do: a "marginal people" built up of tri-racial isolates (719). See Winkler, Vande Brake, Kennedy et al. Curiously at odds with this estimate of the Melungeon population is a report in the Knoxville newspaper, the *News-Sentinel*, that, as of July 2, 1969, declared that: "there's no smaller minority anywhere in America than the Melungeons. And no more mysterious one" (Ivey 87).

2. It is a somewhat interesting aside to note that Burnett, like many other scholars, noted that the term "Melungeon" was likely bestowed upon this people by non-Melungeon whites of the area as a bastardization of the French word *mélange*, of mixed or incongruous elements, but to Burnett simply meaning "mixed" (348) and, in the present indicative, "*melangeons*" (Dunlap and Weslager 83). That racial mixture is, of itself, one of the great debates on the Melungeon people. And one taken up better, and at length, by Vande Brake, Winkler, and Kennedy in their respective studies.

3. As of 1950 (Pollitzer 722).

4. Different spellings of "Melungeon" have been accepted at different times by different scholars, critics, and journalists. For the purposes of this chapter, I will use the default spelling of Melungeon and leave alternate spellings unaltered from their original context. But for a more complete discussion of this, one need only look at A. R. Dunlap and C. A. Weslager's 1948 article "Trends in the naming of Tri-Racial Mixed-Blood Groups in the Eastern United States" from the journal *American Speech* that goes into great geographical detail concerning the differences in spelling by region.

5. A simple Bakthinian concept meaning, literally, "time/space" (Morson and Emerson 366). As opposed to chronologically, I use the term here because it allows me to view Mignola as someone who, in Morson and Emerson's words, acts understanding "the context and the relation of actions and events to it" (367). The action here is constructing Hellboy's

chronology a-chronologically in order to flesh out the character by virtue of filling in his back story, side stories, and even future stories alongside the master narrative, proper, which had been established since chapter one of the *Seed of Destruction* arc in 1994, but, in actuality, began in a short comic composed by Mignola and John Byrne in 1993 (Mignola and Byrne, *Seed of Destruction* TPB).

6. More accurately, according to an unnamed correspondent from *Littell's Living Age* in January-March 1849, "between Powell's Mountain and the Copper Ridge." This article was appropriated and rewritten for the *Knoxville Register* on September 6, 1848, with additions including the first mention of the Portuguese ancestry (Elder 117) and a new marker in Newman's Ridge, which happens to also be in Hancock County (Haywood 45–46).

7. Drumgoole, by trade, was an engrossing clerk in the Tennessee senate who only occasionally wrote poetry and features articles (Winkler "About").

8. It should be noted that Drumgoole spent two weeks among the Melungeons "researching" her article ("About"). Her motivations, as she explained them, were due to her curiosity into their "dialect" and supposed "distilling" practices (Ivey 95).

9. Though many definitions of "fakelore" exist, I will default to Vande Brake, who borrows Richard Dorson's explanation: "The presentation of spurious and synthetic writings under the claim that they are genuine folklore . . . rewritten from earlier literary and journalistic sources in an endless chain of regurgitation" (137).

10. In 1944, near the end of the Second World War, Hellboy is "summoned" to the "real" world in a ritual performed by the otherwise historically dead Grigory Rasputin in Scotland (Mignola and Byrne, "Seed of Destruction"). Rasputin overcame the encumbrance of death and worked with Nazi scientists who required his skills as a mystic for their project Ragna Rok, which, as the name implies and is popularly misinterpreted, is tantamount to biblical apocalypse or, simply put, the end of days.

11. Particularly parodic as, though he does not know it at this point in the timeline, Hellboy himself is only half-demon; his mother was a witch (Blake and Edidin 61).

12. "Outwardly" because the idea of Cora Fisher being "witched" appears in the opening exchange between Hellboy and locals in *Crooked Man* #1 (2). While, the Melungeons are not named, references to "Turkey Creek" (1:2) and a depiction of The Crooked Man who happened to be "behind half the trouble between the whites an the Indians" (13) certainly *could* mark enough speculations concerning Melungeon lore. During the initial discussion I considered between Tom and Hellboy from *Crooked Man* #2, Corben illustrates a grotesque caricature of two Croatoans with dislocated jaws, misplaced eyes, and ritualistic regalia and pose (bone and bead coverings while the more dominant female is depicted stretching out a bat) playing into legends concerning the origins of the Melungeons (5).

13. A quick note here as to graphic depiction: Effie is drawn, seemingly, to an almost precision by Corben, as coming out of the Drumgoole account: "Their dress is ordinary calico, or cotton, short blouse, without buttons or other fastenings than brass pins conspicuously arranged" (qtd. in Winkler 268), but I do not make mention of either her or the Crooked Man's appearance in constructing them as Melungeons due to the wide disparity in actual visual accounts of them. Price notes that they have "a distinctly brown complexion and straight black hair, who generally lack Negroid features but whose ancestry might be Indian" (259), while, later in the same piece, he claims that Virginian Melungeons have "curly black hair and lean faces with rounded features" (260). Ivey claims that the difference in appearance are so accentuated that she agrees with Winkler's proposition saying that they

"may scarcely be spoken of as a race" (95). As no one distinctive agreement on appearance seems possible or appreciated, I have chosen to disregard any racial or ethnic markers ascribed to Witkins or Kolb, particularly as they are given to exaggerated characteristics associated with the grotesque parody Bakhtin suggests would occur in subversive commentary such as Mignola's.

Works Cited

Allen, S. D. "More on the Free Black Population of the Southern Appalachian Mountains: Speculations on the North African Connection." *Journal of Black Studies*. 25.6 (1995): 651–71. Print.

Bakhtin, M. M. *The Dialogic Imagination*. Austin: U of Texas P, 1981. Print.

———. *Rabelais and his World*. Bloomington: Indiana UP, 1984. Print.

Ball, Bonnie. *The Melungeons*. Johnson City, TN: Overmountain P, 1992. Print.

Beale, Calvin. "An Overview of the Phenomenon of Mixed Racial Isolates in the United States." *American Anthropologist* 74.3 (1972): 704–10. Print.

Berry, Brewton. *Almost White*. New York: Macmillan, 1963. Print.

Blake, Victoria and Rachel Edidin. "Character Profiles." *Mike Mignola's Hellboy: The Companion*. Milwaukie, OR: Dark Horse Comics, 2008. 15–132. Print.

Bloch, Robert. "Introduction." *Hellboy: Seed of Destruction*. Milwaukie, OR: Dark Horse Comics, 2003. Print.

Burnett, Swan. "A Note on the Melungeons." *American Anthropologist* 2.4 (1889): 347–50. Print.

Cohen, David Steven. "The Origin of the "Jackson Whites": History and Legend among the Ramapo Mountain People." *Journal of American Folklore* 85 (1972): 260–66. Print.

Elder, Pat. *Melungeons: Examining an Appalachian Legend*. Blountville, TN: Continuity P, 1999. Print.

Dunlap, A. R. and C. A. Weslager. "Trends in the Naming of Tri-Racial Mixed-Blood Groups in the Eastern United States." *American Speech* 22. 2 (1947): 81–87. Print.

Gianni, Gary. "Introduction." *Hellboy: Strange Places*. Milwaukie, OR: Dark Horse Comics, 2006. Print.

Haywood, John. *The Civil and Political History of the State of Tennessee*. Nashville, TN: Barbee & Smith, 1891. Print.

Hirschman, Elizabeth. *Melungeons: The Last Lost Tribe in America*. Macon, GA: Mercer UP, 2005. Print.

Holquist, Michael. "Prologue." *Rabelais and his World*. Bloomington: Indiana UP, 1984. xiii–xxiii. Print.

Ivey, Saundra Keyes. "Ascribed Ethnicity and the Ethnic Display Event: The Melungeons of Hancock County." *Western Folklore* 36.1 (1977): 85–107. Print.

Kennedy, Brent. N. *The Melungeons: The Resurrection of a Proud People*. Macon, GA: Mercer UP, 1997. Print.

MacPherson, Don. "By Hook or By Crook: *Hellboy—The Crooked Man*." *Eye on Comics*. November 2008. 1 October 2009. Web.

Mignola, Mike. "Mike Mignola's Hellboy: World's Greatest Paranormal Investigator." *Hellboy: Seed of Destruction*. Milwaukie, OR: Dark Horse Comics, 2003. Print.

Mignola, Mike (w) and Richard Corben (a). *Hellboy: The Crooked Man #1* (July 2008). Milwaukie, OR: Dark Horse Comics. Print.

———. *Hellboy: The Crooked Man #2* (Aug 2008). Milwaukie, OR: Dark Horse Comics. Print.

———. *Hellboy: The Crooked Man #3* (Sep 2008). Milwaukie, OR: Dark Horse Comics. Print.

Mignola, Mike and John Byrne. *Hellboy: Seed of Destruction*. Milwaukie, OR: Dark Horse Comics, 2003. Print.

Moore, Alan. "Introduction." *Hellboy: Wake The Devil*. Milwaukie, OR: Dark Horse Comics, 2003. Print.

Morson, Gary and Caryl Emerson. *Mikhail Bakhtin: Creation of a Prosaics*. Stanford: Stanford UP, 1990. Print.

Pollitzer, William. "The Physical Anthropology and Genetics of Marginal People of the Southeastern United States." *American Anthropologist*. 74.3 (1972): 719:734. Print.

Price, Edward. "The Melungeons: A Mixed-Blood Strain of the Southern Appalachians." *Geographical Review* 41.2 (1951): 256–71. Print.

Professor Fury. "On Ethnicity and Appalachia in *Hellboy—The Crooked Man*." *Pretty Fakes*. November 2008. 1 October 2009. Web.

Russell, David. *Literature for Children*. Boston: Pearson, 2009.

Schrift, Melissa. "Melungeons and the Politics of Heritage." *Southern Heritage on Display*. Ed. Celeste Ray. Tuscaloosa: U of Alabama P, 2003. 106–29. Print.

Sovine, Melanie. "The Mysterious Melungeions: A Critique of the Mythical Image." Diss. U of Kentucky, 1982. Ann Arbor: UMI, 1982. Print.

Tindall, George. "Beyond the Mainstream: The Ethnic Southerners." *Journal of Southern History* 40.1 (1974): 3–18. Print.

Vande Brake, Katherine. *How They Shine: Melungeon Characters in the Fiction of Appalachia*. Macon, GA: Mercer UP, 2001. Print.

Weiner, Stephen. "The Literary Heritage of Hellboy." *Mike Mignola's Hellboy: The Companion*. Milwaukie, OR: Dark Horse Comics, 2008. 209–21. Print.

Winkler, Wayne. "About the Melungeons." *Melungeon Heritage Association*. February 2004. 1 October 2009. Web.

———. *Walking Toward the Sunset: The Melungeons of Appalachia*. Macon, GA: Mercer UP, 2004. Print.

Worden, William. "Sons of the Legend." *Saturday Evening Post* 18 October 1947: 28+. Print.

Yolen, Jane. "Introduction." *Hellboy: Darkness Calls*. Milwaukie, OR: Dark Horse Comics, 2008. Print.

Meat Fiction and Burning Western Light

The South in Garth Ennis and Steve Dillon's *Preacher*

—Nicolas Labarre

Published from 1995 to 2000, Preacher is a violent, provocative, and influential series. It was one of the defining titles of the Vertigo imprint, a division of DC Comics aiming at adult readers that emerged from the successes of Alan Moore's *Swamp Thing* and Neil Gaiman's *Sandman*. Scripted by an Irishman, Garth Ennis, and drawn by an Englishman, Steve Dillon, it is a deliberately blasphemous, violent, and profane epic, a quest for an indecisive God in a southern landscape saturated with popular culture.

With a narrative center located between Louisiana and Texas, *Preacher* belongs to the field of southern fiction. The physical geography of the series is secondary, however, to its representation of the South as a mythic and mass-culture-saturated place. The series equates the South with a mode of identity, with a way of seeing the world, and it questions the South's representations in mass culture. The series acknowledges the dominant representation of the South through what Tara McPherson calls a "stock set of recurring icons" and characters, but it severs these icons from their historical roots, using them as freestanding signifiers that it reconstructs or discards (76).

The South, in *Preacher*, is a set of representations only loosely connected to geography. It is close to becoming what Scott Romine—borrowing from Baudrillard—announced as a potential final development for southern literature in general: to construct a South that is "a weightless simulacrum," creating its own reality through the deployment of conspicuously southern elements borrowed not from the "natural" world but from preexisting cultural objects (43). In her study of photography in contemporary southern writing, Katherine Henninger shows how representations of the South have

11.1. From *Preacher* #1 (April 1995). Written by Garth Ennis with art by Steve Dillon. Copyright © 1995 Garth Ennis and Steve Dillon.

been naturalized to hide the power struggles that have shaped those representations (180–81). By deliberately conflating fiction and reality, *Preacher* negates this naturalization and creates a space where symbols and representations of the South can be freely examined and reevaluated, placed into conversation and conflict. Further, *Preacher* attempts to clear the ground for a renovated hybrid fiction that would blend the iconography of the South and the West in order to redefine both the limitations and the possibilities of southern identity, offering a version of the South self-consciously in dialogue with its popular representations and with the real histories those representations both reveal and conceal. From this dialogue comes the possibility for a new, more complex South, one that acknowledges its histories and representations without being constrained by familiar narratives.

The ostensible southernness of the series is established in its very first issue with broad strokes, relying on the reader's familiarity with a set of symbols codifying the South. In this issue, most places (a diner, a street in Dallas, a flying structure in Heaven, a cave) are drawn as blank spaces, devoid of details, with the notable exception of Annville, Texas. There, pickups are parked outside the "Long Trailer" bar, decorated with a Budweiser emblem; a Dallas Cowboys helmet is prominently displayed inside. Steve Dillon, a penciller with a tendency to standardize the look of secondary characters, lavishes unusual details on the crowd to emphasize the many twisted and subhuman figures who inhabit the place (see figure 11.1).

These visual clues establish a familiar vision of a certain South, with some support from non-diegetic captions (the lyrics to Willie Nelson's song "Time of the Preacher"), thematic elements (the eschatological theological vision, reminding the reader of the Bible Belt setting through visions of fiery apocalypse), emphasized accents for comic effect, and some easily identified xenophobic southern road police. In this first issue, Ennis and Dillon bring together familiar visual or aural markers of southernness, borrowed from innumerable popular culture products, from *Easy Rider* (1969) to *Thelma and Louise* (1991) or *Blood Simple* (1984), and used here as a functional background, a place stocked with beefy extras, without children, elders, or any aspiration to realism. This setting is in fact disposable, destined to be burned to the ground when Jesse Custer, a white-clad preacher, becomes the vessel of a god-like entity, Genesis, an event that initiates a 66-issue quest for God.

This use of identifiable genres is not limited to the representation of the South in the series. *Preacher* presents its many pop cultural references openly and uses them as part of an ongoing meta-fictional discourse. Most characters are popular culture experts, and even European villains know their Westerns well enough to make casual reference to them: the narrative universe of the series is, by many respects "right outta the movies" (35:13), although Steve Dillon's stiff, semi-realistic graphical treatment always keep these references at a distance. The range of these references is vast—from buddy cop movies (issues #5–7, a *Lethal Weapon* parody) to Rob Reiner's *Spinal Tap* ("Who turned the volume of ignorance up to eleven?" Tulip asks [29:7]) to advertisements, such as when the Irish vampire Cassidy refers to the United States as "Marlboro country" (29:17)—but they generally fall into two broad categories. Some of them function merely as in-jokes or narrative shortcuts, a quick way to characterize the protagonists, à la *Pulp Fiction*.

The other set of references is central to the narrative and theme of the series since, taken together, they outline the complex and conflicting representations of the South in popular culture. The cumulative weight of these references casts a doubt about the possibility of reading *Preacher*'s world as a self-contained, coherent, diegetic universe. While characters in *Preacher* never acknowledge the fact that they are comic book creations, Custer nevertheless accepts his role as a character in a fiction. He is mentored from his early age on by a faceless but easily recognizable John Wayne whom no one but him can see or hear but who is nevertheless capable of helping him. In one striking instance, Custer's drugged trip into his unconscious takes the form of a visit to a movie theater, where he once again meets John Wayne.

This sequence bears further scrutiny: drugged, sitting on a tombstone in a graveyard, Custer starts his inner voyage through a six-panel sequence (32:6; see figure 11.2), a series of tightening close-ups that lead us into Jesse's film-structured unconscious. In each successive panel (excepting an over-the-shoulder view of Custer's guide), the frame closes in on Custer's face, grimacing, with his eyes rolled upward, while he goes through the credits of the movie to come: "Voodoo features presents / A Mind's Eye production / Of a Jesse Custer film / God almighty / The Saint of Killers / Those damn angels / and the Duke / in." These six panels create a very short temporal unit, one that follows a staccato rhythm signaled by the minute changes from one panel to the next and the fracturing of the text into brief word balloons. The moment-to-moment transitions, to use Scott McCloud's terminology (69–75), use such small increments that they come to suggest the successive frames of a film's tracking shot. Thus, even though the presence of word balloons, the narrowness of the panels, and Dillon's style prevent any confusion with actual film frames, the word "Genesis" that appears on top of the next page (see figure 11.3) in huge serif type, cannot be interpreted as anything but a movie title (32:7). McCloud suggests that moment-to-moment transitions

11.2. From *Preacher* #32 (December 1997). Written by Garth Ennis with art by Steve Dillon. Copyright © 1997 Garth Ennis and Steve Dillon.

11.3. From *Preacher* #32 (December 1997). Written by Garth Ennis with art by Steve Dillon. Copyright © 1997 Garth Ennis and Steve Dillon.

require little closure, little effort from the reader. Here, they are used to guide this reader through a paradoxical change of medium, from the "reality" of the comic world to Custer's unconscious, drawn in the form of a movie theater with Jesse as an audience member. John Wayne appears in the center panel, an image on a movie screen, his face heavily shadowed as he faces the reader while framed against an open, brightly colored canyon landscape.

In *Preacher*, Dillon uses ragged panel borders and numerous overlapping or borderless panels, a strategy that prevents any easy identification between the comic page and movie stills, but he draws the screen in Custer's mind with straight lines, in sharp contract with the erratic borders of the page on which it appears. In the last panel of the page, Custer himself is drawn almost as he was at the beginning of the six-panel sequence of the previous page, but the narrow panel in which he had been inscribed is now as wide as the page itself. He wears the same costume, and his black hair still stands out on a black background thanks to a white outline, but he now looks relaxed, smiling, with a soda and a popcorn bucket in his hands. The introduction to the movie world as Custer's unconscious thus also foreshadows the opposition between the constraining world of the South and the open space of the West.

The scene demonstrates that there is no bright line between what is accepted as "reality" and what is considered "fiction" in *Preacher*. Dillon's graphic treatment is identical on both sides of the straight line of the movie screen; Custer is not drawn in a different visual style from the John Wayne he sees. Thus, Dillon draws the attention to the theoretical separation of the two media, only to unite them as part of a continuous narrative universe. The sequence is in effect a reversal of critic Irving Howe's famous dismissive judgment of cinema: "The movie-house is a psychological cloakroom, where one checks one personality" (498). Mass culture critics such as Howe perceived the movies as an external force that threatened the individual. Custer's psyche is, on the contrary, entirely bound within the theater's wall, emphasizing the role of popular conventions in the shaping of one's identity and of southern identity in particular—although at this point, a shift toward other genres and regional representations is already apparent.

This erasure of boundaries and the lack of a diegetic universe in which "reality" could be separated from "fiction" implies that the stereotypical characters and situations Custer confronts in the course of the series should not be considered simply as embodiments of stereotypes, but, to a certain extent, as the stereotypes themselves. Custer's quest is also a *genre-shaping* endeavor, in which a fiction based in exploring and enacting the most familiar clichés of the South's representation explicitly reshapes itself from issue to issue. Southern identity is thus constructed through a visual adventure narrative rather than purely through written or spoken language. Significantly, Custer is awarded a word-based power early in the series: he has the capacity to utter self-fulfilling prophecy, inescapable orders. However, when he is confronted with powerful southern clichés—notably a fallen belle in a crumbling plantation manor and a Klansman—that power of simply rephrasing the world is shown to be either ineffective or inappropriate. The conflict has to be played out as a violent and visual struggle, a fact that underscores how thoroughly common conceptions of the South are constructed and negotiated through visual images.

As *Preacher* became a success, Steve Dillon and Garth Ennis shifted the emphasis of the series, downplaying its religious elements and turning their attention to an investigation of the nature of the United States and the South in particular.[1] The first covers of the series (Custer in prayer, with a burning church in the foreground for #1, Custer angrily questioning an angel for #4, and so on) sketched a blasphemous religious approach that was conceived as the selling point of the series, judging from the promotional material preceding it: "Jesse Custer was a young small-town preacher slowly losing his faith . . . until he merged with a supernatural being called Genesis. Now endowed with a strange ability, Jesse sets out on the biggest mission a preacher could imagine: to find God—literally" (*Absolute Vertigo* inside front cover). However, after a brief episode in New York, *Preacher* moves back to the South. If the southern background was an ephemeral creation in the first story arc, borrowed wholesale from Hollywood to be destroyed after a few pages, it becomes much more elaborate from this point in the series. This added complexity is not, however, a shift to "realism," for the South is consistently treated as a set of representations more than as an actual place.

The narrative arc that begins with the story "All in the Family" (#8) opens with a flashback to a moment in 1974 when Jesse had to watch his father being shot in the head.[2] Only toward the end of the issue does the reader discover that the scene and most of the issue took place in Louisiana, in a plantation of all places, "the privileged site of southern history and feminity," as Tara McPherson puts it (44). Significantly, this is also the first issue of the series where Ennis deals with the backstories of its characters, as Custer and his girlfriend, Tulip, tell each other about their past. This visit to the South is thus positioned first and foremost as a trip to the past, a trip through history: this South is a place of memory and the source of Custer's identity rather than just a geographical place.

These episodes revolve around the L'Angelle family: a decadent southern clan living in Angelville, a decaying plantation set on the border of Texas and Louisiana, where they are held in the thrall of an anachronistic and horrifying matriarch. The L'Angelles are Custer's family on his mother's side, from whom he had run away in his teens and who now seek to return him to the plantation. Even more than in the series opening, Ennis and Dillon deploy identifiable icons of the South. Issue #8 has three splash pages: a swearing Custer, the plantation, and Marie L'Angelle, a fallen belle. These full-page illustrations hint at the ambiguous status of these images. Not only are they part of the narrative sequence, but they also stand on their own as icons do. The clichés are presented as such—they are not naturalized. As seen in figure 11.4, Marie L'Angelle, most often referred to as "Grandma," is always shown wearing the same white negligee as Vivien Leigh in Kazan's *A Streetcar Named Desire*, herself a broken version of the belle, a similarity further underlined by her French name and her habit of setting genteel social codes against human feelings. According to critic Kathryn Seidel, Blanche DuBois in Tennessee Williams's play is an anachronism who "withdraws into a world of illusion and madness" (166). Marie L'Angelle in *Preacher* follows the same path, but in the preserved southern plantation where she lives with her two adopted sons, T. C. and Jody, this world of illusion becomes the accepted common ground. Unlike Blanche Dubois, these characters are shown as powerful within their realm. This power is made clearer by the presence within the narrative of another southern family, a swamp-dwelling clan whose physical deformities indicate generations of incest and whose son, Billy-Bob, becomes a friend to the young Jesse Custer. Angry but passive victims of the L'Angelles' violence, their helplessness emphasizes by contrast the power that a similar character, T. C., can wield once he is integrated into a power structure such as the L'Angelle family. T. C. is known for his indiscriminate sexual appetites, including his lust for chickens. Yet though he is arguably no less sexually deviant than the incestuous swamp-dwellers, he occupies a position of power and authority. The plantation may not be intrinsically superior to the swamp-dwellers' home, but it is immediately presented as dominant, in a literal interpretation of the relative power these narratives have in popular representations of the South.

The power of the plantation owners, of southern aristocracy, and the power of the stereotypes themselves in popular culture are thus reaffirmed through three issues (#8–10) during which the outsiders, Custer and Tulip, are tied and helpless. Blanche DuBois was powerless to impose her will and values upon Stanley Kowalski and his friends, but the constant threat of

11.4. From *Preacher* #8 (November 1995). Written by Garth Ennis with art by Steve Dillon. Copyright © 1995 Garth Ennis and Steve Dillon.

violence in Angelville makes even Custer adopt a deferent attitude in front of Marie L'Angelle. However, as soon as he frees himself, he can claim his identity back. He does not long for a lost past, he does not acknowledge the faded beauty of the belle. Instead, he challenges the coherence of the fictional world delineated by these "treasured icons" of the South (McPherson 5).

Custer's point of view, in this instance, is that of the outsider. While he remains a southerner throughout the series, he does not belong among these decaying representations of southern icons; rather, he brings to the narrative oppositional readings of the power structure within the family. His role in revealing the inherent tensions in the southern plantation narrative is first made clear in the way his presence affects the belle herself. The stereotype of the fallen belle is first taken to the extreme of having Marie reprimand Custer on his language, even when he is protesting a genuine act of horror—his dog having been nailed to a post (9:20)—a reprimand that contrasts her attachment to formality with her monstrous appearance. Set in the past, the scene also functions as a powerful anti-nostalgic device. When Marie is first introduced, the full-page panel presents her as a disheveled bald monster in a wheelchair, with long claw-like fingers, retaining formality and dignity in her speech alone: "Hello Jesse, won't you please introduce me to your young ladyfriend?" (8:21). At this point, the fallen belle merges with the terrifying image of the paralyzed cannibal patriarch in another southern family, that of Tobe Hooper's *The Texas Chainsaw Massacre*. The sense of ritual seen in the dinner scene of Hooper's film, in which a young girl is offered to the sub-human patriarch, is reproduced here with several pages during which Custer and Jesse wait for Marie L'Angelle to appear, before being presented to her. In both cases, members of the family submit to the elder, even though the elder's physical state betrays his or her decrepitude, especially when opposed to the youth of their victims.

Assisting Marie L'Angelle are her two adopted sons: T. C. and Jody. Both are violent, both have a twisted sexuality, and both evoke a conjunction of familiar images, from John Boorman's *Deliverance* to Cormac McCarthy's *Child of God*: zoophile monsters, half-beasts of the bayou, degenerates living with burning crosses on their lawns. They embody a familiar type in Deep South narrative, described by David Bell as "the badlands of the rural; its sick, sordid, malevolent, *nasty* underbelly" (91). They are, in other words, the flip side of the rural utopia of plantation fictions, just as Marie L'Angelle's role as a fallen belle, pushed to grotesque extremes, displays its similarities with the cannibalistic elders of *The Texas Chainsaw Massacre*. The L'Angelles are not just a southern family; instead, they encompass most of the negative imagery associated with the South. All the characteristics commonly attributed to southern society—its sense of place, of family, of history, of *belonging*—are presented as potential sources of horror—to the heroes and to the reader. There is a horror in being assimilated by this version of the South, as Marie L'Angelle makes explicit in this exchange:

> **Marie L'Angelle:** You've still got plenty of that Texas white trash father of yours in you, haven't you? That worthless waste of life who left you nothing but his name.
> **Jesse:** That's all I'll ever need.
> **Marie L'Angelle:** Well, Perhaps I'll take that from you too, Jesse. I'm taking everything else. Perhaps I'll change your name like I changed my own, when that useless cretin I married went and fell in the gumbo. Jesse L'Angelle. Hm. (8:22)

Being devoured by the swamp and being devoured by the L'Angelles are here equated, as they are on several other occasions: the mode of punishment favored by the family for its rebellious members is a stay in an underwater coffin. Cannibalism and body horror become metaphors for an identity crisis. In *Reconstructing Dixie*, Tara McPherson mentions her surprise at discovering an ad for a Scarlett O'Hara doll, "a mythologized image of innocence and purity" presented in an elaborately ornate box, in the very same issue of the *Los Angeles Times* that featured an article about James Allen's collection of lynching photographs and the horrors they revealed. For McPherson, the coincidence serves "as a powerful illustration of our cultural schizophrenia about the South," a condition that allows us to idealize the southern belle without considering the monstrous violence that enabled her coveted lifestyle (3). "All in the Family" challenges that schizophrenia through an organized destruction of the symbols (the plantation is burned, the family is an artificial one, the belle is monstrous) that culminates in a reduction of the bodies to pure flesh and meat.

The Texas Chainsaw Massacre, from which this aesthetic of the body horror seems to have been partly borrowed, has been described by critic Lew Brighton as the "*Gone with the Wind* of Meat Movies" (qtd. in Bloom). "Meat movies," a term sometimes simply referring to especially gory horror films, applies more strictly to a subset of late sixties and seventies releases focused on cannibalism, movies that have also been called "hillbilly horror" for their insistence on opposing rural and urban settings, North and South (Bell 97–99). *Preacher* brings to light the paradoxical cultural identity of a region defined simultaneously by the plantation myth and by such violent representations.³ It exposes the "tensions, ambivalences and ruptures" that exist in these narrations of the regions (McPherson 235).

Just as the L'Angelle plantation is located on the border of Louisiana and Texas, *Preacher* shows the place from the perspective of two apparently incompatible codes: plantation mythology and meat fiction. Such a mash-up of hitherto incompatible southern representations is not new, and Jon Smith notably delineated a similar process of juxtaposition in his study of punk appropriation of diverse southern narrative. For Smith, drawing on Dick Hebdige's study of subculture, a renewed sense of southern identity can be achieved through a borrowing and reconfiguring of "plundered" icons and codes of the region (86–89). However, *Preacher* does not always present this diversity of representations as enabling creative reconstructions, but often as obstacles to such reconstruction. Horrified by both visions, Custer destroys his enemies by fire, suggesting the possibility of a renovated southern identity that would forgo these reified genres and representations. Two similarly depicted brawls signal this reversal (#10 and #12): a young Custer is shown grievously hurt by his uncle Jody, then a later fight plays out in symmetrical fashion, while Custer only asks, "Getting old?" (12:9). What is at stake here is not so much a defeat of the South, but a defeat of a familiar depiction of the South as a place of submission and decay, a defeat that makes possible a renovated conception of the region, a transition for which Custer is but a means.

Having thus exposed the limits of a mythologized conception of feminity and family in the South, Ennis and Dillon again use meat fiction as a counterpoint when they address the issue of race relations in a story arc focusing on the Ku Klux Klan. Narratively and thematically, the two episodes are connected: in one of the establishing scenes of this arc (#41–48) Custer encounters a member of the inbred family who used to live near the plantation, and even more significantly, he later finds his mother, who was supposed to have died at Angelville; further, the plantation itself serves as the background of the cover for #43. Salvation, where the story is set, is a Texas town, and again a frontier, for *Preacher* positions Texas alternatively as belonging to the South and to the West. While Custer could not live in Angelville, in Louisiana, his connection with Salvation proves more ambiguous; while nothing could be saved in Angelville, Salvation can—unsurprisingly—be salvaged; while African Americans were conspicuously absent from the L'Angelle plantation, their fate is immediately called to attention in Salvation. This is a segregated South, where one Mexican idiot can be befriended, but where the "colored folks" mostly live in a place nicknamed "Coontown"

(41:19). When Custer consents to be the sheriff of the town, he discovers the city is in the hands of a diminutive meat-packer, Odin Quincannon. However, when Custer gathers the population to resist Quincannon (45:14), the first question raised is about the presence of African Americans, previously absent from both the city center and the visual space of the comics.

While the Angelville episode was an open parody of plantation romances, the focus here seems to be on an actual historical issue. However, segregation in Salvation is so open, so close to a caricature (Quincannon's lawyer is also a Nazi fetishist, for instance) that it functions once more as a pure signifier, a conflagration of familiar structures and images, from the tyrannical industrial leader to the gathering of the Klan. Tara McPherson notes that post-Civil Rights popular fiction about the South tends to use a "covert" or "lenticular" approach to racial logics (73). *Preacher*, in contrast, resurrects a more "overt" approach, drawing from *Birth of a Nation* in a manner similar to the way in which the Angelville episode reconstructed *Gone with the Wind* (which also includes a Klan raid in the novel, although not in Selznick's adaptation). From the onset of the episode, this social order is an anachronism, surviving only through the passivity of the locals, but one bound to collapse under an outsider's gaze.

Once more, the bodies and flesh serve as metaphors for the corruption of the social order. The meat packing plants were the setting for the *Texas Chainsaw Masscacre*, and Quincannon is presented as a diminutive Meat God, a minuscule Odin talking about himself in the third person, first introduced to the reader in an episode entitled "The Meat-Man Cometh." As with the plantation and Grandma L'Angelle, his first appearance takes place in a splash page (42:4): he comes out of a hangar, wearing his glasses, white briefs, socks, garters, and shoes, covered in blood. The blood forms a red X on his white chest, and taken together wih the blue door behind him, they evoke a fragmented Confederate flag. Quincannon stands for this mythical Griffithian South: he is a klansman (*Birth of a Nation* was initially released as *The Clansman*, the title of the Thomas Dixon novel it adapts), and he is also a grotesque parody of a man whose body—short, bald, and myopic— is contrasted with the power he assumes. His lawyer's sadistic habits frequently incapacitate his workers and his plant pollutes the region; but most shocking of all, his love for brutalized flesh is demonstrated by his habit of making love to a matronly shaped stack of meat from his abattoir, a hideous effigy he even abuses verbally.

Here, as in the L'Angelle story arc and in more minor episodes, such as a visit to a cult of "vampires" in New Orleans (#30–33), stock representations of the South are embodied by unambiguous villains, united by a taste for violence inscribed in the flesh. Carnality and brutalized flesh exist in a state of tension, of unstable equilibrium with the idealized plantation-centered narrative that is still the dominant popular representation of the region. What emerges from this conflict is not the complex, dialogic narrative hoped for by scholars such as McPherson (254–55), but a succession of horrifying tableaux (the aforementioned splash pages) that will be ended by Custer's arrival. This South, conceived not as a place but as a field of conflicting representations, is unsustainable because the gap between these conceptions cannot be bridged. Custer declares as much when he discovers a badly wounded Quincannon making love to his meat girl and decides to kill him: "This ain't a mercy killing, I'd sure like to know what is"(48:8). Like the L'Angelle plantation, the meat packing plants are also thoroughly razed by fire. The fire acts as a powerful symbol, placed as it is in opposition with the tainted flesh presented before; Custer cauterizes these old wounds, but *Preacher* suggests that his intervention is only incidental. Before the destruction of his plant, a lightning bolt strikes Odin (himself a distorted thunder God) at a time when he is threatening to destroy Salvation. His pretentions to divinity are denied, but this *deus ex machina* (to quote Custer, "that was pretty fuckin' lucky" [47:19]) is more than a narrative trick: Odin, Marie L'Angelle, and their subordinates are characters out of their time, bound to be eventually destroyed. Custer's presence, once more, reveals the tensions and exposes the contradictions of representations already bound to fall apart.

These two episodes, and a few ancillary moments beyond the scope of this essay, suggest the impossibility of getting to a unified notion of southernness through established popular representations. They accomplish within the comic a task similar to that undertaken by academics such as Barabara Ladd, in pointing out the "anxiety" surrounding a conception of the South, based around a litany of all-too familiar places—"working plantations . . . tobacco fields and tobacco barns, small towns, 'niggertowns'"—that "animate southern literature, that construct memory and shape the future" (47). These episodes also hint at the problematic relationship between southerness and place, through the emphasis on frontier and on Texas, a state belonging at once to two different regions. Yet, just as Barbara Ladd concludes that "the South continues to mean something" (57) in spite of its perpetual construction and reconstruction, *Preacher* suggests the possibility of reinventing southerness through a questioning of authority and a displacement of some of the most conventional representations of the region, with values and codes of the Western as a suggested alternative.

What Ennis proposes, through Custer, is first a shift of emphasis from symbolic structures, erected to maintain a decaying status quo, to individuals. When Custer arrives in Salvation and hears a group of drunks verbally abusing a Mexican man in a bar, the reader comes to expect a bar fight, a recurring motif in *Preacher*. The composition of the panel itself, recalling that of Custer's arrival in Annville's bar, reinforces this expectation. This time, however, he is stopped by the good-looking and evidently intelligent barmaid (later revealed to be his mother) who advises him to look at the scene from another perspective: "Hector's a little slow, doesn't know too many people. And those dicks are pretty good to him, most of the time. Hell, sometimes it's even his turn to go home with Cora" (41:18). Thus, Custer's and the reader's attentions are drawn to the necessity of going beyond superficial representations, to focus on individual point of view: to move away from a stereotypical situation (the racist comments) and encompass oppositional, individual readings of the same scene. The racism is not denied, the stereotype is not without basis, but the politics of the interaction cannot be reduced to a superficial reading. Custer, an outsider, is unable at first to perceive what the insider points out. Custer's deputy later emphasizes the difference when she notes:

Custer: Time to venture forth an' do battle on behalf of the good folks of Salvation.
Deputy: They may be rednecks, but they're *our* rednecks. (46:11)

This dialogue hinges on a speech made by Custer in the previous issue—when rousing the people of Salvation to unite and resist Quincannon—in which the word "redneck" had a more controversial context:

It's up to you to decide what ["Texan" is] gonna mean here. Is it a buncha fat, bigoted rednecks givin' in to crooks and corporations, 'cause they're too big to fight an' we kinda like 'em in charge of us anyhow? Way the Yankees see us? Or is it drawin' a line in the dust an' sayin' *no further*. [emphasis in the original] (45:16)

Being from the South is not a problem *per se*, but behaving in accordance to southern clichés is. The disparaging notion here is not that these people are rednecks, but that in being complacent, they conform to a stereotype defined by the outside world. Custer's speech incites them to act as independent individuals and not as byproducts of an established symbolic order.

Preacher therefore seems to answer McPherson's call for a "model of southern mixedness ... rooted in everyday life in the South, a life that is not finally reducible to the iconic status of certain southern symbols" (31). This liberal creed of the preeminence of individual over the system often takes the form of anarchistic outburst in *Preacher*, with a forcible and often violent rejection of any authority figures, in a series that ends with the murder of God himself. A striking example of this rebellion of the individual is provided in a full-page illustration of an immense "fuck you" dug into the Mojave Desert: this is a message to NASA and the world, from a failed astronaut, refusing to accept the fact that he wasn't chosen by the institution. "I showed them. I spelt it out for them. And I made sure they could see it on their goddamn fucking shuttle" (39:16).

This stand for the individual against the symbol is refined at a late point in the series, after the Salvation story arc (#53), through the case of Elvis Presley. The cover of the issue, by Glenn Fabry, is a pastiche of a Jasper Johns American flag, and the self-contained episode tells the story of a road trip from Salvation to New York, during which Custer meets several hitchers. While the tone is mostly farcical, the common topic of these stories is the American dream. A series of rags-to-riches narratives exemplifies the possibility of escaping one's origin and predestined path. The last hitcher in the story, drawn as a faceless figure, a silhouette, is set up as a foil to Custer's worries that the country may not be able to sustain the weight of its accumulated dreams. In this context, the dreams are also to be understood as the various power structures, real and symbolic, against which Custer has been pitted.

> Yore concern is touchin'; mighty touching [...] But this here's the greates' an' fines' country ever was or will be, yessir. Ain't no needa be afraid for her. Juz 'cause she openza gates to th' stars, that don't mean ever' man steps through emz gonna climb that high. All 'merica does is show th' way. (53:22)

Through allusions to Colonel Parker, notably, it is clear at this point that the hitcher is none other than Elvis Presley, a southern icon to be sure, but also an actual individual. By blanking out his image, presenting him as a silhouette and by having him point out the freedom an individual has within a symbolic representation, Ennis and Dillon dissociate Elvis the individual from Elvis the icon. This Elvis walked away from his iconic status: "Ah juz live ma own dreamz, 'steada worryin 'all tie 'bout ever'body else's" (53:21).

Through a symmetrical disposition of Elvis and Custer in four consecutive panels, Dillon posits equivalence between Elvis's role and Custer's, while the narrow framing creates a resemblance between the two profiles: Elvis's resignation from his iconic status is more than an individual act; it shows the way to Custer, and potentially to others (53:20–21).

This reduction of the icon to the individual is not, however, the only escape from reified representations of the South in *Preacher*. As pointed out earlier, the diegetic universe of the series is a meta-fictional one, with no direct aspiration to realism. Thus, this reduction to the individual is channeled through the replacement of a set of conflicting codes, the multiple southern genres that make it impossible to fashion a coherent identity, by a more unified genre, one that is more focused on the individual than on a social order. In short, the southerner becomes a westerner. Robert Brinkmeyer has shown that this strategy of displacement, of seeking in the West an alternative to the constraining values of the South, has been adopted by a wide range of authors as a way to shed a new perspective on southern fiction. According to Brinkmeyer, this shift has consequences on the "cultural myths shaping America's conception of itself" (3) in the way it allows these authors to negotiate the opposition between movement and immobility, between the American pioneer and the southern hero bound to a specific location. Though not created by southern authors, *Preacher* fits this description well, but it also fits with Brinkmeyer's refusal to reduce the use of the Western to an *escape* from the South. The Western used in a southern context is a powerful instrument of cultural critique: in other words, these narratives are still about the South, even when they seem to displace it entirely (Brinkmeyer 112–13).

The West is present, in *Preacher*, predictably, through popular culture references and especially through allusions to the Western movie tradition, including John Ford's or Howard Hawks's classics (Quincannon is the name of a character in Ford's *She Wore a Blue Ribbon*, for example) as well as the spaghetti Western, but stopping before the revisionist reversal of the seventies. In *Preacher*, motherly advice is generic formula, as exemplified by Christina's recommendation to Custer in Salvation: "Tradition demands you start cleaning this place up. Run the bad guys out of town on a rail, fall in love with the town beauty, acquire a drunken but amusing sidekick. How about it, stranger?" (42:6). Later, remarking on one of the more mundane aspects of his job, he sarcastically jokes, "It's just like *High Noon*. I knew it would be" (45:8). From its very beginning, *Preacher* brings identifiable elements from the West into its southern fiction: from the ethereal John Wayne, to the Saint of Killers—a character whose appearance is straight from a spaghetti Western. Explaining why the letter column is called "Gone to Texas," Ennis firmly ascribes a Western tropism to the series:

> It's called *Gone to Texas*—not just because Jesse Custer is himself from Texas, or because the first four issues of the book are set there [...] but because it is a Sodding Great Title for anything. It sounds big and wide and epic and downright American, like the kind of thing John Wayne himself probably said on a regular basis. (1:41)

Through quotations, borrowings, and numerous visual markers (guns, hats, showdowns in deserted towns, and so on), this connection to the Western is regularly reaffirmed. Custer himself is a Western hero by his own admission and in the evaluation of people close to him: quick with his fists, apt to start a bar brawl, loyal to the extreme to his friends. He even owns a lighter given to his father by John Wayne himself. He is, or tries to be, the "solitary figure breaking free from his community" identified by Robert Brinkmeyer Jr. as the archetypal westerner (4). However, this identification with the Western hero remains incomplete or at least ambiguous. While his behavior is that of the westerner, Custer is visually set apart from the stereotype in his black and white preacher suit. Moreover, he hates guns and is thus set in sharp contrast with a true-to-type Western character, the Saint of Killers.

More importantly, Custer identifies himself as a southerner on several occasions, notably when discussing American culture with Tulip or when aligning with the people of Salvation. He takes pride in being a southerner who disproves southern clichés, notably when he rebuffs Tulip for putting too much faith in preestablished images of the region (in this case, *Deliverance*):

> **Tulip:** Considering your upbringing, I'm surprised you don't just drool all day and play the banjo.
> **Custer:** That's just your damn yankee stereotype of the South. You don't start rapin' canoeists 'cause you had grits for breakfast. (34:13)

Custer's identity is therefore ostensibly southern, yet not completely beholden to popular representations of the region, and the Western is used as an alternative source of self-definition. *Preacher* does not forgo the relation to place that has long been seen as crucial to southern fiction, but it expands on the ambiguity of its main locale, Texas, as part both of the South and the West, as affirming and defining community and empty frontier simultaneously.

This dual identity plays out throughout the series. Custer's way to fight the southern stereotypes is often to resort to a Western behavior, pitting one genre, one set of conventions against another. In a telling passage in the Salvation story arc, Klansmen besiege the sheriff office where Custer and his assistant are holed up. The siege recalls the confrontation in Howard Hawks's Texas Western *Rio Bravo* (1959), especially in light of John Wayne's importance in *Preacher*, but the Klansmen are reenacting classical southern scenes, complete with burning crosses and white robes (45:22–23). The issue of southern feminity, first addressed through the grotesque figure of Marie L'Angelle, is also reframed through the use of a Western prop: Custer's assistant in Salvation is a beautiful African American woman, initially confined to a predictably marginal role. When Custer invites her to buy an ostensibly oversized firearm, she is able to turn the table on the Klan and seize power over the town. She does not renounce her feminity nor her blackness, but at the end of the Salvation arc, she is the new sheriff. Custer's transformation of a southern town in a Western setting does not only transform his own identity, but is also shown as a vector for profound cultural transformations, with a shift of power from a fat male white character to a fit African American woman.

This progressive replacement of the codes of southern fiction with Western images finds its logical conclusion in the epilogue of the series. After a showdown at the Alamo (the setting of the John Wayne film of the same name), the series ends with a cowboy gunning down God and his angels in Paradise, Custer and Tulip escaping the city on a horse, riding toward the sunset, with Custer half-confessing that he wanted to be a cowboy all along. The issue also opens with three epigraphs all dealing with dreams, cowboys, and the West. Western values have thoroughly replaced the southern imagery that defined the early stages of Custer's quest.

However, for all its appearance of westward movement, *Preacher* still remains bounded in the intermediate State of Texas. For one thing, it leaves its main protagonist remarkably unchanged, or *unmoved*: apart from his preacher collar, his appearance is very similar to what it was in the first episode, and even the eye he lost along the way has been restored by God. Steve Dillon's graphical treatment in *Preacher* is kept deliberately simple (Osborne), with few other clues to the characters' state of mind than their immediate appearance (their state of mind is not reflected in the background, and the page layouts are relatively straightforward, for instance). In this context, this graphical continuity denotes the limited range of the transformations that took place in the course of the 66 issues. Noticeably, Custer may also kiss his attractive African American assistant in Salvation and install her in a position of power, but he nevertheless leaves her to go and find his white girlfriend.

This stability underlines the fact that *Preacher* does not ultimately go West. In the course of the series, Custer goes East, North, but also West (Los Angeles) to no avail. Even a trip to the South of France, to an alternative South, only triggers more fights and violence: the only place he can find first salvation then closure is Texas. Going East is identified with Europe, a region associated with evil in *Preacher* (the villains include a Nazi-worshipping secretary, the treacherous Herr Starr, a European religious organization, a De Sade, and so on), but the West outside Texas is not satisfying either. Custer's journey is a short one: from one border of Texas, where the L'Angelle plantation was located, to the other, toward which he rides at the end of the last issue. The old South and its decaying meat have been verbally and visually assaulted into non-existence, but the South remains. The Western is offered as an alternative model for a southern identity, but this alternative is only sketched through preexisting images and situations from the canon of the genre. When Custer and Tulip ride into the sunset, they are actually riding into something very close to a blank, empty page. The two consecutive two-page spreads in the issue feature a shot-reverse shot framing that might be the closest approximation of cinema techniques in the series, but the fact is that, as depicted in figure 11.5, at the end of the journey, the protagonists ride into emptiness and not a fully realized Western setting. Having denounced the stifling effect of southern representations at length, *Preacher* does not construct a new fully defined southern identity from the Western genre. To paraphrase the blanked-out Elvis in the road trip episode, all the Western does is "show the way." It does not produce a new hegemonic set of representations.

This analysis does not exhaust the possible readings of *Preacher*, but it does suggest that far from being simply the "100% old-fashioned narrative" described by Ennis, it addresses the cultural identity of the South, exposing the discrepancies and omissions in some of the most enduring representations of the region, then offering a smaller, less ambitious, and less hegemonic set of codes, the Western, as a source for a possible reinvention of this identity. A key difference between this endeavor and other uses of the West to reinvent the South, such as those identified by Brinkmeyer, lies

11.5. From *Preacher* #66 (October 2000). Written by Garth Ennis with art by Steve Dillon. Copyright © 2000 Garth Ennis and Steve Dillon.

in the fact that both creators of *Preacher* are outsiders. Their vision of the South is from its very start a self-conscious cultural construction, crafted together from various sources and media, and they choose freely which of these images will be retained in their reconstruction. Thus, like the punks studied by Jon Smith, they foreground the "arbitrariness" of these codes and images, severing their historical significance to focus on the way they coexist and contradict themselves in contemporary popular culture (95). Though *Preacher* bears no connection to the "actual" South, its irreverent use of pre-existing images, conventions, and genres, over an extended period and page count, reconnects it with some of the powerful tropes of southern fiction and southern identity. The ironical and grotesque moments in the narrative merely underline its tenacious exploration of the myth-making and cultural-shaping possibilities in the interface between regions. At the end of her study of southern representations Tara McPherson expresses her hope for "models for change that help us narrate different futures, models often beginning at the level of the micro and the personal, although they mustn't end here" (255). Through its anarchistic outburst against a reified vision of the South, *Preacher* does seem to offer such a model, even though its solution to a reification of a romanticized history often involves nothing more than a fistfight and a cleansing fire.

Notes

1. Following the end of Neil Gaiman's *Sandman*, the series established itself as the top seller of the Vertigo imprint, and reached respectable sales of approximately 50,000 copies per issue, while top-selling comic books of the period sold around 200,000 copies (Miller et al 827–28).

2. Although this essay cites individual issues, the stories discussed here are also available in trade paperback collections. The issues focusing on the L'Angelles are included in *Preacher: Until the End of the World*, and the issues focusing on Jesse's adventures in Salvation are included in *Preacher: Salvation*.

3. Another example of the link between *Preacher* and the Southern meat movies is to be found in another episode of cannibalistic mutant hillbillies (#39, "For All Mankind"), recalling Wes Craven's seminal *The Hills Have Eyes* (1977).

Works Cited

Absolute Vertigo #1. New York: DC Comics, 1995. Print.

Bell, David. "Anti Idyll, Rural Horror." *Contested Countryside Cultures: Otherness, Marginalisation, and Rurality.* Ed. Paul Cloke and Jo Little. New York: Routledge, 1997. 91–104. Print.

Bloom, John. "They Came, They Sawed." *Texas Monthly* November 2004. Web.

Brinkmeyer Jr., Robert H. *Remapping Southern Literature, Contemporary Southern Writers and the West.* Athens: U of Georgia P, 2007. Print.

Deliverance. Dir. John Boorman. Warner Bros., 1972.

Ennis, Garth (w) and Steve Dillon (a). "The Time of the Preacher." *Preacher* #1 (April 1995). New York: DC Comics. Print.

———. "All in the Family." *Preacher* #8 (November 1995). New York: DC Comics. Print.

———. "When the Story Began." *Preacher* #9 (December 1995). New York: DC Comics. Print.

———. "How I Learned to Love the Lord." *Preacher* #10 (January 1996). New York: DC Comics. Print.

———. "Until the End of the World." *Preacher* #12 (March 1996). New York: DC Comics. Print.

———. "Old Familiar Faces." *Preacher* #29 (September 1997). New York: DC Comics. Print.

———. "Snakes in the Grass." *Preacher* #32 (December 1997). New York: DC Comics. Print.

———. "Once Upon a Time." *Preacher* #34 (February 1998). New York: DC Comics. Print.

———. "You and Me against the World." *Preacher* #35 (March 1998). New York: DC Comics. Print.

———. "For All Mankind." *Preacher* #39 (July 1998). New York: DC Comics. Print.

———. "The Man from God Knows Where." *Preacher* #41 (September 1998). New York: DC Comics. Print.

———. "The Meatman Cometh." *Preacher* #42 (October 1998). New York: DC Comics. Print.

———. "Southern Cross." *Preacher* #45 (January 1999). New York: DC Comics. Print.

———. "White Mischief." *Preacher* #46 (February 1999). New York: DC Comics. Print.

———. "Jesse Get Your Gun." *Preacher* #47 (March 1999). New York: DC Comics. Print.

———. "Goodnight and God Bless." *Preacher* #48 (April 1999). New York: DC Comics. Print.

———. "Too Dumb for New York City and Too Ugly for L.A." *Preacher* #53 (September 1999). New York: DC Comics. Print.

———. "A Hell of a Vision." *Preacher* #66 (October 2000). New York: DC Comics. Print.

Gabilliet, Jean-Paul. *Des comics et des hommes: Histoire culturelle des comic books aux Etats-Unis*. Nantes: Editions du temps, 2005. Print.

Henninger, Katherine. *Ordering the Facade: Photography and Contemporary Southern Women's Writing*. Chapel Hill: U of North Carolina P, 2007. Print.

Howe, Irving. "Notes on Mass Culture." *Mass Culture: The Popular Arts in America*. Ed. Bernard Rosenber and David Manning White. Glencoe: Free Press, 1957. 496–503. Print.

Ladd, Barbara. "Dismantling the Monolith: Southern Places—Past, Present, and Future." *South to a New Place: Region, Literature, Culture*. Ed. Suzanne W. Jones and Sharon Monteith. Baton Rouge: Louisiana State UP, 2002. 44–57. Print.

McCloud, Scott. *Understanding Comics: The Invisible Art*. New York: Harper, 1994. Print.

McPherson, Tara. *Reconstructing Dixie. Race, Gender, and Nostalgia in the Imagined South*. Durham: Duke UP, 2003. Print.

Miller, John Jackson, et al. *The Standard Catalog of Comic Books*. Iola, Wi.: Krause Publication, 2002. Print.

Osborne, S. L. "Drinking With the Boys: An Evening with Garth Ennis and Steve Dillon" *Sequential Tart*. September 27, 1998. Web.

Romine Scott. "Where is Southern Literature? The Practice of Place in a Postsouthern Age." *South to a New Place: Region, Literature, Culture*. Ed. Suzanne W. Jones and Sharon Monteith. Baton Rouge: Louisiana State UP, 2002. 23–43. Print.

Seidel, Kathryn Lee. *The Southern Belle in the American Novel*, Tampa: U of South Florida P, 1985. Print.

Smith, Jon. "Southern Culture on the Skids: Punk, Retro, Narcissism, and the Burden of Southern History." *South to a New Place: Region, Literature, Culture*. Ed. Suzanne W. Jones and Sharon Monteith. Baton Rouge: Louisiana State UP, 2002. 76–95. Print.

The Texas Chainsaw Massacre. Dir. Tobe Hooper. Bryanston Distributing Company, 1974.

IV.

Revisualizing Stories, Rereading Images

A Visitation of Narratives

Dialogue and Comics in Randall Kenan's *A Visitation of Spirits*

—Alison Mandaville

Kenan, Comics, and Community Memory

In his book of essays *The Fire This Time* (2007), North Carolina author Randall Kenan writes, "Comic books were my original vice, and they still have more allure to me than sex or drugs. To spend too much time reading was a sign of laziness or worse. Decided evidence of bad character. Surely in my case this was true" (82). Kenan's statement associating sex, comics, and sin are echoed in a short anthologized essay he wrote about North Carolina published in 2008. In it he again associates comics and sex by way of his relationship with two older cousins who, he says, "were my educators about all those things grown-ups were never going to explain to me. Grown-up things. The birds and the bees sorts of things. Subterranean, hidden things were our major topics after basketball and comics" ("North Carolina" 340). Although he is never explicit about their influence in his writing life, comics are, at times, both backdrop to and metaphor by which Kenan writes of the power and significance of language itself. When in *Fire*, he ruminates on the use of the word "nigger," lauding, despite Richard Pryor's eventual rejection of the word, the force with which that comedian wielded it, he compares Pryor to a superhero, questioning how we can possibly disregard his use of the word: "All those times he had unfurled the word 'nigger' as if it were Superman's Cape? Used it as a knife to White America's carotid artery?" He goes on to ask, "Are words so fixed in their original meanings that they cannot be reappointed, recharged, resurrected, born again?" (106). One might ask the same question of a narrative form once associated with vice and degradation—comics.[1] For Kenan, comics, like the word "nigger," might carry problematic connotations, might be something sinful or imply deviance, but nevertheless the highly tangible, sensual form "still" offers him an aesthetic with compelling narrative power—especially when working with themes of marginalized bodies and sensualities in the southeastern United States.

Given the association of comics, sex, and language for Kenan, when teenage Horace Cross, the central character in Kenan's prose novel *A Visitation of Spirits* (1989), struggles to articulate what he feels is the consummate sin of his queer sexual desires, it seems appropriate that from the beginning of the novel "comics" are offered as a strategy of constructing both content and perspective. Full-color superhero posters decorate Horace's bedroom walls like giant frames of a comic:

> On the white walls of his room hung his many friends[;] . . . the Sorcerer [with] . . . his hands . . . surrounded by an electric blue glow[;] . . . a huge green monster-man so muscled he appeared to be a green lump[;] . . . a woman whirling a golden lasso[;] . . . a Viking with long yellow hair and bulging muscles. (17)

As the tale progresses, these colorful figures, electric blue, huge green, golden, and yellow, leak their bright and larger-than-life presence into Horace's everyday world. This fascination with physically different comics figures and the alternate narratives they inhabit is not unproblematic for Horace. Rooted as these forms are in dominant culture, they set up a narrative dissonance between small-town Horace's natal African American (and homophobic) community and the white (racist) community. As Scott McCloud discusses in *Understanding Comics*, comics is a narrative form dependent on iconic imagery. Icons are, by nature, highly generalized images, and comics has often relied on problematic iconic images of difference, as Franz Fanon early observed and many others, including Marc Singer and Brannon Costello, have continued to explore. These are stereotypes that reflect and even perpetuate the very prejudices that readers outside the dominant culture groups experience. The marginalized form of comics has nevertheless long offered those from minority groups in the United States an appealing alternative to "authorized" or "high" literature. The characters in early comics were often working class or immigrant, "ethnic" or physically different. For the last hundred years, from characters such as the Yellow Kid through Superman and the X-Men, comics have offered a narrative home for a wide variety of misfits of all ages. In his discussion of racial identity theory and comics, Singer concludes that while "the potential for superficiality and stereotyping here is dangerously high . . . some comics creators have demonstrated that the superhero genre's own conventions can invite a more nuanced depiction of minority identity" (107). He concludes, "super-hero comics . . . possess a highly adaptable set of conventions . . . [that can] . . . externalize and dramatize the conditions of minority identity in the United States" (118). Brannon Costello marks this double-edged relation-ship between superhero comics characters and southern African American queer male embodiment as reflected in the life of Horace Cross in *Visita-tion*, writing, "these [superhero] characters are not—or at least not *only*—emblems of a fantasy of freedom from a restrictive South; they are crucial to his making sense of a body dilemma that is rooted in the history of his race and region" (140).

Further, Costello notes Horace's own perception of this cruel narrative dilemma as the teen looks over the "representations of white heroes crowd-ing black figures to the margins in the poster for the summer theater pro-duction he once worked on, an ahistorical jumble . . . called *Ride the Freedom Star*" (137). Horace's awareness of narrative violence is not only a matter of content—of white male heroes who appear "hearty and robust like comic book characters, their chests barreled and near to bursting through their shirts" (*Visitation* 211). His frustration is also expressed in terms of narrative framing, positioning, and space on the page—Horace sees that the white characters are in the center of the poster, the black characters off to one side.

Horace's awareness of the gendered and racial narrative this poster spa-tially depicts reflects Kenan's sense of profoundly visual and spatial dimen-sions in narrative construction. In a 1998 interview he said,

I believe you have a vision of what you want to accomplish, which is largely inarticulate. The vision is composed of the sense. It is composed of panoramas. It is composed of people getting together. It is composed of all the things that happen when a human being interacts with a landscape. That is what you see in your mind's eye. The challenge, then, is putting that vision down in sentences. In a word. In such a way that you can best convey, though language, what your mind beheld . . . what order of sentences, what order of paragraphs, what order of chapters, will best relate that vision to a reader. (Rowell 136)

Kenan's sense of narrative is both visual—literally "a vision composed of sense"—and it is interactive—"composed of people getting together" and "of all the things that happen when a human being interacts with a land-scape." This is a spatial sense of narrative both visual and kinesthetic—of "landscape" and the "order" of things ("order" is repeated three times in the quote above), of the "mind's eye" and "putting that vision down in sentences. In a word." When read through McCloud's definition of comics as "[j]uxtaposed pictorial and other images in deliberate sequence, intended to convey information and/or produce an aesthetic response in the viewer" (9), what Kenan here expresses appears to reflect a narrative sensibility in close kinship with comics.[2] Reading the form and the content of *Visitation* through a "comics" lens reveals a particularly material narrative of detection, a search for the story of Horace's problematic gay African American body, rooted in a place (The South), that is at once sensible (especially visual) and spiritual (the Word). It is a landscape made not only of ground and trees, houses and schools, but of words and scripture as tangible as the images they invoke. This text uses several key comics-like strategies: explicit framing, with the accompanying requirement of intensive reader participation in the narrative to "close" on the gutters those frames create; a strong visual and spatial dimension for both place and time; and a heightened sense of the materiality of words themselves to explore themes of embodiment, belonging, and difference.

Comics and Orality

By definition, a regional literature is a local literature and, thematically, *Visitation* is firmly rooted in a southern agrarian landscape with particularly strong imagery drawn from a world of tobacco farming and hog butchering, where issues of family and community are set against a history of conflict and social justice structured through ideas of embodiment (such as race, gender, sexuality). Though drawn from globalized popular literature, the stories of superhero characters referenced most often by the novel—including Wonder Woman, the Hulk, and Superman—also take up these regional themes. Although superhero comics are most commonly associated with urban environments, it is worth remembering that Clark Kent grew up in an agrarian setting, his adoptive family's farm in Kansas. And although much superhero action takes place in cities, no matter where superhero characters find themselves, they are confronted with issues of body and belonging, as, for example, in cases of the X-Men, the Hulk, and Spider-Man. Marc Singer discusses how comics offer a "highly adaptable" form with the potential to register marginal identity (118). And in a fascinating study of superhero comics, Tek K. Bhatia remarks on this reputably "American" form's potential for a kind of "hyperlocalization" in places like Pakistan, where Western globalized characters are given costumes and language modified to reflect a very local environment and culture (291).

Localization and adaptability of narrative are of particular concern in *Visitation*. The novel raises difficult questions of linguistic constitution, of how the individual body is connected to communal words, and of its survival in and through narrative—including history. In his exploration of the role of science fiction in the novel, Costello writes, "Examining *A Visitation of Sprits* in the context of [William Gibson's novel] *Neuromancer* throws into sharp relief how artificial, managed, and constructed Horace's body is in its role as a carrier of his family's history" and that "though obviously Horace does resemble his biological family, the way in which his family codes the elements of that resemblance—as never belonging to Horace, as though he is merely their custodian—is purely discursive" (135). Horace struggles to narrate and depict his own body and the life it holds and experiences, fighting an increasingly losing battle with the "Word" of a community that overwrites him to create their history, their—to use oral historian Melissa Walker's term—"community of memory" (5). In an ongoing play with form suggestive of explicitly visual and plastic comics narrative strategies, the text engages potentially violent effects of such narrative for the individuals figured within it, drawing and framing the genesis and shape of Horace, the marginal narrator.

The youngest in a long line of church-leading men, Horace has been raised within a strong narrative tradition of sin and salvation and achievement drawn from religious community and family histories of slavery and disempowerment circulated and negotiated through oral forms. This sense of communal, ongoing storytelling, in which the listeners/readers participate in "bridging" the gaps (holding the story together between installments/tellings and further, responding directly to the storyteller, projecting their imaginations into the spaces *between* tellings and *within* the tale) is reminiscent of how Randall Kenan characterizes his upbringing in the story:

I was literally raised up by people who were in their seventies and eighties and they were very loquacious. That was the world in which I moved, in which people told stories, in which people understood the world they lived in through talking about it, through relating not only the events that happened to them but to their forefathers ... *my life was structured by these oral narratives* .... My kinfolk were not writers, but that fundamental impetus to create a story, whether it's on the page, or through your mouth, was the milieu in which spent my first seventeen years. (Rowell 138, emphasis added)

In the same interview, Kenan explicitly draws the connection between his own fiction and oral storytelling (139). As Eva Tettenborn observes, "he has expressed that his North Carolina-based fiction in part aims to create 'some sort of record' of his ancestors' and relatives' oral culture so that their 'stories would be guaranteed to be known to other people'" (250). That one of the epigraphs for *Visitation* is drawn from Charles Dickens's *A Christmas Carol* connects not only the themes of the two texts but also their segmented forms, for while *A Christmas Carol*, unlike many of Dickens's longer novels, was not published serially, like Kenan's novel, it nevertheless advances through a series of "visitations" implying not only the oral, but the physical movement of the storyteller to tell: the journey, the *visit*.

In "Oral Culture and Southern Fiction," Jill Terry asserts that "Orality may well be one of the most significant characteristics of writing described as 'Southern'" (519). Defining the narrative significance of orality for the South, she writes, "Orality—that which has the quality of being spoken or otherwise orally communicated—has had a vital role in representing not only the rooted past but also the changing places of the South." In his 2007 study of southern writing, *A Web of Words: The Great Dialogue of Southern Literature* (2007) Richard Gray argues that "[w]riters make their work out of their reading, caught in a web of relationships with earlier writers that is partly a matter of influence and homage and partly one of conflict, antagonism, and struggle" (2). Against Harold Bloom's characterization of this influence on writing as "anxiety," or, in Gray's words, "a kind of Freudian wrestling match," he draws on the sense of voiced interchange that orality implies to define this "web of relationships" in the literature of the U.S. South as a dialogue, albeit a sometimes contentious one. Read through this idea of the importance of orality in southern literature, *Visitation* appears to be no exception to this presumed tradition of voluble exchange in southern literature.

Like comics, early oral literature was, and in many cultures and contexts (including modern theater) continues to be, a rich and interactive form encompassing both the sensual—visual, aural, and kinesthetic—and the textual or verbal-symbolic dimensions through word, voice, gesture, iconic costume, and set. In this sense, rather than the hybrid form many comics scholars have termed it (Chute and DeKoven, 769; Pratt 107; Gravett 619; Bhatia 284), comics might better be considered, like many forms of oral literature, a *dialogic* form. In comics, word and image, reader and text, are in continual dialogue, sometimes "visiting," sometimes "staying away"; sometimes converging on perspective, sometimes diverging, altogether creating a kind of dynamic journey of "call and response" that offers both confirmation of and friction within narrative content. I make the connection between prose novel formats, comics, and oral literature because it illuminates important connections between these narrative media in Kenan's work. For if Kenan explicitly credits his most fundamental narrative impulse to the rich oral culture of story in which he was raised, he chooses to voice his own narrative in print. And it is in comics, I would argue, that the rich media of southern oral literary forms, forms as visual and kinesthetic as the storyteller's body and as worded and symbolic as her voice and language, find their print corollary.

While orality remains a powerful marker by which to characterize southern literature, and oral storytelling is an obvious and key element in Kenan's fiction, critics have begun to complicate the easy stereotyping and generalization of southern literature through "talk." As Walker demonstrates in her study of oral histories told among Southern U.S. farmers, "[t]hough rural Southerners created a recognizable community of memory through their oral history narratives, that community was by no means monolithic" (5). There are many different communities and groups within the large geographic region called "The South," with many different oral traditions (and written literary traditions employing orality) and differing historical relationships to those traditions. And while the word "oral" is most often paired with "tradition," Terry notes that, in southern literature, orality may indeed more commonly be deployed as a strategy of resistance to oppressive traditions. She argues, for example, that "it is in women's writing concerned with representations of female identity in a historically patriarchal South that orality is especially prioritized" (519). Moreover, after W. J. T. Mitchell's elaboration on this idea in *Picture Theory*, Katherine Henninger writes of how "Formal division often stands in for greater cultural tensions and the cultural desire for borders" and goes on to specify that "[t]his is clear in the South, where formal divisions—especially the choice between visual or oral expression—are intimately intertwined in the constructions of gender, race, and class distinction so crucial to, and contested within, southern identities" (13).

Indeed, in African American culture, the relationship to orality is complicated by the fact that it was a form to which slaves were long officially limited while writing was perceived as the more privileged—and powerful—narrative form throughout the U.S. In response, many African Americans have claimed and re-characterized oral culture as a centerpiece of African

American survival and resistance. Further, Uzzie T. Cannon sees potential for orality as a strategy of critique within the African American community. She writes of Kenan's deployment of orality in his short story collection *Let the Dead Bury the Dead* that "through the subversive use of oral storytelling in his short story collection, [he] disturbs the traditional African-American community by defamiliarizing the geographical and abstract aspects of Tims Creek as a community" (107). In an analysis especially relevant to the character Horace's tragic search for the "one Voice," she argues that Kenan's fiction deploys orality in part to caution against its uncritical glorification in the African American community, for "Kenan stresses [that] . . . African Americans fail to consider the unstable formal and thematic attributes of storytelling when ordering their lives around story. They may look for one 'master reality' in the story for the sake of community and disregard the myriad versions therein" (107). In her analysis of *Visitation*'s gothic tropes, Maisha Wester also observes the potential violence these communal narratives do to individuals who embody difference, saying that "the social processes and institutions that define these bodies as aberrant monstrosities are the actual horrors," and that "the habit of naming and locating monstrosity is itself monstrous in Kenan's text" (1039).

Whether a strategy of limitation or resistance, too much attention to orality may, in fact, be obscuring other important strategies in southern narrative forms. In thinking about the interplay of photographic images and southern U.S. fiction by women, Henninger discusses the use of "fictional photographs," that is, photos described and referenced in the words of a story, as a strategy of cultural critique. She claims that the entrenchment of orality in criticism of southern fiction overshadows the significance of the visual, arguing that this bias is a "blindness" that obscures raced and gendered constructions of power naturalized through visual differences, that, while not unique to the South, find valence through historical imagery there. With relevance to my discussion of the function of comics in Kenan's work, she suggests, through her examination of these "fictional photographs," that they "may stand in for the visible/iconic/spatial aspect of written text" and that "in calling attention to the visual aspect of text, *realigning written text with icon*, fictional photographs may stand in for . . . what is beyond the power of the text to represent—a metaphor for the textual unrepresentability of time and voice" (21, emphasis added). Comics are not photographs (though they may include them, both actual and "drawn"), and indeed Henninger explicitly distinguishes between the drawn and the photographed image in important ways. Nevertheless, reading, as Henninger does, for comics palpable visual associations in *Visitation*'s themes and narrative strategies similarly and helpfully complicates Kenan's use of orality and the novel's relationship to oral storytelling.

Costello persuasively argues that reading *Visitation* through its allusions to cyberpunk science fiction and superhero comics—both speculative fictional genres often hinging on themes of body and difference—helps point to a critical theme in the novel: the main character Horace's longing for alternate forms of embodiment. Yet comics are not only *about* alternate bodies, but are themselves alternative narrative forms—an observation that simultaneously points to the ways in which story, as a community endeavor, not only creates its members' identities, but fashions a space for them to belong and houses them. It is clear that Horace not only seeks a new body, he seeks the right "spell" to create that body—a narrative alternative to the one and only "Word" in which he has been brought up. In a community that holds "the Word" sacred above all but within which Horace cannot find belonging, perhaps even more than a new body, he seeks a self-story that can offer a livable container and articulation of his body and its desires *within his community*. Coming out of an oral storytelling upbringing, trying to come to terms with the dominant and exclusive modes of narrative yet deeply influenced and drawn to "alternative" literary modes of expression, in *Visitation* Kenan's use of comics directly engages questions of narrative construction. Of comics' front-and-center use of "frames" to create perspective, Hillary Chute says that the form "is highly conscious of the artificiality of its selective borders, which diagram the page into an arrangement of encapsulated moments." This is not unlike Kenan's narrative, where scene changes are anything but seamless, advanced through and highlighted by pronounced shifts in perspective and from which call attention to the very constructedness of narrative itself ("Comics as Literature" 455).

As Kenan notes of his own grandparents' lives constructed through story, in his imaginary town of Tims Creek "The Word" is closely linked to daily material life and deemed absolutely necessary to community survival. Narrative itself matters deeply, to return to Kenan's words, to "people [who] understood the world they lived in through talking about it." Growing desperate in the face of the internalized and bounding rules and expectations of this tradition of "The Word," by which he feels he cannot live, but that he cannot live without, yet committed to the place he feels is "home"—the rural South—the young Horace seeks an alternate narrative shape, literally a "spell" of physical transformation, a new "image" through which to survive. From his reading of superhero comics and science fiction, Horace realizes that "[t]here are no moral laws that say: You must remain human. And he would not" (Kenan 12). He decides to become a species of a hawk indigenous to the southeastern United States. After carefully collecting and burning the ingredients of the spell he has devised,

> [h]e smiled and reached into the mud, into the soggy sod where the ashes had melted, and in one motion smeared his face with them, as though to reacquaint himself with the sensation of touch. . . . listening, listening for the voice that now seemed his only salvation. Salvation? Was that it, now? Beyond hope, beyond faith? Just to survive in some way. To live. (27)

Horace enacts a "spell" that is, like comics, both sensual and worded: "sensation" and "voice." Sensation and articulation are linked as "in one motion" he simultaneously "reacquaint[s] himself with the sensation of touch" and "listen[s] for the voice that now seemed his only salvation." He seeks in "the voice" a narrative that will enable a transformation by which he can "live" in a sensory body. Though the teen ultimately fails in his attempt, Sheila Smith McKoy argues that the novel successfully "revises the image of black gay portraitures in southern literature" (33). Further, while Horace's physical transformation seems to fail, he has, in this ritual binding together body and word, reopened himself to sensation, and in so doing he articulates the very demonic and ultimately untenable body from which he sought escape.

The Space-Time Continuum in Tims Creek

Horace's search for "voice" sets orality and oral narrative at the core of *Visitation*'s prose. Orality, a matter of three-dimensional spaces and proximate bodies, explicitly draws the past into the present to project a tale into the future. In her study of "communities of memory" among farmers in the southern U.S., Walker looks at the non-linear use of time in oral narrative, writing of how "Rural Southerners . . . used their stories to address serious matters in their present worlds . . . . [M]emories of the past provided narrators with a tool to convey a sense of what was possible—of what the future might look like if it combined the best features of past and present" (5–6). While neither orality nor non-linear narrative is unique to the South, and, in fact, as I have discussed, this is a characterization of southern literature that many find limiting, its presence in *Visitation* is significant—and even as he critiques these orally based stories by which Horace tries to, but cannot, live,

Kenan also finds their forms useful. For in this sense of story, past, present, and future are not only contiguous but they can be tangibly mixed together and renegotiated. Walker writes of how "[g]roups develop their communities of memory by talking with each other over time with repeated conversation" (5). Dialogue between past and present, between teller and listener creates a literature not only situated in history but dynamic and responsive to its current times and people. This sense of a literature being continually reinvented by both its writers and its readers—and its critics—is the subject of Michael Kreyling's study *Inventing Southern Literature* in which he underscores the idea of southern literature, and indeed the idea of the South itself, as an ongoing and dynamic project of "fabrication" (x).

Visitation, like comics, explicitly invokes just such temporally plastic, dialogic sense of narrative throughout. In comics, characters' material images and their words continually gesture to and reinvent (or imprint) each other. George Hovis optimistically observes this process of fabrication and narrative negotiation modeled by how Horace's grandfather "Zeke Cross' tale is an organic part of the oral tradition from which it sprang, and, as such, with every performance it is constantly changing, revisiting the past, but open to new possibilities. Ruth's (Horace's Aunt) periodic interruptions, which challenge the details of Zeke's tale signal that both she and he have heard numerous revisions" (*Vale of Humility* 264). Also recalling strategies common to comics, this is a dialogic narrative that moves readily back and forth in time. Placing quotes from *A Christmas Carol* and *Neuromancer* together as epigraphs to the novel, one story from the past, one set in the future, both drawing on the idea of timeless spirits who move across and outside linear time to explore themes of human transformation, control, and resistance through story, effectively sets up a novel of cross-time "visitations" that collapse past and future into a "present" narrative that, like comics, projects time as a space in which the reader can wander at will. As when reading comics frames on a page, the reader of *Visitation* moves materially back and forth in this spatial arrangement of time, keeping "all times" past, present, and future in play at once to spell a genealogy of the violation Horace experiences through the continual refabrication of stories on which individual and community identity is based. The novel offers no linear walk into the future, but rather multiple painful recursions through existing spaces or frames—visitations and dialogues that, like the panels of comics, are ordered, yet open to recursive reading.

Attention to the visual or spatial in prose literature is nothing new. W. J. T. Mitchell's introductory essay to the 1980 special issue of *Critical Inquiry*,

"The Language of Images," and his longer treatment in the same issue, "Spatial Form in Literature," both sought to reestablish the visual as an integral part of literature and fiction. He writes of "a symbiotic relationship between verbal and pictorial modes in modern art and literature" ("Language of Images" 359) and argues that "spatial form is a crucial aspect of the experience of and interpretation of literature in all ages and all cultures" ("Spatial Form in Literature" 541). The especially spatial nature of Kenan's work has been noted by others. Robert McRuer in "Queer Locations, Queer Transformations" and Sharon Patricia Holland in "(Pro)Creating Imaginative Spaces" both explore the construction of queer identity through space and/or place in the novel. McKoy links together place and race in the novel, saying that it is "not so much a book about gay 'outing' but about 'racial and spatial outings,' the exposure of black Southern gay desire and experience" (18). Similarly, pointing to a cartography of queerness, Keith Clark calls Kenan's fiction a "remapping of the constructed psychic and geographic regions to which his predecessors consigned African-American gay men" (7). Observing that in both *Visitation* and his volume of short stories, *Let the Dead Bury Their Dead*, Kenan is concerned with boundaries, Lindsey Tucker writes, "[he] is intent on showing [that] . . . control—often imaged in tropes of spatiality—is unrealistic, unworkable, and only serves to underscore the permeability of all borders" (306). Significantly, Tucker connects Kenan's focus on narrative form itself with such "spatiality" and notes that "Kenan has also foregrounded a range of spatial problems that involve the processes of textual production" (307).

Visitation's approach to the "spatial problems" associated with "textual production" are strongly reminiscent of comics narrative strategies. As he moves from location to location, from frame to frame, on the night preceding his suicide, Horace's memories of life events and those of his family and community members are triggered by the highly iconic places in the town in which he was raised: Home, School, Theater, Church. The high school triggers memories of his relationships with other students, boys and girls. The church triggers memories of religious sermons, funerals. In each highly symbolic location perspectives of community members weave among Horace's own memories. Interspersed with these scenes from the past and present are those of the "future": the perspectives of Horace's older cousin James Malachai *after* Horace's death, of Horace's grandfather who raised him and dreams of his own funeral, and of his Aunt Ruth's visit to another dying man nearly a year after the teen's death. Like a map, times and events are depicted and connected in spatial rather than chronological relation—a strategy

McCloud claims for the comics form, writing of the placement of consecutive "frames" together in a panel on one page (or two facing pages),

[I]n Comics, the past is more than just *memories* for the audience and the future is more than just *possibilities!* Both past and future are real and visible and *all around us!* Wherever your eyes are focused that's *now.* But at the same time your eyes take in the *surrounding landscape* of *past and future.* (104, emphasis in original)

Visitation's multiplicity of perspectives and sense of all-time as a contiguous and simultaneously present and accessible space are echoed in McCloud's declaration that "In the world of comics, *time and space* are *one and the same*" (100). As perspective on events generated by each location is repeatedly reframed by visitations past, present, and future, time is reinforced as a place and places become icons. It is as if Kenan is "teaching" readers to read prose as they would a comic. As McCloud says, "In learning to read comics we all learned to perceive time *spatially*" (104).

Like comics icons, these highly symbolic "places" in *Visitation* serve both as shorthand for the complex relationships and history each one invokes and as a narrative strategy that impels the audience's participation. For each reader must draw on her own store of "southern" associations to fill out and adjust these generalized and often problematic icons. And in further echo of comics' use of icons, within these "place" frames of Home, School, Church, Theater, the narrative locates the iconic, almost cartoon-like characters of Grandfather, Teacher, Preacher, and Actor, exposing the problematic community figuration of such icons, and complicating those figurations through the multiple perspectives offered by other characters and reader closure. Author and reader symbiotically create a narrative, like comics, in which the reader moves, sees, and actively connects the dots of Horace's demise, offering an immediacy and intimacy of narrative perspective regardless of chronological time or geographic location so that indeed, "Wherever your eyes are focused, that's *now*" (McCloud 104). The narrative very explicitly juxtapositions these "frames" of past, present, and future events *spatially* to illuminate a more complex and viscerally interactive web of responsibility for Horace's death than a linear prose narrative would permit. And this is a web into which the reader is inexorably and sensually drawn.

Echoing the frames and issues of a comic book series, the early Western European novel's serial heritage is still evident in the chapters and episodes, arranged spatially, upon which most novels still depend to reinforce "narrative pull." These chapters and episodes are akin to the frames employed by comics to demand reader participation (and thus maintain reader investment) in that leap from scene to scene. Aligning comics with narratives of violent detection (or detection of violence), McCloud entitles one of his chapters "Blood in the Gutter," playing on the concept of the "gutters" in comics—the term for that space "between" frames (60). He gives a classic example of the work readers must do to "fill in" these gaps in narrative in two side-by-side frames that suggest, but don't actually depict, great violence. The first frame is a close up of two figures: one with an axe raised, saying "Now you die!"; the other with a look of terror on his face saying "No! No!" In the second frame, the scene pulls perspective back to show a city skyline in silhouette, as an iconic scream, "Eeyah!" rings through the night air. What happened? Who did it?

McCloud implies that if there was a murder, it was we, the readers who made it happen. Provoked into closing that gap between the two frames, we draw on what we "know," from experience, from previous narrative, to advance the frame, effectively to kill someone. As McCloud says, "I may have drawn an axe being raised in this example, but I'm not the one who let it drop or decided how hard the blow, or who screamed, or why. That, dear reader, was your special crime, each of you committing it in your own style. All of you participated in the murder . . ." (68). Through this strategy of "closure" associated with comics we are, as readers, fully drawn into the narrative process (pun intended). Frames, gutters, and icons thus make for "a medium where the audience is a willing and conscious collaborator and closure is the agent of change, time and motion" (65). The listener participation that oral storytelling invokes through physical proximity, question and response, rhythm, volume, and silent pauses, is like the reader participation that comics accomplish through drawn framing, discrepancy between image and text, and in closure on symbolic and partial depictions created by icon and frame. As prose, *Visitation* engages the reader by creating "gutters" not only between chapters, but also between shifting perspectives, a variety of narrative forms, and iconic representations that demand elaborated graphic imaginings from its readers.

Building on McCloud's discussion of time as space and reader engagement, Chute writes:

> Comics moves forward in time through the space of the page, through its progressive counterpoint of presence and absence: packed panels (also called frames) alternating with gutters (empty space). Highly

textured in its narrative scaffolding, comics doesn't blend the visual
and the verbal—or use one simply to illustrate the other—but is rather
prone to present the two nonsynchronously; a reader of comics not only
fills in the gaps between panels but also works with the often disjunctive
back-and-forth of *reading* and *looking* for meaning. ("Comics as Literature" 452)

Visitation's use of time as space, juxtapositioning different characters'
points of view in different narrative forms (personal reminiscence, dream,
traditional storytelling, a play script, an autobiography) and in different
textual fonts (sometimes italics and sometimes plain typeface) tangibly
deploys the very strategies of sequence, position, and frame of image and
text that the comics form exploits and centers the significance of narrative
construction itself. The placement, for example, of a "play script" within a
novel narrative (a dialogue between Horace and his older cousin about sex
and religion) showcases the very constructedness of the scene: it presses
the reader not only to bridge the gap between the narrative prose that precedes and follows this section but more specifically shifts her into "reading a play" mode, where she knows, and *keeps in mind*, that, as with any
"script," much of the play is missing—such as casting, sets, and costumes
. . . and direction (110–14). The reader closes on the scene. The form of a
play helps create this section of text as potentially palpable, malleable—
and explicitly dialogic. In a 1995 interview with V. Hunt published in the
African American Review, Kenan discusses his shifts in narrative form, and
specifically the use of the play script within the novel: "It was the best form
to accomplish what I wanted the reader to *see* at that moment. When you
read a play you try to *visualize* it in another way than when you read a well-
written scene in prose . . . . [I]t was *something about the reader's relationship
to the text* I wanted to exploit, the expectations that are brought to it, *the
appearance of the text*" (414, emphases added). And when Hunt asks, "Do
you mean that you were trying to *manipulate* the reader's *visual expectations?*" Kenan answers, "Yes" (414).

Closing on explicitly partial and iconic scenes, the reader, in turn,
"manipulates" what is a tangibly inviting text. *Visitation* everywhere implies
a missing sensible or graphic element. In one of the most obvious examples,
the text of the theater poster Horace looks at is presented graphically on
the pages of the novel, with centered, short lines of text setting up a rectangular "poster format"—but without the actual graphics. Suzanne W. Jones
observes that, at times, "remembered events are so vivid that they erupt

into [Horace's cousin] Jimmy's prose confessions as short dramatic scenes" (291) that are presented as literal play scripts. And a number of critics have observed the detailed description of Horace's suicide as "graphic." Harry Thomas writes that "Horace's violent end is a viscerally horrible thing to behold" (129). Through shifting perspectives, places, and times in the text one can't help but "hear" the shifts in voice and be aware of "seeing"—in my case to the point of actually drawing in the margins: a map tracing Horace's physical journey through his community; a family tree organizing his web of relations; and even a multi-dimensional timeline connecting the events of his life with those of other community members.

In *Visitation*, through Kenan's extensive use of comics imagery and an admitted effort to create a visual dimension with shifts in narrative format, the process of reader visualization is far more explicit than in most prose novels. This complex narrative of disparate memories, perspectives, and genres functions as a kind of hypertextual comic by which the reader may help create and link all these graphic "maps" one to another without ever specifying a single "path" of travel—for reading comics is often a rigorous and highly recursive experience akin to the active listening process involved in oral storytelling.[3] This readerly longing for the tangible graphic that *Visitation* creates echoes Horace's own violent journey through his community's iconic and often deadening stories, his own efforts to link voice and sensibility—his longing for the "reacquaintance" of narrative with "sensation." Simultaneously, this hard work of participation in narrative creation creates a reader deeply invested and complicit in the story web of Horace's community, a web of both survival and violence that raises the question: *Who killed Horace?*

When I gave this question as an essay topic to my class, students developed a wide variety of answers: religion, his parents, his peers, himself, his cousin. Interestingly, none answered, "I did." But in fact, as a reader, one does commit a kind of narrative murder in this novel, shadowing the physical violence of Horace's ending to close on his "blood in the gutters." Indeed, it is vital to this text that we, the readers, do so. Of choosing to write Horace's death, as opposed to his own survival as a gay youth in the rural south, Kenan said, "for a community to change they have to understand the devastation that they're wreaking on certain people" and that "tragedy was much more effective at disturbing, and in moving, people" (Hunt 416). While it is important not to indiscriminately collapse the Tims Creek community and broader social responsibility for Horace's suicide altogether with that of the individual reader, this narrative seeks to nevertheless draw each reader firmly into that narrative web to viscerally experience the particular part she does and can play in maintaining—and changing—such potentially powerful narratives.

Framing the South

Though thoroughly steeped in global popular culture, *Visitation* is a novel relentlessly committed to "staying in the South." Of his place as a southern writer, Kenan says that many texts in the southern literary canon "walk a fine line between revulsion and acceptance," that "[b]eing in the South, writing about it through yourself . . . you're so often reflecting about wanting to get out of the South but at the same time knowing—and it's a horrible paradox—that this is what sustains you, this is what makes you who you are" (Hunt 413). The broader history and politics behind this tension are beyond the scope of this essay but are, in part, explored through the voices of Horace and his cousin James Malachai. Despite his powerful longing to be "other," Horace can "see" no alternative to the deadly spell he casts: "He had no alternative, he kept saying to himself. No other way out" (16). For like his older cousin James who returns to Tims Creek against the advice of Northern friends and colleagues, Horace cannot "get out" of this southern frame, for it gives him shape—it makes him who he is. As his uncle confirms, "He was a son of the community more than most" (188).

Even in selecting the animal into which he hopes to change, Horace decides against non-native species, thinking to himself: "Cats had a physical freedom he loved to watch, the svelte, smooth, sliding motion of the great cats of Africa, but he could not *see* himself transforming into anything that would not *fit* the swampy woodlands of Southeastern North Carolina. He had to stay here" (11, emphases added). This sense of the "frame" into which he can *see* himself *fitting* is both tangible and visual—like comics. His own family and community have, in a sense, raised him to be a local superhero: "He was Horace Thomas Cross, the Great Black Hope, as his friend John Anthony called him" (13). In his "autobiography" Horace writes, "I remember wanting to be a superhero and first trying to design a suit like Iron Man's so I could fly and then a costume like Batman's so I could look tough, and I would come to somebody's rescue, mysteriously, when something went wrong" (247). Horace's identity, built on the idea of seeking justice, cannot survive undamaged outside the space of oppression he was raised to "overcome" and the people he was raised to "rescue."

Kenan writes of how Horace "escaped with Clark Kent, slipping into phone booths and emerging powerful and all-knowing; he followed Bruce Wayne, and he too need only change his clothes and put on a cloak to mask him and give him honor and nobility" (240), and yet, as Costello notes in his discussion of the four characters depicted in posters on Horace's bedroom walls (Dr. Strange, the Hulk, Wonder Woman, Thor), the teen's attraction to these iconic figures has more to do with a longing for alternate embodiment than escape (Costello 138–140). It is no surprise, given the multiple allusions to Superman in both *Visitation* and Kenan's later essays, that Horace not only chooses for his transformation an indigenous species, he chooses to become hawk—a powerful creature who can fly—like Superman, Wonder Woman (with her invisible plane), Iron Man (with his suit), and even some characters in African American folk tales of slavery (see Virginia Hamilton's version of "The People Could Fly").

But flying is not the same as escaping—even in the folk tales of slavery. In a section of *The Fire Next Time* that Kenan titles "Fly, Black Bird, Fly" he explores the meteoric rise of African Americans including Oprah Winfrey and Barack Obama, who is himself a comics fan. Kenan writes, "Obama flies, without a doubt. But his magic, that voodoo that he do so well is bound up in blackness. Not despite, but because of" (137). Clark Kent can change his clothing and mask his identity, but he is forever an alien. For Horace, as for Superman or Wonder Woman, exiled from the world of gods to serve justice in an alien human landscape—relocation is not an option. Indeed, one's very identity is based on sticking around. Like Superman. Like Obama.[4] As if still meditating eighteen years later on Horace's choice of an indigenous American bird over a great African cat, Kenan dubs Obama "Brother Raven" in *The Fire Next Time*, saying "unlike the cat, the Raven can fly" (145). As *Visitation* makes clear, for Kenan, who after a stint in New York City, returned to his home state to live and teach, finally only narrative, or the "spell" can shift—and, if properly caped (oh that trickster), perhaps even fly.

And as the novel progresses, it seems to Horace that there are no narratives of survival by which he can constitute himself as queer and remain in his community. But because of *Visitation*'s fragmented construction, the reader is not so narratively caught. Kenan enacts, not a "way out" exactly, but rather a fracturing and restructuring of the alternate forms and fictions available to Horace to create a way to embody, though not "save" Horace. Sheila Smith McKoy goes so far as to argue that the text is potentially transformative, that it counters the "message" that being gay in the South is impossible, and that, in fact, Kenan "insist[s] that homosexual desire can transform culture and open a space wherein black men can embrace gay identity, even in the rural South" (17). Certainly, paying attention to the forms and themes of comics appearing in *Visitation* helps open one's vision onto a dynamic, dialogic, and global southern vista.

Reading for Kenan's "comics sensibility" can offer the readers of this novel a more nuanced awareness of the narrative shape in which Horace's experience, to mix the senses, is *tangibly seen*—or "beheld." Kenan's call to "remember" the physical labor of yesterday's tobacco farming, "that once upon a time, hands, human hands plucked ripe leaves from stalks . . . that people were bound by this strange activity" (*Visitation* 257) sounds remarkably similar to his claim nearly twenty years later in *The Fire Next Time* when he writes, "Once upon a time, not too very long ago, the debate, the talk, the discussion about race was much more visceral, became physical at times, had more at stake—actually had the ability to change lives" (94). For once it is *beheld*, "all times" remembered in hands and eyes and mouths, then narrative—and the lives defined and experienced through it—can be *talked about* and shaped.

Words that are visible, tangible, that can depict and affect the life of the body, are at the center of this novel. Where the novel and its author clearly survive through just such a narrative sensibility, Horace's belief in the ruling Word, in finding "the one and only voice" that fixes and frames, rather than engaging in "talk" or "dialogic" narrative, results finally in his destruction. By the end of the novel, chronologically just before the violent ritual that opens his story, when Horace has lost one after another of his bids for narrative belonging—through summer theater, at school, in his family, and at church—he comes round to seek a final and desperate medicine in his own words. Unable to accommodate himself in the frames created by family and community narratives of belonging, he writes to house himself:

So he wrote his autobiography, without stopping, one long suspended effort, words upon words flowing out of him, expressing his grief. *But he never read what he had written, hoping rather to exorcise his confusion.* So strong was his belief in words—perhaps they would lead him out of this strange world in which he had suddenly found himself. In the end, after reams and reams of paper and thousands of lines of scribble, he had found no answers. In frustration he burned it. (239, emphasis added)

Subsumed in this sense of one "absolute" voice, trying to cast himself—"his *confusion*"—outside the body and place that gives it shape, Horace can neither hear, read, nor see his own self: *"But he never read what he had written."* Although he turns, finally, to *creating* his own words, he makes no room for a *reading*, for a comics-like recursion into his own story. Horace makes no room for dialogue—even with himself.

In answering a question about teaching new writers, Kenan marks the importance of reading as a dialogue, "The more we've read, the more we have to talk back to and talk back with; the more arsenal we have to use in articulating our vision of the world" (Rowell 11). And in *The Fire Next Time* he characterizes his lifelong desire to write not as a one-way act but as a dialogue: "I wanted to write before I knew I wanted to write, *and write I did, talking back, writing back* to Beatrix Potter, to Louis Stevenson and Edgar Allan Poe and Tom Swift and the Hardy Boys . . ." (81, emphasis added). His comments return us to Gray's argument about the dialogic nature of southern literature: "the great dialogue that characterizes southern literature [is] a chain of communications that entails, not talking *like* other writers but talking *with*, them, talking *to* and sometimes *against*—in short, talking *back*" (244).

For Kenan, a southerner raised on interactive oral storytelling and comics, narrative is at core a dialogic process, a recursive activity of the sensory body. Comics narrative is built on such recursive reading strategies to "articulate" a "vision of the world," and *Visitation* too requires such work of its readers (Rowell 11). McCloud says of this recursive work the form invites that "Closure fosters an intimacy surpassed only by the written word" (69). But I would disagree. As a dialogic, explicitly sensual, and recursive form, comics is closer to oral narrative than prose and so is, potentially *more* intimate. And though Henninger argues that orality comes weighted with a myth of "authenticity," a myth that Cannon argues Kenan critiques, comics, as an explicitly constructed form offers an intimate narrative that does not erase its origins as a constructed thing. In his discussion of comics narrative, particularly against other visual narratives like film, Henry John Pratt concludes:

> The simplicity of the medium entails that comics can offer an individual voice and foster an intimacy between artist and reader that meets the level of literature—or even exceeds it, since comics reflect the artist's visual as well as verbal sensibility. Close connections between artist and reader in a pictorial narrative medium are hard to come by, and it is with good reason that we value their occurrence in comics. (116–17)

Comics may foster "intimacy"—but not because comics is a "simple" medium. Comics—like most narrative media—can be easy or hard. While I agree that comics, through icon and cartoon, can appear simpler—or at least less detailed—than either photorealistic visual or mimetic prose imagery, for this very reason it requires of its readers a more active, and yes, "intimate" engagement in the process of "closure" to "fill in" details and advance the narrative (a process that film, for example, usually does for the reader, and at a predetermined pace). Indeed, this is the very gap—between the lack of obvious reader work required by "actual" photographs and the explicit closure demanded of readers of "fictional" photographs—that Henninger argues southern women writers exploit to illuminate and critique oppressive and naturalized images of race and gender. While offering stories about alternate physical embodiment, comics also affords Kenan a complex narrative template for his prose, a dialogic web of multiple frames that can shape and house that alternate body. It is a narrative home that, on examination, is not so very far away from, even if it is explicitly critical of, the oral narrative structures of his grandparents.

The strong influence of comics in a novel of post-modern prose rooted in the southern U.S. underscores Kenan's efforts to offer a narrative form that can invite the reader to join in picturing, through one young black man's experience, the historical and contemporary specificity of the local South, with all its intersecting and powerfully fricative influences of church, family, homophobia, racism, and agrarian lifestyle *and* the globalized world of total connection into which that region is fast tipping. Comics is dialogic, tangible, bears close relation to old forms of media still so central to ideas of southern literature (visual, oral and dialogic, folk-based), and to new media, already part and parcel of the Global "New South" (also visual, participatory, socially networked, and hyperlinked). In *Visitation* it is clear that southern literature exists *in the world*, spinning, as Gray calls it "a web of words regional in immediate origin and focus but connected dialogically with other webs of words, national and eventually transnational" (244). Comics, a flexible narrative form that "still ha[s] more allure to [Kenan] than sex or drugs," may have its dangers in stereotype, yet the echoes of comics narrative strategy and thematic content in this novel resound as witness to the critical role that narrative itself plays in how communities and individuals within them live—or don't live—by how we frame a life, how we arrange and connect the frames, and what change we bring to its gutters. As Kenan says, "As simple as it seems, it's all about learning how to see" (*Fire* 111).

Being able to fly helps.

Notes

1. Scott McCloud uses the plural of "comic" to refer to the narrative form as whole, a convention I also follow.

2. While the recent exchange between Henry John Pratt and Aaron Meskin in *The Journal of Aesthetics and Art Criticism* (in articles published 2009–2010) makes it clear that the definition of what exactly constitutes "comics" remains under debate, Scott McCloud's foundational work in comics narrative theory almost twenty years ago offers a definition that remains a touchstone in the still emerging field of comics criticism. I use this definition and much of McCloud's terminology for its usefulness in exploring comics in relation to Kenan's prose.

3. Arguably, traditional serial comics often naturalize aspects of the form including iconics and framing, creating a potentially immersive, more passive reading experience. And yet, particularly as contemporary independent comic narratives have shown, while registering this longing for "escape," the form can also offer a profoundly counter-immersive, rigorous reading experience. Though images can "clarify" or intensify the meaning of words in comics narrative (or vice-versa), as Chute notes, discrepancy between word and image is also a powerful strategy creating both friction and complexity, and one used by even very popular comics narratives.

4. Ironically, although Barack Obama is an avowed fan of Spider-Man (among other comics), he does not think much of Superman. In answer to Benjamin Svetkey's 2008 *Entertainment Weekly* interview question "If you could be any superhero, which superhero would you be?", Obama offers the nuanced reply, "I was always into the Spider-Man/Batman model. The guys who have too many powers, like Superman, that always made me think they weren't really earning their superhero status. It's a little too easy. Whereas Spider-Man and Batman, they have some inner turmoil. They get knocked around a little bit."

Works Cited

Bhatia, Tej K. "Super-heroes to super languages: American popular culture through South Asian language comics." *World Englishes* 25.2 (2006): 279–98. Web. 12 Jan 2010.

Cannon, Uzzie T.: "Disturbing the African American Community: Defamiliarization in Randall Kenan's *Let the Dead Bury Their Dead.*" *Southern Literary Journal* 42.1 (2009): 102–21. Print.

Chute, Hillary. "Comics as Literature? Reading Graphic Narrative." *PMLA*. 123.2 (2008): 452–65. Web. 12 Feb 2009.

———. "Decoding Comics." *MFS: Modern Fiction Studies* 52.4 (2006): 1014–27. Web. 12 Feb 2009.

Chute, Hillary and Marianne DeKoven. "Introduction: Graphic Narrative." *MFS: Modern Fiction Studies* 52.4 (2006): 767–82. Web. 12 Feb 2009.

Clark, Keith. Introduction. *Contemporary Black Men's Fiction and Drama.* Ed. Keith Clark. Urbana: U of Illinois P, 2001. 1–14. Print.

Costello, Brannon. "Randall Kenan Beyond the Final Frontier: Science Fiction, Superheroes, and the South in *A Visitation of Spirits.*" *Southern Literary Journal* 43.1 (2010): 125–150. Print.

Gravett, Paul. "Seriously Funny Business." *New Internationalist* 387 (2006): 2–5. Web. 12 Jan 2010.

——. "'Where is the use of a book without pictures or conversations?' Coming to Terms with the Graphic Novel in Europe." *Third Text* 21.5 (2007): 617–25. Web. 12 Jan 2010.

Gray, Richard. *A Web of Words: The Great Dialogue of Southern Literature.* Athens, Georgia: U of Georgia P, 2007. Print.

Hamilton, Virginia. *The People Could Fly: American Black Folktales.* New York: Knopf, 1993. Print.

Henninger, Katherine. *Ordering the Facade: Photography and Contemporary Southern Women's Writing.* Chapel Hill: U of North Carolina Press, 2007. Print.

Holland, Sharon Patricia. "(Pro)Creating Imaginative Spaces and Other Queer Acts: Randall Kenan's *A Visitation of Spirits* and Its Revival of James Baldwin's Absent Black Gay Man in *Giovanni's Room.*" *James Baldwin Now.* Ed. Dwight A. McBride. New York: New York UP, 1999. 265–88. Print.

Hovis, George. *Vale of Humility: Plain Folk in Contemporary North Carolina Fiction.* Columbia, South Carolina: UP of South Carolina, 2007. Print.

——. "'I Contain Multitudes': Randall Kenan's *Walking on Water* as Collective Autobiography." *Southern Literary Journal* 36.2 (2004): 100–25. Web. 2 May 2006.

Hunt, V. "A conversation with Randall Kenan." *African American Review* 29.3 (1995): 411–20. Web. 12 Jan 2010.

Kenan, Randall: "An Interview with Octavia E. Butler." *Callaloo* 14.2 (1991): 495–504. Web. 2 May 2006.

——. *A Visitation of Spirits.* New York: Anchor Doubleday, 1990. Print.

——. "North Carolina." In *State by State: A Panoramic Portrait of America.* Eds. Matt Weiland and Sean Wilsey. New York: Ecco (Harper Collins), 2008. 342–47. Print.

——. *The Fire This Time.* Hoboken, NJ: Melville House P, 2007. Print.

Kreyling, Michael. *Inventing Southern Literature.* Jackson, Mississippi: UP of Mississippi, 1998. Print.

McCloud, Scott. *Understanding Comics.* New York: Harper, 1994. Print.

McKoy, Sheila Smith. "Rescuing the Black Homosexual Lambs: Randall Kenan and the Reconstruction of Southern Gay Masculinity." *Contemporary Black Men's Fiction and Drama.* Ed. Keith Clark. Urbana: U of Illinois P, 2001. 15–36. Print.

McRuer, Robert. "Queer Locations, Queer Transformations: Randall Kenan's *A Visitation of Spirits.*" *South to a New Place: Region, Literature, Culture.* Ed. Suzanne Jones and Sharon Monteith. Baton Rouge, LA: Louisiana State UP, 2002. 184–95. Print.

Meskin, Aaron. "Defining Comics?" *Journal of Aesthetics & Art Criticism* 65.4 (2007): 369–79. Web. 14 May 2010.

Mitchell, W. J. T. "Editor's Note: The Language of Images." *Critical Inquiry* 6.3 (1980): 359–62. Web. 18 May 2010.

——. "Spatial Form in Literature: Toward a General Theory." *Critical Theory* 6.3 (1980): 539–67. Web. 18 May 2010.

Pratt, Henry John. "Narrative in Comics." *Journal of Aesthetics and Art Criticism* 67.1 (2009): 107–17. Web. 14 May 2010.

Rowell, Charles H. "An Interview with Randall Kenan." *Callaloo* 21.1 (1998): 133–48. Web. 2 May 2006.

Singer, Marc. "'Black Skins' and White Masks: Comic Books and the Secret of Race." *African American Review* 36.1 (2002): 107–19. Print.

Svetkey, Benjamin. "The Other Presidential Debate." *Entertainment Weekly* 1006 (2008): 30. Web. 12 May 2010.

Terry, Jill. "Oral Culture and Southern Fiction." *A Companion to the Literature and Culture of the American South*. Ed. Richard Gray and Owen Robinson. Malden, MA: Blackwell, 2007. 518–35. Print.

Tettenborn, Eva: "'But What If I Can't Change?': Desire, Denial, and Melancholia in Randall Kenan's A Visitation of Spirits." *Southern Literary Journal* 40.2 (2008): 249–66. Print.

Thomas, Harry.: "'A Wanderer on the Earth' and 'A Son of the Community': Place and the Question of Queers in the Rural Souths of Lee Smith and Randall Kenan." *North Carolina Literary Review* 17 (2008): 117–30. Print.

Tucker, Lindsey. "Gay Identity, Conjure, and the Uses of Postmodern Ethnography in the Fictions of Randall Kenan." *Modern Fiction Studies* 49.2 (2003): 306–31. Web. 2 May 2006.

Walker, Melissa. *Southern Farmers and Their Stories*. Lexington, Kentucky: UP of Kentucky, 2006. Print.

Wester, Maisha. "Haunting and Haunted Queerness: Randall Kenan's Re-inscription of Difference in *A Visitation of Spirits*." *Callaloo* 30.4 (2007): 1035–53. Print.

A Re-Vision of the Record

The Demands of Reading Josh Neufeld's *A.D.*: *New Orleans After the Deluge*

—Anthony Dyer Hoefer

The images coming out after Hurricane Katrina now haunt southern, U.S. and even global visual cultural, altering collective memories and creating new, or at least newly visible, open wounds. . . . What do we want from pictures of the city, its people and places? What do these pictures "want" from us?
—Katherine R. Henninger, *Ordering the Facade*

No other artform gives so much to its audience while asking so much **from** them as well.
—Scott McCloud, *Understanding Comics*

Near the end of the graphic novel *A.D.: New Orleans After the Deluge*, the author/artist Josh Neufeld recreates an image that was seared into the public consciousness in the fall of 2005: an overhead shot that approximates the vantage point of a cable news helicopter looking down on a crowd of thousands gathered at the doors of New Orleans's Ernest L. Morial Convention Center. This image, like so many that have come to speak for the event, overwhelms its viewer with its sheer scope: nothing in it is easily quantifiable, and so the viewer can only understand the size of the crowd as "many," just as they can only know that the suffering is great, and the chaos, insurmountable. The image tells nothing of a particular event: gone are its individual textures, and the individual identities and stories of the people in that crowd have been effaced.

However, *A.D.* refuses to submit to either the sort of generalization offered by the perspective this image recreates or to its inverse, the easy, coherent narratives of tragedy or triumph—both of which dominated news coverage of the storm and subsequent flood. Neufeld's image evokes the August heat by using only red and gold tones. Amid this scheme, a single un-colored figure stands out in the crowd: Denise, described in the cover text as a "Sixthgeneration New Orleanian poet, singer, and kickboxer with a master's degree in guidance and counseling," and one of six people whose experiences are chronicled in *A.D.* At once recalling both news coverage of the flood and the *Where's Waldo?* series, Neufeld confronts his audience with the delicate, difficult interpretive work the aftermath of Katrina requires. Quickly, the perspective swoops from that aerial vantage point down into the crowd, to provide a sense of its claustrophobia; that image is promptly juxtaposed with a close-up of Denise—crammed into a mass of thousands of others, yet overwhelmed by a sense of isolation and abandonment. Here, Neufeld seeks out an appropriate balance between the particular and the general: the sheer scope of the suffering and destruction threatens to overwhelm and even betray the particular experiences of individuals. Conversely, the pathos of an individual witness's testimony might reduce the magnitude of the event, remove it from its historical context, or diminish the political momentum necessary for action.

Based on interviews Neufeld conducted with six New Orleanians, *A.D.* is an episodic oral history of the storm, from evacuation to flood to exile; the online publication *SMITH Magazine* presented it in regular installments between January 2007 and August 2008; a year later—in time for the fourth anniversary of Katrina's landfall—Pantheon Books released an expanded edition of *A.D.* The comic does not bring to the traumatic experiences of its subjects the same sort of aesthetic innovation of Art Speigelman's *Maus* and *In the Shadow of No Towers*; instead, it adopts an unadorned, relatively conventional aesthetic that mimics the simplicity of the oral history form. Nonetheless, *A.D.* demands much of its readers—if not in form, then in the ethics of reading. Neufeld's multimedia, multimodal graphic oral history of the Great Deluge

- challenges the visual record of a highly mediated event, moving between the iconic and general to the unfamiliar and particular;
- challenges claims to objective representation of reality/experience of trauma and suffering on this scale;
- and, through the inclusion of hyperlinks, discussion threads, and podcasted interviews with its subjects, encourages the audience to move out from the text to begin the difficult work of making some meaning from the event.

Katherine Henninger asks, "what do" photographs of post-Katrina New Orleans "'want' from us?" The answer is, *interpretation*. I contend that Neufeld foregrounds this *want* of interpretation—that it seeks to resolve the ethical contradiction between the impulse to bear witness to these events and the problems of representing the suffering of others by prompting the audience to take on the responsibility of making meaning from that suffering and, in its online form, provides opportunities to engage the world beyond the text.

The result is a work with a profound pedagogical impulse, which nonetheless avoids the pitfalls of pedantry or cliché—obstacles that are, as Henninger notes, difficult to avoid in the highly contested, overdetermined rhetorical ground of the United States South and, more specifically, of post-Katrina New Orleans. The New Orleans of the popular imagination exists as a sort of sensory overload—a heightened reality of jazz, cocktails and Creole cooking, subtropical heat, and brilliant sights of parades and second-lines—that obscures New Orleans's complicated history. In the days following the flood, the veneer was torn away; unfortunately, representations of the destruction wrought by the flood did not provide entry into that complexity and instead, as some critics have argued, forced the event into equally reductive scripts of black suffering and southern abjection. *A.D.* does not obviously engage in these sorts of ideological debates; nor does it directly address the myriad causes and consequences of the suffering it depicts—the peculiar genealogy of New Orleans, the history of African American suffering that was recalled and exposed by the flood, or the continuing disavowal of the decay facing the nation's urban infrastructure.

However, these matters are not absent: Rather than confronting that problem head on, and thus sacrificing the coherence of conventional narrative, *A.D.* subtly exposes the contingency of any representation of the storm, and, in its online form, invites the reader to investigate these issues, to learn more about the city and the storm, and even to interact with its characters—all in order to wrestle with the meaning of the flood and its aftermath. And while the reader may never fulfill these obligations, *A.D.* furthers the critical discussion of how the suffering of others might be ethically represented and read—particularly when the representation necessarily engages such deeply contested discourses as race and region. Those ethics demand the reader participate in the ongoing, labor-intensive processes of researching, listening, and revising the record of the event.

Context, Structure, and Narrative

A.D. emerged from the twinned impulses to take on the near-destruction of the city felt by both writer-artist Josh Neufeld, whose credits include Harvey Pekar's *American Splendor*, and Larry Smith, the founder and editor of *SMITH Magazine*, an online journal devoted to personal narratives. *SMITH* had previously serialized *Shooting War*, Anthony Lappé and Dan Goldman's graphic novel take on the war on terror, and Smith believed that something similar might be done "about the environment or Katrina" (Brophy-Warren). His attention was drawn to Neufeld, whose volunteer work in Biloxi following the storm had inspired a blog and subsequently a self-published memoir, *Katrina Came Calling*. "Having been in New York when the towers fell, I remember that overwhelming feeling of helplessness and displaced anger," Neufeld told the *New York Times* (Gustines). "When Katrina hit, I saw what was happening, and I realized that I, as a single person, could somehow help."

The result of their collaboration was a fascinating text: a web-based work of graphic reportage and oral history that presents the event through six intertwined narratives collected from six different New Orleanians. Originally, *SMITH* presented *A.D.* in a series of thirteen chapters, posted as Neufeld completed them over a twenty-month period. The distinctions between these chapters remain evident in the published book through transitions of color (each chapter is two-toned, dominated by two shades of a single color); rather than listing chapters, however, the book edition is divided into five parts: a Prologue (which offers a wordless overview of the event, from landfall to flood), "The City" (which presents the days leading up to the flood), "The Flood," "The Diaspora," and the greatly expanded conclusion, "The Return."

A.D. offers little in the way of obvious visual innovation or experimentation: its visual style is clear, concise, and relatively unsurprising—that is to say, realistic but not photorealistic. Colors evoke particular emotional content: gold for the "halcyon" days before the storm, a foreboding purple as the storm looms, a sickly green as the water stagnates a deep red for the searing late August heat, exacerbated by a position on a sweltering rooftop or amid the masses crowded at a shelter ("Pulp Secret").

Throughout these episodes, Neufeld recreates the Katrina stories of six New Orleanians. Crucially, none of these characters adhere to the stereotypes that populate popular representations of the city: *A.D.* offers no voodoo priestesses, drag queens, jazz musicians, southern belles, Cajun shrimpers, drug dealers, or corrupt politicians. Instead, these six people were carefully chosen to both represent different New Orleans neighborhoods and, more importantly, to suggest the wide varieties of Katrina-experiences. The characters, in order of their appearance, are:

- Leo, a white 20-something comic book collector, editor of the independent newspaper, *AntiGravity*, and resident of the hipster section of Mid City. Leo evacuates with his girlfriend Michelle.
- The Doctor (Brobson Lutz), a bon vivant, aficionado of all things New Orleans, and a veteran of many storms. The comic's other major white character, the Doctor rides out the storm among friends, dogs, and good wine in his French Quarter apartment.
- Kwame, an African American high school senior in suburban New Orleans East and the son of a minister. He evacuates with his family, and he ultimately finishes high school in California, while his parents return to rebuild their church. As he was a minor at the time of the comic's original publication, he is called "Kevin" in the online edition.
- Abbas (originally "Hamid" and drawn without a mustache in the web-comic), the Iranian-born proprietor of an Uptown grocery store who rides out the flood waters atop a shed in the rear of his store with his friend Mansell. Abbas remains behind to protect the successful business he has built in his adopted community.
- Denise, in many ways, the dominant figure in the text. An African American sixth-generation New Orleanian, she holds a master's degree in guidance and counseling, and lives with her mother, her niece Cydney, and Cydney's daughter R'nae in a small apartment above a boxing club in the economically blighted Central City area.

The six major figures are diverse in every possible way: in terms of geography, race, age, class, and sexual orientation. Furthermore, the differences in their narratives suggest the dramatically different ways in which New Orleanians experienced the storm and flood: Leo and Michelle evacuate but subsequently return to rebuild their lives; Kwame evacuates with his family, but, due to the destruction of the school system, is forced to relocate and finish high school in California; the Doctor stays throughout the storm and flood, but suffers little or no damage to his personal property and works to restore some sense of normalcy to his community; Abbas and Mansell remain to protect their property, but ultimately need to be rescued; Denise evacuates to one of the shelters of last resort and finds herself caught up in the Kafka-esque, post-Katrina bureaucracy of recovery.

This episodic, multiple-narrative structure only hints at the vast possibility of Katrina-experiences. Just as critically, Neufeld takes steps to ensure that the text does not posit these six narratives as wholly representative of the event: each character encounters other people, whose stories are suggested by the text and can be imagined by the audience. For instance, two days after the storm makes landfall, Abbas and Mansell meet two men in a fishing boat, who patrol the flooded streets for stranded residents (97). They offer assistance, but Abbas and Mansell choose to stay behind; in the final image offered of these men, the audience sees them, from Abbas's and Mansell's approximate perspective, drive off into the distance, and can only wonder what happens to them. That image is recalled, to even more dramatic effect, in an illustration that represents something Denise witnessed the following day (1 September 2005) from a balcony at the hospital to which she has evacuated. Denise and her niece Cydney watch as a man wades through chest-deep floodwaters, towing a motor-less johnboat that holds his sick wife and infant child. The hospital is in the midst of being evacuated by National Guardsmen, and the family is turned away. In a full-page panel that follows, Cydney and Denise (and, from their position, the audience) watch the anonymous family as they move out of view. Whatever heroic or tragic events follow, the audience cannot know.

These episodes, like others in the text, remind the audience that hundreds, if not thousands, of survivor narratives remain untold. Thus, nothing about the narratives of *A.D.* is closed, and this openness is matched by the web-based original publication's thrust to move beyond the text itself. Through the inclusion of hyperlinks, the web comic compels the reader to move outward—to investigate a wide variety of online Katrina resources, including simulations, archived news reports, YouTube videos of flood waters, and even the final, independent report on the levee breaches issued by the National Science Foundation and a team from UC-Berkeley. This impulse to educate the audience about the flood is matched by the web-text's effort to teach readers about the vibrant community and culture of New Orleans— a culture that transcends the experiences of tourists on Bourbon Street. Among the links offered by *SMITH*'s edition of *A.D.* are those to a recipe for the Doctor's favorite cocktail, the Sazerac; to *AntiGravity*, the magazine that Leo edits; and to the MySpace page of One Man Machine, a musician who performs at an *AntiGravity* party. Furthermore, podcast interviews with the

Doctor and Leo and a comment function/message board allow readers to interact with each other, the author, and the characters. I will return to these web functions and resources, but for now, their sum total is indicative of the profound pedagogical drive of the text: its mission is not simply to narrate, but to provide a vehicle through which the audience can access an impressive amount of information about New Orleans. These links are not simply web-based footnotes; rather, they are part of a broader strategy to compel the reader to more actively and critically approach the public record and the popular memory of post-Katrina New Orleans—a strategy also evident in the text's engagement with the photographic archive of the event.

Challenging the Visual Archive of Post-Katrina New Orleans

Given the scriptural precedent for flood narratives, it is fitting that *A.D.* begins as it does—cosmically, biblically, with a wide, wordless image of the earth. The Prologue continues without characters, dialogue, or much narration—just brief dates and place names; the perspective from above zooms in tighter, first onto the Gulf of Mexico and then onto an aerial image of the city of New Orleans. Closer-in images follow, depicting a bird's-eye view of life on Bourbon Street, in Jackson Square, and in a neighborhood that lies perilously close to a canal. The representations of New Orleans are matched by similarly bucolic depictions of Biloxi, Mississippi. The serene distance of these aerial images is quickly disrupted by the return to a view from beyond the atmosphere and to an image of a storm moving into and then through the Gulf of Mexico; dates mark the charge of Katrina toward New Orleans, and flashes to a jammed interstate, all lanes headed away from the city, and of crowds gathering at the Superdome remind us of what happened. Stunning visions of the storm's arrival, the ravages of its winds, and the breaching of the levees come next and ultimately give way to a drawing of a body, floating facedown in the flooded streets and finally, a double-page spread of the flooded city, both on Tuesday, August 30—the day after the storm.

The Prologue is stunning in its silence—in the inevitability of the destruction and in the author's refusal to use language to articulate its meaning. That discomfiting quiet is possible because the Prologue does not need to offer the audience any information they do not already possess; *A.D.* depends on the assumption that the audience is familiar, not only with the events, but with specific images and types of images used to portray them. Indeed, in response to a reader comment on the online edition of the prologue, Neufeld wrote that he was "using a lot of photographic reference for this project—especially for the prologue. About half the images are directly from photos, while the others use photos as a resource." The majority of these images approximate either satellite shots of swirling clouds or video and photographs captured from helicopters hovering safely above the city. Certainly, these images offer the utility of panorama—Neufeld can portray the scope of the destruction more easily from above. However, this visual strategy has an added benefit: it immediately locates the narratives that follow within the context of what much of the audience has already seen.

And so, while *A.D.*'s aesthetic is not characterized by the obvious innovation or the postmodern manipulation of visual convention that can be attributed to other notable nonfiction graphic narratives, it is nonetheless visually fascinating: like Spiegelman's work or Ho Che Anderson's graphic autobiography of Martin Luther King Jr., *A.D.* seeks to visually represent events that are already highly visually mediated; in doing so, it recalls, recreates, and revises images that have become part of the public consciousness.[1] The Prologue begins this process—not just locating its story in an historical context, but also by demanding that its readers reconsider the images that may have been presented as documents of facts. As Susan Sontag and others have noted, photographs seems to inspire an impulse to accept them as complete and total representations of reality. Even in a moment in which electronic media is our "surround," writes Sontag, events become "real" for "those who [are] elsewhere, following it as 'news'" once we apprehend them through photographs (21). "[T]he photograph provides a quick way of apprehending something and a compact form for memorizing it," Sontag writes. "The photograph is like a quotation, or a maxim or proverb. Each of us mentally stocks hundreds of photographs, subject to instant recall" (22). Unfortunately, this process too often leads us to deny the subjectivity of photographs and to accept them as "crude," but nonetheless objective, "statement[s] of fact addressed to the eye," as Sontag notes that Virginia Woolf did (26). Consequently, the images offered by mass media displace the event itself, and the representation becomes indistinguishable from the original.

Sontag's observation about our mental stock of images applies to the public understanding of both New Orleans itself and to its flooding in 2005. The city persists through its visual representations within the historical and popular culture imaginary: from the various stage and screen productions of *Streetcar Named Desire* to the images of Mardi Gras revelry supplied by the city's tourism industry to grainy video of Bourbon Street debauchery available on programs like *COPS* and on seamy products like *Girls Gone*

Wild, New Orleans has been and remains spectacularly specular. The archive of these images in the public discourse, however, was deeply unsettled by the images broadcast from New Orleans and published in newspapers and magazines across the globe in the days following Katrina. "The familiar tourist images of old New Orleans—tied up in the blackness of another era—allowed a disavowal of the racism that elsewhere was writ large across our television screens," writes Tara McPherson (331–32); McPherson contends that, prior to deluge, popular representations of New Orleans have "celebrated diversity when it adds flavor to tourist attractions" and to the spectacle of public celebrations like Mardi Gras, public places like Preservation Hall, and public memorials like Louis Armstrong Park, but "remain blind to government policies that put those attractions (not to mention the largely poor, black workers that built and sustained them) at risk" (332). For generations, according to Judith Jackson Fossett, the city has existed in the popular imagination as "'the Big Easy'—good food, good sex, good times, a place that care forgot, a tourist paradise" (327); this "tourist veneer" not only conceals the inequality within the city—it also displaces the manifold ways in which the rest of the nation is implicated in the despair that persists here in this hub of national and global commerce.

As the images poured forth from the flooded city, however, that "tourist veneer" was ripped away. As Fossett writes, "The whole cloth of racial, socioeconomic, and color caste, as well as post-1945 geographic segregation . . . could be seen" (326). These revelations were so stunning that many had trouble making sense of what they suddenly saw. "The scenes were at once familiar and unfamiliar," noted journalist David Halberstam in *Vanity Fair* (385). The American public is accustomed to broadcast footage of hurricanes, as well as images of horrific destruction. Likewise, an audience is familiar with the narrative arcs to which television news attaches such images: "First, there are the tragedy and the tears; then, in time, the redemption, the rejuvenation, and the gratitude." Despite this familiarity, Halberstam—who earned his fame as a reporter in Vietnam—found the images of the flooded city particularly disconcerting:

It was unfamiliar as well, because when the damage is this catastrophic, the people so helpless, the government so weak and clumsy, we expect it to take place somewhere else-on the coast of Sri Lanka or Bangladesh, for instance—somewhere distant and poor. We do not expect to see so many fellow Americans overwhelmed, unable to help themselves and unable to escape the disaster. We do not expect to see our government so impotent and indifferent that it is completely paralyzed at the most critical moment. We do not expect to see the story play out so slowly and the cavalry arrive so late.

Was this really us? Was this really an American city coming apart— or drowning—as we watched? Were all these poor people, whose lives were broken, and some of whom looted their own city, really Americans? Aren't we better than this? Aren't we different? (385)

Halberstam was hardly alone; according to the historian David Brinkley, "Commentators kept asking: Is this America? Analogies were made to Third World countries" (204). In particular, Brinkley cites CNN anchor Anderson Cooper's assessment that "Walking through the rubble, it feels like Sri Lanka, Sarajevo, somewhere else, not here, not home, not America" (204). Unfortunately, while these images unsettled the facade that had previously concealed the deep social problems plaguing the city (and, indeed, the nation), the public reckoning with this newfound knowledge was deeply troubling: too often, the images put forth too easily fit other familiar archives of images—archives that positioned New Orleans, a majority-black city in the deepest part of the U.S. South, as inexorably different from the rest of the nation. Rather than seeing the history of "post-1945 geographic segregation" in the U.S., as Fossett does, these commentators saw something abject, foreign, and inexorably Other—a notion of the region that, as Leigh Anne Duck notes, proved critical to the broader discourses of nation and national identity throughout the twentieth century (7). As Anna Brickhouse notes, the "rotting bodies and sick or starving survivors" of "what the news continually characterized as an incomprehensibly 'Third-World' scene" allowed viewers to disavow any connection to the events they witnessed—and, I would add, any complicity with the suffering depicted (1100). Other explanations of the images emphasized racial difference rather than national identity, locating the images in the context of an archive of the broadest stereotypes of blackness. Consider the uncomfortable description of the scene by Cooper's CNN colleague Wolf Blitzer: "You simply get chills every time you see those poor individuals . . . so many of these people, almost all of them that we see, are so poor, and they're so black" (Brinkley 203–4).

In the months and years since, the visual rhetoric of post-Katrina has proven to be highly contested. Certainly, the images upon which Blitzer commented and that the cable news audience witnessed were overwhelmingly images of black people, many of whom were poor. The critical questions, then, really deal with the consequences and the authenticity of these representations. While reviewing a photo essay by New Orleans *Times-Picayune* photographer Ted Jackson (presented on the website "Nieman Reports," a component of Harvard's Nieman Foundation for Journalism), I noticed two comments near the bottom of the page. Writing on 8 March 2009, "Aurora" asks for permission to use some of the photos for "an essay on Hurrican [sic] Katrina as a reflection of the reality of race and class in America"; in November, "Bruce Tuttle" responds, "Oh lawdy, oh lawdy! Have mercy on mah soul! This papuh is a true inspiration to me and mah children."

Various cultural and literary scholars have sought to make sense of the emergent visual rhetoric of post-Katrina New Orleans. Lloyd Pratt notes "the eerie similarity of those images of massed African Americans lined up along railroad tracks to descriptions of the post-Emancipation South,"[2] and that Ted Jackson's photograph of "a distraught African-American woman in a posture of supplicating prayer beneath the headline, "Help Us, Please," would be "better consigned to the archives of nineteenth-century abolitionism" (264). Fossett contends that, in the mass media coverage of the flood, black residents "go mostly unheard," the "voices or homemade signs entreating help register[ing] briefly on news cameras panning across the squalor of those left behind" (326).

However, it is not helpful or even possible to reject the photographic and media archive of post-Katrina New Orleans. As Katherine Henninger writes, "If the photographs of Katrina's aftermath represent very real bodies in a very real, very damaged place, they represent even more how quickly one facade built of cultured visions can give way to another. There is danger in this, but also power" (185). The power noted by Henninger surges throughout *A.D.*: while a photograph might obscure its own artifice as an historical record, a panel from a graphic novel is more obviously a product of artistic creation. And when a photographic image from the public archive of Katrina is recreated by *A.D.*, the juxtaposition of the two reveals the artifice of both. Thus, by appropriating that archive and reconfiguring it to tell these divergent and unexpected narratives, the comic demands that the audience bring an intense critical gaze to bear on both Neufeld's text and the broader visual archive upon which it is based.

While *A.D.*'s engagement of a general visual Katrina archive is more obvious in the prologue "The Storm," recreated and revised photographs are woven into the main narratives of the text—none more notable than Neufeld's depiction of the horrific days Denise spent waiting for help at the Ernest N. Morial Convention Center in the city's Central Business District. A photograph by the *Times-Picayune*'s Brett Duke on 1 September 2005, presents a wide-angle image of dozens of people, crammed on the sidewalk outside the Convention Center (see figure 13.1). That photograph shares

13.1. Brett Duke. Untitled photograph. *Center of Desperation*. Online photographic archive. NOLA.com. the *Times-Picayune*. 1 Sept 2005. Photo © 2010 The Times-Picayune Publishing Co., all rights reserved. Used with permission of the *Times-Picayune*.

13.2. From *A.D.: New Orleans After the Deluge*. New York: Pantheon, 2009. Copyright © 2009 Josh Neufeld.

topic, perspective, and composition with this image from *A.D.*, a depiction of Denise's mother, niece, and grandniece in the same general location (see figure 13.2; 136). Since the months following the storm, Duke's photograph has been available at the *Times-Picayune*'s Katrina archive, found at its website, NOLA.com; a cursory viewing of this archive alongside *A.D.* suggests that it proved to be a great resource for Neufeld as he created the comic.

13.3. From *A.D.: New Orleans After the Deluge*. New York: Pantheon, 2009. Copyright © 2009 Josh Neufeld.

13.4. Ted Jackson. Untitled Photograph. Online photographic archive. NOLA.com. the *Times-Picayune*. 1 Sept 2005. Photo © 2010 The Times-Picayune Publishing Co., all rights reserved. Used with permission of the *Times-Picayune*.

More striking similarities are evident in other, more gut-wrenching images. One of the most horrific moments of *A.D.* occurs at the Convention Center, when Denise watches a conflict emerge over a bottle of water. The dispute is filled with macho-bravado, but culminates in a revelation of total vulnerability and fear, as one of the men in the dispute collapses and begs for help for his baby (see figure 13.3; 140–41). That image clearly draws inspiration, down to the man's jersey and shorts, from a Ted Jackson photograph from the *Times-Picayune* (see figure 13.4).[3] The differences between the two images are just as important. To begin, the dead woman behind the father is absent from Neufeld's image; in fact, in the chronology of *A.D.*, the woman, Miss Williams, does not die until the following day (152).

The photographs of that frail corpse, a blanket draped across it, were reprinted frequently in the weeks that followed; Neufeld's re-creation of it is no less stirring. By locating Miss Williams's death elsewhere, Neufeld posits a chronology distinct from that suggested by Jackson's photograph: these events are not simultaneous, even if they appear that way in the photo. This revision reminds the audience of the subjectivity of both the narrative of *A.D.* and of the photograph: both have unique, particular perspectives (in the case of the photo, Ted Jackson; in the case of the comic image, Neufeld and his proxy, Denise), and neither can claim to present the total or complete meaning of the event. Finally, both Neufeld's depictions of the father and baby and of Miss Williams's death occur in front of blank backgrounds; indeed, the father and baby are the only figures in that image. The consequence: these individuals and their stories are given primacy; their experiences constitute unique and particular narratives of suffering and injustice, and they demand our individual attention.

The demand Neufeld places on the audience is the demand of interpretation. While the urgency and ethical obligation here is particular to his subject, similar demands are placed by all graphic narratives, according to comics artist and theorist Scott McCloud. "No other artform gives so much to its audience while asking so much *from* them as well," he has famously contended (92). In McCloud's description of the phenomenon he calls "closure," the sequence of various images to articulate a coherent narrative is *more* dependent on a form of self-aware audience participation and interpretation than either film or prose; in order for graphic narrative to work, the reader has to make the cognitive leap from the time and space represented in one panel to the next, and then onward. Thus, a viewer might, like Woolf, consider a photograph—or even video footage—to be unmediated representation of a real moment in time and, consequently, remain unaware of the process of interpreting or reading that image. Comics, on the other hand, remind an audience that their images represent only an artist's rendering of an idea or moment. The conventions of composition and representation in comics (motion lines, thought and dialogue balloons, sound effects, the transition across the "gutter" from one image to the next) are not mimetic, but figurative; as Hilary Chute notes, "[a]n awareness of the limits of representation . . . is integrated into comics through its framed, self-conscious, bimodal form" (457). Consequently, the comics reader should have a heightened awareness of his or her duties of interpretation.

The expectation of interpretation is a powerful tool for comics artists, particularly those creating nonfiction texts that address historical events. Through "its manifest handling of its own artifice, its attention to its seams," graphic narrative unsettles the familiarity, if not banality, of imagery that has become commonplace. Most famously, Art Spiegelman's *Maus* and *In the Shadow of No Towers* trouble the familiar media representations of two highly mediated events—the Holocaust and the attacks of September 11, 2001—in stylistically radical manners. In his *King: A Comics Biography of Martin Luther King Jr.*, Ho Che Anderson appropriates extant visual archives in even more dramatic ways—recreating unseen but nonetheless famous moments in a noir-ish black and white, painting other moments in abstracted watercolors, and inserting collages of reproduced archival news photographs. Through this expressionist and varied use of images, "*King* simultaneously borrows from and disrupts photography's presumed optical truths and claims to objectivity," writes Michael A. Chaney (180); "Anderson's artistry bankrupts assumptions regarding photographic objectivity, the constitutive 'past-ness' of history, and the separation of copy from original" (188).

Because the responsibilities of interpretation are foregrounded, *A.D.*, like *King*, fosters a critical reading of the public memory of visually mediated historical events. It is insufficient to merely destabilize the truth claims, however. Instead, *A.D.* also posits strategies for ethical representations and ethical readings of such images—strategies that, among other things, balance the scale and scope of destruction with the need to consider the particular and individual forms of suffering and trauma. Consider, for instance, an image taken from a helicopter that depicts the crowds pouring out of the Convention Center. The photograph is composed to emphasize a series of parallel lines: the power lines, the red stripe and the lettering on the building, the base of its facade, the division between sidewalk and street, and the median. The crowd is hemmed in between the line of the building and the line of the street. The result is an image that emphasizes the sheer size of the

13.5. From *A.D.: New Orleans After the Deluge*. New York: Pantheon, 2009. Copyright © 2009 Josh Neufeld.

crowd and the idea that they have been abandoned and yet still effectively trapped by the civic institutions of their city.

Certainly, these ideas—people crammed together, nowhere to go—are critical to making sense of the consequences of the government inaction and the awful experience of the victims. However, in representing that reality, this image effaces both the authorial effort of composition *and* the individuality of each of these people: they are part of a nearly inhuman mass, a chaotic group of helpless, deteriorating bodies difficult to identify with. In contrast, the "*Where's Waldo*" image of Denise balances the needs to tell both stories (see figure 13.5). Its composition is fairly consistent; the perspective is a near approximation, and the parallel lines remain constant. The crowd appears even larger in Neufeld's image, but among them, one figure stands out: Denise is colored white, unlike the yellow-shaded crowd around her, and also unlike the others, she has a voice. While she alone has a voice in this story, the image presents her, not as special, but as one among thousands. Just as the six-part narrative structure of the book suggests the multitude of Katrina experiences, so too does this illustration. Though the audience is privy to Denise's experience, it cannot access the experience of the others. However, it is critical that we are at least *reminded* that their stories exist and deserve our listening, and that we know that whatever truth is offered by this image, it is provisional and in need of further consideration. Here, the truth of this moment is not self-evident, but rather, myriad and difficult to grasp. Denise's confusion becomes the audience's: how do we begin to make sense of the crowd? For Denise, no sufficient response exists—she must simply find her way through the crowd to her family. For the reader, however, the image implies an appropriate response: thousands of other stories, similar and still distinct from Denise's, exist in the frame, and the audience is compelled to seek them out and listen whenever the opportunity arises.

Trauma, Image, and Interpretation

Alone, a challenge to photorealism and the objectivity of the archive of Katrina-related images would be an insufficient response to the events *A.D.* chronicles; however, it is a necessary step in the effort to adequately and ethically bear witness to the stories of these six individuals. In this respect, *A.D.* belongs alongside *Maus*, *In the Shadow of No Towers*, Marjane Satrapi's *Persepolis*, and Joe Sacco's *Palestine*—works that, Hilary Chute writes, "explore the conflicted boundaries of what can be said and what be shown at the intersection of collective histories and life stories" (459). Jeff Adams has noted that what he calls "the image text" ("graphic novels, comic books, illustrated texts") has emerged contemporaneously and not coincidentally alongside "a pedagogic impulse, a desire to recount and relay traumatic incidents from the past for a contemporary audience" (35). In particular, *A.D.* suggests that the comics form is uniquely suited to bearing witness to the tragedies and traumas of the Information Age—horrific, highly mediated events that audiences around the globe can witness or even experience through photographs, television, newspapers, and the Internet. Unbounded by the requirements of realism, the confines of language, or the expectations of objectivity, comics like these can offer the coherent articulations necessary to respond to individual and historical traumas without sacrificing the ambiguity, dislocation, and confusion fundamental to these experiences.

In contrast to works like *Maus* and *King*, *A.D.*'s aesthetic is largely conventional and straightforward, but it is not without figurative moments. Consider, for instance, Neufeld's representation of Leo's realization that his home and all of his belongings are underwater. While *A.D.* in many ways fits within the genres of oral history and nonfiction narrative, it shares with other comics the capacity for visual metaphor and representing subjective reality. The prior page relatively realistically portrays Leo seeing an Internet image of his neighborhood (115); his expression indicates his despair. Here, however, is a representation of his internal response to the loss of his comic book collection. In terms of the sort of loss and suffering chronicled elsewhere in the text, this experience may not strike the reader as significant; *A.D.*, however, is careful not to categorize or rank the losses suffered by its characters. This image depicts the trauma of Leo's realization in a way that might not otherwise be clear: though he is safely in Houston, he feels that some element of himself remains with the now-destroyed collection. These comics are touchstones and represent some crucial facet of him—whether the work of collecting them, the influences they had upon him, or perhaps other memories connected to them. Leo is hardly alone in this experience: a deep investment in one's home and physical belongings is natural, and its loss provokes existential angst. Again, if, in another form, Leo were to suggest that the loss of his beloved comic books was tragic, his audience might reasonably respond with little sympathy and see little to mourn in the midst of other suffering; a similar reaction might be elicited from a photograph of a pulpy mass of waterlogged back-issues of *Amazing Spider-Man*. Here, however, the psychological reality of the experience is made apparent.

This panel recalls what Gillian Whitlock terms the "boxes of grief" in Spiegelman's *In the Shadow of No Towers* (969). Interestingly, McCloud's criticism and theorization of comics shares much in common with the ongoing work of trauma studies; the preeminent concern of both critical discourses is the construction of coherent narrative from disparate fragments. The comics reader, as McCloud notes, is conditioned to make the interpretive leaps across the gutter, linking the action of one panel to the next. Our own experience of reality requires the same process of "closure," he contends: "our senses can only reveal a world that is fragmented and incomplete. Our perception of 'reality' is an act of faith, based on mere fragments" (62). In our daily experience of reality, that act of faith is all but invisible—as close to reflex as a cognitive process can be.

Traumatic experiences like those undergone by the characters in *A.D.*, however, disrupt the process of closure and thus, the sense of coherent, objective reality. "Trauma is itself a shattering experience that disrupts or even threatens to destroy experience in the sense of an integrated or at least visibly articulated life," writes Dominick LaCapra; "There is a sense in which trauma is an out-of-context experience that upsets expectations and unsettles one's very understanding of existing contexts" (117). For LaCapra and other trauma theorists, "existing contexts" can include familiar narratives and even language itself. Thus, even an experienced writer like David

Halberstam can struggle to articulate the traumatic experiences of Katrina and the flood, which exposed the contingent, fictive nature of conventional narratives of national identity: his question, "Was this really us?", becomes the existential, "Who are we, really?"

Neufeld's image of the father, pleading for help, prompts a similar response from the reader: who are we who allowed this to happen? It is an image, and a reaction, that disrupts any familiar discourse of community or nation. Other, similarly unsettling images occur during Denise's time at the Convention Center; for instance, Neufeld illustrates the terror felt by the abandoned crowd in a horrifying image of crowded, apparently disembodied heads (150–51). The sweating and terrified faces, the eeriness of these seemingly disembodied heads and disembodied voices, and the confined, askew frame, combine to evoke feelings of claustrophobia, vertigo, and terror—a combination of emotions that transcends language.

Traumatic experience like the one represented in this image has a crippling effect on its victims long after the actual event has occurred. Victims are paralyzed, endlessly reliving an experience that cannot be assimilated into coherent narrative. In order to move forward, the victim must "work through" the experience—that is, integrate it into a coherent narrative that reduces neither its magnitude nor its complexity. The articulation must not do a disservice to the experience or the victim by delimiting it in any way, but it must also provide something coherent enough to allow for the victim to move forward. While the therapeutic models for analyzing and working through trauma pertain specifically to individual victims, theorists like LaCapra (a historian by training) apply them to broad historical, cultural, and social events. In the cases of historical or global traumas, societies suffer collectively from an inability to assimilate traumatic experiences and must work to understand what occurred so that they can move forward and ultimately take action in response.[4] The process of working through traumatic experience does not require or even promise "total redemption of the past or healing its traumatic wounds," according to LaCapra. Instead, "we can work to change the causes of this cause, insofar as they are social, economic, and political and thereby attempt to prevent its recurrence as well as enable forms of renewal" (119).

Trauma theorists like LaCapra and Cathy Caruth suggest that new, experimental, and often non-linear forms are necessary to do this—forms that have little concern with realism and mimesis and are thus better suited to articulate the repetitious, chaotic experience of trauma.[5] The existing archive of Katrina images proves ill-suited to these needs as long as the images remain embedded in the familiar media narratives noted by Halberstam—"the tragedy and the tears; then, in time, the redemption, the rejuvenation, and the gratitude" (385). In its revision of the archive, *A.D.* liberates the images from that context. While Neufeld's text offers a fairly linear, chronological narrative—the dates and times are often noted, allowing the reader to keep track of how events in different parts of the city relate—the comics form foregrounds the subjectivity and mediation of its narrative: the text presents real stories of actual individuals, but places the burden of interpretation on the audience.

Denise's experiences at the Convention Center and her effort to recover her life are among the text's most powerful representations of traumatic events and experiences. The episode at the Convention Center concludes when the rage she has expressed throughout the book finally gives way to resignation and despair (153). Though thousands of other people have crowded onto the narrow sidewalks outside the Convention Center, each panel shows only one adult member of Denise's family. The blank space behind them isolates them from the other citizens of New Orleans and the other members of their de facto community outside the facility; the gutters divide them from their own family members, suggesting the profoundness of their isolation. Though each woman is among thousands, and though she is with the people to whom she is closest, each experience this moment alone. The baby offers a wordless cry—perhaps the most appropriate response—while Denise vacantly states that "They are trying to kill us all," revealing the cause of her alienation (153). From her perspective, the body politic has been irrevocably sundered; the majority have abandoned this minority and left them for dead.

This sense of alienation from others is characteristic of traumatic events: perhaps the victim believes that she alone knows the horrific truth that any sense of coherent experience is a pleasant fiction, and now can no longer stand to be around those who cannot see it too; or perhaps the trauma victim's sense of self is so shattered that he can no longer put forward a coherent self to interact with others. In Denise's case, the aftermath of the storm is horrible: she despises her new life, but cannot see any meaning in the old one. From a new "Habitat for Humanity" home in Baton Rouge a year after the storm, she reports, "I fucking hate it here, but I'm afraid I would hate it in New Orleans more—and I don't want to hate the only place I ever considered home" (176). She continues, "This isn't my life. This is the life of someone I wouldn't even want to shake hands with" (177). In order to fully reckon with the meaning of the near-destruction of New Orleans, the audience must wrestle with these ambiguous and challenging emotions—her anger, abjection, and self-loathing.

Though the stakes are higher, the process of working-through Denise must undergo to move forward (and she does, returning to New Orleans to work as a counselor for victims of domestic abuse) is not unlike the interpretive work required of reading a graphic narrative: both processes require one to take disparate, disconnecting elements to constitute something coherent. In both instances, the reader and the victim must make cognitive leaps of faith in order to make some sense of what has happened. In neither case is the aim to express objective truth, but rather, a contingent, provisional, usable articulation of reality. "Narrative," LaCapra writes, "at best helps one not to change the past through a dubious rewriting of history but to work through posttraumatic symptoms in the present in a manner that opens possible futures" (121–22).

The effort to open those futures requires one to negotiate a contradiction: a coherent narrative is necessary to understand the event and respond, but that coherence can be tainted—and perhaps, harmful—if a "dubious rewriting of history" too easily assigns blame on a scapegoat or if it provides its audience with a sense of catharsis that forestalls necessary action. In the latter case, a survivor narrative can, with the best of intentions, allow an audience to so immediately identify with the character(s) that its members believe that they have suffered and ultimately conquered this traumatic experience alongside the figures from the narrative. In this case, the text may restore a sense that all is well, long before this is the case.

A.D. negotiates this contradiction, as it has throughout, by foregrounding its own artifice. The text bears witness to the events of the flood as well as its psychological consequences, but it does not seek to provide its audience with a virtual experience of the storm and flood. In the final two sections, "The Diaspora" and "The Return" (presented together as a consolidated and reduced Epilogue in the web comic), Josh Neufeld conducts follow-up telephone interviews with the six subjects at various intervals—first, a year and a half later, and then again in February 2008. The artist draws himself as he asks questions, and then illustrates the events that the subjects narrate in response. The voices are theirs, and the audience is unmistakably cast into Neufeld's perspective as an interviewer, an outsider listening to their stories. The people, whom we have come to know as characters in a story, now address us in their own voices, and the reader, like Neufeld, is obligated to tease some coherent meaning out of the disparate narratives.

Opening New Futures Online: Interactivity, Multimodal Functionality, and Bearing Witness to the Stories Beyond the Text

The pedagogical impulse of *A.D.* is predicated on a particular ethics of reading in which critical engagement and sophisticated interpretive work are demanded of the audience. If new futures are to be opened, however, it will be not just because the book offers insight into this trauma—both individual and national—but because the understanding it provides propels the reader to continue to struggle at making sense of the event and even to take action in response. The illustration of the father in the jersey, holding his infant and begging for help, emphasizes the necessity of an ethical response: with no one else in the image, the reader becomes his audience; we, the audience, become the "you" in "You gotta help me." Likewise, Denise calls out to the audience for help in her most desperate moment (146). Denise's head moves out of the panel, as if she is abandoning the two-dimensional page for the three-dimensional world of the audience; her gaze is directed at the audience, and thus, so are her questions. Already, the audience has been deeply engaged in the interpretive work necessitated by the medium; now, it has become implicated in the events it depicts. Sadly, the audience hears neither plea until years later—no earlier than late 2008 for the web comic reader and August of 2009 for the reader of the printed edition. Still, through their cries, *A.D.* calls for the audience to do something. How often, though, does what is represented in a book impel action in the world not bound by its covers? Bearing witness alone is positive and perhaps all that we can demand of a narrative work, but the characters in *A.D.* call for more.

Interestingly, the original web-based form of the comic provides some mechanisms for further investigation, discussion, and, potentially, action: through a series of Internet-enabled functions, the text provides opportunities to investigate the genealogy of the flood, to explore stories untold within the frame of the narrative, and—perhaps most interestingly—to develop a community of readers (and characters). In its online form (via *SMITH Magazine*), *A.D.* propels the reader to the world outside the text, where he or she can, at the very least, continue to participate in the ongoing process of understanding the causes and consequences of the near-destruction of New Orleans and where action might be taken. Many of these functions extend the pedagogical potential of the text. Hyperlinks to Leo's magazine, the menu at the fabeled French Quarter restaurant Galatoire's, and the Wikipedia entry for Sazerac enrich the audience's understanding of the unique and vibrant pre-Katrina cultures of New Orleans—a function that not only establishes setting, but probably more importantly, participates in arguments that cite New Orleans's cultural uniqueness and importance as justification for large national investment in the rebuilding process.[6] Similarly, links to news items, archived updates from the National Weather Service, and to a computer simulation of the levee breaches connect the events of the comic to the broader chronology of the flood. In addition, podcasted interviews with Lutz, Hamid/Abbas, Leo, and Denise supplement the reader's understanding of these individuals and of the city.

But in terms of the processes of bearing witness and working through traumatic experiences, the comment function is among the most compelling elements of *A.D.* Nothing about the particular application should strike the reader as particularly novel; indeed, one finds similar comment functions following nearly every blog posting or news article published online. In the context of work of documentary art, the comments played out in a surprising way: the readers could not only offer their reactions, but in fact, engage with the author and even the subjects of the text. And given the serial form in which *A.D.* first appeared, readers could even offer editorial decisions. For instance, in response to events in Chapter 1 of the web-comic, blogger Cade Roux offered a mild correction: "I hate to be a nitpicker, but NO ONE was thinking about this storm coming to New Orleans until Friday. All the projections were Tampa and then Florida panhandle and then Alabama. It wasn't until Friday evening that the projections changed to New Orleans." Neufeld not only answered Roux's comment, but corrected the inaccuracy: "I feel it's pretty important to get the details right, so in the spirit of the constantly updateable www-world we live in, I've made changes to a couple of panels." Neufeld was not alone in offering explanations: when readers objected to the presence of a New England Patriots poster on the wall of Leo's apartment in Chapter 2, the real Leo felt compelled to explain that, though the poster was in fact in his apartment before the storm, his primary allegiance was to the hometown Saints. While these quibbles may, to paraphrase Roux, seem "nitpicky," the particular textures of the places and events depicted here matter greatly to those who see what they have lost recreated.

More compelling conversations developed through the comments. In response to events in the third chapter of the web-comic, "Amy," a registered nurse from New Orleans, expresses deep concern over the depiction of the treatment Denise and her family received at Memorial Hospital: Denise's mother, a surgical tech at Memorial, had been promised a room for her family, but a doctor or administrator tells her that rooms have been reserved from the families of RNs, whose presence is more critical. The real Denise responds, and a fascinating conversation develops. Amy, too, was "kicked out" of a promised private room at her hospital, and each believes that race informed their particular experiences: Denise notes that all the staff that were asked to move to a common space (including her mother and family) were black, and Amy believes that her whiteness expedited her evacuation from the city a few days after the storm. The conversation is a rare thing in American political discourse: an organic and relatively un-self-conscious discussion about the ways in which race informs our experience.

Concerns about race emerge elsewhere in the comments section; particularly notable is a conversation between Neufeld, Denise, and comics artist Dean Haspiel. In Chapter 5 ("Katrina Comes Calling") of the webcomic, much of the early morning landfall of the storm is presented through the experiences of Denise, who has decided to ride out the storm alone in her Central City apartment. As the hurricane sweeps through town, her building begins to sway, and she becomes terrified. In the final panel, she cries out, "I'm gonna die in this bitch! Damn!" This dialogue concerned comics artist Dean Haspiel, who wrote that the line "felt forced and took me out of the drama. I could almost hear the gangsta drum beats behind her 'rap' and wondered if she really blurted that line when she was alone and scared with her cat in the confines of her compromised position?" (sic). A few hours later, Denise responded:

> Dean,
> That woman is me, and that is exactly what I was thinking at that moment and for many, many moments during the hurricane. I was terrified, and that was my expression of terror, not false bravado.
> And maybe, just maybe, rap music reflects the very real language of a very real people. Because, frankly, I talked like that before I ever heard a rap record.

Haspiel responds awkwardly, attempting to establish his rap bonafides and thus, one supposes, the authenticity and expertise necessary to make such statements. "Fair enough," he writes. "I grew up on the origins of hip-hop in the upper west side of Manhattan and I cherish the music. Just ask Josh." He continues, arguing that, even in this sort of work, the artist-writer has the obligation to edit "certain facts" that might take the audience "OUT of the drama."

While Haspiel's impulse for self-defense is off-putting (really, it is just a step away from "I have plenty of black friends"), his thesis deserves consideration: what is the artist's obligation when an event succumbs to the easy but limited confines of a familiar script or even reinforces a pernicious stereotype? If nothing else, Haspiel seems to argue, that stereotype seems to be an artistic shortcut—a momentary weakness that reduces the power and complexity of the narrative. Denise's response is equally salient, and far more direct: that's the way it happened. And Neufeld, in his response, agrees: "Certainly, as I was writing the scene, I wouldn't have had the Denise character say what she did. . . . I realize that it may take some readers 'out of the story,' but at least in this case, I think it is more important to tell what really happened."

Their discussion is fascinating, because it echoes the concerns about photographs of black New Orleanians articulated by Lloyd Pratt and Judith Jackson Fossett, and because it yields some insight into *A.D.*'s sublimated engagement with race and other political concerns. Wolf Blitzer's description about the masses at the Superdome—"so poor, and . . . so black"—has been almost-universally derided, but it is worth considering why it poses such an affront. What is untrue about it? Did it not accurately describe many of the folks gathered there? Is it troubling because it reduces the more complex reality of who suffered because of the flood? Or because it links "poor" and "black" in a way that resonates with a rhetoric of southern paternalism that we have not yet gotten past? Or perhaps, because it renders the event and its victims as something hopelessly, inexorably Other—reinforcing the people on the screen as a special category, distinct from a not-poor, not-black, not-southern, not-New Orleanian American identity? In the case of Katrina, discussions of race are particularly problematic, posing a set of questions less about *why* we react a certain way than about *how* we move forward: should one minimize race in order to dispel notions this was only a story of black suffering or to challenge the conflation of blackness, poverty, and victimization? Or does that strategy get in the way of a coherent narrative necessary for political action—that is to say, does it reduce the political urgency to address the very real concerns of social inequality that disproportionately affects African Americans and that inform the aftermath of Hurricane Katrina? The answers do not come easily, as Blitzer's misstep and Haspiel's awkward assertion of authenticity attest: our discourses of racial and national identity are messy things, and even when we tread very carefully and speak with the best of intentions, our limitations catch up with us.

I would not suggest that *A.D.* offers any answers to these difficult questions; indeed, Neufeld seems to avoid such missteps by hardly mentioning issues of race or ethnicity. However, this is not a cop-out, but in fact a
far more complex and potentially successful strategy for working through
the particular challenges of this topic. Certainly, the diversity of the city
is reflected in the selection of characters, but the specific ways in which
identity (whether figured in terms of class, race, gender, sexuality, or religious affiliation) informed the particular Katrina-experiences of these
individuals are never directly addressed. These concerns, however, are
made present through a variety of cues that give these characters shape.
Such cues might be as simple as names (Abbas/Hamid is, for instance, an
Iranian immigrant). Others are not as obvious to readers without specific
knowledge of the city: when we first meet Denise, she wears a sweatshirt
emblazoned with "Xavier University"—a reference to the New Orleans-
based institution, which is the nation's only Roman Catholic historically
black university. Similarly, each character's affiliation to his or her particular neighborhood provides contextual clues about race and class: Kevin/
Kwame is from New Orleans East, a suburban community that was, prior
to the storm, a haven for the city's black middle and upper middle classes,
while Denise's neighborhood—Central City—was among the city's most
impoverished. This willingness to let the evidence of identity and position
emerge through the narrative, rather than explicitly detailing it, implicitly
recognizes the complexities of race and ethnicity—and of class within race:
Kwame's story—evacuated to a much better high school in Berkeley, then
onto a college at an elite institution in Ohio—has little in common with
Denise's experience, but it is no less authentic or authentically black. And
while Abbas's ethnicity seems to have no impact on the textures of their
particular Katrina story,[7] Neufeld does not succumb to the easy cliché of a
hard-working immigrant to tell his story.

   A.D.'s engagement with race is not limited to implicit clues or to the
online discussions of its readers; while the text itself does not delve deeply
into these topic, the hyperlinks embedded in the webcomic locate the events
within the context of race, introducing relevant and even critical information that informs our reading. The most significant example of this can be
found in *A.D.*'s reference to what has come to be called the "Gretna incident."
On September 1, according to the historian Douglas Brinkley, a group of
some two hundred people (whom Brinkley estimates to be about 95-percent
black) decided to leave the chaos of the shelters of last resort and walk over
the Mississippi River to the neighboring and relatively undamaged town

of Gretna. Near the midpoint of the bridge (known locally as the Crescent City Connection), the group was turned away at gunpoint—complete with warning shots—by the Gretna police. They were told, Brinkley writes, that "'there would be no Superdomes in their city.' That was shorthand for the fact that there would be *no disorder* in Gretna"—an understanding of the status of the city dependent solely on reports in the national news media (470). Brinkley probably could, and should, take this further: whether it was articulated or not, that statement was ultimately shorthand for their aim to ensure that there would be no more *black people* in Gretna.

This incident is given only a few panels in *A.D.*; the infuriated group returns to the Convention Center and is met by Denise, who prompts their apparent leader to tell their story. Conversations begin in the crowd, and people begin to offer explanations of their situation that, however, improbable, seem more reasonable than simple neglect: "They won't let us go! We trapped here!" one terrified woman exclaims (149). In response, one man proffers a theory held at one time by some members of New Orleans's African American community and controversially discussed in Spike Lee's documentary, *When the Levees Break*: "Y'know, I hear they blew up that levee in the Ninth Ward to flood us out!" the man shouts (149).

Both the Gretna incident and the conspiracy theory are fraught with the histories and language of racial strife and oppression. The printed edition of *A.D.*, however, never addresses those implications; the identity of the "they" that "won't let us go" and that "blew up the levee" is never made clear, but by positioning statements of black disenfranchisement so close together, the text recognizes that race informs this moment. More importantly, the hyperlinks of the webcomic allow the reader to further pursue this line of inquiry. Beneath the panels addressing the Gretna episode is a link to a *60 Minutes* story about the event by the late Ed Bradley. Likewise, the man's claim about the possible dynamiting on the levee—which might strike the reader as the unlikely assumptions of man in an unbelievable situation—is made more reasonable through a (now inactive) link to a December 2005 report from the NBC Nightly News that investigated the circulation of similar claims within the city's black community. Together, these reports about the ways race influenced individual experiences and interpretations of Katrina and its aftermath provide critical context for the events of the book; once one reads them, the identity of "they" becomes clear, and the horror of the image that follows—a two-page spread focused on the desperate faces of the crowd as they confront the possibility that no one is coming for them— is made more intense (150–51). In this moment, with those reports in mind, the divide between "they" and "us" is not about where one sits, inside or outside the city, stranded or safe: it is unavoidably racial.

This strategy for addressing race and other concerns has a number of benefits for Neufeld and the reader. In moments like those I described above, the text can focus squarely on generating the emotions of frustration, despair, isolation, and abandonment felt by these characters, rather than diverging into historical complexities that, as Haspiel says, "take" the audience "out of the drama." These emotions are universalized and thus challenge the "Othering" effect of media representations of the Superdome and Convention Center, of the sort evident in Wolf Blitzer's "so poor ... so black" comment. At the same time, the reader can access that context, come to a more complete understanding of the particular experience of these individuals, and begin to construct a genealogy of the event by considering factors Neufeld does not directly address. Ultimately, this approach is not unlike the *Where's Waldo* image, in that it balances the particular and the general: Neufeld's images and narrative emphasize the particularity of these characters, but the links allow the reader to investigate the scale, the causes, and the consequences of the event.

Unfortunately, the additional functionality of the web-based text is no panacea. The conversations in the comment section, for instance, never realize what we can see in retrospect as their potential: instead of discussion of potential action, the comments are most often platitudes for Neufeld's work; the community created by these discussions is fleeting and offers little additional testimony by victims. Nonetheless, the possibility is dormant within the text, and as long as the webcomic remains active, readers may still interact with each other. Despite its relative novelty and ephemerality, the webcomic form offers great utility for the historical trauma of hurricane Katrina: it bears witness to the event in a way that gives voice to victims without fetishizing their suffering; it challenges the conventional representation of the event, demands an interpretive and engaged reader, and (in the web-form) it provides a vehicle through which an audience can both learn about the event and interact with others in a community of mutual interest. *A.D.* is thus more than a chronicle of an event; it is a call for action. Action might not be taken in response to this work, but it might come from other writers who find in *A.D.* new strategies for representing those things that do not easily yield to conventional forms of storytelling.

Notes

1. In response to a commenter on the original web comment, Neufeld wrote that he was "using a lot of photographic reference for this project—especially for the prologue. About half the images are directly from photos, while the others use photos as a resource" (http://www.smithmag.net/afterthedeluge/2007/01/01/prologue-1/).

2. I would argue that these images most immediately recall photographs of black men conscripted by the Mississippi National Guard to work on the levees during the 1927 flood.

3. In the course of teaching *A.D.*, several of my students noted that the woman above and behind the corpse (out of focus, dark T-shirt with red lettering and white oval) bears such a striking resemblance to a woman in Abbas/Hamid's store much earlier (32) that it cannot be a coincidence.

4. According to LaCapra, "working through trauma does not imply the possibility of attaining total integration of the self, including the retrospective feat of putting together seamlessly (for example, through a harmonizing or fetishistic narrative) the riven experience of the past trauma. Any such retrospective 'suturing' would itself by phantasmatic or illusory. *Working-through means work on posttraumatic symptoms* in order to mitigate the effects of trauma . . . , thereby enabling a more viable articulation of affect and cognition or representation, as well as ethical and sociopolitical agency, in the present and future" (118–19).

5. "Narrative at best helps one not to change the past through a dubious rewriting of history but to work through posttraumatic symptoms in the present in a manner that opens possible futures. It also enables one to recount events and perhaps evoke experience, typically through nonlinear movements that allows trauma to register in language and its hesitations, indirections, pauses, and silences. And particularly, by bearing witness and giving testimony, narrative may help performatively to create openings in existence that did not exist before" (La Capra 121–22).

6. Other examples of works that participate in this argument include Tom Piazza's *Why New Orleans Matters*, Andrei Codrescu's *New Orleans, Mon Amour*, and essay collections like *Do You Know What it Means to Miss New Orleans?* The argument on the other side has been less sustained, but perhaps more pernicious: advocates include engineers (Klaus Jacob, "Time for a Tough Question: Why Rebuild?"), and media commentators like *Slate's* Jack Shafer ("Don't Refloat: The Case Against Rebuilding New Orleans"—playing, I think, the devil's advocate) and former CNN and current Fox News talking head Glenn Beck ("Big Easy a Lost Cause?").

7. Unlike the title figure in Dave Egger's nonfiction work, *Zeitoun*, who, despite deep connections to the New Orleans Community, finds himself in the custody of Homeland Security operatives after the storm.

Works Cited

Adams, Jeff. "The Pedagogy of the Image Text: Nakazawa, Sebald and Spiegelman Recount Social Traumas." *Discourse: Studies in the Cultural Politics of Education* 29.1 (2008): 35–49. Print.

Anderson, Ho Che. *King: A Comics Biography of Martin Luther King, Jr.* Seattle: Fantagraphics Books, 2005. Print.

Beck, Glenn. "Big Easy a Lost Cause?; Did Idaho Senator Hide Gay Behavior?; Castro Endorses Hillary-Obama." Transcript. *CNN.com.* CNN. 29 August 2007. Web. 28 March 2010.

Brickhouse, Anna. "'L'Ouragan de Flammes' ('The Hurricane of Flames'): New Orleans and Transamerican Catastrophe, 1866/2005." *American Quarterly.* 59.4 (2007): 1097–1130. Print.

Brinkley, Douglas. *The Great Deluge: Hurricane Katrina, New Orleans, and the Mississippi Gulf Coast.* New York: William Morrow, 2006. Print.

Brophy-Warren, Jamin. "Capturing a Disaster in Cartoons." *WSJOnline. Wall Street Journal.* 17 July 2009. Web. January 2010.

Caruth, Cathy. *Unclaimed Experience: Trauma, Narrative, and History.* Baltimore, MD: Johns Hopkins UP, 1996. Print.

Chaney, Michael A. "Drawing on History in Recent African American Graphic Novels." *MELUS: The Journal of the Society for the Study of the Multi-Ethnic Literature of the United States* 32.3 (2007): 175–200. Print.

Chute, Hillary. "Comics as Literature? Reading Graphic Narrative." *PMLA: Publications of the Modern Language Association.* 123.2 (2008): 452–65. Print.

Codresu, Andrei. *New Orleans, Mon Amour.* New York: Algonquin Books, 2006. Print.

"Denise." Comment RE: 'Chapter 5: Katrina Comes Calling.'" *A.D.: New Orleans After the Deluge. SMITH Magazine.* SMITH Mag. 21 July 2007. Web. January 2010.

Duck, Leigh Anne. *The Nation's Region: Southern Modernism, Segregation, and U.S. Nationalism.* Athens, GA: University of Georgia Press, 2006. Print.

Duke, Brett. Untitled photograph. *Center of Desperation.* Online photographic archive. NOLA.com. *New Orleans Times-Picayune.* 1 September 1, 2005. Web, photograph. January 2010.

Fossett, Judith Jackson. "Sold Down the River." *PMLA: Publications of the Modern Language Association of America* 122.1 (2007): 325–30. Print.

Gustines, Georges Gene. "Graphic Memories of Katrina's Ordeal." *New York Times* 24 August 2009: BOOKS 1. Print.

Halberstam, David. "Hell and High Water-American Apocalypse: New Orleans 2005." *Vanity Fair* November 2005: 358. Print.

Haspiel, Dean. Comment RE: 'Chapter 5: Katrina Comes Calling.'" *A.D.: New Orleans After the Deluge. SMITH Magazine.* SMITH Mag. 21 July 2007. Web. January 2010.

———. "Comment RE: "Prologue Part I: 'In the Beginning. . . .'" *A.D.: New Orleans After the Deluge. SMITH Magazine.* SMITH Mag. 25 January 2007. Web. January 2009.

Henninger, Katherine. *Ordering the Facade: Photography and Contemporary Southern Women's Writing.* Chapel Hill, NC: U of North Carolina P, 2007. Print.

Jacob, Klaus. "Time for a Tough Question: Why Rebuild?" *Washington Post.* 6 September 2005: A25. Print.

Jackson, Ted. *A Tragedy Illuminates the Ethical Dimensions of Picture Taking: An Essay in Words and Pictures. Nieman Reports.* Nieman Foundation for Journalism at Harvard. N.D. Web. 28 March 2010.

———. Untitled photographs. Online photographic archive. NOLA.com. *New Orleans Times-Picayune.* 1 September 1, 2005. Web, photograph. January 2010.

LaCapra, Dominick. *History in Transit: Experience, Identity, Critical Theory*. Ithaca, NY: Cornell UP, 2004. Print.

McCloud, Scott. *Understanding Comics: The Invisible Art*. Northampton, MA: Kitchen Sink, 1993. Print.

McPherson, Tara. "No Natural Disaster: New Orleans, Katrina, and War." *PMLA: Publications of the Modern Language Association of America* 122.1 (2007): 331–35. Print.

Neufeld, Josh. *A.D.: New Orleans After the Deluge*. New York: Pantheon Books, 2009. Print.

———. *A.D.: New Orleans After the Deluge*. *SMITH Magazine*. SMITH Mag. Web. January 2010.

Piazza, Tom. *Why New Orleans Matters*. New York: Harper, 2005. Print.

Pool, David. Untitled photograph. Online AP Archive. MSNBC.com. January 2010. Web.

Pratt, Lloyd. "New Orleans and Its Storm: Exception, Example, or Event?" *American Literary History* 19.1 (2007): 251–65. Print.

Pulp Secret. "Comic Book News and Reviews: Pulp Secret Report 05/15/07." 15 May 2007. YouTube. Web video clip. Accessed on 22 December 2009.

Rutledge, David, ed. *Do You Know What it is to Miss New Orleans?* Seattle: Chin Music Press, 2008. Print.

Sacco, Joe. *Palestine*. New York: Fantagraphics, 2002. Print.

Satrapi, Marjane. *The Complete Persepolis*. New York: Pantheon, 2007. Print.

Shafer, Jack. "Don't Refloat: The Case Against Rebuilding New Orleans." *Slate*. Slate.com. 7 September 2005. Web. 28 March 2010.

Sontag, Susan. *Regarding the Pain of Others*. New York, NY: Picador, 2003 Print.

Spiegelman Art. *In the Shadow of No Towers*. New York: Pantheon, 2004. Print.

———. *The Complete Maus*. New York: Pantheon, 1996. Print.

Tuttle, Bruce. "Comment RE: *A Tragedy Illuminates the Ethical Dimensions of Picture Taking*." *A Tragedy Illuminates the Ethical Dimensions of Picture Taking*. *Nieman Reports*. Nieman Foundation for Journalism at Harvard. 16 November 2009. Web. January 2009.

Whitlock, Gillian. "Autographics: The Seeing 'I' of the Comics." *MFS: Modern Fiction Studies* 52.4 (2006): 965–79. Print.

About the Contributors

Tim Caron is the associate dean of the Macaulay Honors College of the City University of New York. He earned his Ph.D. from Louisiana State University. His research and teaching interests include comics and graphic novels and the intertwined issues of race and religion in writers from the American South.

Brannon Costello is associate professor of English at Louisiana State University, where he specializes in southern literary studies and comics studies. He has published essays on authors including Jack Butler, Randall Kenan, Eudora Welty, and Richard Wright, and he is the author of *Plantation Airs: Racial Paternalism and the Transformations of Class in Southern Fiction, 1945–1971* (Louisiana State UP, 2007) and the editor of *Howard Chaykin: Conversations* (UP of Mississippi, 2011). His ongoing research projects include a critical study of Chaykin's work and an examination of the role of "geek culture" in contemporary southern fiction.

Brian Cremins is an assistant professor of English at Harper College in Palatine, Illinois. He earned his Ph.D. in English from the University of Connecticut in 2004 and has contributed essays on comics to publications including the *International Journal of Comic Art* and *The Jack Kirby Collector*. His current project involves a study of depersonalization, memory, and mourning in the works of John Porcellino and Carrie McNinch. He lives in Chicago.

Conseula Francis, associate professor of English and director of African American studies at the College of Charleston, earned her Ph.D. at the University of Washington. Her research interests include African American genre fiction and black intellectual thought. She is the editor of *Conversations with Octavia Butler* (UP of Mississippi, 2009) and the author of the forthcoming *An Honest Man and a Good Writer: The Critical Reception of James Baldwin*.

Anthony Dyer Hoefer was recently named director of the University Scholars Program at George Mason University, where he also teaches undergraduate seminars in the Honors College. He lives in Virginia with his family.

M. Thomas Inge is the Blackwell Professor of Humanities at Randolph-Macon College, where he teaches and writes about American humor and comic art, film and animation, southern literature and culture, William Faulkner, and Asian literature. He has been publishing essays and books on comics for over thirty years, including *Comics as Culture* (1990), and more recently an edition of *My Life with Charlie Brown* (2010) by Charles Schulz. Inge is the general editor of the Great Comics Artists and the Conversations with Comic Artists series for the University Press of Mississippi. He wanted to be a cartoonist but got diverted into teaching.

Nicolas Labarre received his Ph.D. from the Université de Haute-Bretagne, in Rennes, and he is currently an assistant professor at the Université Michel de Montaigne in Bordeaux. After a few years dedicated to the study of mass culture theories, he has shifted his interest to comic books and cultural hierarchies. He also writes children's books.

Alison Mandaville teaches literature and writing at Pacific Lutheran University. Her articles on comics have appeared in the *International Journal of Comics Literature*, the *Comics Journal, Philology*, and the book *Teaching the Graphic Novel* (MLA, 2009). She received a Fulbright lectureship to Azerbaijan in 2007–08, where she explored contemporary literature and comic art of the region.

Gary Richards, assistant professor of English at the University of Mary Washington, is the author of *Lovers and Beloveds: Sexual Otherness in Southern Fiction, 1936–1961* (Louisiana State UP, 2005) and a contributor to *Beth Henley: A Casebook* (Routledge, 2002) and *Faulkner's Sexualities* (UP of Mississippi, 2010). He has also published essays addressing regional and sexual identity in the works of Alfred Uhry, Tennessee Williams, Truman Capote, Allan Gurganus, and Jim Grimsley, among others. His current scholarship focuses on literary representations of gay New Orleans and on images of the U.S. South in contemporary musical theater.

Joseph Michael Sommers is an assistant professor of English at Central Michigan University where he teaches courses in children's and young adult literature. He received his Ph.D. from the University of Kansas and has published essays on figures such as Gary Paulsen, Hunter Thompson, Denise Levertov, and Judy Blume. Over the next year he will bring out chapters and articles on the culture of children in nineteenth-century lady's journalism, the maturation of Marvel Comics' characters in the Post 9/11 Moment, and *Twilight*. His future projects include a book-length collection investigating the work of Alan Moore, an essay interrogating the underpinnings of Christopher Nolan's *The Dark Knight*, and the idea of children as monsters in filmic representation.

Christopher Whitby earned an M.A. in American cultural studies from the University of Manchester, where he wrote a thesis on the work of Doug Marlette. His research focuses on notions of southern identity in editorial and comic strips.

Qiana J. Whitted is associate professor of English and African American studies at the University of South Carolina. She earned her Ph.D. from Yale University. She is the author of *"A God of Justice?": The Problem of Evil in Twentieth-Century Black Literature* (U of Virginia P, 2009), and her publications have appeared in *African American Review, Southern Literary Journal,* and the *Encyclopedia of Comics and Graphic Novels*. Her current research and teaching interests focus on postmodern black American literature and the intersections of race, history, and censorship in comics.

Index